M000121767

Atlanta

streetatlas

Contents

Introduction

Cover photo: One Atlantic Center in Atlanta. Photo © Heinz H. Hansen/Emporis GmbH

RAND McNALLY

Rand McNally Consumer Affairs
P.O. Box 7600
Chicago, IL 60680-9915
randmcnally.com
For comments or suggestions, please call
(800) 777-MAPS (-6277)
or email us at:
consumeraffairs@randmcnally.com

Using Your Street Atlas

The PageFinder™ Map

> Turn to Page C to locate the PageFinder™ Map. Each of the small squares outlined on this map represents a different map page in the Street Atlas.

> Locate the specific part of the metropolitan area that you're interested in.

> Note the appropriate map page number.

> Turn to that map page.

The Index

> The Street Atlas includes separate indexes for streets, schools, parks, shopping centers, golf courses, and other points of interest.

> In the street listings, information is presented in the following order: city, map page number, and grid reference.

STREET		
City	Map #	Grid
N Monticello Av		
CHCG	2976	C2
CHCG	3032	C3
LNWD	2920	C2
Montrose Av		
CHCG	2917	A7
SRPK	2917	A7
SRPK	2973	C1

> A grid reference is a letter-number combination (B6 for example) that tells you precisely where to find a particular street or point of interest on a map.

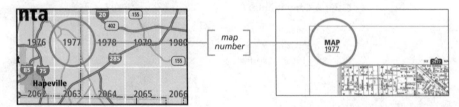

missing pages?

Please note that map pages in this book are numbered according to Rand McNally's page numbering system, not according to traditional page numbering. For this reason, your book may look as though it is missing pages. For example, one page might contain map number 3034 while the following page has map number 3089. The quickest way to resolve any confusion over page numbering is to consult the PageFinder™ Map in the front portion of the Street Atlas.

The Detail Maps

> Each detail map is divided into a grid formed by rows and columns. These rows and columns correspond to letters and numbers running horizontally and vertically along the edges of the map.

> To use a grid reference from the index, search horizontally within the appropriate row and vertically within the appropriate column. The destination can be found within the grid square where the row and column meet.

> Adjacent map pages are indicated by numbers that appear at the top, bottom, and sides of each map.

> The legend explains symbols that appear on the maps.

PageFinder™ Map

PAGE
C

PageFinder™ Map
U.S. Patent No. 5,419,586
Canadian Patent No. 2,116,425
Patente Mexicana No. 188186

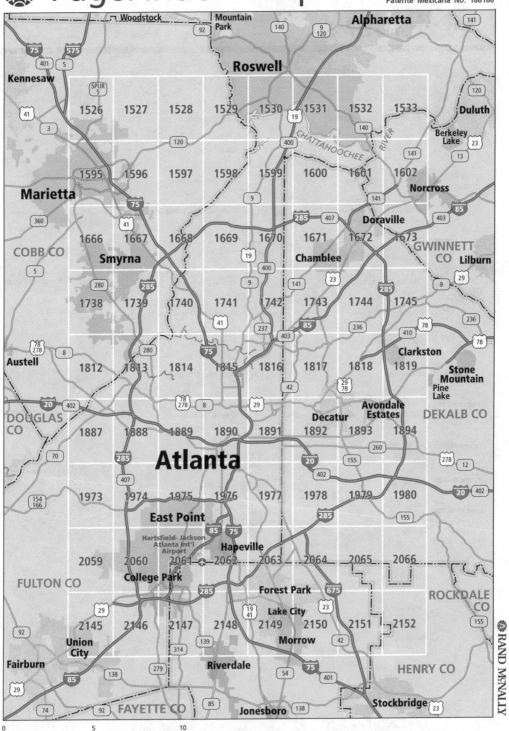

LEGEND

123	Interstate Highway
BUS 123	Interstate (Business) Highway
123	U.S. Highway
123	State/Provincial Highway
123	Secondary State/Provincial Highway/County Highway
1	Trans-Canada Highway
123	Canadian Autoroute
123	Mexican Highway
123	Other Highway Designation
456	Exit Number
	Free Limited Access Highway (with Tunnel)
	Toll Limited Access Highway Toll Plaza
	Interchange
	Ramp
	Highway
	Primary Road
	Secondary Road
	Minor Road, Unpaved Road
	Walkway, Trail

	Trolley
	Ferry, Waterway
	Lock, Levee
	Gate, One-Way Road
	Railroad, Mass Transit Line and Station
	Bus Station
P	Park and Ride
P	Parking Lot/Parking Garage
1200	Block Number
	International Boundary State Boundary
	County Boundary City Boundary
H	Hospital
	Police, Sheriff etc.
FS	Fire Station
?	Information/Visitor Center/ Welcome Center

	City/Town/Village Hall & other Government Buildings
	Courthouse
	Post Office
Lib	Library
	Museum
	School
	University or College
	Rest Area
	Service Area
	Border Crossing or Port of Entry
	Theater/Performing Arts Center
	Golf Course
	Other Point of Interest

CITIES & COMMUNITIES

Community Name	Abbr.	County	Map Page	Community Name	Abbr.	County	Map Page
Adams Park		Fulton	1975	-- Henry County	HryC		
* Alpharetta	ALPT	Fulton	1531	* Lake City	LKCY	Clayton	2150
* Atlanta	ATLN	Fulton	1890	La Vista		DeKalb	1745
* Avondale Estates	AVES	DeKalb	1893	Leafmore		DeKalb	1818
Brookhaven		DeKalb	1743	* Marietta	MRTA	Cobb	1595
Cedar Grove		DeKalb	2065	Mechanicsville		Gwinnett	1673
* Chamblee	CMBL	DeKalb	1671	* Morrow	MRRW	Clayton	2149
* Clarkston	CLKN	DeKalb	1819	Mountain View		Clayton	2062
-- Clayton County	ClyC			Newtown		Fulton	1532
-- Cobb County	CobC			Nickajack		Cobb	1813
* College Park	CGPK	Fulton	2061	* Norcross	NRCS	Gwinnett	1602
Conley		Clayton	2064	Oakdale		Cobb	1740
Constitution		DeKalb	1977	Oak Grove		DeKalb	1744
* Decatur	DCTR	DeKalb	1892	Panthersville		DeKalb	2065
-- DeKalb County	DKbC			Pendley Hills		DeKalb	1894
* Doraville	DRVL	DeKalb	1672	* Pine Lake	PNLK	DeKalb	1819
Druid Hills		DeKalb	1892	Plaza		Clayton	2148
Dunaire		DeKalb	1819	Red Oak		Fulton	2146
Dunwoody		DeKalb	1600	Rehoboth		DeKalb	1818
Eastland Heights		DeKalb	1977	Rex		Clayton	2151
* East Point	EPNT	Fulton	1975	* Riverdale	RVDL	Clayton	2148
Eastwood		DeKalb	1978	* Roswell	RSWL	Fulton	1530
Edgemoor East		Clayton	2149	Sandy Plains		Cobb	1527
Ellenwood		Clayton	2151	Sandy Springs		Fulton	1670
Embry Hills		DeKalb	1672	Scottdale		DeKalb	1818
Fair Oaks		Cobb	1666	* Smyrna	SMYR	Cobb	1666
Flintwoods		Clayton	2148	South Decatur		DeKalb	1893
* Forest Park	FTPK	Clayton	2149	Toco Hills		DeKalb	1817
-- Fulton County	FulC			Tucker		DeKalb	1745
Gilmore		Cobb	1739	* Union City	UNCT	Fulton	2145
Glen Haven		DeKalb	1894	Vinings		Cobb	1740
-- Gwinnett County	GwnC			Vista Grove		DeKalb	1744
* Hapeville	HPVL	Fulton	2062	Westoak		Cobb	1526

*Indicates incorporated city

MAP
F

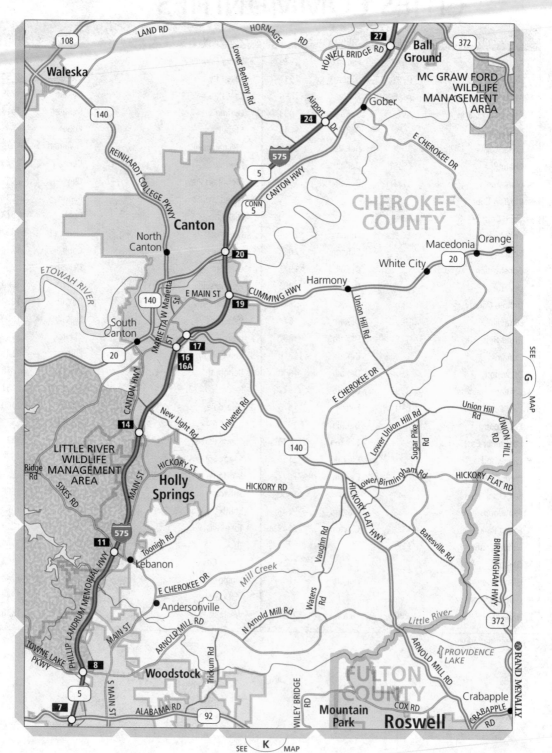

1:150,800
1 in. = 2.4 mi.

0   1.0   2.0
                  miles

108   LAND RD   HORNAGE   RD   27   Ball Ground   372

Waleska   Lower Bethany Rd   HOWELL BRIDGE RD

MC GRAW FORD WILDLIFE MANAGEMENT AREA

140   Airport Dr   Gober

24   575   E CHEROKEE DR

5   CANTON HWY   CHEROKEE COUNTY

REINHARDT COLLEGE PKWY   CONN 5

North Canton   Canton   Macedonia   Orange

ETOWAH RIVER   20   White City   20

140   W Marietta St   E MAIN ST   CUMMING HWY   Harmony

South Canton   19   Union Hill Rd

20   17   E CHEROKEE DR

CANTON HWY   16   16A

New Light Rd   Univeter Rd   Union Hill Rd

Lower Union Hill Rd   UNION HILL RD

14   Sugar Pike Rd

LITTLE RIVER WILDLIFE MANAGEMENT AREA   140   HICKORY FLAT RD

Ridge Rd   HICKORY ST   Lower Birmingham Rd

SIXES RD   MAIN ST   Holly Springs   HICKORY RD   HICKORY FLAT HWY   Batesville Rd

BIRMINGHAM HWY

11   575   Vaughn Rd

PHILLIP LANDRUM MEMORIAL HWY   Toonigh Rd   Lebanon   Mill Creek   Waters Rd   Little River   372

E CHEROKEE DR   PROVIDENCE LAKE

Andersonville   N Arnold Mill Rd

TOWNE LAKE PKWY   MAIN ST   ARNOLD MILL RD   Arnold Mill Rd   FULTON COUNTY   Crabapple

8   Trickum Rd   COX RD

S MAIN RD   Woodstock   WILEY BRIDGE RD   Mountain Park   Roswell   CRABAPPLE RD

5   ALABAMA RD   92

7

SEE   G   MAP

RAND MCNALLY

SEE   K   MAP

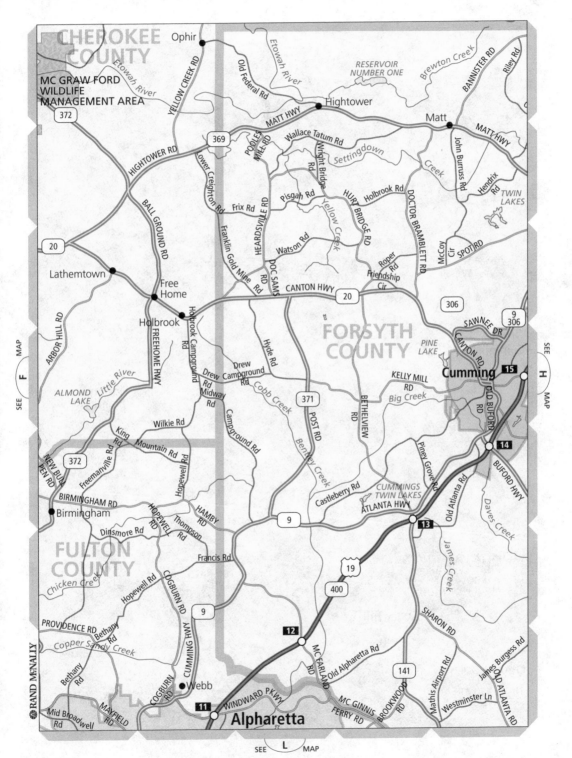

N

1:150,800
1 in. = 2.4 mi.

0   1.0   2.0
miles

CHEROKEE COUNTY

Ophir

MC GRAW FORD WILDLIFE MANAGEMENT AREA

Etowah River

YELLOW CREEK RD

372

HIGHTOWER RD

369

Old Federal Rd

Etowah River

POOLES MILL RD

MATT HWY

Hightower

Wallace Tatum Rd

Settingdown Creek

RESERVOIR NUMBER ONE

Brewton Creek

BANNISTER RD

Riley Rd

Matt

MATT HWY

John Burruss Rd

Hendrix

TWIN LAKES

Wright Bridge Rd

Lower Creighton Rd

Frix Rd

Pisgah Rd

HURT BRIDGE RD

Holbrook Rd

DOCTOR BRAMBLETT RD

McCoy Cir

SPOT RD

20

BALL GROUND RD

Lathemtown

Free Home

Holbrook

FREEHOME HWY

Holbrook Campground Rd

Franklin Gold Mine Rd

HEARDSVILLE RD

DOC SAMS

Watson Rd

Yellow Creek

CANTON HWY

Roper Rd

Friendship Cir

20

FORSYTH COUNTY

306

9 306

SAWNEE DR

CANTON RD

OLD BUFORD RD

Cumming

15

PINE LAKE

ARBOR HILL RD

ALMOND LAKE

Little River

Drew Campground Rd

Hyde Rd

Cobb Creek

371

BETHELVIEW RD

KELLY MILL RD

Big Creek

SEE F MAP

SEE H MAP

Midway Rd

Wilkie Rd

King Mountain Rd

Campground Rd

POST RD

Bentley Creek

Piney Grove Rd

Old Atlanta Rd

14

BUFORD HWY

Daves Creek

372

NEW BULL PEN RD

Freemanville Rd

Hopewell Rd

BIRMINGHAM RD

HOPEWELL RD

Thompson Rd

HAMBY RD

Castleberry Rd

CUMMINGS TWIN LAKES

ATLANTA HWY

9

13

James Creek

Birmingham

Dinsmore Rd

Francis Rd

FULTON COUNTY

Chicken Creek

Hopewell Rd

COGBURN RD

9

19

400

SHARON RD

PROVIDENCE RD

Bethany Rd

Copper Sandy Creek

Bethany Rd

12

MC FARLAND RD

Old Alpharetta Rd

141

BROOKWOOD RD

Mathis Airport Rd

Westminster Ln

James Burgess Rd

OLD ATLANTA RD

Bethany Rd

Mid Broadwell Rd

MAYFIELD RD

COGBURN RD

CUMMING HWY

Webb

11

WINDWARD PKWY

Alpharetta

MC GINNIS FERRY RD

RAND McNALLY

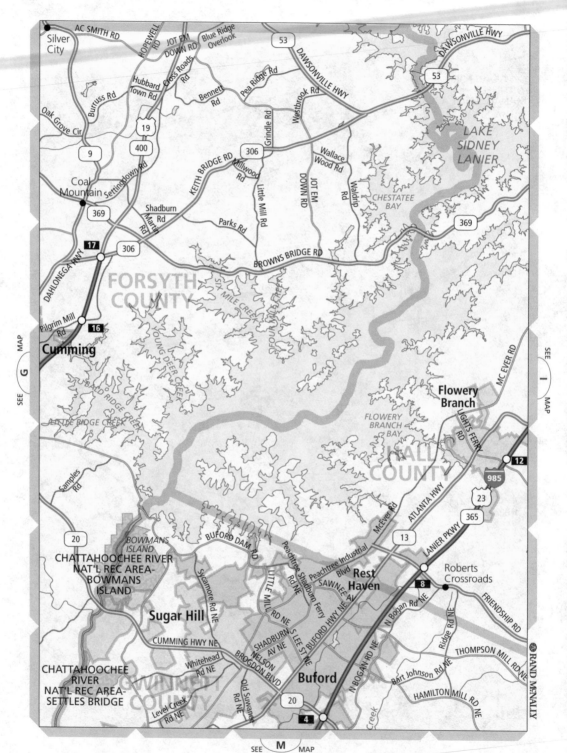

N

Silver City

AC SMITH RD

HOPEWELL RD
JOT PM DOWN RD
Blue Ridge Overlook

53

DAWSONVILLE HWY

Cross Roads Rd

Hubbard Town Rd

Bennett Rd

Pea Ridge Rd

Westbrook Rd

DAWSONVILLE HWY

53

Burruss Rd

Oak Grove Cir

19

400

9

Gruipije Rd

306

Wallace Wood Rd

LAKE SIDNEY LANIER

Coal Mountain

Settingdown Rd

Millwood Rd

Little Mill Rd

JOT EM DOWN RD

Waldrip Rd

CHESTATEE BAY

369

Shadburn Rd

369

Martin Rd

KEITH BRIDGE RD

Parks Rd

BROWNS BRIDGE RD

DAHLONEGA HWY

17

306

FORSYTH COUNTY

SIX MILE CREEK

Pilgrim Mill Rd

16

Cumming

FOUR MILE CREEK

YOUNG DEER CREEK

BALD RIDGE CREEK

Flowery Branch

MC EVER RD

LITTLE RIDGE CREEK

FLOWERY BRANCH BAY

LIGHTS FERRY RD

12

HALL COUNTY

Samples Rd

985

23

20

BOWMANS ISLAND

BUFORD DAM RD

Peachtree Industrial Blvd

Shadburn Ferry Rd NE

McEver Rd

ATLANTA HWY

365

CHATTAHOOCHEE RIVER NAT'L REC AREA- BOWMANS ISLAND

Sycamore Rd NE

LITTLE MILL RD NE

SAWNEE AV

Rest Haven

13

LANIER PKWY

Roberts Crossroads

8

FRIENDSHIP RD

Sugar Hill

S LEE ST NE

BUFORD HWY NE

N BOGAN RD NE

Ridge Rd NE

THOMPSON MILL RD NE

CUMMING HWY NE

SHADBURN AV NE

NELSON BROGDON BLVD

Whitehead Rd NE

N BOGAN RD NE

Bart Johnson Rd NE

CHATTAHOOCHEE RIVER NAT'L REC AREA- SETTLES BRIDGE

GWINNETT COUNTY

Old Suwanee Rd NE

Buford

20

HAMILTON MILL RD NE

Level Creek Rd NE

4

Creek

MAP

I

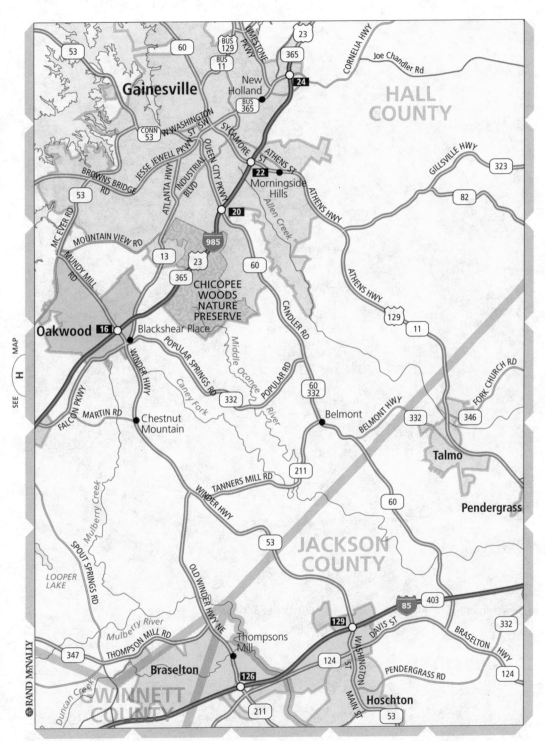

MAP
J

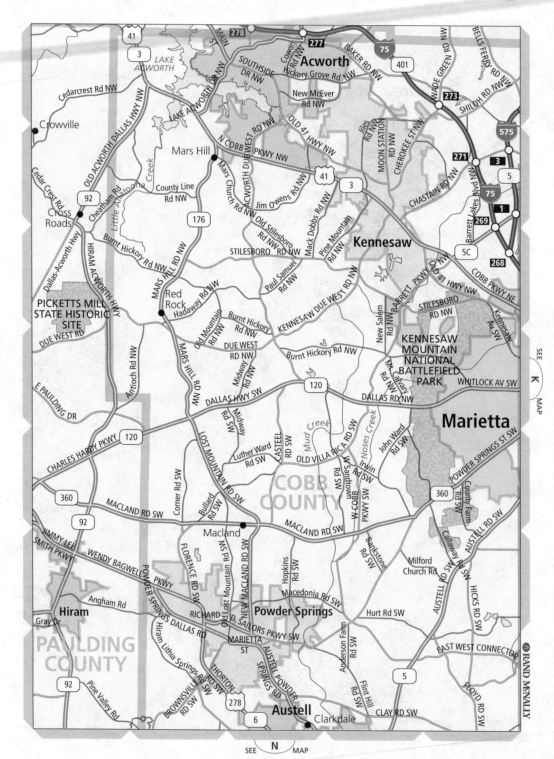

1:150,800
1 in. = 2.4 mi.

0   1.0   2.0
miles

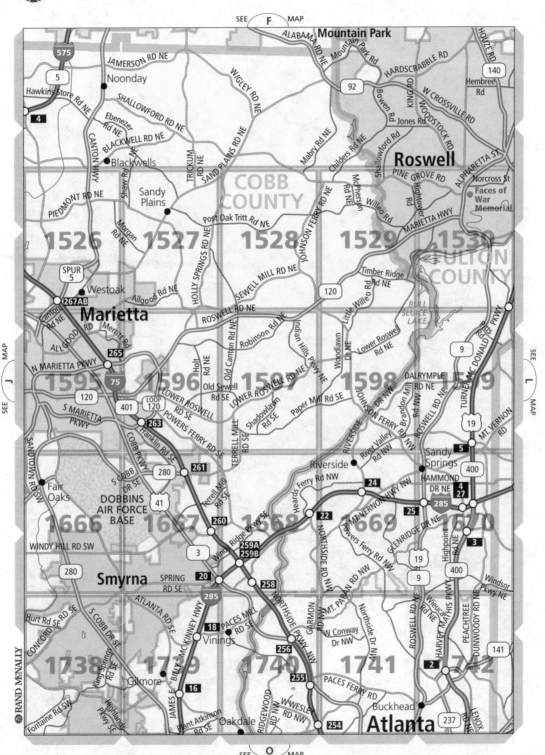

N

1:150,800
1 in. = 2.4 mi.
0   1.0   2.0
miles

SEE F MAP

575
5
4

JAMERSON RD NE
Noonday
Hawkins Store Rd NE
SHALLOWFORD RD NE
Ebenezer Rd NE
CANTON HWY
BLACKWELL RD NE
Blackwells
Shaw Rd NE
TRICKUM RD NE
SAND PLAINS RD NE
WIGLEY RD NE
ALABAMA RD NE
Mountain Park Rd
Mountain Park
92
HARDSCRABBLE RD
HOLTZ RD
140
Hembree Rd
W CROSSVILLE RD
KING RD
Bowen Rd
Jones Rd
WOODSTOCK RD
Mabry Rd NE
Childers Rd NE
Shallowford Rd
McPherson Rd NE
Roswell
Norcross St
PINE GROVE RD
ALPHARETTA ST
Faces of War Memorial

Piedmont Rd NE
Sandy Plains
Morgan Rd NE
Post Oak Tritt Rd NE
COBB COUNTY
Willeo Rd
Highower
MARIETTA HWY

1526   **1527**   **1528**   **1529**   **1530**

SPUR 5
Westoak
267AB
Marietta
Canton Rd NE
ALLGOOD RD
Merritt Rd
265
Allgood Rd NE
HOLLY SPRINGS RD NE
SEWELL MILL RD NE
Roswell Rd NE
120
Timber Ridge Rd NE
Little Willeo Rd
Lower Roswell Rd NE
9
FULTON COUNTY
BULL SLUICE LAKE
Pitts Pkwy

SEE J MAP

75
120
401
LOOP 120
263
Franklin Rd SE
POWERS FERRY RD SE
LOWER ROSWELL RD SE
Old Canton Rd NE
Robinson Rd NE
Indian Hills Pkwy NE
Holt Rd NE
Old Sewell Rd NE
LOWER ROSWELL RD NE
Woodlawn Dr NE
Shadowlawn Rd SE
Paper Mill Rd SE
JOHNSON FERRY RD NE
DALRYMPLE RD NE
Brandon Mill Rd NW
ROSWELL RD NE
TURNER MC DONALD PKWY
19
MT. VERNON RD

1595   **1596**   **1597**   **1598**   **1599**

S MARIETTA PKWY
S COBB DR SE
COBB PKWY
280
261
TERRELL MILL RD SE
RIVERSIDE DR NW
Riverside
River Valley Rd NW
JOHNSON FERRY RD
Sandy Springs
5
400
HAMMOND DR NE

SEE L MAP

SANDTOWN RD SW
Fair Oaks
DOBBINS AIR FORCE BASE
41
Terrell Mill Rd SE
260
Heards Ferry Rd NW
24
MT VERNON HWY NW
285
27
GLENRIDGE DR NE
Highpoint Rd NE
3

1666   **1667**   **1668**   **1669**   **1670**

WINDY HILL RD SW
280
Smyrna
SPRING RD SE
20
Windy Ridge Pkwy SE
259A 259B
258
3
22
NORTHSIDE RD NW
Powers Ferry Rd NW
25
19
9
400

ATLANTA RD SE
285
18
PACES MILL RD SE
Vinings
256
NORTHSIDE PKWY NW
GARMON
MT. PARAN RD NW
W Conway Dr NW
Northside Dr NW
ROSWELL RD NE
Wieuca Rd NE
HARVEY MATHIS PKWY
PEACHTREE DUNWOODY RD NE
Windsor Pkwy NE
141

Hurt Rd SE
CONCORD RD SE
S COBB DR SE
King Springs Rd SE
Fontaine Rd SW
Highlands Pkwy SE
JAMES E "BILLY" MC KINNEY HWY
16
Plant Atkinson Rd SE
Gilmore
255
RIDGEWOOD RD NW
W WESLEY RD NW
254
PACES FERRY RD
Buckhead
2
Atlanta
237
LENOX RD NE
Oakdale

1738   **1739**   **1740**   **1741**   **1742**

RAND MCNALLY

SEE O MAP

MAP
L

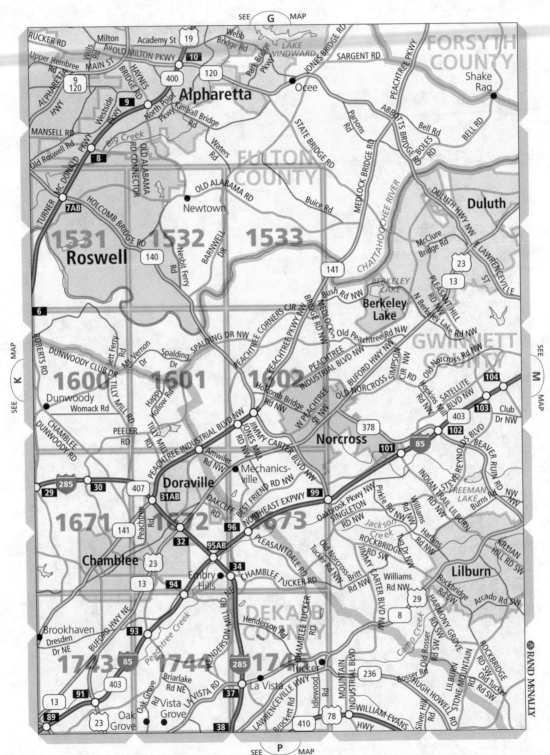

1:150,800
1 in. = 2.4 mi.

0   1.0   2.0
miles

N

FORSYTH COUNTY

RUCKER RD
Milton
Academy St   19
Webb Bridge Rd
LAKE WINDWARD
JONES BRIDGE RD
SARGENT RD

Wills Rd
OLD MILTON PKWY   10
Upper Hembree Rd
MAIN ST
HAYNES BRIDGE RD
400
120

Shake Rag

ALPHARETTA HWY
9 120
Westside Pkwy
North Point Pkwy
Kimball Bridge Rd
Ocee
Parsons Rd
PEACHTREE PKWY
ABBOTTS BRIDGE RD
Bell Rd
BELL RD

MANSELL RD
Big Creek
9
8

Old Roswell Rd
OLD ALABAMA RD CONNECTOR
Waters Rd
State Bridge Rd
FULTON COUNTY
MEDLOCK BRIDGE RD
BOLES RD

TURNER MC DONALD PKWY
7AB
HOLCOMB BRIDGE RD
OLD ALABAMA RD
Newtown
Buice Rd
CHATTAHOOCHEE RIVER
DULUTH HWY NW
E LAWRENCEVILLE
Duluth

1531   1532   1533
Roswell
140
BARNWELL DR
Nesbit Ferry Rd
141
McClure Bridge Rd
BERKELEY LAKE
23
13
ST

6

ROBERTS RD
DUNWOODY CLUB DR
Jett Ferry Rd
Mt Vernon Dr
Spalding Dr
SPALDING DR NW
PEACHTREE CORNERS CIR
Bush Rd NW
MEDLOCK BRIDGE RD NW
Berkeley Lake
N Berkeley Lake Rd NW
Old Norcross Rd NW
GWINNETT COUNTY

1600   1601   1602
Dunwoody
Womack Rd
TILLY MILL RD
Happy Hollow Rd
PEACHTREE INDUSTRIAL BLVD NW
Holcomb Bridge Rd NW
PEACHTREE INDUSTRIAL BLVD
BUFORD HWY NW
OLD NORCROSS
SIMPSON CIR NW
SATELLITE BLVD NW
104
103
Club Dr NW

CHAMBLEE DUNWOODY RD
PEELER RD
TILLY MILL RD
JONES MILL RD NW
JIMMY CARTER BLVD NW
W PEACHTREE ST NW
Norcross
378
403
102
85
REYNOLDS BLVD

29
285
30
407
Amwiler Rd NW
Mechanics-ville
101
INDIAN TRAIL LILBURN
FREEMAN LAKE
BEAVER RUN RD NW
Burns Rd NW

1671   1672   1673
Doraville
31AB
OAKCLFF RD
BEST FRIEND RD NW
NORTHEAST EXPWY
99
Oakbrook Pkwy NW
SINGLETON RD NW
Pirkle Rd NW
Williams Harbins Rd NW
Jackson Creek
ROCKBRIDGE RD SW
STEVE REYNOLDS BLVD

141
32
96
95AB
PLEASANTDALE RD
Old Norcross Tucker Rd NW
Tug Dr NW
KILLIAN HILL RD SW
Lilburn

Chamblee
23
13
94
Embry Hills
34
CHAMBLEE TUCKER RD
Britt Rd NW
Williams Rd NW
JIMMY CARTER BLVD NW
Rockbridge Rd SW
Arcado Rd SW

Brookhaven
Dresden Dr NE
93
Peachtree Creek
HENDERSON MILL RD NE
Henderson Rd NW
CHAMBLEE TUCKER RD
29
8
HARMONY GROVE RD SW
LILBURN STONE MOUNTAIN RD SW
ROCKBRIDGE RD SW
Old Tucker Rd SW

DEKALB COUNTY

1743   1744   1745
85
403
Briarlake Rd NE
LA VISTA RD
285
Tucker
236
Rosser Rd Old Rosser Rd SW
HUGH HOWELL RD
Silver Hill Rd SW

13
91
Oak Grove Rd NE
La Vista
37
Brockett Rd
Idlewood Rd
MOUNTAIN INDUSTRIAL BLVD
78
WILLIAM EVANS HWY

89
23
Oak Grove
Vista Grove
38
LAWRENCEVILLE HWY
410

RAND McNALLY

SEE K MAP

SEE M MAP

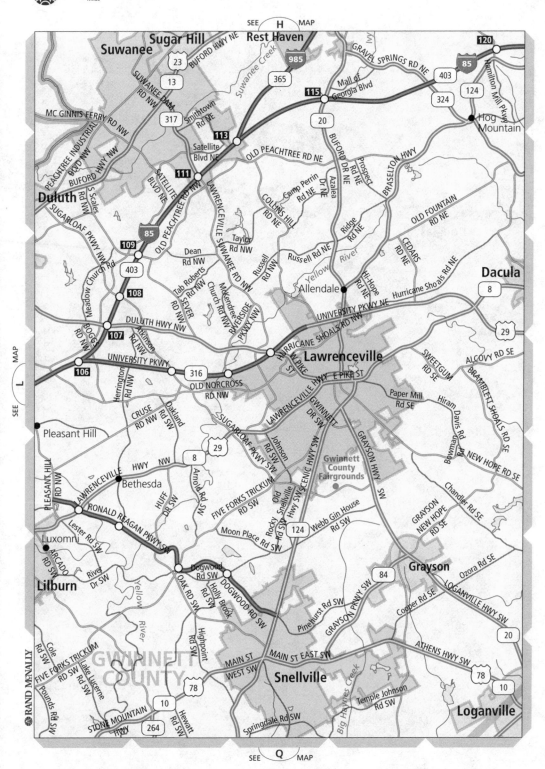

1:150,800
1 in. = 2.4 mi.
0   1.0   2.0
miles

N

SEE H MAP

Suwanee
Sugar Hill
Rest Haven

23
13
985
365
115
20
403
324
120
85
124

Hog Mountain

MC GINNIS FERRY RD NW
SUWANEE DAM RD NW
BUFORD HWY NE
Smithtown Rd NE
317
Satellite Blvd NE
113
GRAVEL SPRINGS RD NE
Mall of Georgia Blvd

PEACHTREE INDUSTRIAL BLVD NW
BUFORD HWY NW
S Scales Rd NW
SATELLITE BLVD NE
111
OLD PEACHTREE RD NE
OLD PEACHTREE RD NE
LAWRENCEVILLE RD NW
Camp Perrin Rd NE
Azalea Dr NE
BUFORD DR NE
Prospect Rd NE
BRASELTON HWY
OLD FOUNTAIN RD NE

Duluth
SUGARLOAF PKWY NW
85
109
403
108
107
106
BOGGS RD NW
Meadow Church Rd
Atkinson Rd NW
DULUTH HWY NW
UNIVERSITY PKWY
316
University Pkwy NE
University Pkwy NE

COLLINS HILL RD NE
Taylor Rd NW
Dean Rd NW
Tab Roberts Rd NW
SEVER RD NW
McKendree Church Rd NW
RIVERSIDE PKWY NW
LAWRENCEVILLE SUWANEE RD NW
Russell Rd NW
Russell Rd NE
Ridge Rd NE
Hi-Hope Rd NE
CEDARS RD NE
Yellow River

Allendale
Dacula
8
29

Hurricane Shoals Rd NE
HURRICANE SHOALS RD NW
N PIKE ST
Lawrenceville
E PIKE ST
LAWRENCEVILLE HWY
SWEETGUM RD SE
ALCOVY RD SE
BRAMBLETT SHOALS RD SE

OLD NORCROSS RD NW
CRUSE RD NW
Oakland Rd SW
SUGARLOAF PKWY SW
Johnson Rd SW
GWINNETT DR SW
GRAYSON HWY SW
Paper Mill Rd SE
Hiram Davis Rd
Bowman Rd
NEW HOPE RD SE

Pleasant Hill
Herrington Rd NW
8
29
Gwinnett County Fairgrounds
GRAYSON NEW HOPE RD SE
Chandler Rd SE

LAWRENCEVILLE HWY NW
Bethesda
RONALD REAGAN PKWY SW
HUFF DR SW
Arnold Rd SW
FIVE FORKS TRICKUM RD SW
Old Snellville Hwy SW
Rocky Rd SW
SCENIC HWY SW
Webb Gin House Rd SW
124
GRAYSON PKWY SW
Grayson
84
Ozora Rd SE
Cooper Rd SE
LOGANVILLE HWY SW
20

Luxomni
Lester Rd SW
ARCADO RD SW
River Dr SW
Dogwood Rd SW
OAK RD SW
Holly Brook Rd SW
DOGWOOD RD SW
Highpoint Rd SW
Moon Place Rd SW
Pinehurst Rd SW
ATHENS HWY SW
78
10

Lilburn
Cole Rd SW
FIVE FORKS TRICKUM RD SW
Lake Lucerne Rd SW
Pounds Rd SW
GWINNETT COUNTY
78
MAIN ST WEST SW
MAIN ST EAST SW
Snellville
Big Haynes Creek
Temple Johnson Rd SW
Loganville
10
264
Hewatt Rd SW
STONE MOUNTAIN HWY
Springdale Rd SW

RAND MCNALLY

SEE L MAP

SEE Q MAP

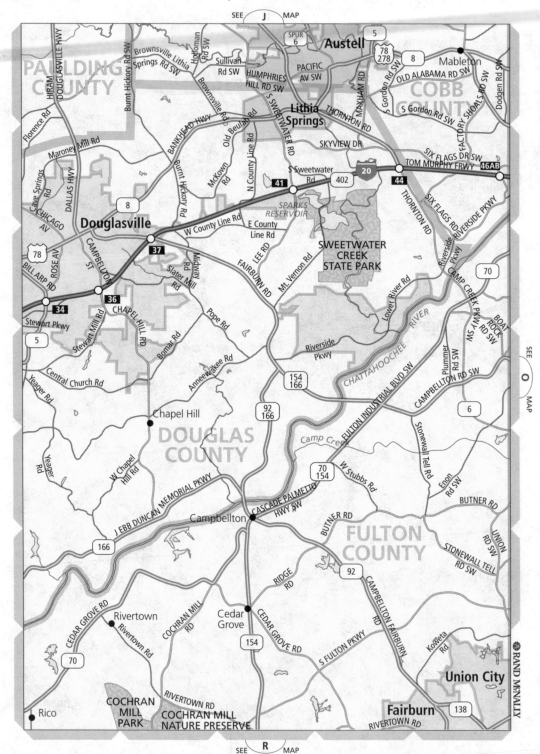

1:150,800
1 in. = 2.4 mi.

0   1.0   2.0
miles

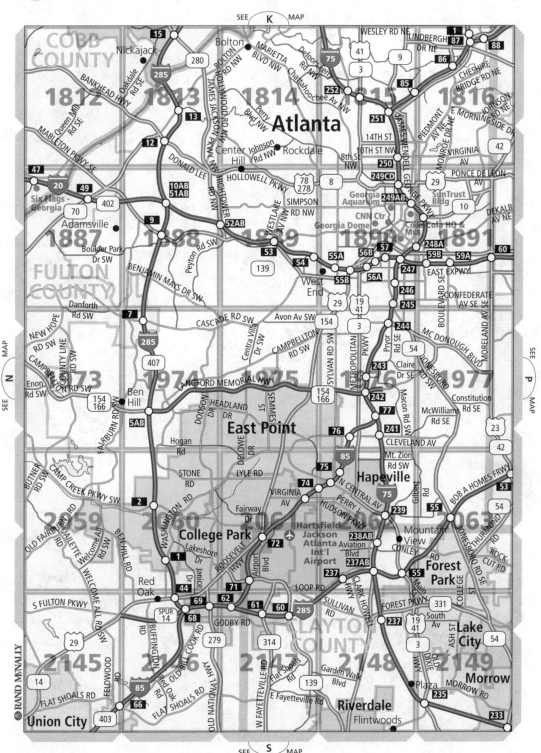

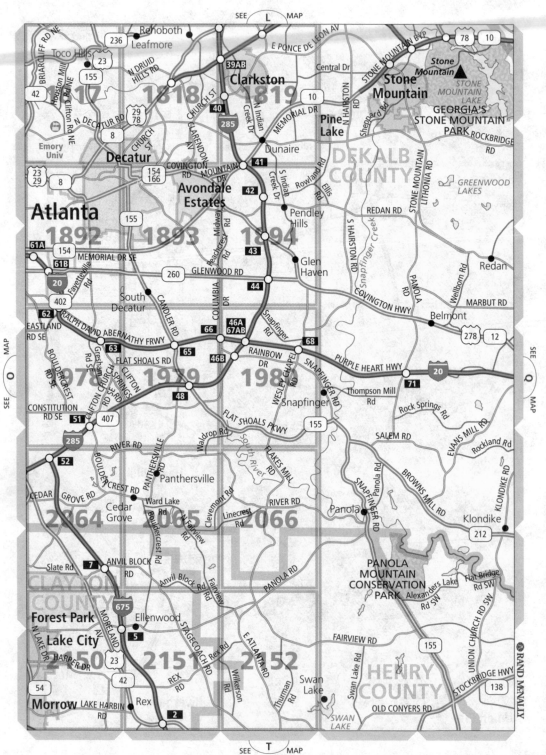

SEE L MAP

236   Rehoboth
Leafmore

E PONCE DE LEON AV

78   10

Toco Hills
23

155

BRIARCLIFF RD NE
Houston Mill Rd NE
N Pat Clifton Rd NE

N DRUID HILLS RD

39AB

Clarkston

Central Dr

Stone
Mountain

STONE
MOUNTAIN
BVP

Stone
Mountain

78   10

2817   **2818**   **2819**

42

155

N DECATUR RD

29
78

8

CHURCH ST

40

285

CLARENDON AV

N Indian Creek Dr

10

MEMORIAL DR

N HAIRSTON RD

Sheppard Rd

Stone
Mountain

STONE
MOUNTAIN
PARK   ROCKBRIDGE
RD

GEORGIA'S
STONE MOUNTAIN
PARK

Emory
Univ

CHURCH ST

Dunaire

41

DEKALB
COUNTY

STONE MOUNTAIN RD

LITHONIA RD

GREENWOOD
LAKES

23
29

8

Decatur

154
166

COVINGTON
RD

MOUNTAIN DR

Avondale
Estates

42

S Indian Creek Dr

Rowland Rd

Ellis

S HAIRSTON RD

REDAN RD

Snapfinger Creek

Redan

Atlanta
1892   **1893**   **1894**

155

Peachcrest Rd

Midway Rd

43

Pendley
Hills

Glen
Haven

COVINGTON HWY

PANOLA RD

Wellborn Rd

Redan

61A

154
61B

MEMORIAL DR SE

260

GLENWOOD RD

CANDLER RD

COLUMBIA DR

44

S HAIRSTON RD

MARBUT RD

20

Fayetteville Rd

South
Decatur

Snapfinger Rd

Belmont

278   12

402

62

EASTLAND
RD SE

RALPH DAVID ABERNATHY FRWY

63

Gresham Rd SE

CHURCH ST

CLIFTON SPRINGS RD SE

66

46A
67AB

68

PURPLE HEART HWY

20

BOULDERCREST RD SE

FLAT SHOALS RD

65

46B

RAINBOW DR

WESLEY CHAPEL RD

SNAPFINGER RD

Thompson Mill Rd

71

1978   **1979**   **1980**

CONSTITUTION
RD SE

51

48

Snapfinger

Rock Springs Rd

285

407

RIVER RD

FLAT SHOALS PKWY

155

SALEM RD

EVANS MILL RD

Rockland Rd

52

BOULDERCREST RD

PANTHERSVILLE RD

Panthersville

Waldrop Rd

South River

FLAKES MILL RD

Snapfinger Rd

Panola Rd

BROWNS MILL RD

KLONDIKE RD

CEDAR
GROVE RD

Cedar
Grove

Ward Lake Rd

BOULDERCREST RD

Fairview Rd

Clevemont Rd

Linecrest Rd

RIVER RD

Panola

Klondike

2064   **2065**   **2066**

212

Slate Rd

7

ANVIL BLOCK RD

Anvil Block Rd

Fairview Rd

PANOLA RD

PANOLA
MOUNTAIN
CONSERVATION
PARK

Alexanders Lake Rd SW

Flat Bridge Rd SW

CLAYTON
COUNTY

675

Ellenwood

MORELAND AV

STAGECOACH RD

E ATLANTA RD

FAIRVIEW RD

UNION CHURCH RD SW

Forest Park

N LAKE DR

Lake City

5

23

Rex Rd

Wilkerson Rd

155

2150   **2151**   **2152**

HARPER DR

42

Thurman Rd

Swan Lake

HENRY
COUNTY

STOCKBRIDGE HWY

54

Morrow   LAKE HARBIN RD

Rex

2

REX RD

SWAN
LAKE

OLD CONYERS RD

138

RAND MCNALLY

SEE T MAP

SEE O MAP

SEE Q MAP

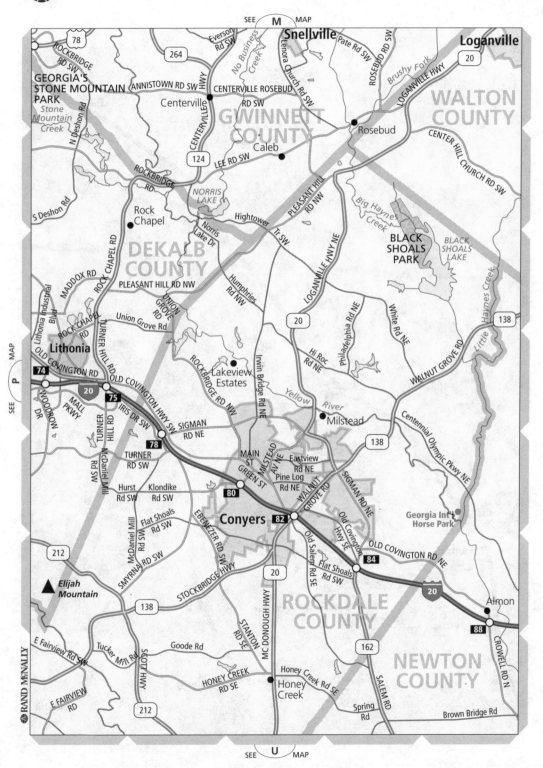

MAP
R

1:150,800
1 in. = 2.4 mi.

0   1.0   2.0
miles

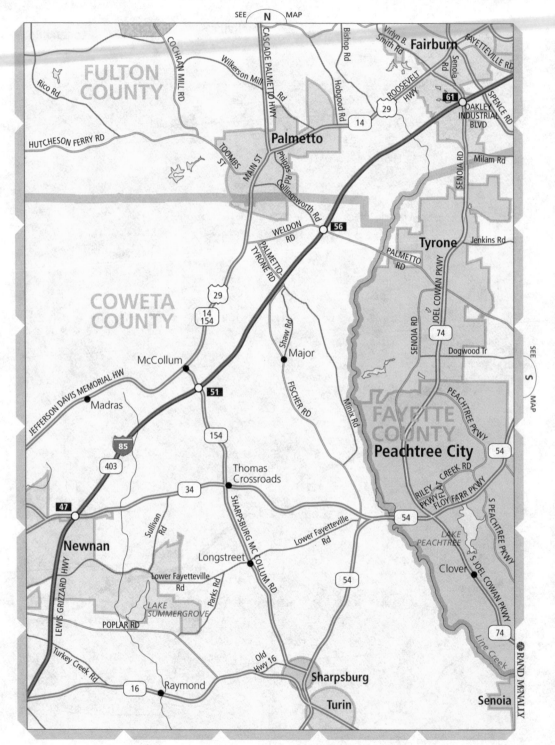

FULTON COUNTY

Rico Rd

COCHRAN MILL RD

HUTCHESON FERRY RD

Wilkerson Mill Rd

CASCADE PALMETTO HWY

TOOMBS ST

MAIN ST

Bishop Rd

Hobgood Rd

Virlyn B. Smith Rd

Fairburn

ROOSEVELT HWY

FAYETTEVILLE RD

Senoia Rd

29

14

61

OAKLEY INDUSTRIAL BLVD

SPENCE RD

Palmetto

Philips Rd

Collingsworth Rd

WELDON RD

PALMETTO-TYRONE RD

SENOIA RD

Milam Rd

56

PALMETTO RD

Tyrone

Jenkins Rd

COWETA COUNTY

29

14 154

McCollum

Madras

JEFFERSON DAVIS MEMORIAL HW

51

85

403

47

Newnan

LEWIS GRIZZARD HWY

Shaw Rd

Major

FISCHER RD

Minix Rd

JOEL COWAN PKWY

74

Dogwood Tr

FAYETTE COUNTY

Peachtree City

PEACHTREE PKWY

54

154

Thomas Crossroads

34

Sullivan Rd

SHARPSBURG MC COLLUM RD

Longstreet

Lower Fayetteville Rd

Parks Rd

Lower Fayetteville Rd

LAKE SUMMERGROVE

POPLAR RD

Turkey Creek Rd

16

Raymond

Old Hwy 16

Sharpsburg

Turin

RILEY PKWY

FLAT CREEK RD

FLOY FARR PKWY

LAKE PEACHTREE

54

54

S PEACHTREE PKWY

Clover

S JOEL COWAN PKWY

74

Line Creek

Senoia

RAND MCNALLY

1:150,800
1 in. = 2.4 mi.

0   1.0   2.0

miles

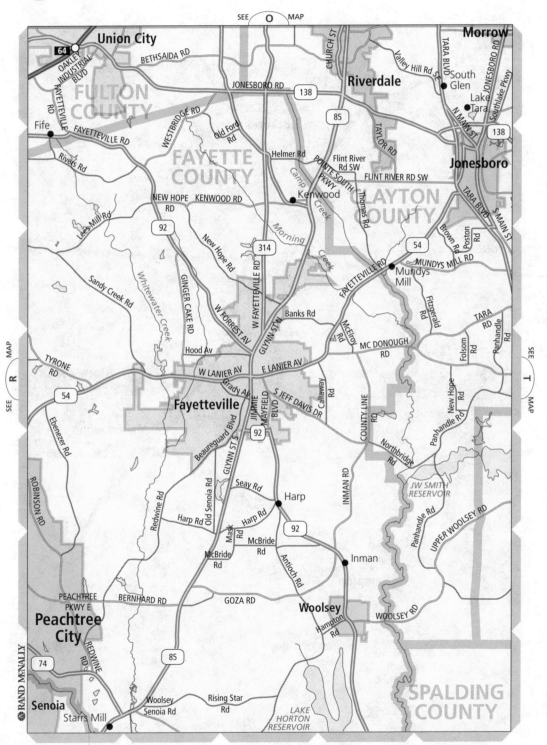

SEE O MAP

Union City

64

OAKLEY INDUSTRIAL BLVD

FAYETTEVILLE RD

BETHSAIDA RD

Morrow

TARA BLVD

Valley Hill Rd SE

CHURCH ST

Riverdale

South Glen

JONESBORO RD

138

Lake Tara

N MAIN ST

JONESBORO RD

Southlake Pkwy

FULTON COUNTY

85

TAYLOR RD

138

WESTBRIDGE RD

Old Ford Rd

Fife

FAYETTEVILLE RD

Rivers Rd

FAYETTE COUNTY

Helmer Rd

Flint River Rd SW

FLINT RIVER RD SW

Jonesboro

NEW HOPE RD

KENWOOD RD

POINTE SOUTH PKWY

Camp Creek

Kenwood

Thomas Rd

CLAYTON COUNTY

TARA BLVD

S MAIN ST

Lees Mill Rd

92

New Hope Rd

314

Morning Creek

54

Brown Rd

Poston Rd

MUNDYS MILL RD

Sandy Creek Rd

GINGER CAKE RD

W FORREST AV

W FAYETTEVILLE RD

Banks Rd

FAYETTEVILLE RD

Mundys Mill

Fitzgerald Rd

Whitewater Creek

Hood Av

GLYNN ST N

McElroy Rd

MC DONOUGH RD

TARA RD

Panhandle Rd

Folsom Rd

SEE R MAP

TYRONE RD

W LANIER AV

E LANIER AV

Callaway Rd

SEE T MAP

54

Grady Av

S JEFF DAVIS DR

COUNTY LINE RD

New Hope Rd

Fayetteville

Ebenezer Rd

JIMMIE MAYFIELD BLVD

92

Panhandle Rd

Beauregard Blvd

GLYNN ST S

Seay Rd

Harp

INMAN RD

Northbridge Rd

JW SMITH RESERVOIR

ROBINSON RD

Redwine Rd

Harp Rd

Old Senoia Rd

Harp Rd

92

Panhandle Rd

UPPER WOOLSEY RD

Mask Rd

McBride Rd

Inman

McBride Rd

Antioch Rd

PEACHTREE PKWY E

BERNHARD RD

GOZA RD

Woolsey

WOOLSEY RD

Peachtree City

REDWINE RD

85

Hampton Rd

SPALDING COUNTY

74

Woolsey Senoia Rd

Rising Star Rd

LAKE HORTON RESERVOIR

RAND MCNALLY

Senoia

Starrs Mill

MAP
T

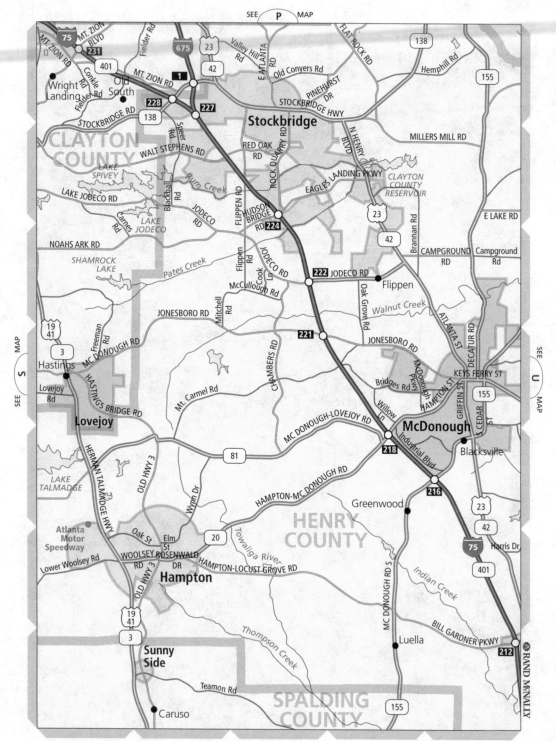

1:150,800
1 in. = 2.4 mi.

0   1.0   2.0
miles

N

SEE **P** MAP

75 MT. ZION BLVD
MT. ZION RD
231
Fielder Rd
675
23
Valley Hill Rd
E ATLANTA
FLATROCK RD
138
401
42
Old Conyers Rd
Hemphill Rd
155
Wright Landing
Conkle Rd
Fielder Rd
Old South
MT. ZION RD
1
PINEHURST DR
STOCKBRIDGE HWY
228
227
STOCKBRIDGE RD
138
Speer Rd
Stockbridge
N HENRY BLVD
MILLERS MILL RD

CLAYTON COUNTY
WALT STEPHENS RD
RED OAK RD
ROCK QUARRY RD

LAKE SPIVEY
Rum Creek
EAGLES LANDING PKWY
CLAYTON COUNTY RESERVOIR
E LAKE RD

LAKE JODECO RD
Blackhall Rd
JODECO RD
FLIPPEN RD
HUDSON BRIDGE RD
224
23
Brannan Rd

Carnes Rd
LAKE JODECO
42
CAMPGROUND RD
Campground Rd

NOAHS ARK RD
Pates Creek
Flippen Rd
JODECO RD
Oak Grove Rd
Walnut Creek

SHAMROCK LAKE
McCullough Rd
Cook Ln
222 JODECO RD
Flippen

JONESBORO RD
Mitchell Rd
221
JONESBORO RD
ATLANTA ST
DECATUR RD

19 41
McFreeman
CHAMBERS RD
McDonough Pkwy
KEYS FERRY ST

3
Hastings
MC DONOUGH RD
HAMPTON ST
GRIFFIN ST
155
S CEDAR ST

Lovejoy Rd
HASTINGS BRIDGE RD
Mt. Carmel Rd
Bridges Rd
McDonough
Lovejoy
Willow Ln
218
Industrial Blvd
Blacksville

HERMAN TALMADGE HWY
OLD HWY 3
81
MC DONOUGH-LOVEJOY RD
216

LAKE TALMADGE
Wynn Dr
HAMPTON-MC DONOUGH RD
Greenwood
23
42

Atlanta Motor Speedway
Oak St
Elm St
20
Towaliga River
HENRY COUNTY
75
Harris Dr

Lower Woolsey Rd
WOOLSEY RD
ROSENWALD DR
HAMPTON-LOCUST GROVE RD
401

OLD HWY 3
Hampton
MC DONOUGH RD S
Indian Creek

19 41
Luella
BILL GARDNER PKWY

3
Sunny Side
Thompson Creek
212
RAND MCNALLY

Teamon Rd

Caruso
SPALDING COUNTY
155

SEE **S** MAP

SEE **U** MAP

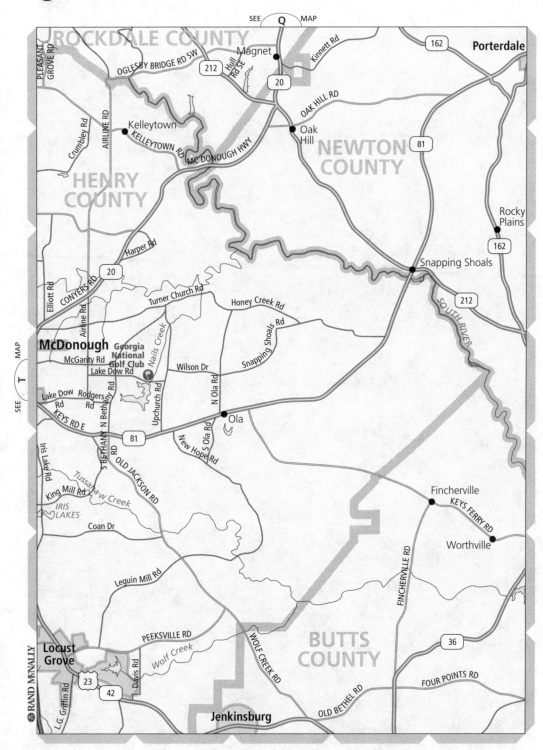

1:150,800
1 in. = 2.4 mi.
0   1.0   2.0
miles

SEE Q MAP

ROCKDALE COUNTY

PLEASANT GROVE RD
OGLESBY BRIDGE RD SW
212
Hull Rd SE

Magnet
Kinnett Rd
162
Porterdale
20

OAK HILL RD

Crumbley Rd
AIRLINE RD
Kelleytown
KELLEYTOWN RD
MC DONOUGH HWY

Oak Hill
81

NEWTON COUNTY

HENRY COUNTY

Rocky Plains
162

Harper Rd

Snapping Shoals
212

Elliott Rd
CONVERS RD
20

Turner Church Rd
Honey Creek Rd

SOUTH RIVER

Airline Rd
Nails Creek
Snapping Shoals Rd

McDonough
Georgia National Golf Club
McGarity Rd
Lake Dow Rd
Wilson Dr

Lake Dow Rd
Rodgers Rd
N Bethany RD
Upchurch Rd
N Ola Rd
Ola

KEYS RD E
81
S BETHANY RD

Iris Lake Rd
New Hope Rd
S Ola Rd
OLD JACKSON RD

King Mill Rd
Tussahaw Creek
IRIS LAKES

Fincherville
KEYS FERRY RD

Coan Dr

Worthville

FINCHERVILLE RD

Leguin Mill Rd

BUTTS COUNTY

Locust Grove
PEEKSVILLE RD
Wolf Creek
WOLF CREEK RD
36

23
42
Davis Rd

L.G. Griffin Rd
Jenkinsburg
OLD BETHEL RD
FOUR POINTS RD

RAND McNALLY

SEE T MAP

MAP
1526

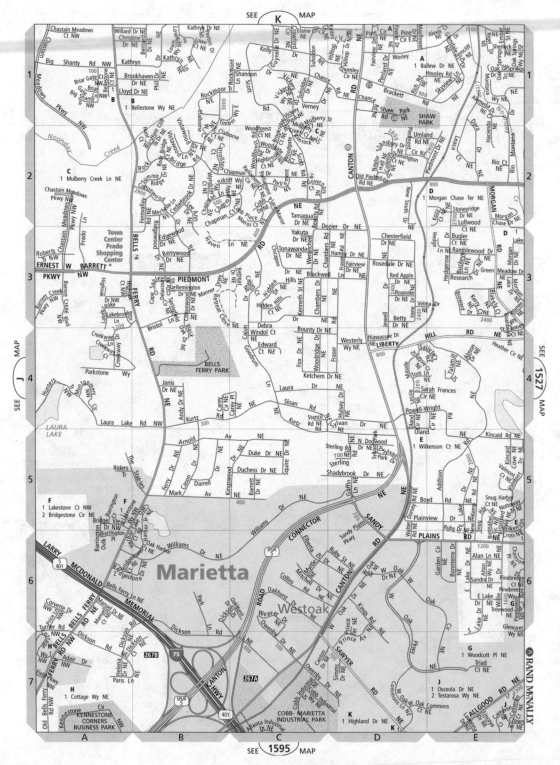

1:30,000
1 in. = 2500 ft.

0   0.25   0.5
miles

SEE K MAP

SEE J MAP

SEE 1527 MAP

RAND McNALLY

Marietta

Westoak

MAP
1527

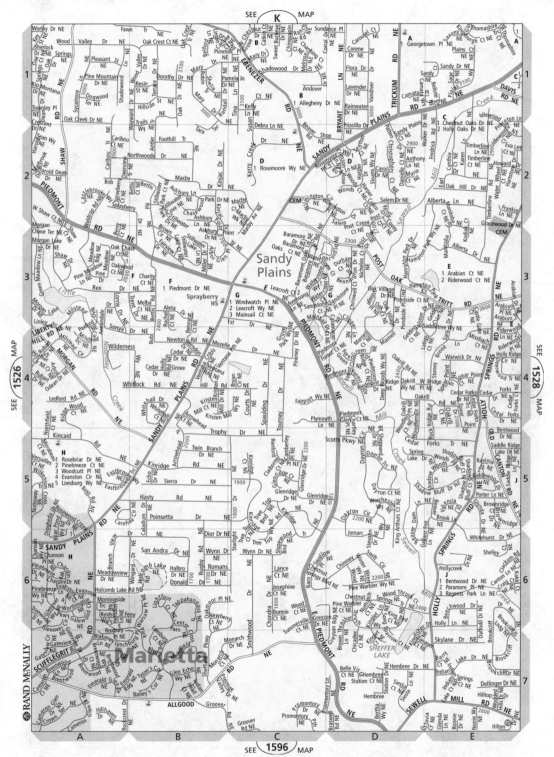

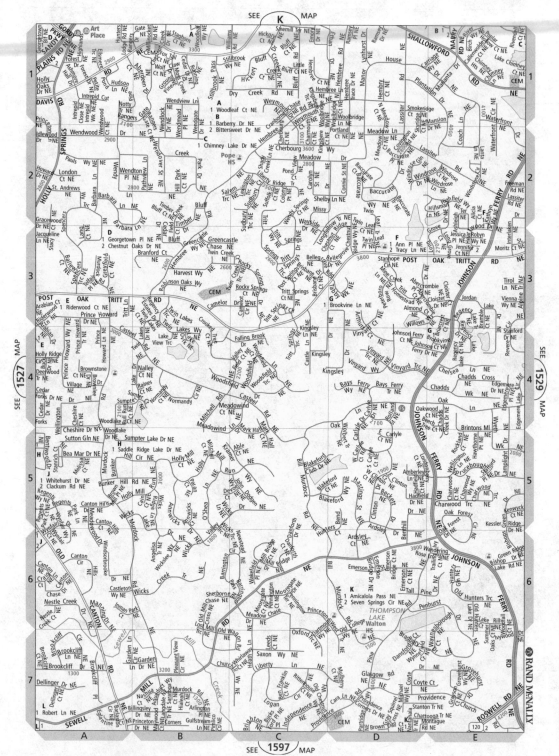

MAP
1528

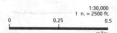

1:30,000
1 n. = 2500 ft.

0   0.25   0.5
miles

SEE K MAP

SEE 1527 MAP

SEE 1529 MAP

SEE 1597 MAP

RAND M!NALLY

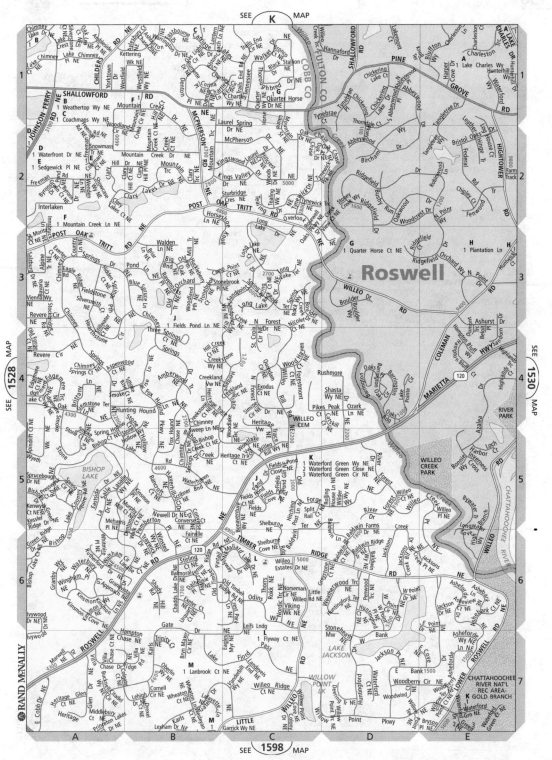

MAP
1529

1:30,000
1 in. = 2500 ft.

0   0.25   0.5
miles

SEE K MAP

Roswell

SEE 1528 MAP

SEE 1530 MAP

SEE 1598 MAP

RAND M\!NALLY

MAP
1530

1:30,000
1 in. = 2500 ft.

0   0.25   0.5
miles

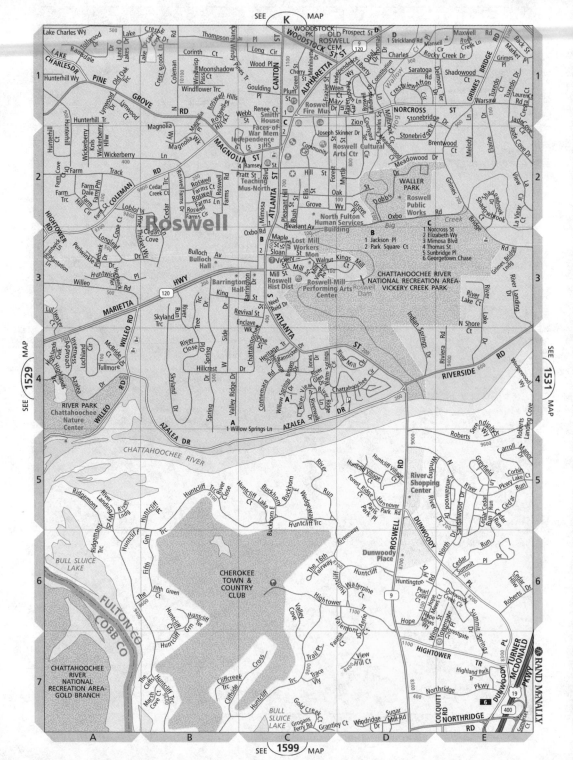

Roswell

SEE 1529 MAP

SEE 1531 MAP

CHATTAHOOCHEE RIVER

CHATTAHOOCHEE RIVER NATIONAL RECREATION AREA-VICKERY CREEK PARK

RIVER PARK Chattahoochee Nature Center

CHATTAHOOCHEE RIVER NATIONAL RECREATION AREA-GOLD BRANCH

BULL SLUICE LAKE

CHEROKEE TOWN & COUNTRY CLUB

RIVERSIDE RD

River Shopping Center

Dunwoody Place

NORTHRIDGE RD

RAND McNALLY

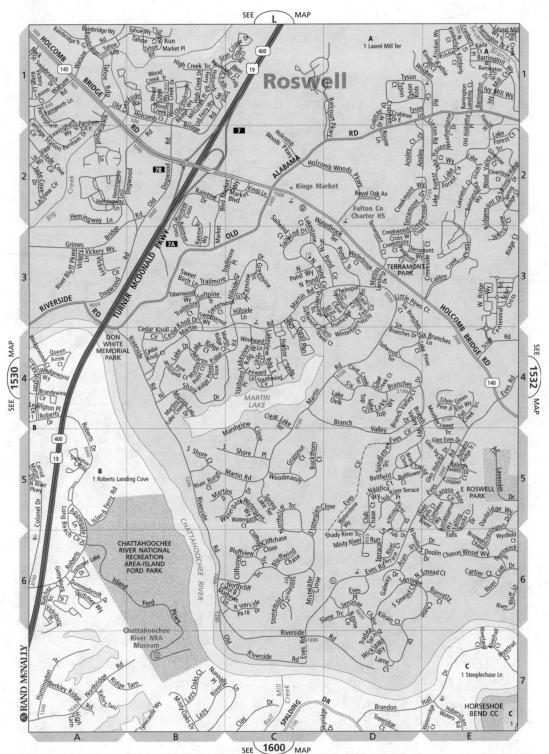

MAP
1531

1:30,000
1 in. = 2500 ft.

miles

SEE — L — MAP

Roswell

SEE 1530 MAP

SEE 1532 MAP

SEE 1600 MAP

RAND M°NALLY

MAP
1532

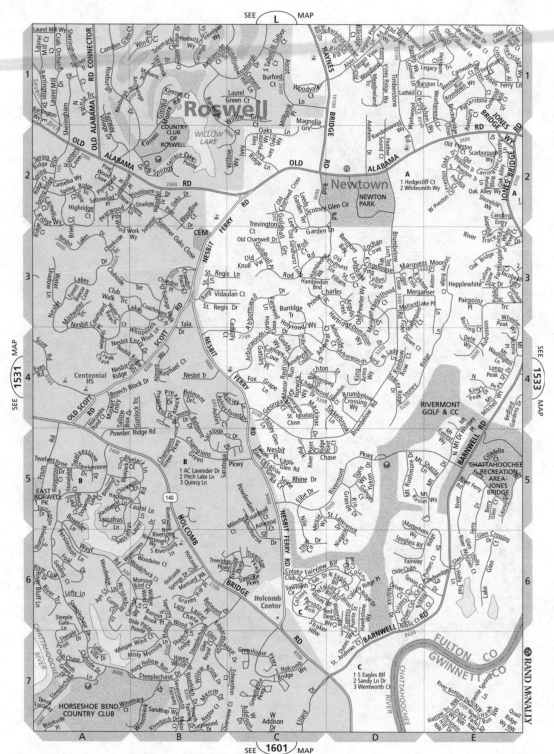

1:30,000
1 n. = 2500 ft.
0   0.25   0.5
miles

Roswell

Newtown

SEE 1531 MAP

SEE 1533 MAP

RAND McNALLY

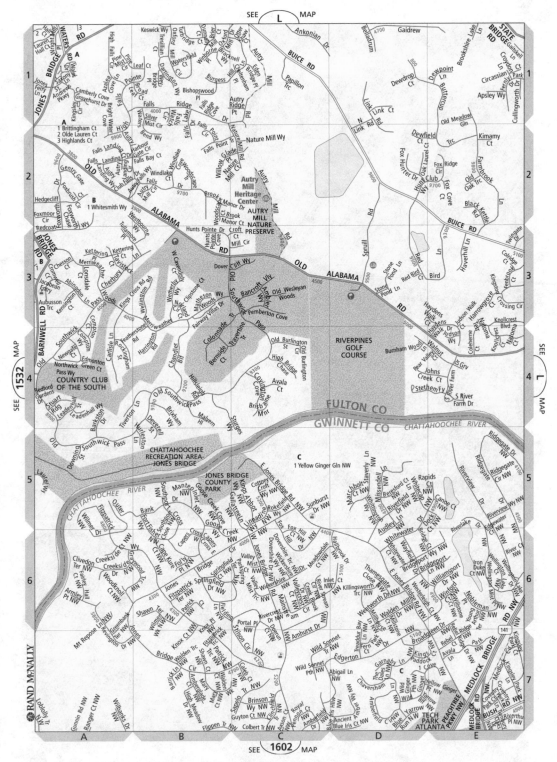

MAP
1533

1:30,000
1 in. = 2500 ft.

0   0.25   0.5
miles

N

SEE L MAP

SEE 1532 MAP

SEE L MAP

SEE 1602 MAP

RAND McNALLY

MAP
1595

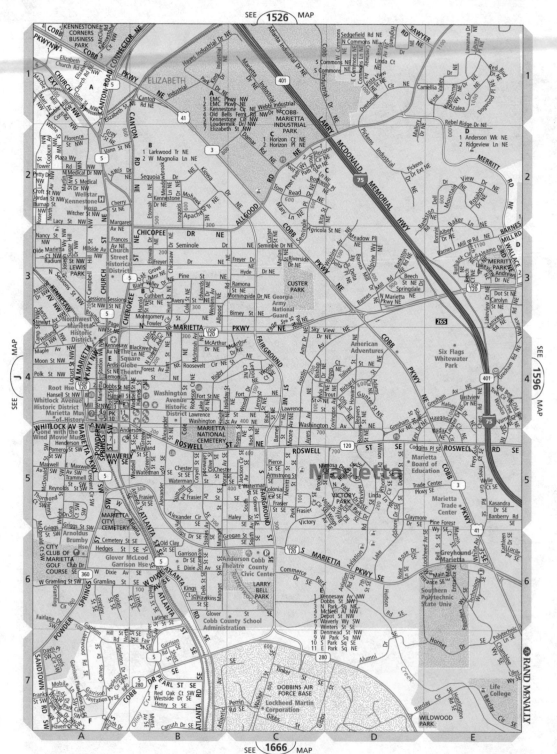

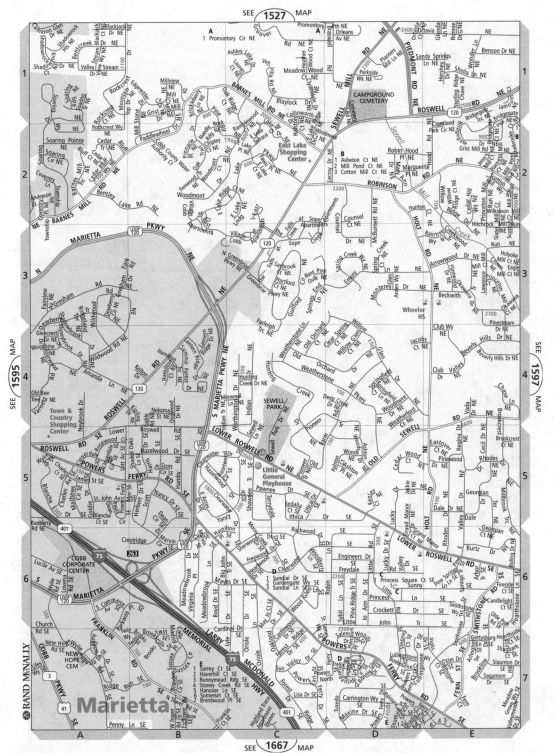

MAP
1596

MAP
1597

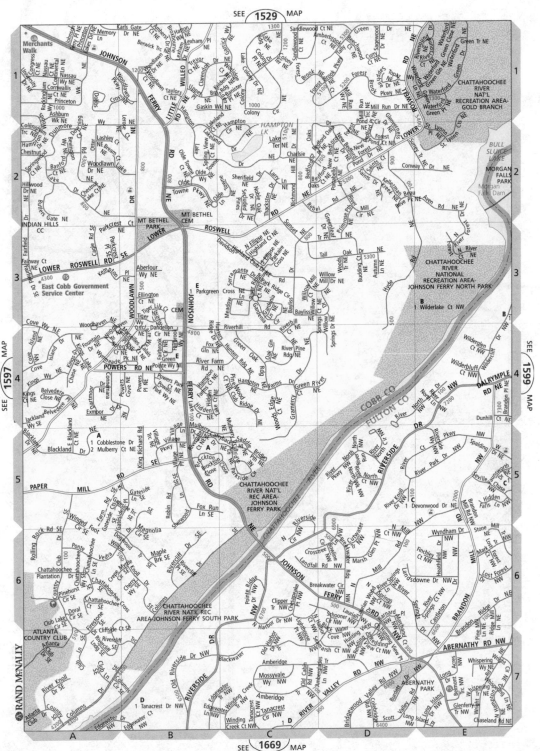

MAP 1598

1:30,000
1 in. = 2500 ft.
0   0.25   0.5
miles

RAND McNALLY

CHATTAHOOCHEE RIVER NAT'L RECREATION AREA-GOLD BRANCH

BULL SLUICE LAKE

MORGAN FALLS PARK

Morgan Falls Dam

CHATTAHOOCHEE RIVER NATIONAL RECREATION AREA-JOHNSON FERRY NORTH PARK

B 1 Wilderlake Ct NW

COBB CO / FULTON CO

INDIAN HILLS CC

MT BETHEL PARK

MT BETHEL CEM

East Cobb Government Service Center

Merchants Walk

CHATTAHOOCHEE RIVER NAT'L REC AREA-JOHNSON FERRY PARK

A 1 Cobblestone Dr
  2 Mulberry Ct NE

C 1 Devonwood Dr NE

CHATTAHOOCHEE RIVER NAT'L REC AREA-JOHNSON FERRY SOUTH PARK

ATLANTA COUNTRY CLUB

ABERNATHY PARK

D 1 Tanacrest Dr NW

C 1 Tanacrest Dr NW

MAP
1599

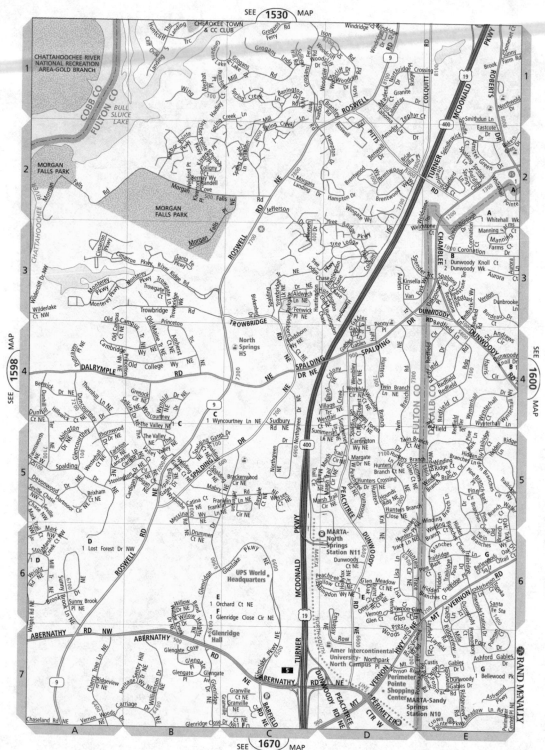

1:30,000
1 in. = 2500 ft.
0   0.25   0.5
miles

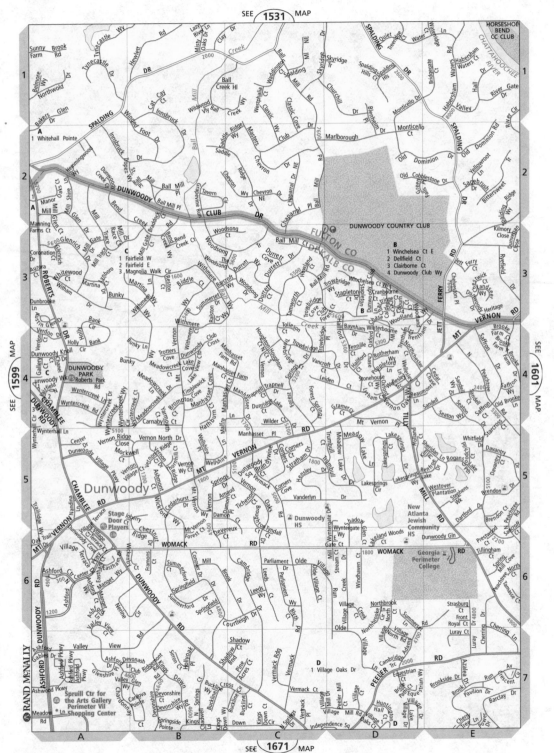

MAP
1600

1:30,000
1 in. = 2500 ft.

0   0.25   0.5
miles

SEE 1599 MAP

SEE 1601 MAP

RAND MCNALLY

MAP
1601

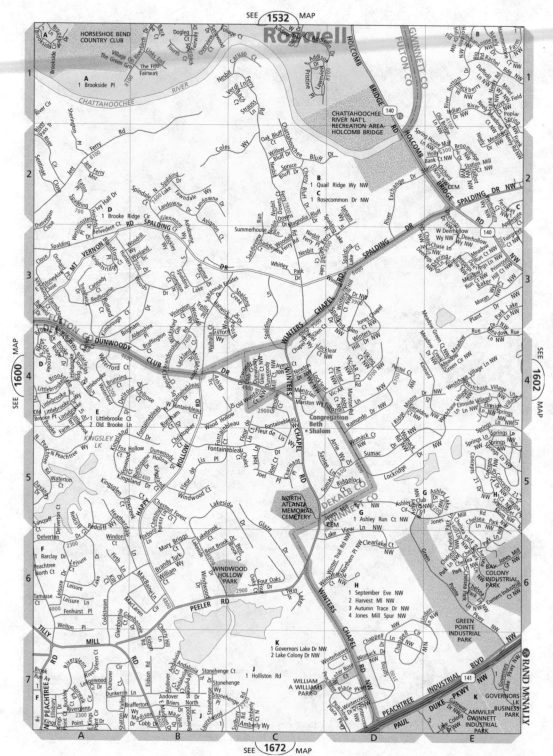

1:30,000
1 in. = 2500 ft.

0   0.25   0.5
miles

Roswell

HORSESHOE BEND
COUNTRY CLUB

CHATTAHOOCHEE
RIVER NAT'L
RECREATION AREA-
HOLCOMB BRIDGE

CHATTAHOOCHEE RIVER

A
1 Brookside Pl

B
1 Quail Ridge Wy NW

C
1 Rosecommon Dr NW

D
1 Brooke Ridge Cir

E
1 Littlebrooke Ct
2 Old Brooke Ln

Congregation
Beth
Shalom

NORTH
ATLANTA
MEMORIAL
CEMETERY

WINDWOOD
HOLLOW
PARK

KINGSLEY LK

F
1 Barclay Dr

PEELER RD

G
1 Ashley Run Ct NW

H
1 September Eve NW
2 Harvest Ml NW
3 Autumn Trace Dr NW
4 Jones Mill Spur NW

K
1 Governors Lake Dr NW
2 Lake Colony Dr NW

J
1 Holliston Rd

WILLIAM
A WILLIAMS
PARK

GREEN
POINTE
INDUSTRIAL
PARK

BAY
COLONY
INDUSTRIAL
PARK

AMWILER
GWINNETT
INDUSTRIAL
PARK

GOVERNORS
BUSINESS
PARK

DUKE PKWY

PAUL

PEACHTREE INDUSTRIAL BLVD

RAND McNALLY

SEE 1600 MAP

SEE 1602 MAP

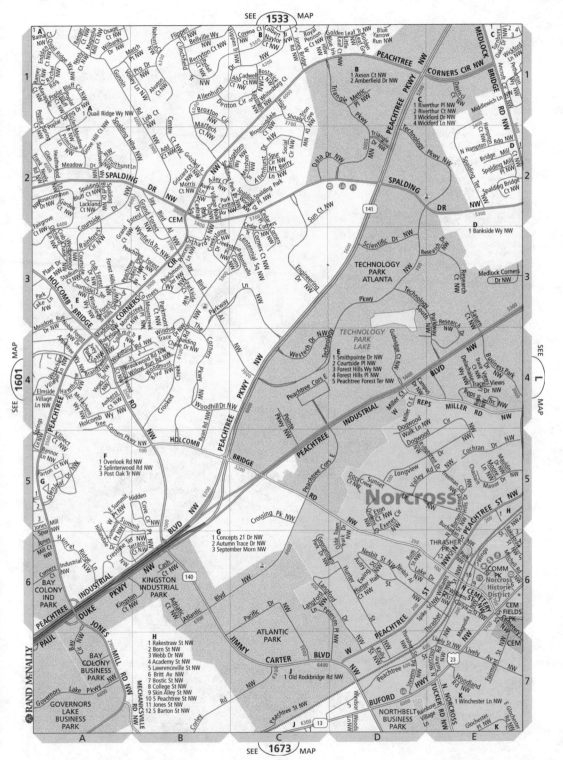

MAP
1602

1:30,000
1 in. = 2500 ft.

0   0.25   0.5
miles

N

SEE 1533 MAP

SEE 1601 MAP

SEE L MAP

SEE 1673 MAP

RAND McNALLY

Norcross

B
1 Axson Ct NW
2 Amberfield Dr NW

C
1 Riverthur Pl NW
2 Riverthur Ct NW
3 Wickford Dr NW
4 Wickford Ln NW

D
1 Bankside Wy NW

E
1 Smithpointe Dr NW
2 Courtside Pl NW
3 Forest Hills Wy NW
4 Forest Hills Pl NW
5 Peachtree Forest Ter NW

F
1 Overlook Rd NW
2 Splinterwood Rd NW
3 Post Oak Tr NW

G
1 Concepts 21 Dr NW
2 Autumn Trace Dr NW
3 September Morn NW

H
1 Rakestraw St NW
2 Born St NW
3 Webb Dr NW
4 Academy St NW
5 Lawrenceville St NW
6 Britt Av NW
7 Bostic St NW
8 College St NW
9 Skin Alley St NW
10 S Peachtree St NW
11 Jones St NW
12 S Barton St NW

J
1 Old Rockbridge Rd NW

K
1 Winchester Ln NW

TECHNOLOGY
PARK
ATLANTA

TECHNOLOGY
PARK
LAKE

ATLANTIC
PARK

KINGSTON
INDUSTRIAL
PARK

BAY
COLONY
IND
PARK

BAY
COLONY
BUSINESS
PARK

GOVERNORS
LAKE
BUSINESS
PARK

NORTHBELT
BUSINESS
PARK

Norcross
Historic
District

MAP
1666

SEE 1595 MAP

1:30,000
1 in. = 2500 ft.
0   0.25   0.5
miles

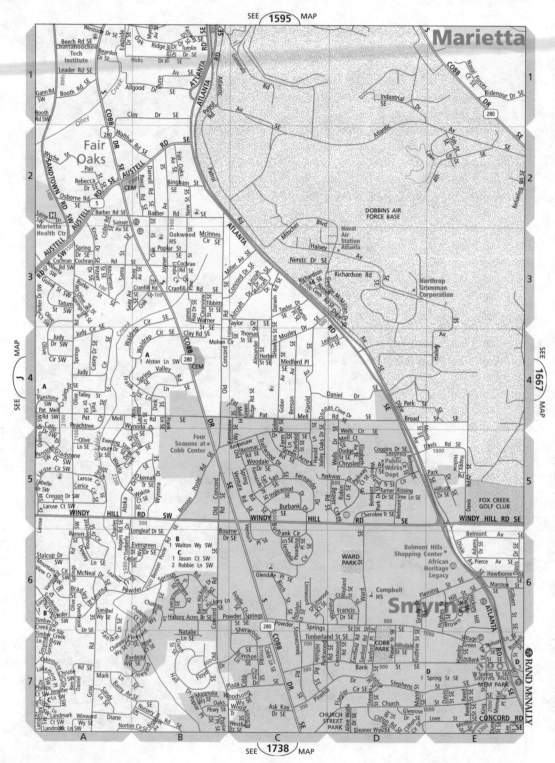

Marietta

Fair
Oaks

Smyrna

SEE J MAP

SEE 1667 MAP

SEE 1738 MAP

RAND McNALLY

MAP
1667

1:30,000
1 in. = 2500 ft.

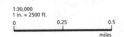

0   0.25   0.5
miles

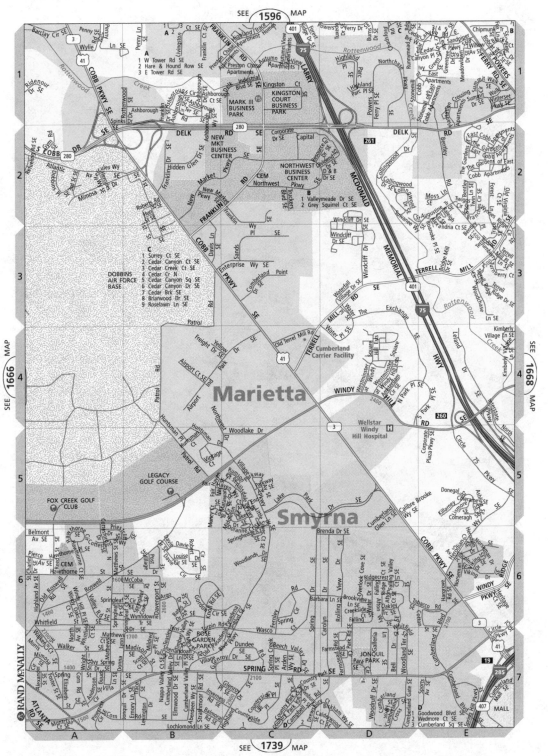

SEE 1596 MAP

SEE 1666 MAP

SEE 1668 MAP

SEE 1739 MAP

A
1 W Tower Rd SE
2 Hare & Hound Row SE
3 E Tower Rd SE

B
1 Valleymeade Dr SE
2 Grey Squirrel Ct SE

C
1 Surrey Ct SE
2 Cedar Canyon Ct SE
3 Cedar Creek Ct SE
4 Cedar Cr N
5 Cedar Canyon Sq SE
6 Cedar Canyon Dr SE
7 Cedar Brk SE
8 Briarwood Dr SE
9 Roselawn Ln SE

D
1 Goodwood Blvd
2 Wedmore Ct SE
3 Cumberland Sq SE

DOBBINS
AIR FORCE
BASE

Marietta

Smyrna

MARK III
BUSINESS
PARK

KINGSTON
COURT
BUSINESS
PARK

NEW
MKT
BUSINESS
CENTER

NORTHWEST
BUSINESS
CENTER

Cumberland
Carrier Facility

Wellstar
Windy
Hill Hospital

LEGACY
GOLF COURSE

FOX CREEK GOLF
CLUB

ROSE
GARDEN
PARK

JONQUIL
PARK

MALL

RAND MCNALLY

MAP
1668

1:30,000
1 n. = 2500 ft.

0   0.25   0.5
miles

SEE 1597 MAP

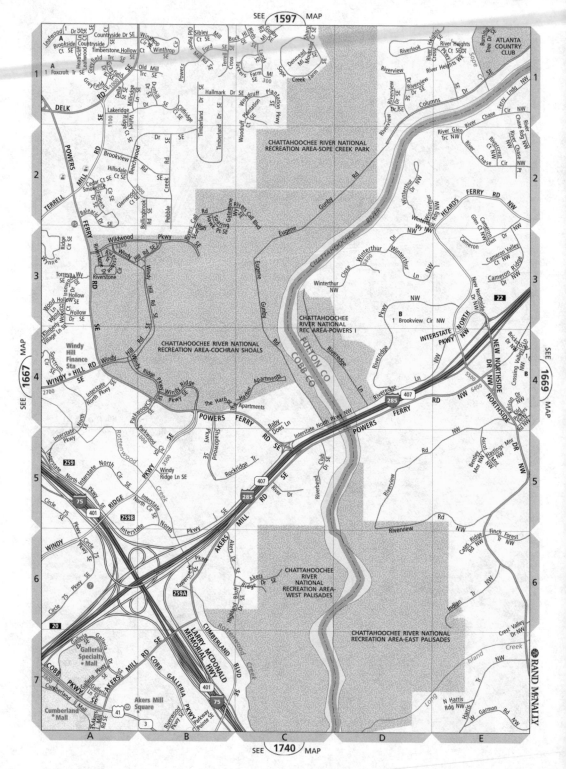

SEE 1667 MAP

SEE 1669 MAP

SEE 1740 MAP

RAND McNALLY

CHATTAHOOCHEE RIVER NATIONAL
RECREATION AREA-SOPE CREEK PARK

CHATTAHOOCHEE
RIVER NATIONAL
REC AREA-POWERS I

CHATTAHOOCHEE RIVER NATIONAL
RECREATION AREA-COCHRAN SHOALS

CHATTAHOOCHEE
RIVER
NATIONAL
RECREATION AREA-
WEST PALISADES

CHATTAHOOCHEE RIVER NATIONAL
RECREATION AREA-EAST PALISADES

ATLANTA
COUNTRY
CLUB

MAP
1669

N

1:30,000
1 in. = 2500 ft.

0   0.25   0.5
miles

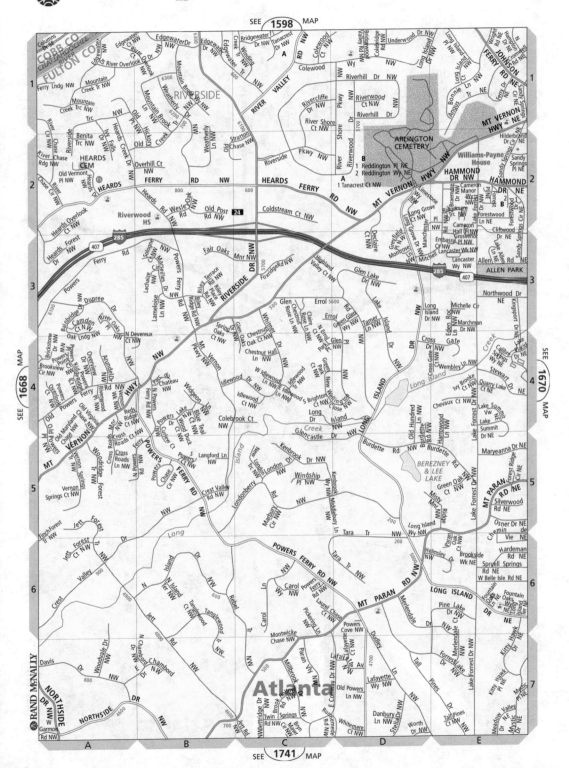

SEE 1598 MAP

SEE 1668 MAP

SEE 1670 MAP

SEE 1741 MAP

RAND McNALLY

Atlanta

MAP
1670

1:30,000
1 n. = 2500 ft.

N

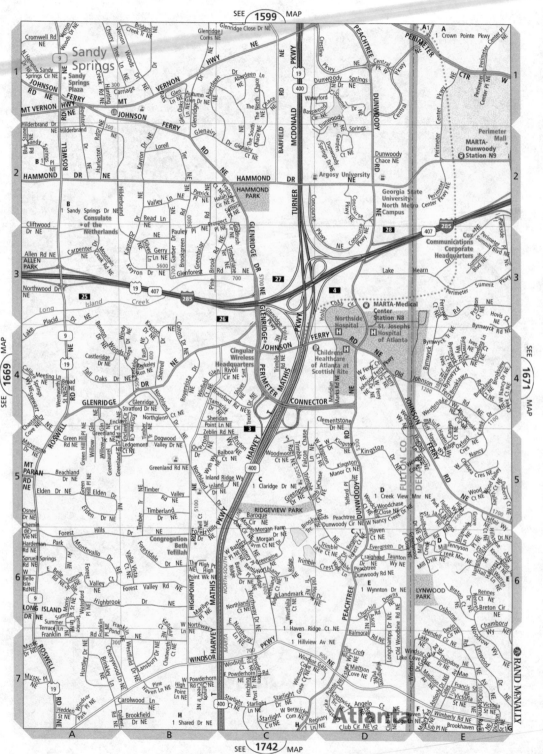

SEE 1599 MAP

SEE 1669 MAP

SEE 1671 MAP

SEE 1742 MAP

RAND M°NALLY

Atlanta

MAP
1671

1:30,000
1 in. = 2500 ft.

0 0.25 0.5
miles

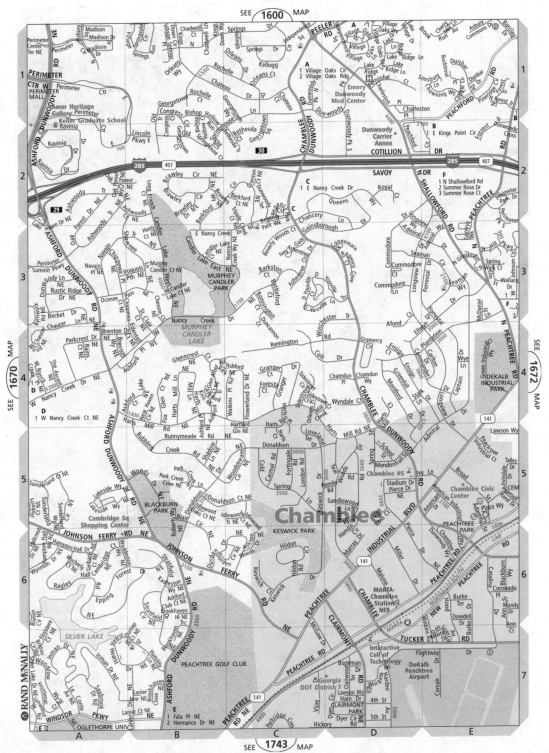

SEE 1600 MAP

SEE 1670 MAP

SEE 1672 MAP

SEE 1743 MAP

MAP
1672

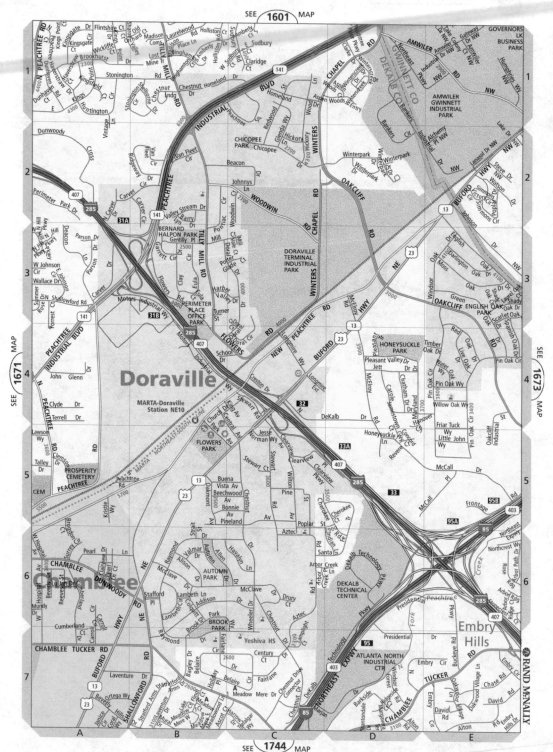

RAND MCNALLY

MAP
1673

N

1:30,000
1 in. = 2500 ft.

0   0.25   0.5
miles

SEE 1602 MAP

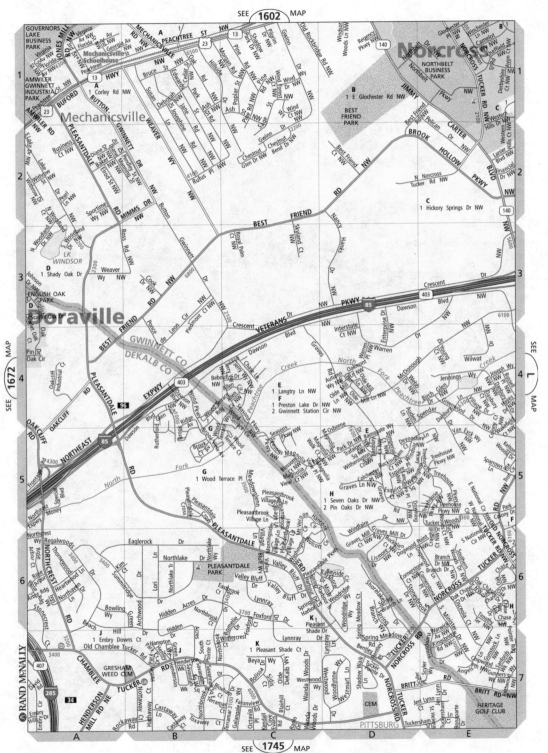

SEE 1672 MAP

SEE L MAP

SEE 1745 MAP

RAND MCNALLY

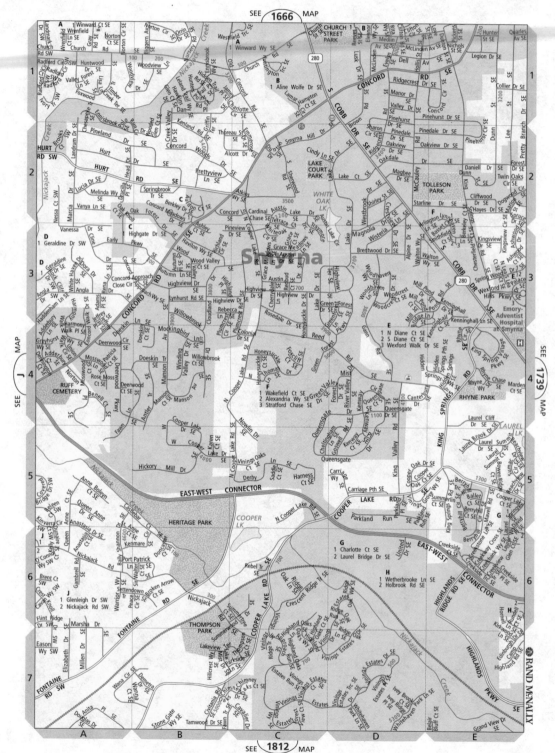

MAP
1738

SEE J MAP

SEE 1739 MAP

1:30,000
1 n. = 2500 ft.

0   0.25   0.5
miles

N

RAND McNALLY

MAP
1739

1:30,000
1 in. = 2500 ft.

0   0.25   0.5
miles

SEE 1667 MAP

SEE 1738 MAP

SEE 1740 MAP

SEE 1813 MAP

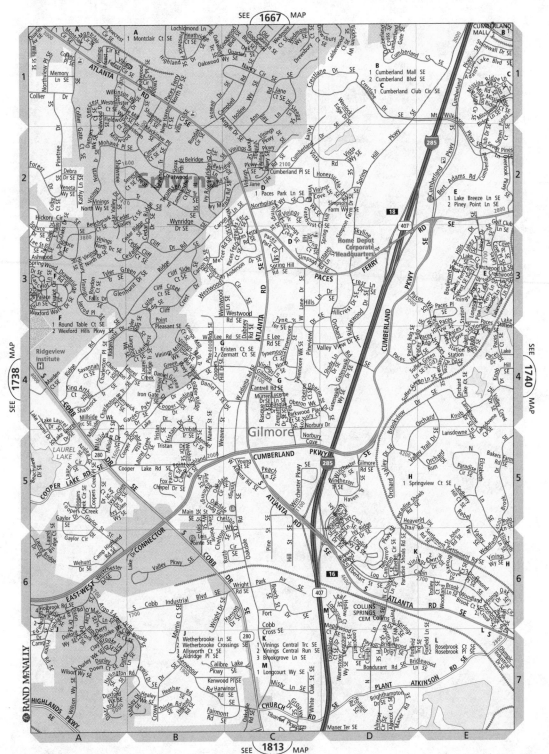

RAND McNALLY

MAP
1740

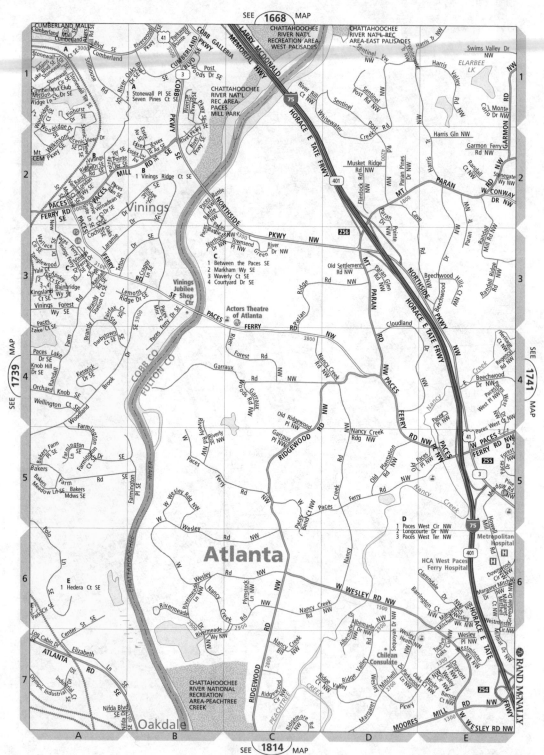

1:30,000
1 n. = 2500 ft.

0   0.25   0.5
miles

N

SEE 1668 MAP

SEE 1739 MAP

SEE 1741 MAP

SEE 1814 MAP

Vinings

Atlanta

Oakdale

RAND McNALLY

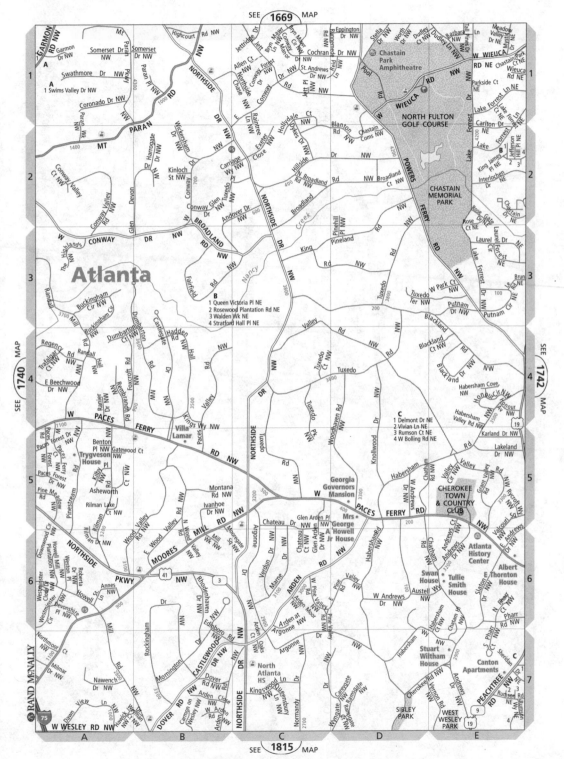

MAP
1741

1:30,000
1 in. = 2500 ft.

0   0.25   0.5
miles

SEE 1669 MAP

SEE 1740 MAP

SEE 1742 MAP

SEE 1815 MAP

Atlanta

B
1 Queen Victoria Pl NE
2 Rosewood Plantation Rd NE
3 Walden Wk NE
4 Stratford Hall Pl NE

C
1 Delmont Dr NE
2 Vivian Ln NE
3 Rumson Ct NE
4 W Bolling Rd NE

NORTH FULTON
GOLF COURSE

CHASTAIN
MEMORIAL
PARK

Chastain
Park
Amphitheatre

Georgia
Governors
Mansion

CHEROKEE
TOWN
& COUNTRY
CLUB

Atlanta
History
Center

Swan
House

Tullie
Smith
House

Albert
E Thornton
House

Stuart
Wiltham
House

Canton
Apartments

SIBLEY
PARK

WEST
WESLEY
PARK

Mrs
George
A Howell
Jr House

Trygveson
House

Villa
Lamar

RAND McNALLY

A   B   C   D   E

MAP
1742

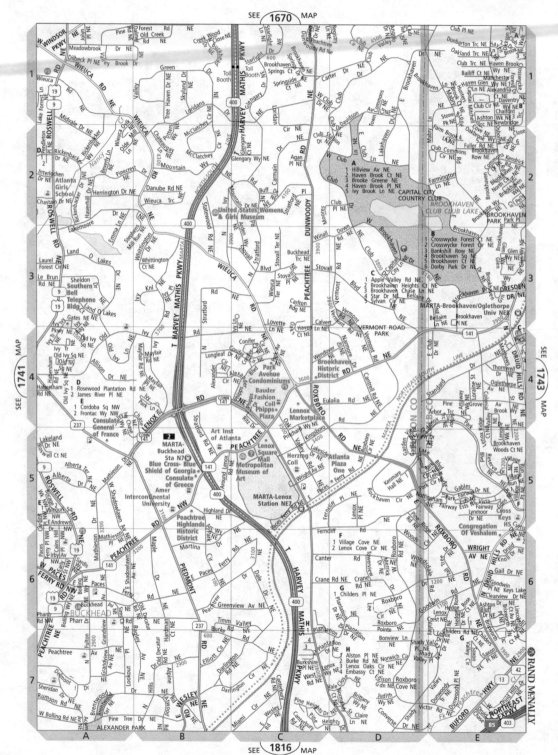

1:30,000
1 in. = 2500 ft.
0   0.25   0.5
miles

RAND McNALLY

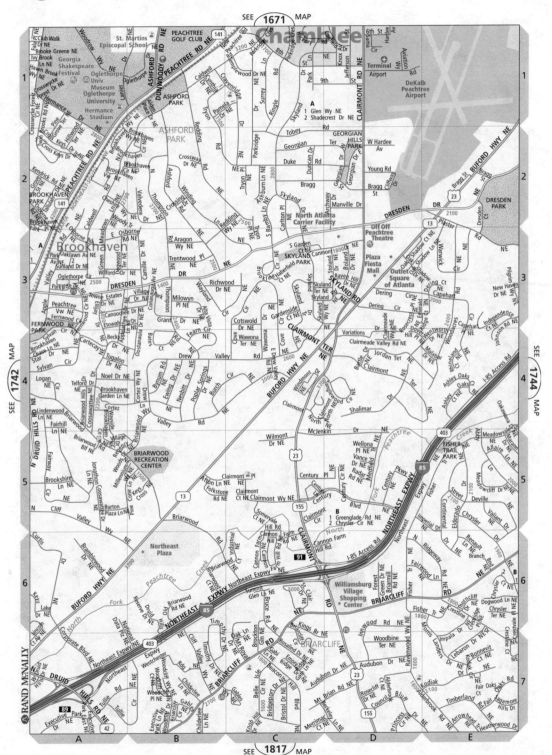

MAP 1743

MAP
1744

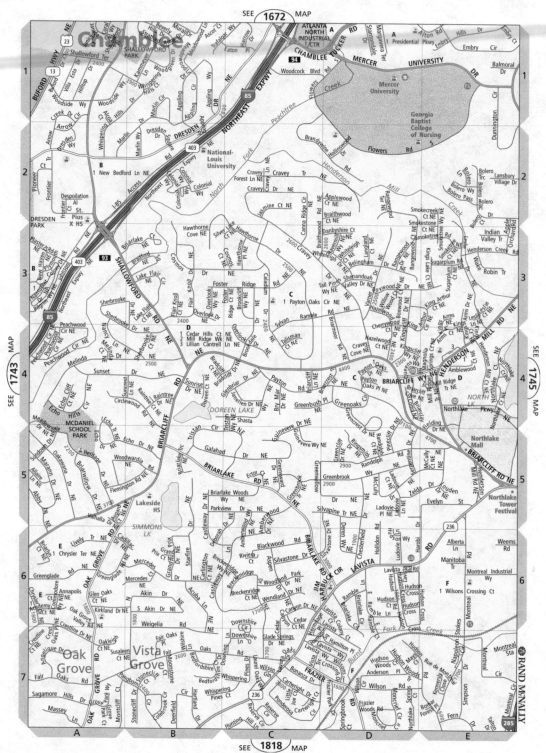

SEE 1672 MAP

SEE 1743 MAP

SEE 1745 MAP

SEE 1818 MAP

RAND McNALLY

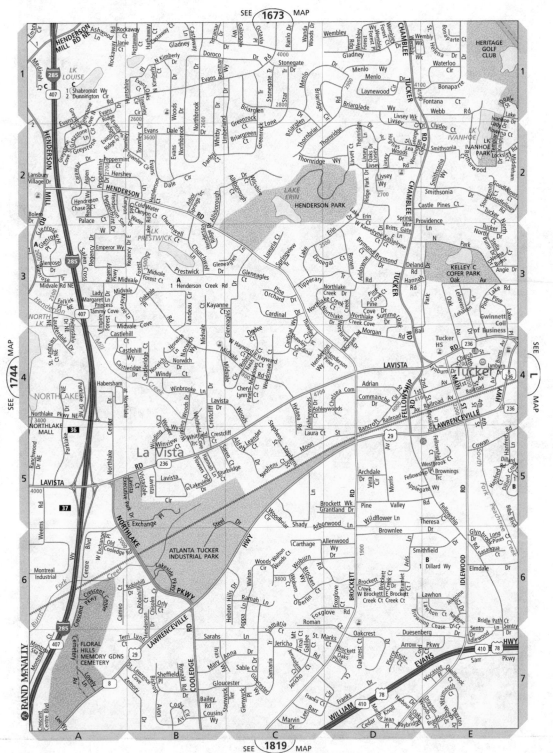

MAP
1745

SEE **1673** MAP

SEE **1744** MAP

SEE **L** MAP

SEE **1819** MAP

HERITAGE GOLF CLUB

LK LOUISE

C 1 Shabromat Wy
C 2 Dunnington Cir

HENDERSON MILL RD NE

HENDERSON MILL RD

LAKE ERIN

HENDERSON PARK

LK PRESTWICK

A 1 Henderson Creek Rd

KELLEY C COFER PARK

Gwinnett Coll of Business

NORTHLAKE

NORTHLAKE MALL

La Vista

LAVISTA

Tucker HS

Tucker

LAWRENCEVILLE

ATLANTA TUCKER INDUSTRIAL PARK

Montreal Industrial

FLORAL HILLS MEMORY GDNS CEMETERY

B 1 Dillard Wy

BROCKETT

IDLEWOOD

WILLIAM

EVANS

MAP
1812

1:30,000
1 n. = 2500 ft.

0   0.25   0.5
miles

N

SEE 1738 MAP

Smyrna

Atlanta

SEE N MAP

SEE 1813 MAP

SEE 1887 MAP

RAND MCNALLY

A
1 Whitehall Pl SE

B
1 Leland Dr SW
2 Strickland Dr SW

C
1 Vinings Place Cove SE

D
1 Riverline Wy SE

E
1 Sheraton Wy SW

F
1 Riverline Ct SE
2 N Brookside Dr SE

G
1 Clearstream Ln SW

H
1 Plantation Hill Rd SE

J
1 Silver Mine Tr SE
2 Six Flags Pkwy SW

SUMMERLIN LK

QUEENS LAKE

Fulton County Airport-Brown Field

CHATTAHOOCHEE RIVER

COBB CO
FULTON CO

FULTON CO INDUSTRIAL PARK

MABLETON PKWY 139

MARTIN LUTHER KING JR DR SW

LEE INDUSTRIAL BLVD

BANKHEAD HWY 8 SE

BANKHEAD HWY SW

BANKHEAD HWY 8

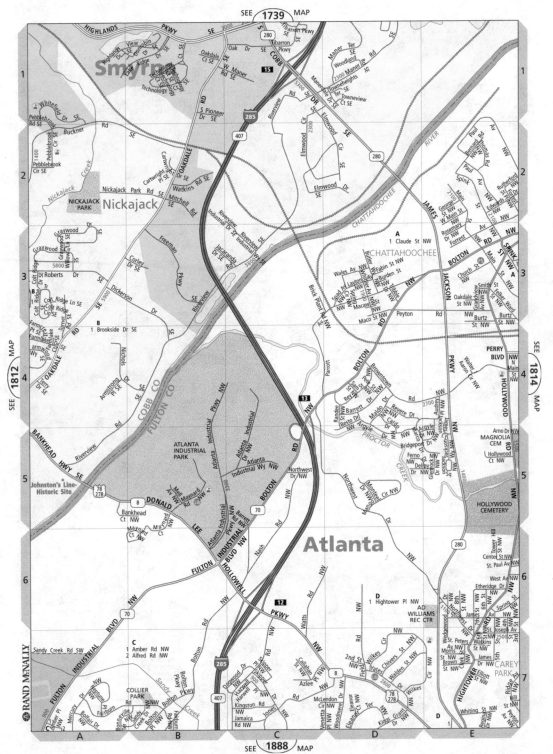

MAP
1813

N

1:30,000
1 in. = 2500 ft.

0   0.25   0.5
miles

SEE 1739 MAP

SEE 1812 MAP

SEE 1814 MAP

SEE 1888 MAP

Smyrna

Nickajack

NICKAJACK PARK

CHATTAHOOCHEE

Atlanta

ATLANTA INDUSTRIAL PARK

COBB CO
FULTON CO

Johnston's Line-
Historic Site

PROCTOR

MAGNOLIA CEM

HOLLYWOOD CEMETERY

AD WILLIAMS REC CTR

COLLIER PARK

CAREY PARK

RAND MCNALLY

A   1 Claude St NW

B   1 Brookside Dr SE

C   1 Amber Rd NW
     2 Alfred Rd NW

D   1 Hightower Pl NW

MAP
1814

SEE 1740 MAP
SEE 1813 MAP
SEE 1815 MAP
SEE 1889 MAP

Atlanta

A
1 Bassett Hall Pl NW
2 Market Square Pl NW
3 Iron Bound Pl NW
4 Queen Anne Pl NW
5 Palace Green Pl NW
6 Newport Pl NW
7 Surry County Pl NW
8 Middle Plantation Rd NW
9 Westover Plantation Pl NW
10 Paper Mill Pl NW
11 Walnut Hill Pl NW
12 George Wythe Pl NW
13 Spring Green Pl NW
14 Spinning House Pl NW

B
1 Forrest Av NW
2 Rutherford St NW

C
1 Felker Ward St NW
2 Moore St NW

D
1 Defoors Mill Pl NW
2 Defoors Mill Cir NW
3 Defoors Mill Wy NW
4 Defoors Mill Dr NW
5 Defoors Mill Ct NW
6 Defoors Ct NW
7 Defoors Cross NW
8 Defoors Wk NW

E
1 Woodmere Sq NW
2 Adrian Pl NW
3 Lamsden Ln NW
4 Maribeau Sq NW
5 La Parc NW
6 Monte Sq NW
7 Chaumont Sq NW
8 Acacia St NW

F
1 Church St NW
2 Warfield St NW

FULTON CO.
COBB CO.
CHATTAHOOCHEE RIVER NAT'L RECREATION AREA-PEACHTREE CREEK
BOLTON
CRESTLAWN CEMETERY
MAGNOLIA CEM
PROCTOR CREEK
HOLLYWOOD CEMETERY
GUN CLUB PARK
ROCKDALE
ROCKDALE PARK
CENTER HILL PARK
Inman Yard
Tilford Station
KNIGHT PK
CROSS CREEK GOLF CLUB
Seaboard Industrial Blvd
Atlanta Evening HS
Fulton County Jail

RAND McNALLY

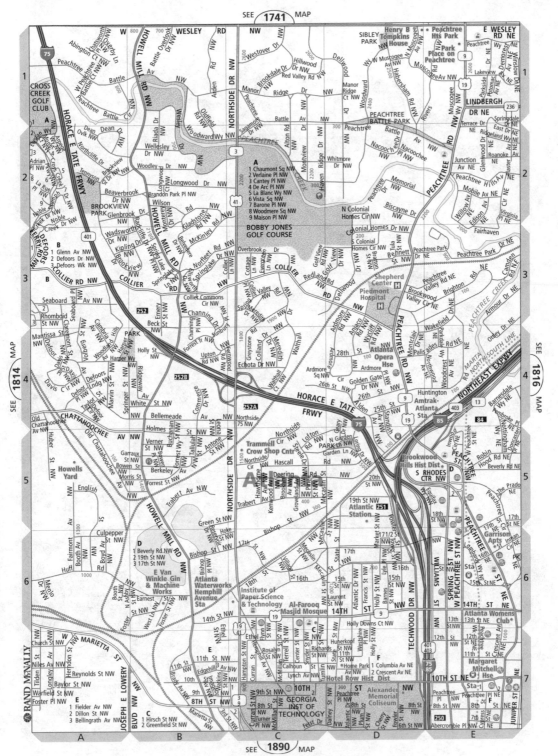

MAP 1815

1:30,000
1 in. = 2500 ft.
0   0.25   0.5
miles

SEE 1814 MAP

SEE 1816 MAP

RAND McNALLY

MAP
1816

1:30,000
1 n. = 2500 ft.

0   0.25   0.5
miles

SEE 1815 MAP

SEE 1817 MAP

Atlanta

SEE 1891 MAP

RAND McNALLY

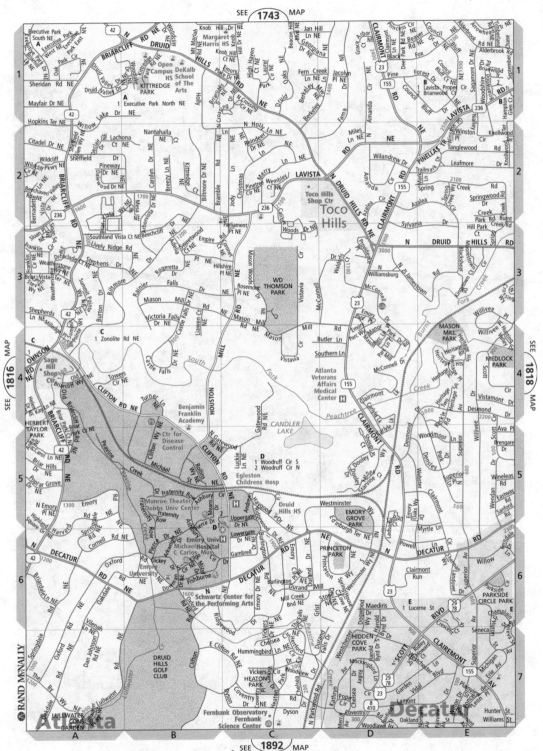

MAP
1817

1:30,000
1 in. = 2500 ft.

0   0.25   0.5
miles

N

SEE 1743 MAP

SEE 1816 MAP

SEE 1818 MAP

SEE 1892 MAP

RAND MCNALLY

Atlanta

Decatur

Toco Hills

DRUID HILLS

WD THOMSON PARK

MASON MILL PARK

MEDLOCK PARK

CANDLER LAKE

Atlanta Veterans Affairs Medical Center

EMORY GROVE PARK

PRINCETON PARK

PARKSIDE CIRCLE PARK

HIDDEN COVE PARK

HEATON PARK

DRUID HILLS GOLF CLUB

LULLWATER CONS GARDEN

Fernbank Observatory · Fernbank Science Center

MAP
1818

1:30,000
1 n. = 2500 ft.

0   0.25   0.5
miles

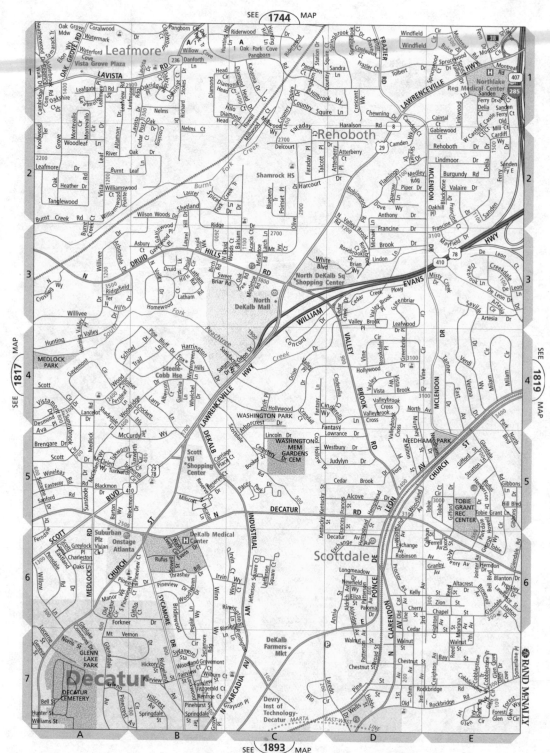

SEE 1817 MAP

SEE 1819 MAP

RAND McNALLY

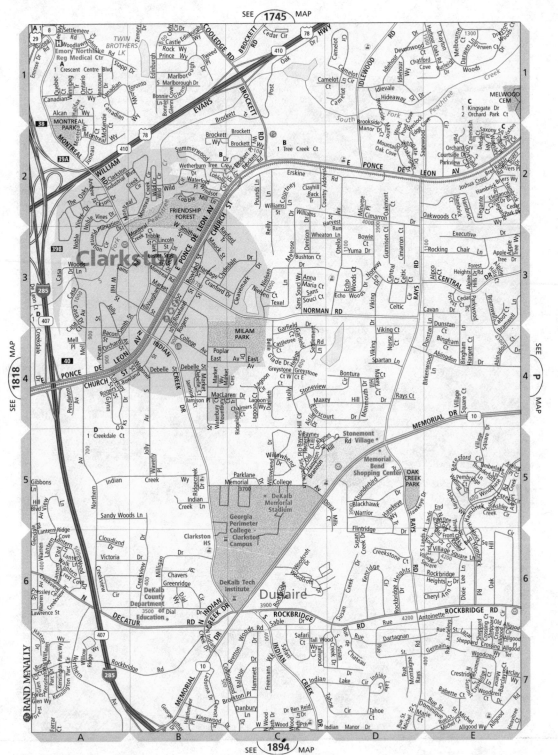

MAP
1819

1:30,000
1 in. = 2500 ft.

0   0.25   0.5
miles

RAND McNALLY

MAP
1887

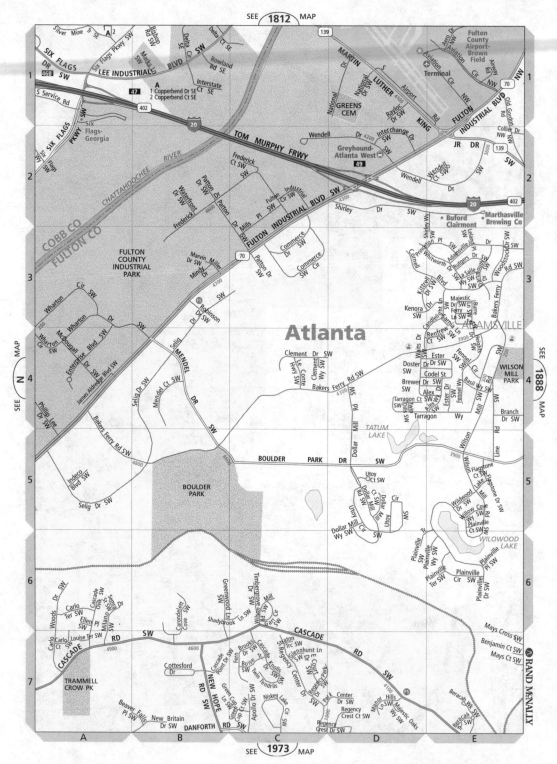

MAP
1887

1:30,000
1 in. = 2500 ft.

0   0.25   0.5
miles

SEE (1812) MAP

Atlanta

SEE (1973) MAP

ADAMSVILLE

SEE (1888) MAP

RAND McNALLY

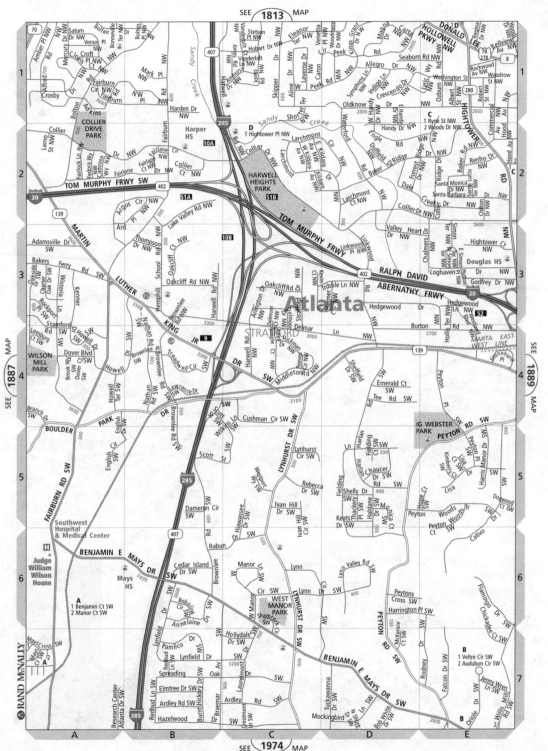

MAP
1888

MAP
1889

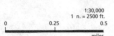

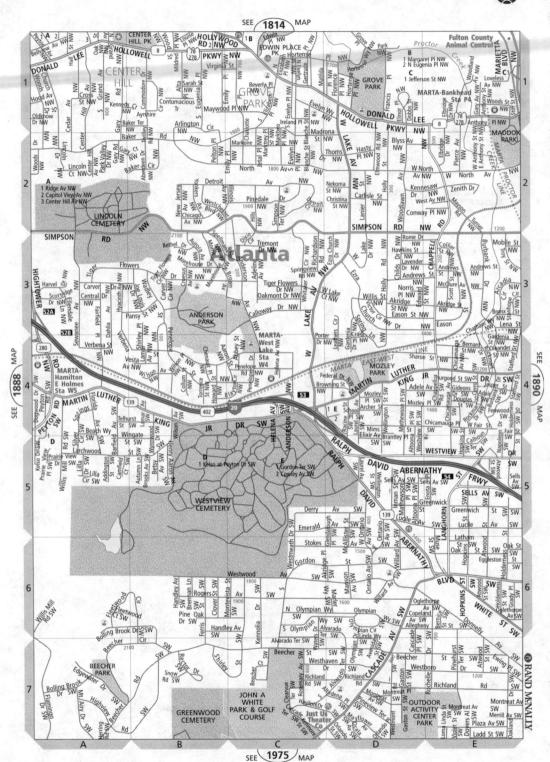

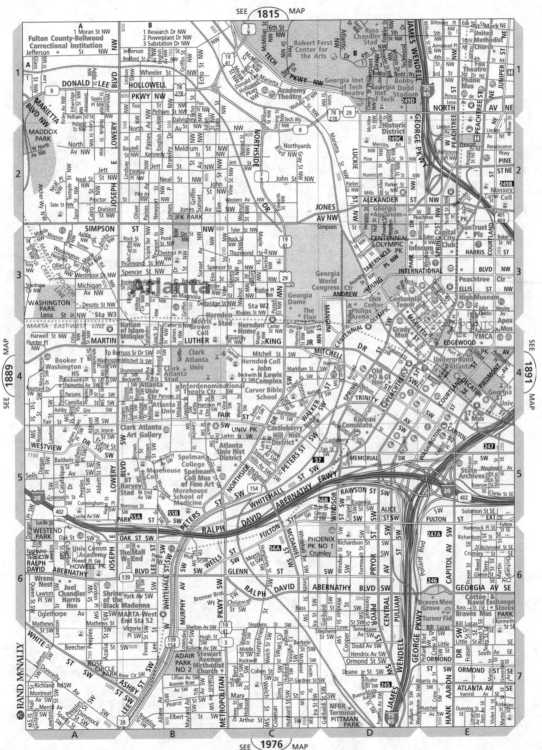

MAP
1890

1:30,000
1 in. = 2500 ft.

0   0.25   0.5
miles

N

SEE 1815 MAP

SEE 1889 MAP

SEE 1891 MAP

SEE 1976 MAP

RAND McNALLY

MAP
1891

1:30,000
1 n. = 2500 ft.
0   0.25   0.5
miles

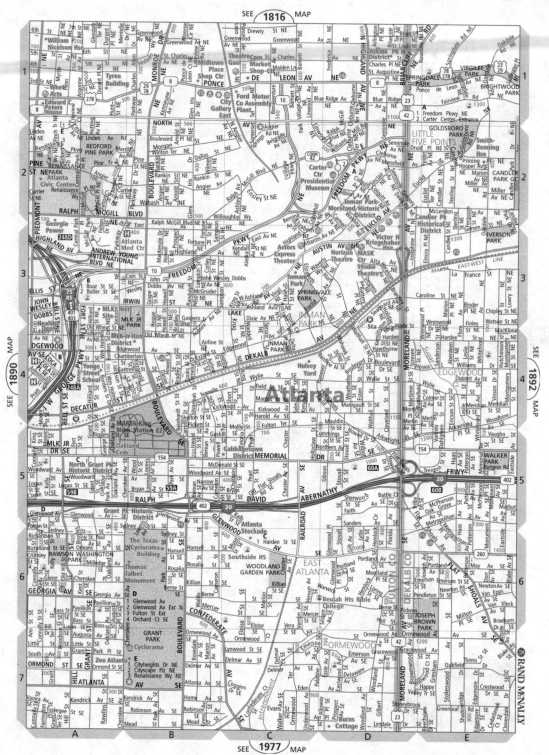

Atlanta

SEE 1890 MAP

SEE 1892 MAP

RAND McNALLY

MAP
1892

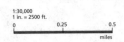
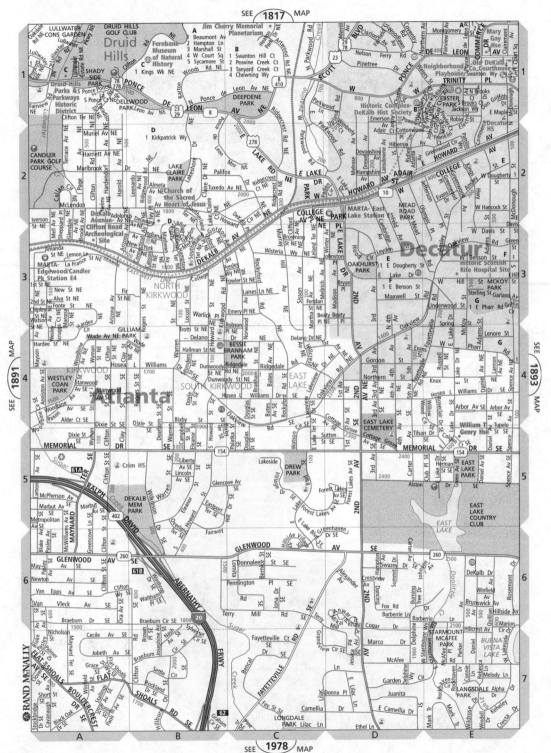

MAP
1893

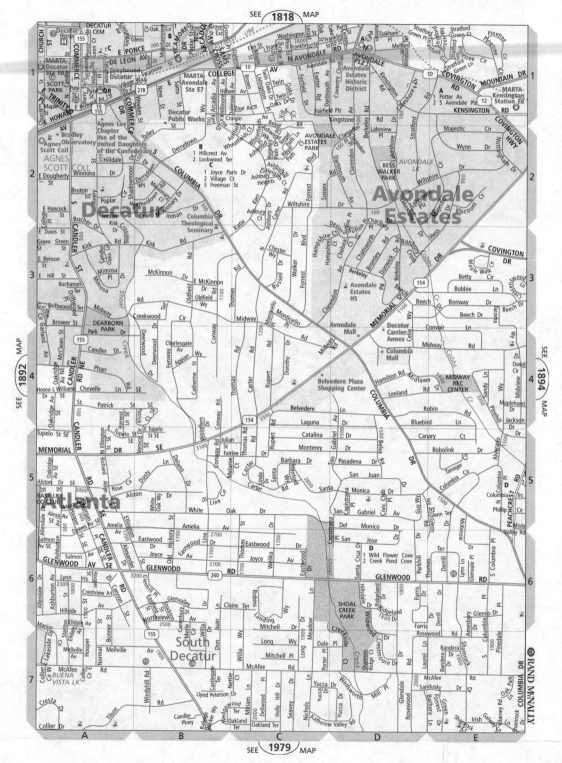

SEE **1818** MAP

SEE **1892** MAP

SEE **1894** MAP

SEE **1979** MAP

RAND McNALLY

A   B   C   D   E

1   2   3   4   5   6   7

Decatur

Avondale Estates

Atlanta

South Decatur

MAP
1894

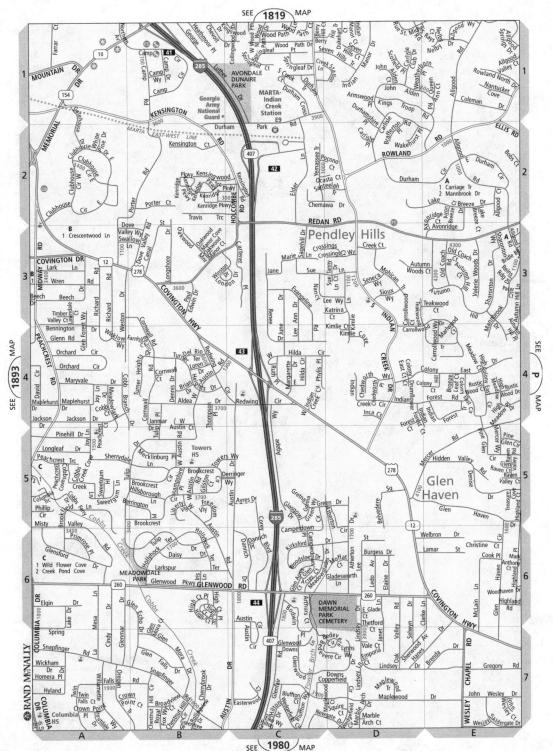

SEE 1819 MAP

SEE 1893 MAP

SEE P MAP

SEE 1980 MAP

Pendley Hills

Glen Haven

1:30,000
1 in. = 2500 ft.
0   0.25   0.5
miles

MAP
1973

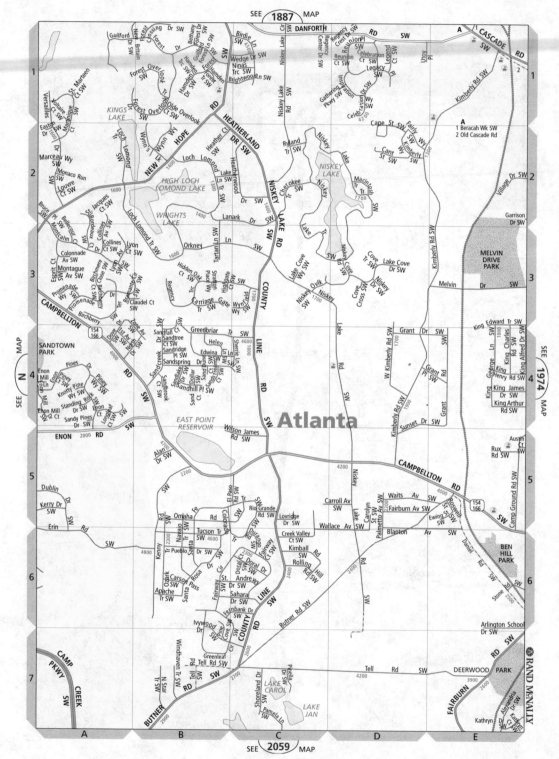

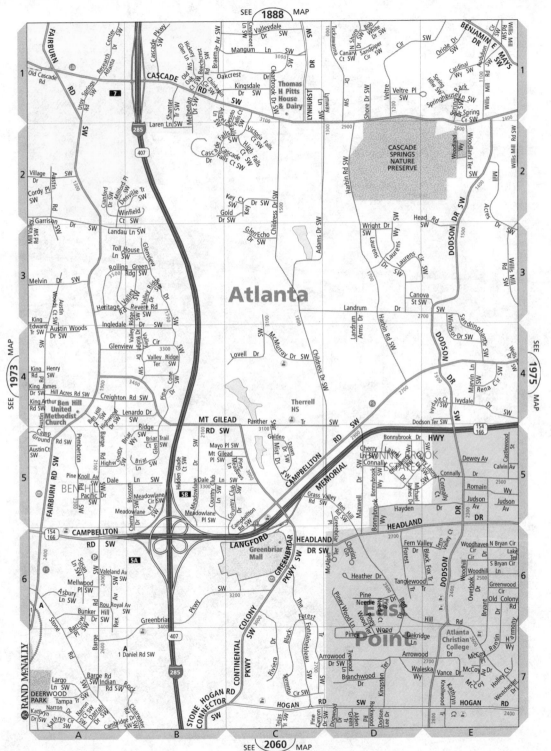

MAP 1974

1:30,000
1 in. = 2500 ft.

0   0.25   0.5
miles

SEE **1888** MAP

Atlanta

CASCADE
SPRINGS
NATURE
PRESERVE

Thomas
H Pitts
House
& Dairy

BEN HILL

Ben Hill
United
Methodist
Church

MT GILEAD
RD SW

Therrell
HS

WINTHROP

East
Point

Greenbriar
Mall

LANGFORD   HEADLAND

Atlanta
Christian
College

DEERWOOD
PARK

SEE **1973** MAP

SEE **1975** MAP

SEE **2060** MAP

MAP
1975

1:30,000
1 n. = 2500 ft.
0   0.25   0.5
miles

SEE 1889 MAP

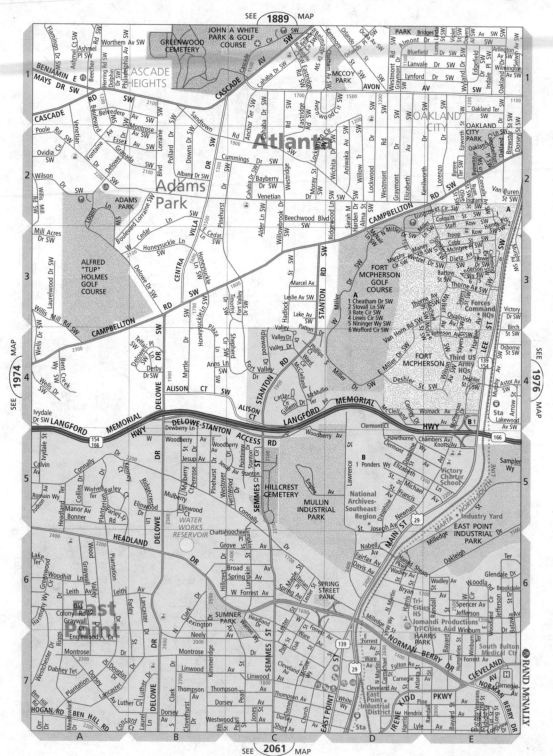

SEE 1974 MAP

SEE 1976 MAP

SEE 2061 MAP

RAND MCNALLY

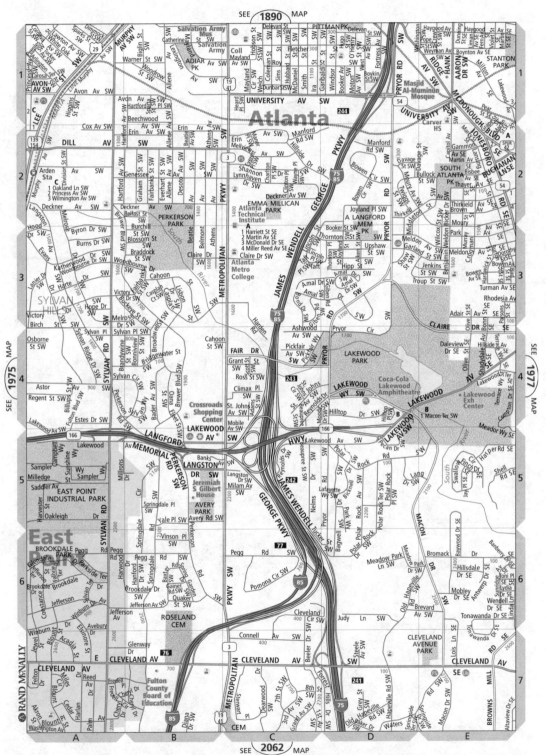

MAP
1976

MAP
1977

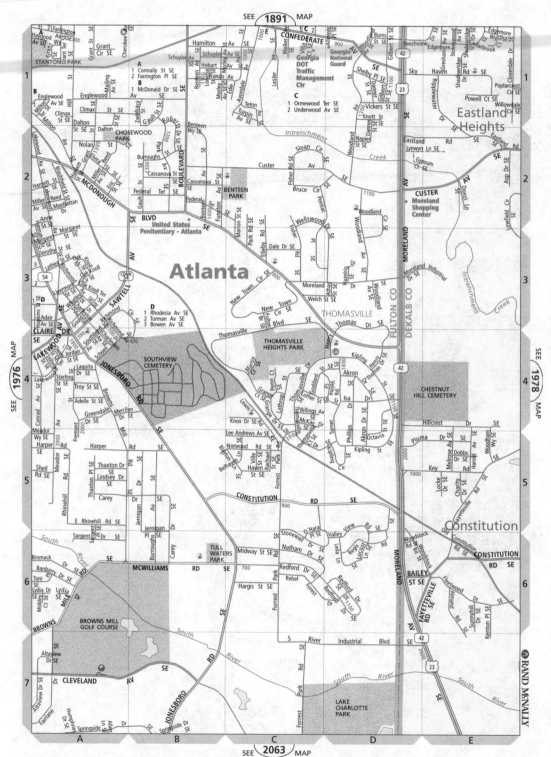

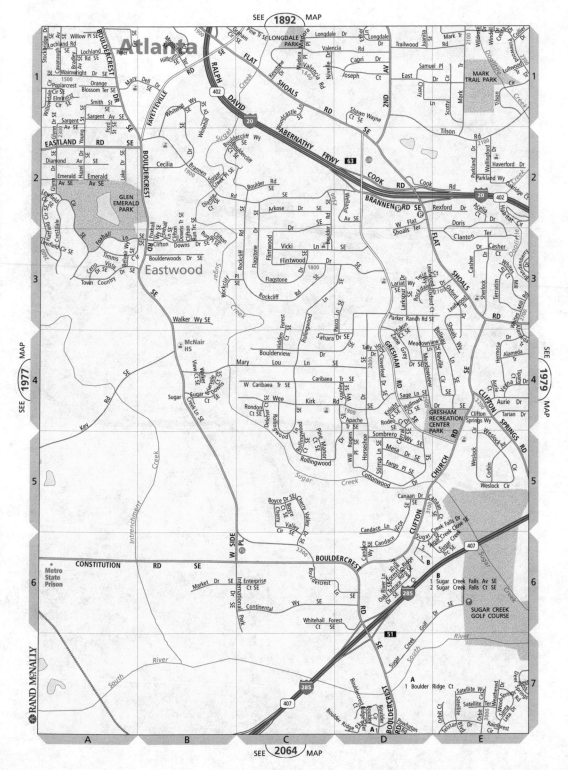

MAP
1978

N

1:30,000
1 in. = 2500 ft.
0   0.25   0.5
miles

SEE 1892 MAP

Atlanta

LONGDALE PARK

MARK TRAIL PARK

EASTLAND RD SE

GLEN EMERALD PARK

Eastwood

SEE 1977 MAP

McNair HS

SEE 1979 MAP

GRESHAM RECREATION CENTER PARK

CLIFTON SPRINGS RD

CHURCH RD

Metro State Prison

CONSTITUTION RD SE

BOULDERCREST

B
1 Sugar Creek Falls Av SE
2 Sugar Creek Falls Ct SE

SUGAR CREEK GOLF COURSE

South River

A
1 Boulder Ridge Ct

BOULDERCREST RD SE

RAND McNALLY

SEE 2064 MAP

A   B   C   D   E

MAP
1979

1:30,000
1 in. = 2500 ft.

0   0.25   0.5
miles

N

SEE 1893 MAP

SEE 1978 MAP

SEE 1980 MAP

SEE 2065 MAP

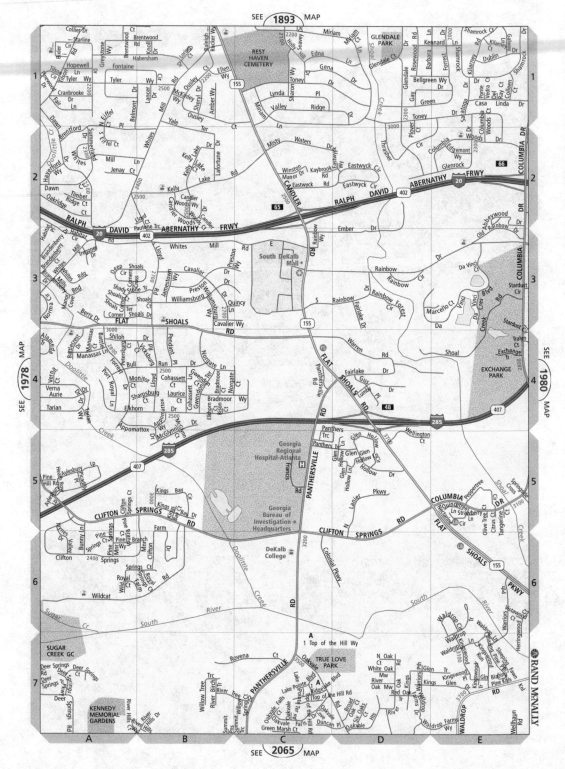

RAND McNALLY

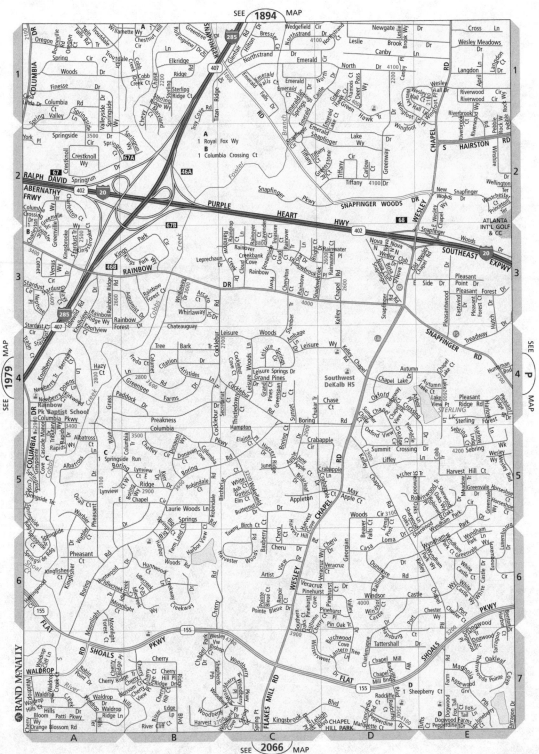

MAP
1980

SEE 1894 MAP

1:30,000
1 in. = 2500 ft.

0   0.25   0.5
miles

SEE 1979 MAP

SEE P MAP

RAND McNALLY

SEE 2066 MAP

MAP
2059

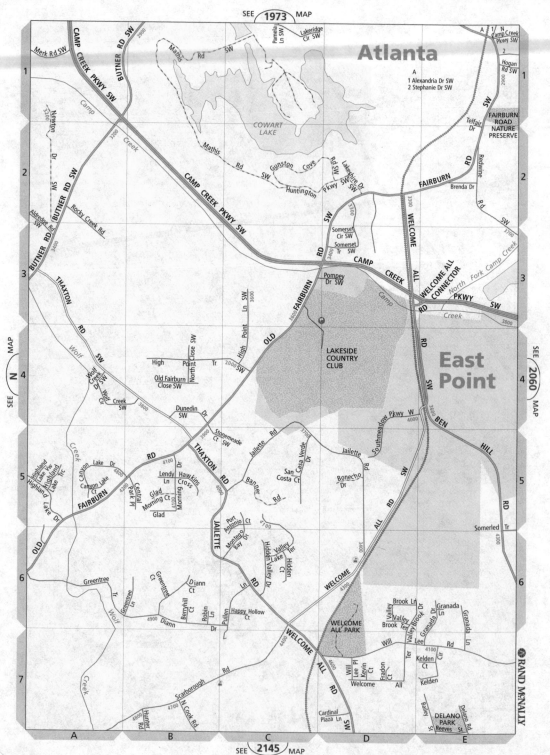

1:30,000
1 n. = 2500 ft.

0   0.25   0.5
miles

Atlanta

A
1 Alexandria Dr SW
2 Stephanie Dr SW

**East
Point**

LAKESIDE
COUNTRY
CLUB

FAIRBURN
ROAD
NATURE
PRESERVE

WELCOME
ALL PARK

DELANO
PARK

RAND MCNALLY

A   B   C   D   E

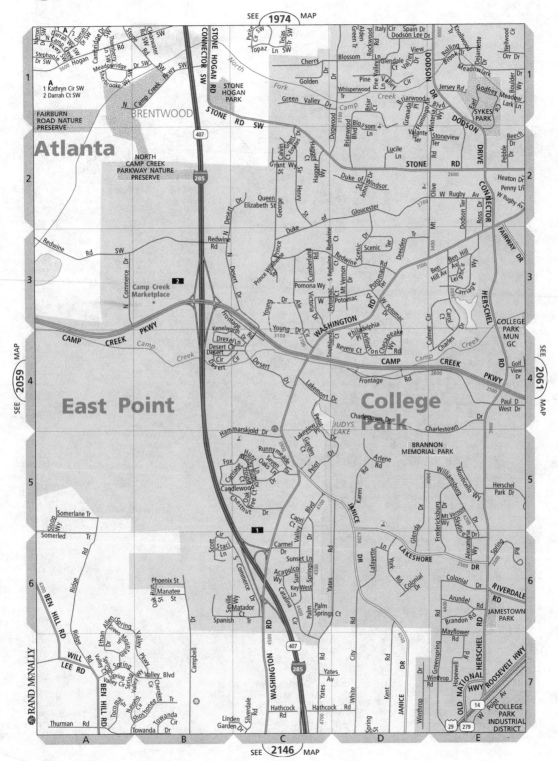

MAP
2060

1:30,000
1 in. = 2500 ft.

0   0.25   0.5
miles

N

SEE 1974 MAP

SEE 2059 MAP

SEE 2061 MAP

SEE 2146 MAP

Atlanta

East Point

College Park

BRENTWOOD

FAIRBURN ROAD NATURE PRESERVE

NORTH CAMP CREEK PARKWAY NATURE PRESERVE

STONE HOGAN PARK

SYKES PARK

Camp Creek Marketplace

JUDYS LAKE

BRANNON MEMORIAL PARK

COLLEGE PARK MUN GC

JAMESTOWN PARK

Herschel Park Dr

COLLEGE PARK INDUSTRIAL DISTRICT

RAND McNALLY

A
1 Kathryn Cir SW
2 Darrah Ct SW

MAP
2061

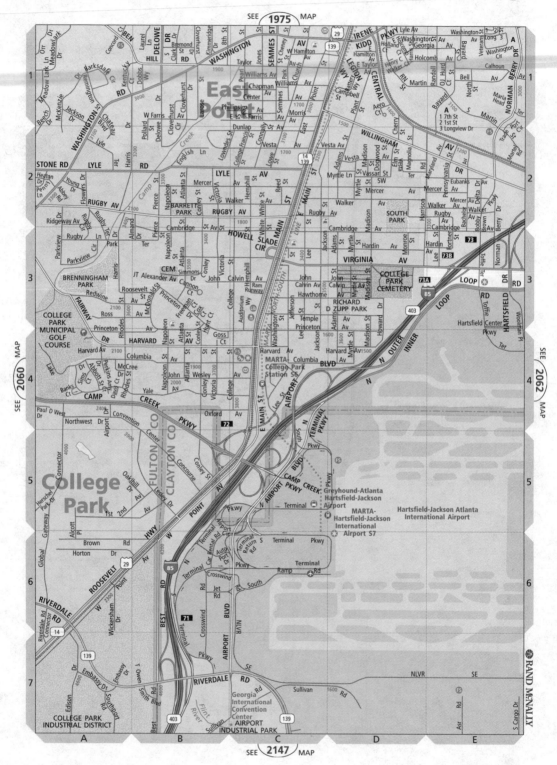

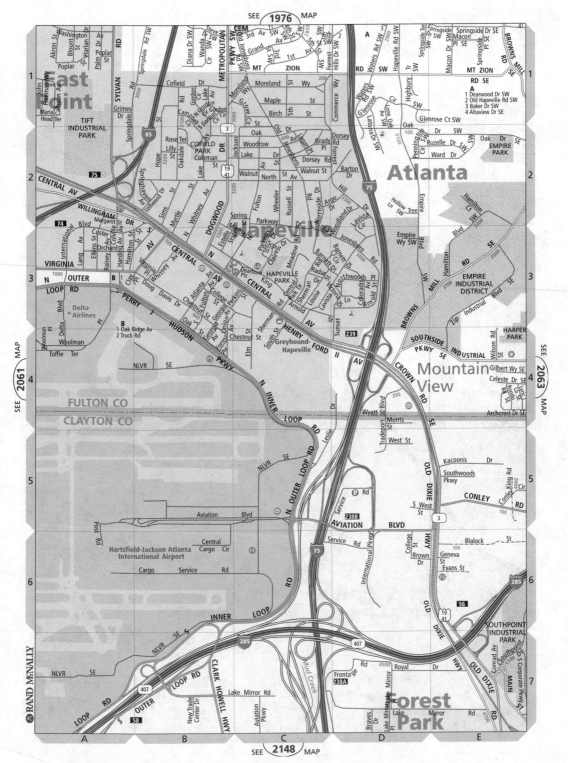

MAP
2062

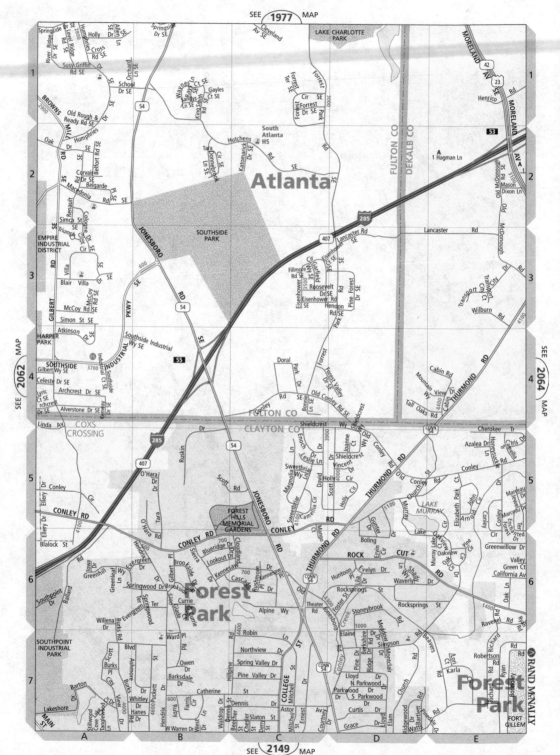

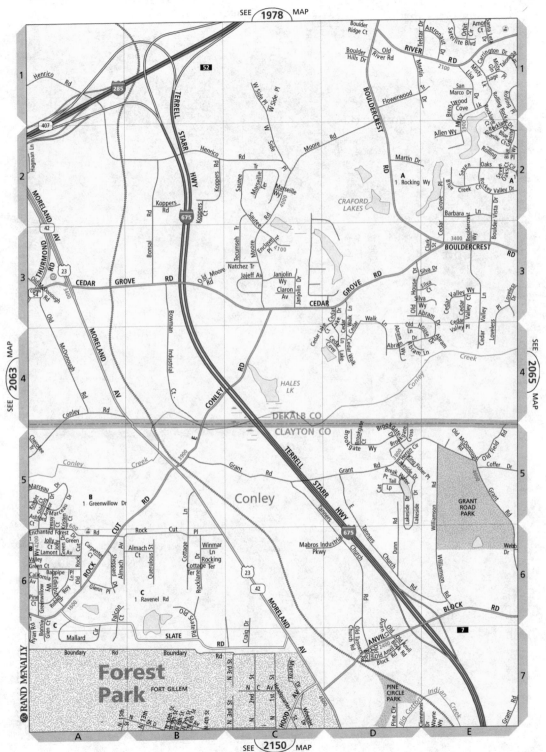

MAP
2065

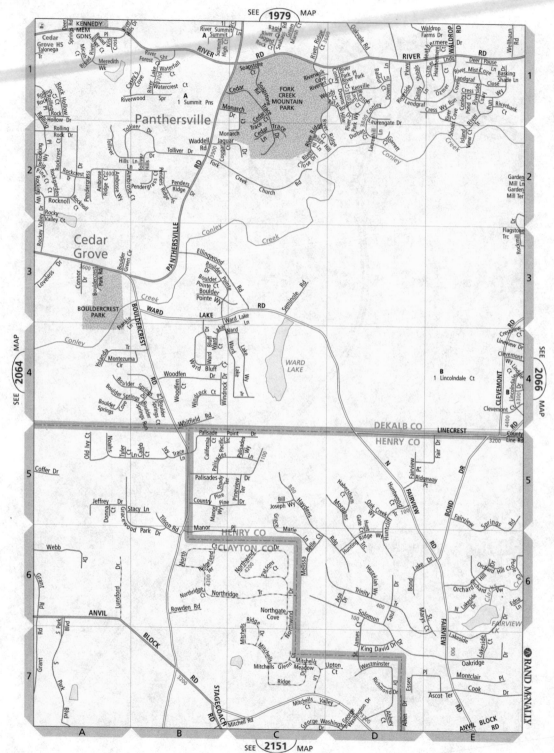

MAP
2066

SEE 1980 MAP

SEE 2065 MAP

SEE P MAP

SEE 2152 MAP

1:30,000
1 in. = 2500 ft.

RAND MCNALLY

MAP
2145

1:30,000
1 n. = 2500 ft.

0   0.25   0.5
miles

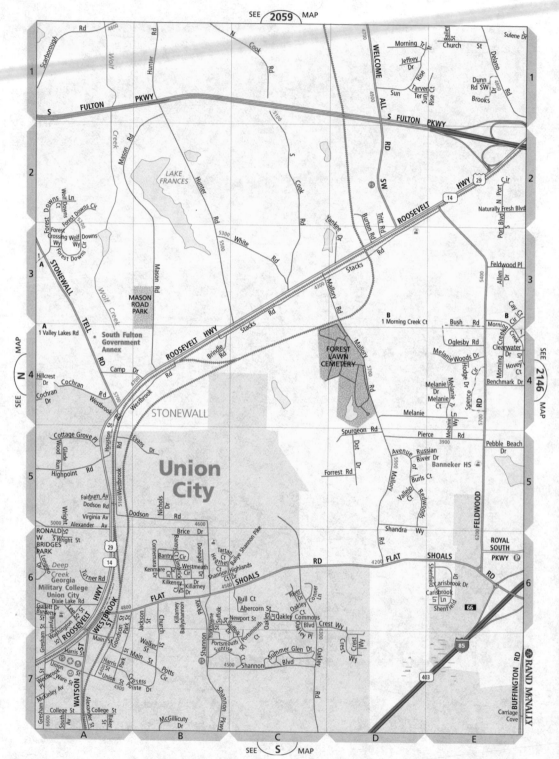

SEE N MAP

SEE 2146 MAP

Union City

STONEWALL

MASON ROAD PARK

LAKE FRANCES

FOREST LAWN CEMETERY

South Fulton Government Annex

A 1 Valley Lakes Rd
B 1 Morning Creek Ct

Banneker HS

Georgia Military College Union City

RONALD W BRIDGES PARK

Deep Creek

ROYAL SOUTH PKWY

RAND McNALLY

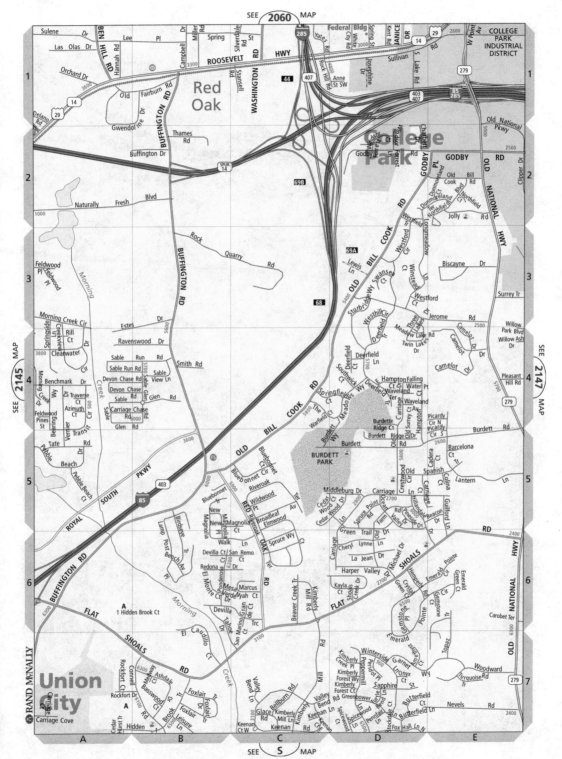

MAP
2146

N

1:30,000
1 in. = 2500 ft.
0   0.25   0.5
miles

SEE 2060 MAP

COLLEGE
PARK
INDUSTRIAL
DISTRICT

Red
Oak

College
Park

BURDETT
PARK

Union
City

RAND McNALLY

Carriage Cove

SEE 2145 MAP

SEE 2147 MAP

SEE S MAP

A   B   C   D   E

MAP
2147

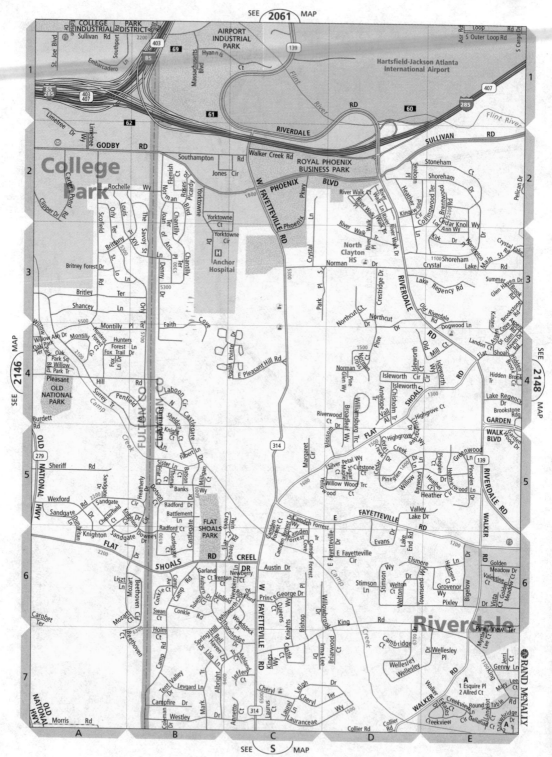

1:30,000
1 in. = 2500 ft.

0   0.25   0.5

miles

SEE 2061 MAP

SEE 2146 MAP

SEE 2148 MAP

SEE S MAP

College Park

Riverdale

RAND McNALLY

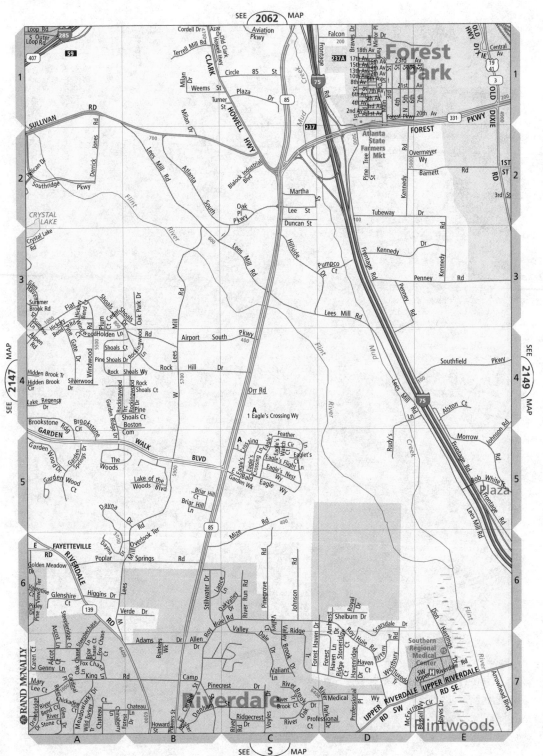

MAP
2148

1:30,000
1 in. = 2500 ft.

0   0.25   0.5
miles

SEE 2062 MAP

SEE 2147 MAP

SEE 2149 MAP

SEE S MAP

Forest Park

Riverdale

FAYETTEVILLE

UPPER RIVERDALE

Flintwoods

RAND McNALLY

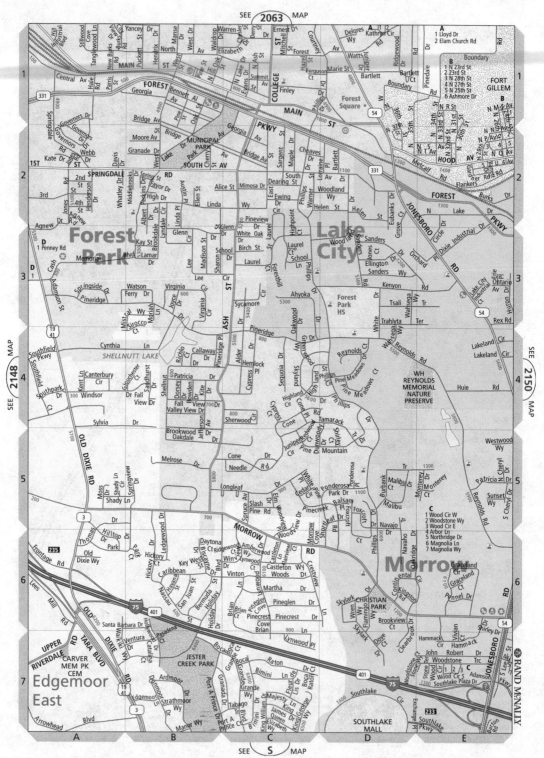

MAP
2149

1:30,000
1 in. = 2500 ft.

0   0.25   0.5
miles

SEE 2063 MAP

A
1 Lloyd Dr
2 Elam Church Rd

B Boundary
1 N 23rd St
2 23rd St
3 N 28th St
4 N 27th St
5 N 25th St
6 Ashmore Dr

FORT GILLEM

Forest Square

Forest Park

Lake City

Forest Park HS

WH REYNOLDS MEMORIAL NATURE PRESERVE

SHELLNUTT LAKE

SEE 2148 MAP

SEE 2150 MAP

C
1 Wood Cir W
2 Woodstone Wy
3 Wood Cir E
4 Arbor Ln
5 Northridge Dr
6 Magnolia Ln
7 Magnolia Wy

Morrow

MORROW RD

UPPER RIVERDALE

CARVER MEM PK CEM

Edgemoor East

JESTER CREEK PARK

CHRISTIAN PARK

SOUTHLAKE MALL

RAND McNALLY

SEE S MAP

A   B   C   D   E

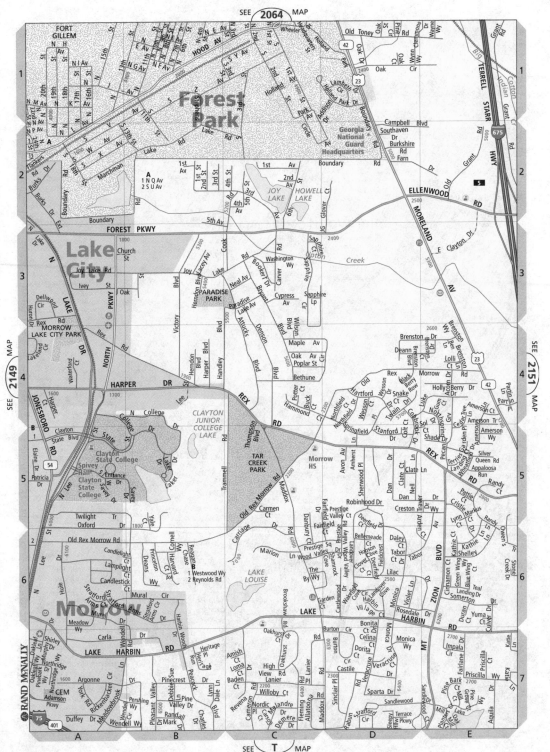

MAP
2151

1:30,000
1 in. = 2500 ft.

0   0.25   0.5
miles

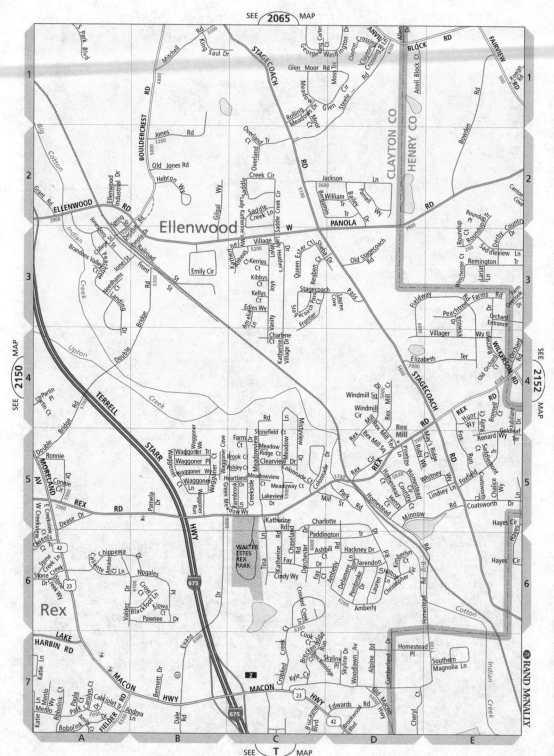

SEE 2150 MAP

SEE 2152 MAP

Ellenwood

ELLENWOOD

PANOLA

CLAYTON CO

HENRY CO

Rex

WALTER
ESTES
REX
PARK

Rex
Mill

RAND MC NALLY

A   B   C   D   E

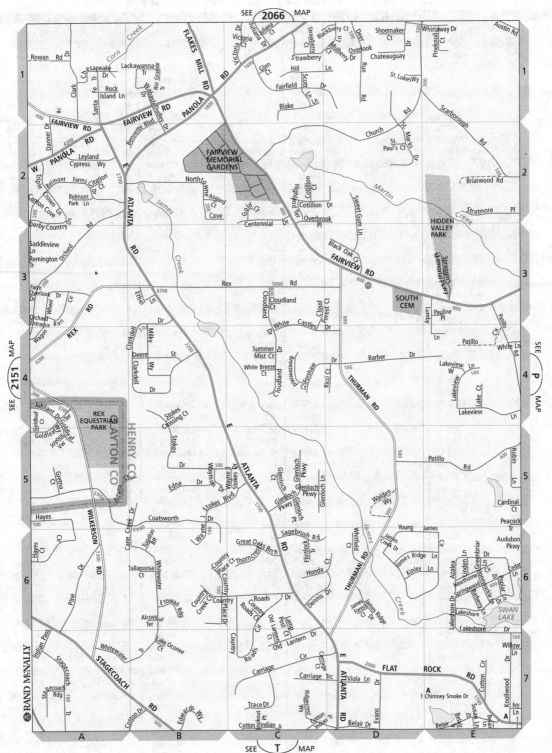

MAP
2152

LIST OF ABBREVIATIONS

Admin	Administration	Cr	Creek	Jct	Junction	PO	Post Office
Agri	Agricultural	Cres	Crescent	Knl	Knoll	Pres	Preserve
Ag	Agriculture	Cross	Crossing	Knls	Knolls	Prov	Provincial
AFB	Air Force Base	Curv	Curve	Lk	Lake	Rwy	Railway
Arpt	Airport	Cto	Cut Off	Lndg	Landing	Rec	Recreation
Al	Alley	Dept	Department	Ln	Lane	Reg	Regional
Amer	American	Dev	Development	Lib	Library	Res	Reservoir
Anx	Annex	Diag	Diagonal	Ldg	Lodge	Rst	Rest
Arc	Arcade	Div	Division	Lp	Loop	Rdg	Ridge
Arch	Archaeological	Dr	Drive	Mnr	Manor	Rd	Road
Aud	Auditorium	Drwy	Driveway	Mkt	Market	Rds	Roads
Avd	Avenida	E	East	Mdw	Meadow	St.	Saint
Av	Avenue	El	Elevation	Mdws	Meadows	Ste.	Sainte
Bfld	Battlefield	Env	Environmental	Med	Medical	Sci	Science
Bch	Beach	Est	Estate	Mem	Memorial	Sci	Sciences
Bnd	Bend	Ests	Estates	Metro	Metropolitan	Sci	Scientific
Bio	Biological	Exh	Exhibition	Mw	Mews	Shop Ctr	Shopping Center
Blf	Bluff	Expm	Experimental	Mil	Military	Shr	Shore
Blvd	Boulevard	Expo	Exposition	Ml	Mill	Shrs	Shores
Brch	Branch	Expwy	Expressway	Mls	Mills	Skwy	Skyway
Br	Bridge	Ext	Extension	Mon	Monument	S	South
Brk	Brook	Frgds	Fairgrounds	Mtwy	Motorway	Spr	Spring
Bldg	Building	ft	Feet	Mnd	Mound	Sprs	Springs
Bur	Bureau	Fy	Ferry	Mnds	Mounds	Sq	Square
Byp	Bypass	Fld	Field	Mt	Mount	Stad	Stadium
Bywy	Byway	Flds	Fields	Mtn	Mountain	St For	State Forest
Cl	Calle	Flt	Flat	Mtns	Mountains	St Hist Site	State Historic Site
Cljn	Callejon	Flts	Flats	Mun	Municipal	St Nat Area	State Natural Area
Cmto	Caminito	For	Forest	Mus	Museum	St Pk	State Park
Cm	Camino	Fk	Fork	Nat'l	National	St Rec Area	State Recreation Area
Cap	Capitol	Ft	Fort	Nat'l For	National Forest	Sta	Station
Cath	Cathedral	Found	Foundation	Nat'l Hist Pk	National Historic Park	St	Street
Cswy	Causeway	Frwy	Freeway	Nat'l Hist Site	National Historic Site	Smt	Summit
Cem	Cemetery	Gdn	Garden	Nat'l Mon	National Monument	Sys	Systems
Ctr	Center	Gdns	Gardens	Nat'l Park	National Park	Tech	Technical
Ctr	Centre	Gen Hosp	General Hospital	Nat'l Rec Area	National Recreation Area	Tech	Technological
Cir	Circle	Gln	Glen	Nat'l Wld Ref	National Wildlife Refuge	Tech	Technology
Crlo	Circulo	GC	Golf Course	Nat	Natural	Ter	Terrace
CH	City Hall	Grn	Green	NAS	Naval Air Station	Terr	Territory
Clf	Cliff	Grds	Grounds	Nk	Nook	Theol	Theological
Clfs	Cliffs	Grv	Grove	N	North	Thwy	Throughway
Clb	Club	Hbr	Harbor/Harbour	Orch	Orchard	Toll Fy	Toll Ferry
Cltr	Cluster	Hvn	Haven	Ohwy	Outer Highway	TIC	Tourist Information Center
Col	Coliseum	HQs	Headquarters	Ovl	Oval	Trc	Trace
Coll	College	Ht	Height	Ovlk	Overlook	Trfwy	Trafficway
Com	Common	Hts	Heights	Ovps	Overpass	Tr	Trail
Coms	Commons	HS	High School	Pk	Park	Tun	Tunnel
Comm	Community	Hwy	Highway	Pkwy	Parkway	Tpk	Turnpike
Co.	Company	Hl	Hill	Pas	Paseo	Unps	Underpass
Cons	Conservation	Hls	Hills	Psg	Passage	Univ	University
Conv & Vis Bur	Convention and Visitors Bureau	Hist	Historical	Pass	Passenger	Vly	Valley
Cor	Corner	Hllw	Hollow	Pth	Path	Vet	Veterans
Cors	Corners	Hosp	Hospital	Pn	Pine	Vw	View
Corp	Corporation	Hse	House	Pns	Pines	Vil	Village
Corr	Corridor	Ind Res	Indian Reservation	Pl	Place	Wk	Walk
Cte	Corte	Info	Information	Pln	Plain	Wall	Wall
CC	Country Club	Inst	Institute	Plns	Plains	Wy	Way
Co	County	Int'l	International	Plgnd	Playground	W	West
Ct	Court	I	Island	Plz	Plaza	WMA	Wildlife Management Area
Ct Hse	Court House	Is	Islands	Pt	Point		
Cts	Courts	Isl	Isle	Pnd	Pond		

Atlanta Street Index

SR-154 Knotts Av

STREET City Map # Grid

SR-154 Langford Memorial Hwy
ATLN 1974 C5
EPNT 1974 E5
SR-154 Lee St SW
ATLN 1890 B7
ATLN 1975 E4
SR-154 Main St
ATLN 1975 E4
EPNT 1975 E4
SR-154 Memorial Dr
AVES 1893 D3
AVES 1894 A1
DKbC 1893 D3
SR-154 Memorial Dr SE
ATLN 1890 E5
ATLN 1891 E5
ATLN 1893 A5
DKbC 1892 B5
DKbC 1893 B5
SR-154 Memorial Dr SW
ATLN 1890 E5
SR-154 Peters St SW
ATLN 1890 D4
SR-154 Trinity Av SW
ATLN 1890 C5
SR-154 W Whitehall St SW
ATLN 1890 B7
SR-154 Womack Av
EPNT 1975 E4
SR-155
ATLN 1893 A4
DCTR 1817 E7
DKbC 1743 C5
DKbC 1817 E7
DKbC 1893 B7
DKbC 1979 C1
DKbC 1980 A6
SR-155 Candler Rd
DKbC 1893 A6
DKbC 1979 C1
SR-155 Candler Rd NE
ATLN 1893 A4
DCTR 1893 A4
SR-155 Candler Rd SE
ATLN 1893 A4
DKbC 1893 A5
SR-155 S Candler St
DCTR 1893 A4
SR-155 Clairemont Av
DCTR 1817 E7
DKbC 1817 D6
SR-155 Clairmont Rd
DKbC 1817 D6
SR-155 Clairmont Rd NE
DKbC 1743 C5
DKbC 1817 D1
SR-155 E College Av
DCTR 1893 A1
SR-155 Commerce Dr
DCTR 1893 A1
SR-155 Flat Shoals Pkwy
DKbC 1979 E6
SR-155 Flat Shoals Rd
DKbC 1979 C4
SR-160
FTPK 2149 D1
SR-160 Jonesboro Rd
FTPK 2149 D1
SR-166
ATLN 1973 E5
ATLN 1974 E5
EPNT 1974 E5
FulC 1973 A4
SR-166 Campbellton Rd SW
ATLN 1973 E5
FulC 1973 A4
SR-166 Langford Memorial Hwy
ATLN 1974 C5
EPNT 1974 E5
SR-236
ATLN 1815 E1
ATLN 1816 A1
DKbC 1744 C7
DKbC 1745 B5
DKbC 1816 E2
DKbC 1817 C2
SR-236 Hugh Howell Rd
DKbC 1745 E4
SR-236 Lavista Rd
DKbC 1744 C7
DKbC 1745 B5
DKbC 1817 E1
SR-236 Lavista Rd NE
ATLN 1816 D2
DKbC 1816 D2
DKbC 1817 C2
SR-236 Lawrenceville Hwy
DKbC 1745 E4
SR-236 Lindbergh Dr NE
ATLN 1815 E1
SR-236 Lindbergh Wy NE
ATLN 1816 B2
SR-237
ATLN 1742 B6
ATLN 1816 B1
SR-237 Piedmont Rd NE
ATLN 1742 B6
ATLN 1816 B1
SR-260
ATLN 1891 E6
ATLN 1892 A6
ATLN 1893 B6
DKbC 1892 A6
DKbC 1893 B6
SR-260 Glenwood Av SE
ATLN 1891 E6
ATLN 1892 E6
DKbC 1892 E6
SR-260 Glenwood Rd
DKbC 1893 A6
SR-260 Ralph D Abernathy Frwy
ATLN 1892 B6
DKbC 1892 B6
SR-279
CGPK 2060 E7
CGPK 2146 E1
FulC 2146 E1
SR-279 Old National Hwy
CGPK 2060 E7
CGPK 2146 E4
FulC 2146 E7
FulC 2147 A5
SR-280
ATLN 1813 D2
ATLN 1888 E1
ATLN 1889 A4
CobC 1595 B7
CobC 1666 A2
CobC 1667 A2
CobC 1739 A5
CobC 1813 C1
MRTA 1667 A2
SMYR 1666 B4
SMYR 1738 C1
SMYR 1813 C1
SR-280 S Cobb Dr SE
ATLN 1813 D2
CobC 1595 B7
CobC 1666 A2
CobC 1667 A2
CobC 1739 A5
CobC 1813 C1
MRTA 1667 A2
SMYR 1666 B4
SMYR 1738 C1
SMYR 1813 C1
SR-280 Delk Rd SE
CobC 1667 C2
MRTA 1667 C2
SR-280 Hightower Rd NW
ATLN 1888 E2
ATLN 1889 A4
SR-280 James Jackson Pkwy NW
ATLN 1813 E7
SR-314
CGPK 2147 C5
ClyC 2147 C5
SR-314 W Fayetteville Rd
CGPK 2147 C5
ClyC 2147 C5
SR-331
ClyC 2148 E1
FTPK 2148 E1
LKCY 2149 D2
SR-331 Forest Pkwy
ClyC 2148 E1
FTPK 2148 E1
LKCY 2149 D2
SR-360
MRTA 1595 A6
SR-360 Powder Springs St SW
MRTA 1595 A6
SR-400
ATLN 1742 C1
ATLN 1816 C1
FulC 1530 E7
FulC 1670 C5
RSWL 1531 C1
SR-400 T Harvey Mathis Pkwy
ATLN 1742 C6
ATLN 1816 C1
FulC 1670 C3
SR-400 Turner McDonald Pkwy
FulC 1530 E7
FulC 1670 C5
RSWL 1531 C1
SR-401
ATLN 1740 D2
ATLN 1815 E7
ClyC 2149 B6
CobC 1526 A6
CobC 1667 D3
CobC 1740 D2
MRRW 2149 B6
MRTA 1526 B7
MRTA 1667 C1
SR-401 Horace E Tate Frwy
ATLN 1740 E6
ATLN 1815 A3
FulC 1740 D2
SR-401 James W George Pkwy
ATLN 1815 D7
SR-401 Larry McDonald Mem Hwy
CobC 1526 A6
CobC 1667 D3
CobC 1740 C1
MRTA 1526 B7
MRTA 1667 C1
SR-402
ATLN 1887 E2
ATLN 1978 B1
CobC 1887 E2
DKbC 1892 A5
DKbC 1978 B1
SR-402 Purple Heart Hwy
DKbC 1980 D3
SR-402 Ralph D Abernathy Frwy
ATLN 1888 D3
ATLN 1978 B1
DKbC 1892 A5
DKbC 1978 B1
SR-402 Southeast Expwy
DKbC 1980 A2
SR-402 Tom Murphy Frwy
ATLN 1887 E2
CobC 1887 E2
SR-403
ATLN 1815 E4
CGPK 2061 D3
CGPK 2146 D1
DKbC 1672 D7
DKbC 1742 E7
DKbC 1816 D1
FulC 2145 D7
UNCT 2145 D7
SR-403 James W George Pkwy
ATLN 1815 D7
SR-403 Northeast Expwy
ATLN 1815 E4
DKbC 1672 D7
DKbC 1742 E7
DKbC 1816 A4
SR-403 Northeast Expwy NE
ATLN 1816 D1
SR-403 Veterans Pkwy
GwnC 1673 B4
SR-407
ATLN 1813 C2
ATLN 1974 B2
ATLN 2060 C7
CGPK 2146 D1
ClyC 2062 D7
ClyC 2147 E1
CobC 1667 E7
CobC 1739 D3
CobC 1813 C2
DKbC 1670 E3
DKbC 1744 E7
DKbC 1818 E1
DKbC 1978 E6
DKbC 2064 A2
DRVL 1672 A2
EPNT 2060 B2
FTPK 2062 D7
FulC 1669 A3
FulC 1888 B6
FulC 1974 B2
FulC 2060 C7
FulC 2146 D1
SMYR 1667 E7
SMYR 1813 C2
SR-410
DCTR 1817 D7
DKbC 1745 D7
DKbC 1817 D7
DKbC 1818 E3
DKbC 1892 C1
SR-410 Lawrenceville Hwy
DKbC 1818 A5
SR-410 Ponce de Leon Av NE
DKbC 1892 C1
SR-410 Scott Blvd
DCTR 1817 D7
DKbC 1817 D7
SR-410 William Evans Hwy
DKbC 1745 D7
DKbC 1818 E3
US-19
ATLN 1741 E4
ATLN 1742 A1
ATLN 1815 E1
ATLN 1890 C1
ATLN 1976 C1
ATLN 2062 B2
ClyC 2062 E6
ClyC 2149 A7
FTPK 2062 E6
FTPK 2148 E1
FulC 1530 E7
FulC 1670 C1
FulC 1742 A1
HPVL 2062 B2
RSWL 1531 C1
US-19 14th St NW
ATLN 1815 E6
US-19 N Central Av
ATLN 2062 D4
HPVL 2062 D4
US-19 Crown Rd SE
ATLN 2062 D4
US-19 Dogwood Dr
HPVL 2062 B1
US-19 Metropolitan Pkwy SW
ATLN 1890 C7
ATLN 1976 C1
ATLN 2062 B2
US-19 Northside Dr NW
ATLN 1815 C6
US-19 Northside Dr SW
ATLN 1890 C6
US-19 Old Dixie Rd
ClyC 2062 E7
ClyC 2149 A4
FTPK 2062 E7
FTPK 2148 E1
US-19 Peachtree Rd NE
ATLN 1742 A6
US-19 Peachtree Rd NW
ATLN 1741 E7
ATLN 1815 E1
US-19 W Peachtree St NW
ATLN 1815 C6
US-19 Peachtree St NW
ATLN 1815 E5
US-19 Ralph D Abernathy Frwy
ATLN 1890 C6
US-19 Roswell Rd NE
ATLN 1741 E4
ATLN 1742 A1
FulC 1670 A4
FulC 1742 A1
US-19 Spring St NW
ATLN 1815 E6
US-19 Tara Blvd
ClyC 2149 A7
US-19 Turner McDonald Pkwy
FulC 1530 E7
FulC 1670 C1
RSWL 1531 C1
US-23
ATLN 1891 D1
ATLN 1892 B1
ATLN 1977 E7
ClyC 2150 D1
ClyC 2151 A6
CMBL 1672 A7
CMBL 1744 A1
DCTR 1817 D7
DKbC 1672 D4
DKbC 1743 C5
DKbC 1744 A1
DKbC 1817 D6
DKbC 1977 E7
DKbC 2063 E1
DRVL 1672 B5
FTPK 2064 C6
FTPK 2150 D1
GwnC 1602 E7
GwnC 1673 B1
NRCS 1602 E7
US-23 Buford Hwy NE
CMBL 1672 A7
CMBL 1744 A1
DKbC 1672 B5
DKbC 1743 C5
DKbC 1744 A1
DRVL 1672 B5
US-23 Buford Hwy NW
DRVL 1672 D3
GwnC 1602 E7
GwnC 1672 D3
NRCS 1602 E7
US-23 Clairemont Av
DCTR 1817 D6
DKbC 1817 D6
US-23 Clairmont Rd
DKbC 1817 D6
US-23 Clairmont Rd NE
DKbC 1743 C5
DKbC 1817 D1
US-23 Macon Hwy
ClyC 2151 A7
US-23 Moreland Av
ClyC 2064 A3
ClyC 2150 D1
ClyC 2151 A6
DKbC 2063 E1
FTPK 2064 C6
FTPK 2150 D1
US-23 Moreland Av NE
ATLN 1891 D1
US-23 Moreland Av SE
ATLN 1891 D4
ATLN 1977 E7
DKbC 1977 E7
DKbC 2063 E1
US-23 Ponce de Leon Av NE
ATLN 1891 E1
ATLN 1892 B1
DKbC 1892 D1
US-23 Scott Blvd
DCTR 1817 D7
DKbC 1892 D1
US-29
ATLN 1890 D1
ATLN 1891 B1
ATLN 1892 B1
ATLN 1975 D5
CGPK 2060 E7
CGPK 2146 E1
DCTR 1817 D7
DKbC 1745 B7
DKbC 1817 E6
DKbC 1818 B5
DKbC 1819 A1
DKbC 1892 D1
EPNT 1975 D7
EPNT 2061 A6
FulC 2145 A6
FulC 2146 E1
UNCT 2145 A6
US-29 Chapel St SW
ATLN 1890 B5
US-29 Church St
EPNT 1975 D7
US-29 East Point St
EPNT 1975 D7
EPNT 2061 D1
US-29 Juniper St NE
ATLN 1890 E1
US-29 Lawrenceville Hwy
DKbC 1745 B7
DKbC 1818 B5
DKbC 1819 A1
US-29 Lee St SW
ATLN 1890 B7
ATLN 1975 D5
US-29 Legion Wy
EPNT 2061 D1
US-29 Main St
ATLN 1975 E5
CGPK 2061 A6
EPNT 1975 E4
EPNT 2061 A6
US-29 North Av NE
ATLN 1890 E1
US-29 North Av NW
ATLN 1890 D1
US-29 Northside Dr NW
ATLN 1890 C4
US-29 Northside Dr SW
ATLN 1890 C5
US-29 Peters St SW
ATLN 1890 B5
US-29 Piedmont Av NE
ATLN 1891 A1
US-29 Ponce de Leon Av NE
ATLN 1891 E1
ATLN 1892 B1
DKbC 1892 D1
US-29 Roosevelt Hwy
CGPK 2060 E7
CGPK 2146 E1
FulC 2145 A6
FulC 2146 E1
UNCT 2145 A6
US-29 Scott Blvd
DCTR 1817 D7
DKbC 1817 E6
DKbC 1818 A5
DKbC 1892 D1
US-29 W Whitehall St SW
ATLN 1890 B7
US-41
ATLN 1740 E5
ATLN 1741 B6
ATLN 1815 C2
ATLN 1890 C7
ATLN 1976 C1
ATLN 2062 B2
ClyC 2062 E7
ClyC 2149 A7
CobC 1595 B1
CobC 1667 A1
CobC 1668 A7
CobC 1740 B1
FTPK 2062 E6
FTPK 2148 E1
HPVL 2062 B2
MRTA 1595 B1
MRTA 1596 A7
MRTA 1667 A1
SMYR 1667 E7
US-41 N Central Av
ATLN 2062 D4
HPVL 2062 D4
US-41 Cobb Pkwy NE
CobC 1595 B1
MRTA 1595 B1
US-41 Cobb Pkwy NW
CobC 1595 A1
US-41 Cobb Pkwy SE
CobC 1667 A1
CobC 1668 A7
CobC 1740 B1
MRTA 1595 E5
MRTA 1667 A1
SMYR 1667 E7
US-41 Crown Rd SE
ATLN 2062 D4
US-41 Dogwood Dr
HPVL 2062 B1
US-41 Metropolitan Pkwy SW
ATLN 1890 C7
ATLN 1976 C1
ATLN 2062 B2
US-41 Northside Dr NW
ATLN 1741 C7
ATLN 1815 C2
ATLN 1890 C1
US-41 Northside Dr SW
ATLN 1890 C7
US-41 Northside Pkwy NW
ATLN 1740 E5
ATLN 1741 B6
CobC 1740 B2
US-41 Old Dixie Rd
ClyC 2062 E7
ClyC 2149 A4
FTPK 2062 E7
FTPK 2148 E1
US-41 Ralph D Abernathy Frwy
ATLN 1890 C6
US-41 Tara Blvd
ClyC 2149 A7
US-78
ATLN 1813 D7
ATLN 1892 A1
CobC 1812 C3
DCTR 1817 D7
DKbC 1745 D7
DKbC 1817 E6
DKbC 1818 E3
DKbC 1892 D1
US-78 Bankhead Hwy SE
CobC 1812 C3
US-78 Bankhead Hwy SW
CobC 1812 A3
US-78 D L Hollowell Pkwy NW
ATLN 1813 D7
US-78 Juniper St NE
ATLN 1890 E1
US-78 Lawrenceville Hwy
DKbC 1818 B5
US-78 North Av NE
ATLN 1890 E1
US-78 North Av NW
ATLN 1890 C2
US-78 Northside Dr NW
ATLN 1890 D1
US-78 Piedmont Av NE
ATLN 1891 A1
US-78 Ponce de Leon Av NE
ATLN 1891 E1
ATLN 1892 A1
DKbC 1892 D1
US-78 Scott Blvd
DCTR 1817 D7
DKbC 1817 E6
US-78 William Evans Hwy
DKbC 1745 D7
DKbC 1818 E3
US-278
ATLN 1813 D7
ATLN 1892 A1
AVES 1893 B1
CobC 1812 C3
DCTR 1892 C2
DKbC 1892 C2
DKbC 1893 B1
US-278 N Avondale Plz
AVES 1893 D1
US-278 N Avondale Rd
AVES 1893 B1
US-278 Bankhead Hwy SE
CobC 1812 C3
US-278 Bankhead Hwy SW
CobC 1812 A3
US-278 E College Av
AVES 1893 C1
DCTR 1892 E2
DKbC 1893 C1
US-278 W College Av
DCTR 1892 E2
US-278 College Av NE
ATLN 1892 C2
US-278 Covington Hwy
AVES 1893 E1
DKbC 1893 E1
US-278 Covington Rd
AVES 1893 E1
DKbC 1893 E1
US-278 D L Hollowell Pkwy NW
ATLN 1813 D7
US-278 Juniper St NE
ATLN 1890 E1
US-278 E Lake Dr
DCTR 1892 D2
DKbC 1892 D2
US-278 E Lake Rd NE
DKbC 1892 C2
US-278 North Av NE
ATLN 1890 E1
US-278 North Av NW
ATLN 1890 C2
US-278 Northside Dr NW
ATLN 1890 D1
US-278 Park Pl
DCTR 1892 D2
US-278 Park Pl NE
ATLN 1892 C2
DCTR 1892 D2
US-278 Piedmont Av NE
ATLN 1891 A1
US-278 Ponce de Leon Av NE
ATLN 1891 E1
ATLN 1892 A1
DKbC 1892 A1

A

Aaron St NW
ATLN 1889 B4
Abberley Wy
DKbC 1819 E5
Abbey Cir
DKbC 2066 C3
Abbey Ct
ClyC 2065 D7
Abbey Rd
EPNT 2061 A2

INDEX 4

Abbey St NW — Amberfield Dr NW

Atlanta Street Index

Street	City	Map #	Grid
Abbey St NW	ATLN	1889	C4
Abbeywood Dr	DKbC	1979	E2
	RSWL	1529	D1
N Abbeywood Pl	RSWL	1529	D1
S Abbeywood Pl	RSWL	1529	D1
Abbott St	CGPK	2061	A4
Abbott St SW	ATLN	1890	A4
Abbottswell Dr	FulC	1532	C3
	RSWL	1532	C3
Abby Ct NW	GwnC	1601	D4
Abby Ln NE	DKbC	1743	E5
Abercorn St	UNCT	2145	C6
Abercrombie Pl NE	CobC	1528	D3
Abercrombie Pl NW	ATLN	1815	E7
Aberdeen Ct NE	CobC	1528	B1
Aberdeen Dr NE	FulC	1670	B1
Aberdeen Dr NW	ATLN	1889	B2
Aberdeen Ln NE	FulC	1670	C1
Aberdeen St NE	ATLN	1891	E4
Aberdeen Wy SE	SMYR	1667	B7
Aberlour Wy NE	CobC	1598	B3
Abernathy Rd NE	FulC	1599	B7
Abernathy Rd NW	FulC	1598	E7
Abigail Ln NW	GwnC	1533	D7
Abilene Ct	DKbC	2066	D2
Abingdon Ct	DKbC	1819	E4
Abingdon Dr	DKbC	1819	E4
Abingdon Ln	FulC	1533	A3
Abingdon Wy NE	FulC	1599	C6
Abington Ct NW	ATLN	1815	A1
Abington Dr NE	FulC	1599	A5
Able Ct NE	CobC	1528	C5
Abner Ct NW	ATLN	1814	A4
Abner Pl NW	ATLN	1814	A4
Abner Ter NW	ATLN	1814	A4
Abram Dr	DKbC	2064	E3
Abram Ln	DKbC	2064	D4
Abram Wy	DKbC	2064	D4
Acacia Ct	DKbC	1818	C3
Acacia Ln SE	CobC	1812	C6
Acacia St NW	ATLN	1814	D7
Academy Ct NE	DKbC	1744	A6
Academy St NW	NRCS	1602	E6
Acadia St	EPNT	1976	A7
Acapulco Wy	EPNT	2060	C6
Acaro Ct	HryC	2066	D7
Acelia Ct	DKbC	1978	E2
AC Lavender Dr	RSWL	1531	E5
Acorn Av NE	ATLN	1742	A7
	ATLN	1816	A1
Acorn Dr	ClyC	2150	E4
E Acres Dr SE	CobC	1596	B5
Acuba Ln NE	DKbC	1744	B6
Ada Av NW	ATLN	1814	A7
Adair Av NE	ATLN	1816	C7
Adair Av SE	ATLN	1976	E3
Adair Ct	DCTR	1892	D2
Adair Dr NW	CobC	1526	A7
	MRTA	1526	A7
Adair St	DCTR	1892	D2
Adair St SW	ATLN	1889	E4
Adams Cir NE	MRTA	1595	D4
Adams Ct	ClyC	2152	A5
Adams Dr	ClyC	2148	B7
	RVDL	2148	B7
Adams Dr NW	ATLN	1814	B2
Adams Dr SE	CobC	1666	E6
Adams Dr SW	ATLN	1974	C3
Adams Ovlk NW	ATLN	1814	B3
Adams Pl SE	CobC	1738	A3
Adams Rd	DKbC	1600	D7
Adams Run NW	ATLN	1814	B3
Adams St	CGPK	2061	D2
	CMBL	1671	E5
	DCTR	1892	E3
Adams St SW	ATLN	1976	C4
Adams Lake Blvd SE	CobC	1739	E1
Adamson Pkwy	MRRW	2149	E7
Adamson St	FTPK	2149	A3
Adamson St SW	ATLN	1890	D7
Adamsville Dr SW	ATLN	1887	E3
Add Ct NW	GwnC	1602	B2
Adderbury Ct SE	SMYR	1738	A4
Adderbury Ln SE	CobC	1738	A4
	SMYR	1738	A4
Addie Ln NE	CobC	1597	E1
Addie St NW	ATLN	1890	A1
Addington St SW	ATLN	1889	A5
Addison Dr	DRVL	1672	B6
	FTPK	2150	D1
E Addison Dr	RSWL	1601	C1
W Addison Dr	RSWL	1532	C7
	RSWL	1601	C1
Addison Pl NW	ATLN	1814	A4
Addison Rd NE	CobC	1526	E5
Adele Av SW	ATLN	1889	D4
Adelia Pl NE	DKbC	1817	B3
Adeline Av NW	ATLN	1889	C3
Adelle St SE	ATLN	1977	A4
Adina Dr NE	ATLN	1816	C2
Adkins Rd NW	ATLN	1888	A1
Admiral Dr	CMBL	1671	E5
	DKbC	1671	E5
Admiral Wy	DKbC	1671	E3
Admiral Wy SE	CobC	1812	A1
Adolphus Av NE	ATLN	1892	A2
Adrian Pl NW	ATLN	1815	A2
Adrian St	DKbC	1745	D4
Adriatic Ct NW	GwnC	1602	B6
Aerie Ct	FulC	1530	D6
Aero Ct	EPNT	2061	D1
Aero Dr NW	FulC	1812	E7
Afond Ct	DKbC	1671	D4
Afton Ct SE	SMYR	1667	D6
Afton Dr	RSWL	1530	D1
Afton Ln NE	DKbC	1743	B5
Afton Wy SE	SMYR	1667	D6
Agan Pl NE	ATLN	1742	C2
Agape Wy	DKbC	1894	C5
Agnes Jones Pl SW	ATLN	1890	A5
Agnew Dr	FTPK	2149	A3
Agnew Rd	FTPK	2149	A2
Agricola St NE	MRTA	1595	C3
Ahyoka Dr	LKCY	2149	C3
Aiken St SW	ATLN	1976	D3
Ailey Ct NW	GwnC	1602	B2
Aircraft Dr N	CobC	1666	C3
Aircraft Dr S	CobC	1666	C3
Aircraft Dr SE	CobC	1666	C3
Airlie Dr	DKbC	1819	C4
Airline St NE	ATLN	1891	B4
Airline St SE	ATLN	1891	B4
Airport Blvd	CGPK	2061	B7
Airport Cir	CGPK	2061	B5
Airport Ct SE	MRTA	1667	B4
Airport Dr	CGPK	2061	A5
Airport Rd	CMBL	1743	D1
	DKbC	1743	D1
S Airport Rd	FulC	1887	D1
Airport Ind Park Dr SE	MRTA	1667	B4
Airport South Pkwy	ClyC	2148	B4
Airway Rd	FulC	1887	E1
Ajax Dr NW	ATLN	1814	A5
Akers Dr SE	CobC	1668	B6
Akers Mill Rd SE	CobC	1668	A7
	CobC	1740	A1
Akers Ridge Dr SE	CobC	1668	C6
N Akin Dr NE	DKbC	1744	B6
S Akin Dr NE	DKbC	1744	B6
Akridge Pl SW	ATLN	1889	D6
Akridge St NW	ATLN	1889	E3
Akron Dr SE	ATLN	1977	D4
Akron St	EPNT	1976	A7
	EPNT	2062	A1
Alabama St SW	ATLN	1890	D4
Alameda Tr	DKbC	1978	E3
Alan Dr SW	ATLN	1973	B5
Alan Ln NE	CobC	1526	E6
Alapaha Ct	FulC	1532	E2
Alaska Av NE	ATLN	1891	C3
Albany Dr SW	ATLN	1975	B2
Albatross Ct	DKbC	1980	A5
Albatross Ln	DKbC	1980	A5
Albemarle Dr NW	ATLN	1740	D6
Alberson Ct	DKbC	1818	B4
Albert Dr	FTPK	2149	B2
Albert Dr NE	MRTA	1595	E3
Albert St NW	ATLN	1888	E1
Alberta Dr NE	ATLN	1742	A5
	CobC	1527	E3
Alberta Ln	DKbC	1744	E6
Alberta Ln NE	CobC	1527	E2
Alberta Ter NE	ATLN	1742	A5
Albion Av NE	ATLN	1891	D2
Albright Tr	ClyC	2147	B7
Alcan Wy	DKbC	1819	A1
Alchemy Pl NW	GwnC	1672	E2
Alco St NE	ATLN	1816	D2
Alcoa Ct	DKbC	1744	A1
Alcott Dr SE	CobC	1738	B2
	SMYR	1738	B2
Alcott Pl	CGPK	2061	A6
Alcove Dr	DKbC	1818	D5
Alcovy Ter	HryC	2152	B6
Aldah Dr	DKbC	1745	C5
Aldea Dr	DKbC	1894	B4
Alden Av NW	ATLN	1815	D4
Alden Green Tr	EPNT	1974	D7
	EPNT	2060	D1
Alden Place Dr NE	DKbC	1743	B1
Aldenshire Pl	FulC	1601	B4
Alder Ct SE	ATLN	1892	A4
Alder Dr	FTPK	2149	C4
Alder Ln SW	ATLN	1975	C3
Alderbrook Ct NE	DKbC	1743	D7
Alderbrook Rd	DKbC	1817	E1
Alderbrook Rd NE	DKbC	1743	D7
	DKbC	1817	E1
Aldergate Dr	DKbC	1894	E7
Alderman Trc SE	CobC	1812	A7
Aldred Pl SE	CobC	1812	B4
Aldredge Rd SW	FulC	2059	A2
Aldrich Av	DKbC	1818	D6
Aldridge Av	DKbC	1818	D6
Aldridge Pl SE	SMYR	1739	B7
Aldwych Ln NE	FulC	1599	C3
Ale Cir	EPNT	2060	C3
Aleamo Dr NE	MRTA	1595	E3
Alemeda Dr NE	CobC	1526	E1
Aleta Dr NE	CobC	1527	B3
Alex Dr SW	ATLN	1887	E4
Alex Wy SW	ATLN	1887	E4
Alexa Av SE	ATLN	1893	A5
Alexander Av	DKbC	1892	D6
	UNCT	2145	A5
Alexander Cir NE	ATLN	1742	B4
Alexander Cir SE	MRTA	1595	B5
Alexander Dr	DKbC	1893	A6
Alexander Dr NE	ATLN	1816	A1
Alexander St	UNCT	2145	A7
Alexander St NE	ATLN	1890	E2
	MRTA	1595	B5
Alexander St NW	ATLN	1890	D2
Alexander St SE	CobC	1666	C4
	MRTA	1595	B5
	SMYR	1667	A7
Alexandria Ct NE	DKbC	1742	E1
Alexandria Ct SE	CobC	1667	E2
Alexandria Dr SW	ATLN	1973	E7
	ATLN	2059	D1
Alexandria Wy	CGPK	2060	E6
Alexandria Wy SE	SMYR	1738	C4
Alexis Ct NE	CobC	1526	E1
Alfred Rd NW	ATLN	1813	B7
Alice St	FTPK	2149	B2
Alice St SW	ATLN	1890	D5
Alicia Ct	DKbC	2066	C3
Alicia Ct NE	CobC	1528	E2
Aline Dr NW	ATLN	1888	C1
Aline Wolfe Dr SE	SMYR	1666	D7
	SMYR	1738	C1
Alison Ct	EPNT	1975	C4
Alison Ct SW	ATLN	1975	B4
Alison Dr	DRVL	1672	B6
Allaire Ln NE	DKbC	1743	E5
Allatoona Rd	ClyC	2150	C7
Allegheny Dr NE	CobC	1527	C1
Allegheny St SW	ATLN	1889	D6
Allegro Dr NW	ATLN	1888	D1
Allen Cir NW	GwnC	1673	C4
Allen Ct NW	ATLN	1741	C1
Allen Dr	ClyC	2065	D7
	ClyC	2151	D1
	DRVL	1672	B6
	FulC	2145	E3
	RVDL	2148	B7
Allen Ln SE	ATLN	1977	A7
	ATLN	2063	A1
N Allen Rd SE	CobC	1812	B2
Allen Rd NE	ATLN	1816	B4
	FulC	1669	E3
Allen Rd SE	CobC	1812	A3
Allen Rd SW	CobC	1812	A4
Allen Wy	DKbC	2064	E2
Allendale Dr	ATLN	1893	A6
	DKbC	1893	A6
Allendale Dr SE	ATLN	1893	A6
	DKbC	1893	A6
Allene Av SW	ATLN	1890	B7
	ATLN	1976	B1
Allenhurst Dr NW	GwnC	1602	C2
Allen Temple Ct NW	ATLN	1888	C4
Allenwood Wy	DKbC	1745	D6
Allgood Cir	DKbC	1819	E7
Allgood Ct	DKbC	1894	E2
Allgood Dr SE	CobC	1666	A1
Allgood Pl	DKbC	1819	E7
Allgood Rd	DKbC	1819	E7
Allgood Rd NE	CobC	1527	B7
	MRTA	1526	E7
Allgood Ter	DKbC	1819	E7
Allgood Wy	DKbC	1819	E7
Allgood Springs Dr	DKbC	1894	E1
Allgood Valley Ct	DKbC	1894	E1
Allison Dr NE	ATLN	1742	A4
Alloway Pl SE	ATLN	1891	D7
	ATLN	1977	D1
Allsborough Ct	DKbC	1745	C2
Allsborough Dr	DKbC	1745	B2
Allsworth Ct SE	SMYR	1739	B7
Alma St NW	ATLN	1814	C4
Alma St SW	ATLN	1975	D2
Almach Av	ClyC	2064	A6
Almach Ct	ClyC	2064	B6
Almand Dr	CGPK	2061	B3
Almand Rd SE	DKbC	1977	E6
Almeta Av NE	ATLN	1892	B2
Almon Dr NE	CobC	1526	E4
Almond Ct NE	CobC	1528	D3
Almont Dr SW	ATLN	1975	D1
Almont Wy	RSWL	1532	B4
Alpco Ct	DKbC	1819	E3
Alpha Dr	DKbC	1892	E7
Alpharetta St	RSWL	1530	C1
Alpharetta St SR-9	RSWL	1530	C1
Alpharetta St SR-120	RSWL	1530	C1
Alpine Dr SE	SMYR	1738	D3
Alpine Rd	ClyC	2151	D7
Alpine Rd NE	ATLN	1742	B7
Alpine Tr NE	CobC	1528	E3
Alpine Wy	FTPK	2063	C6
Alpine Wy NE	MRTA	1595	D3
Alpine Hills Ct	DKbC	1819	E3
Alpine Hills Dr	DKbC	1819	E3
Alston Ct	ClyC	2148	E4
Alston Ct NE	CobC	1529	B1
Alston Dr	DKbC	1893	A5
Alston Dr NE	CobC	1527	D3
Alston Dr SE	ATLN	1892	D5
	DKbC	1892	D5
	DKbC	1893	A5
Alston Ln SW	CobC	1666	B4
Alston Pl NE	ATLN	1742	D7
Alta Av NE	ATLN	1891	D3
Alta Pl NW	ATLN	1889	B1
Altacrest Dr	DKbC	1818	E6
Altadena Pl SW	ATLN	1889	C7
Altamont Dr	DKbC	1818	A2
Altaview Dr SE	ATLN	1976	E7
	ATLN	2062	E1
Alta Vista Dr NE	DKbC	1743	B3
Altheas Ct	ClyC	2151	C3
Alto Ct NW	GwnC	1602	C1
Alton Rd	DKbC	1672	D7
	DKbC	1744	D1
Alton Rd NW	ATLN	1815	C2
Alton Wy NE	CobC	1526	E6
Altoona Pl SW	ATLN	1889	D5
Alumni Dr SE	CobC	1595	D7
	MRTA	1595	D7
Alva St NE	ATLN	1892	A3
S Alvarado Ter SW	ATLN	1889	D7
Alvarado Ter SW	ATLN	1889	C6
Alvaton Ct NW	GwnC	1602	B1
Alvecot Cir SE	CobC	1739	D7
	CobC	1813	D1
Alverado Wy	DKbC	1893	E5
Alverstone Dr SE	ATLN	2063	A4
Alvin Dr NW	ATLN	1814	B6
Alvin Rd	FulC	1532	D1
Amado Ct	ClyC	2151	A6
Amador Cir	FulC	1599	D2
Amal Dr SW	ATLN	1976	C3
Amanda Cir	DKbC	1817	D2
N Amanda Cir NE	DKbC	1817	D1
Amanda Ln NE	MRTA	1596	A4
Amanda St NE	ATLN	1892	A3
Ambage Ln	DKbC	1980	C4
Amber Pl NW	ATLN	1813	A7
Amber Rd NW	ATLN	1813	B7
Amber Wy	DKbC	1979	B1
Amberbrook Ct NE	CobC	1598	D1
Amberfield Cir NW	GwnC	1533	D7
Amberfield Dr NW	GwnC	1533	C7
	GwnC	1602	D1

INDEX 5

Amberglade Ct NW — Ashbill Ct

Atlanta Street Index

STREET	City	Map #	Grid
Amberglade Ct NW	GwnC	1533	B7
Amberglades Ln NW	FulC	1598	D7
Amberidge Tr NW	FulC	1598	C7
Amberley Ln NE	CobC	1528	D5
Amberly Ct N	DKbC	1601	C7
Amberly Ct S	DKbC	1672	C1
Amberly Dr	DKbC	1672	B1
Amberly Rd	ClyC	2151	D6
Amberly Wy	DKbC	1601	C7
Amberside Ct	RSWL	1532	B1
Amberwood Dr NE	DKbC	1744	C6
Amberwood Tr NE	CobC	1529	B4
Amberwood Wy	ClyC	2149	C6
Amberwood Wy NE	DKbC	1744	C6
Ambler Wy	FulC	1533	C3
Ambleside Pl NE	CobC	1529	A1
Amblewood Ct NE	DKbC	1744	E4
Ambrose Ct	DKbC	2065	A2
Ambrose Wy	DKbC	2065	A2
Ambrose Ridge Ct	DKbC	2065	A2
Amelia Av	DKbC	1893	A5
Amelia Ln	ClyC	2151	C3
American Dr	CMBL	1671	E5
American Industrial Wy	CMBL	1671	E5
Amerson Ct	ClyC	2150	E4
Amerson Ln	ClyC	2150	E5
Amerson Tr	ClyC	2150	E4
Amerson Wy	ClyC	2150	E5
Amesbury Dr	DKbC	1893	E7
Amethyst Ct	FulC	2146	D7
Amethyst Cove	FulC	1532	C4
Amherst Ct NE	CobC	1598	B1
	FulC	1599	B4
Amherst Ct NW	GwnC	1602	A4
Amherst Dr	ClyC	2148	D6
Amherst Ln	ClyC	2150	D5
Amherst Pl NW	ATLN	1814	E2
Amhurst Dr NW	ATLN	1888	C1
	GwnC	1533	C7
Ami St SE	ATLN	1891	A7
Amicalola Pass NE	CobC	1528	D6
Amish Ct	ClyC	2150	C7
Amity Ct	ClyC	2151	A7
Amor Ct	DKbC	2064	E1
Amsler Rd	DKbC	2066	C6
Amsterdam Av NE	ATLN	1816	B6
	DKbC	1816	C6
Amsterdam Cir SE	CobC	1667	D4
	MRTA	1667	D4
Amster Green Dr	FulC	1599	E2
Amwiler Ct NW	GwnC	1672	E1
Amwiler Rd NW	DKbC	1672	D1
	GwnC	1673	A1
Amwiler Industrial Dr NW	GwnC	1672	E1
Amy Ct	CGPK	2061	A4
Amy Dr NE	MRTA	1595	C4
Anaheim Dr	FulC	1532	D1
Anastasia Ct SE	CobC	1738	A6
Anastasia Dr SE	CobC	1738	A5
Anchor Ter SW	ATLN	1975	C2
Anchorage Pl	RSWL	1532	B1
Ancient Amber Wy NW	GwnC	1533	D7
Ancient Oak Ct SE	CobC	1597	C5
Ancroft Cir NW	GwnC	1602	E1
Andalusia Ct	DKbC	1601	B7
Andalusia Pl	DKbC	1601	B7
Andalusia Tr	DKbC	1601	B7
Anderson Av NW	ATLN	1889	C3
Anderson Cir SE	SMYR	1667	A7
Anderson Ct	MRTA	1596	A2
Anderson Dr SE	CobC	1739	B3
Anderson Pl	DKbC	1744	D7
Anderson St SE	MRTA	1595	A5
Anderson Wk NE	CobC	1596	A2
	MRTA	1595	E2
Anderson Wy SW	ATLN	1975	E3
Andover Ct	DKbC	1601	B7
Andover Dr	DKbC	1601	B7
Andover Dr NE	CobC	1527	C1
Andover Dr NW	ATLN	1741	B2
Andrea Ln	ClyC	2151	A7
Andrew Jackson Dr	CLKN	1819	A2
Andrews Cir	DKbC	1817	C5
Andrews Ct NW	ATLN	1741	E6
E Andrews Dr NW	ATLN	1741	E6
W Andrews Dr NW	ATLN	1741	D5
Andrews Dr NE	MRTA	1595	E3
Andrews Dr NW	ATLN	1741	E7
Andrews St NW	ATLN	1889	D3
Andrew Young Int'l Blvd NE	ATLN	1890	E3
	ATLN	1891	A3
Andrew Young Int'l Blvd NW	ATLN	1890	D3
Andy Dr NE	CobC	1526	B4
Angel Falls Ln SW	ATLN	1974	B1
Angelique Dr	DKbC	1744	A7
Angelisa Tr NE	CobC	1528	B6
Angelo Ct NE	CobC	1812	A5
Angelo Dr NE	ATLN	1670	D7
	ATLN	1742	D1
Angels Ln NW	GwnC	1673	E7
Angie Dr	DKbC	1745	E3
N Angier Av NE	ATLN	1891	C2
Angier Av NE	ATLN	1891	A2
Angier Ct NE	ATLN	1891	A2
Angier Pl NE	ATLN	1891	B2
Angier Springs Rd NE	ATLN	1891	C2
Angla Dr SE	CobC	1738	A3
	SMYR	1738	A3
Angla Dr SW	CobC	1738	A3
Angus Tr NE	FulC	1669	E1
Anita Pl NE	DKbC	1816	E5
Anita Pl SE	CobC	1738	A7
	CobC	1812	A1
Aniwaka Av SW	ATLN	1975	D2
Anjaco Rd NW	ATLN	1815	D4
Ankonian Dr	FulC	1533	C1
Ann Ct	CMBL	1671	E7
Ann Pl NE	CobC	1528	D3
Ann Rd SE	SMYR	1739	C1
Ann St	CMBL	1671	E6
Anna Maria Ct	DKbC	1819	C3
Annandale Dr NE	CobC	1527	A4
Annapolis Ct NE	DKbC	1744	A6
Anne Dr SE	CobC	1812	C3
Anne St NW	ATLN	1814	C2
Anne St SE	ATLN	1977	A2
Anne St SW	FulC	2146	D1
Anne Boleyn Ct SE	CobC	1738	A5
Annelaine Dr SW	ATLN	1888	B6
Annette Ct	ClyC	2147	C7
Annie St	DKbC	1818	D6
Annie St NW	ATLN	1814	D4
Anniston Av SE	ATLN	1892	A4
Anniston Ct SE	CobC	1597	E4
Anns Ln SW	ATLN	1975	B4
Annwicks Ct NE	CobC	1528	B5
Annwicks Dr NE	CobC	1528	B5
Ansley Bnd	DKbC	2066	C3
Ansley Ct	RSWL	1531	D2
Ansley Dr	RSWL	1531	D2
Ansley Dr NE	ATLN	1816	A5
Ansley St	DCTR	1892	E2
Ansley Villa Dr NE	ATLN	1816	A4
Ansley Walk Ter NE	ATLN	1816	A5
Antelope Tr	ClyC	2147	D4
Anthony Dr	DKbC	1818	D2
Anthony Ln NE	CobC	1527	D2
Anthony Pl NW	ATLN	1889	E1
E Anthony St NW	ATLN	1889	E2
W Anthony St NW	ATLN	1889	E2
Anthony St NW	ATLN	1889	E1
Antioch Dr NE	DKbC	1670	E7
Antler Tr NE	CobC	1527	B2
Antler Tr SE	SMYR	1738	B4
Antone St NW	ATLN	1815	B5
Antwerp Dr SE	ATLN	1976	E6
Anvil Block Ct	HryC	2151	D1
Anvil Block Rd	ClyC	2064	D7
	ClyC	2151	D1
Anwar Tr	DKbC	1892	D6
Apache Tr NE	MRTA	1595	B2
Apache Tr SE	DKbC	1978	D4
Apache Tr SW	ATLN	1973	B6
Apollo Dr SW	FulC	1887	C7
Appalachee Dr NE	DKbC	1743	A4
Appaloosa Run	ClyC	2150	E5
Appian Wy	DKbC	1893	B4
Applegate Ct NW	GwnC	1601	E2
Applegate Ln	FulC	1531	A5
Applegate Wy	DKbC	1745	D5
Apple Orchard Rd	DKbC	1744	E3
Appleton Cir SE	CobC	1595	A7
Appleton Ct	DKbC	1980	C5
Appleton Dr SE	CobC	1595	A7
Apple Tree Dr	DKbC	1819	E3
Apple Tree Wy	DKbC	1819	E3
Appletree Wy NW	GwnC	1602	A4
Apple Valley Rd NE	DKbC	1742	D3
	DKbC	1743	A3
Applewood Ct NE	DKbC	1744	D2
Appling Cir	DKbC	1744	B1
Appling Dr	DKbC	1744	B1
Appling Pl	DKbC	1744	B1
Appling Wy	DKbC	1744	B1
Appomattox Dr	DKbC	1979	A4
Appomattox Wy	DKbC	1979	B4
Approach Ct	RSWL	1601	B1
April Ln	DKbC	1980	E1
Apsley Ct SE	CobC	1740	A3
Apsley Wy	FulC	1533	E1
Aquamist Dr	DKbC	1980	B3
Aqueduct Wy NE	CobC	1528	B7
Aquila Dr	ClyC	2150	E7
Arabian Ct NE	CobC	1527	E3
Arabian Dr NE	CobC	1527	E3
Arabian Pl NE	CobC	1527	E3
Arabian Tr NE	CobC	1527	E3
Aragon Wy NE	DKbC	1743	B3
Aran Dr	RSWL	1531	D6
Arbor Av SE	ATLN	1892	E4
Arbor Ct NE	CobC	1527	A4
Arbor Ln	MRRW	2149	E6
Arbor Pl	DKbC	1980	D4
Arbor Rdg	DKbC	1672	E6
Arbor Tr SE	CobC	1596	E6
Arbor Trc NE	DKbC	1742	E4
Arbor Chase	DKbC	1818	D1
Arbor Creek Ln	DKbC	1672	C6
Arbor Creek Pt	DKbC	1672	C6
Arborcrest Dr	DKbC	1818	C5
Arbordale Dr	DKbC	1818	A3
Arboreal Ct	FulC	1532	C4
Arbor End SE	SMYR	1667	C5
Arbor Gate Dr SW	CobC	1812	A5
Arbor Gates Dr NE	ATLN	1816	C1
Arbor Glen Pl NE	CobC	1527	B3
Arbor Path Dr	DKbC	1672	E6
Arbor Ridge Ct	DKbC	1672	E6
Arborside Ct	FulC	1532	D4
Arbor Springs Trc	DKbC	1745	B2
Arborvista Dr NE	DKbC	1817	B3
Arborwood Ln	DKbC	1745	C6
Arborwoods Dr	FulC	1532	C4
Arc Wy NE	ATLN	1742	B5
Arcadia Av	DKbC	1893	B1
N Arcadia Av	DCTR	1818	B7
	DKbC	1818	C7
Arcadia Cir NW	ATLN	1889	E3
Arcadia St NE	ATLN	1816	C7
Arcaro Ct	DKbC	1980	B3
Archcrest Dr SE	ATLN	2062	E4
Archdale Dr	DKbC	1745	D5
Archer St SW	ATLN	1889	D4
Archer Tr	DKbC	1980	D5
Archer Wy NW	ATLN	1890	A2
Archway Dr	DKbC	1743	D2
Archwood Dr	DKbC	1673	B6
Ard Pl NW	ATLN	1888	A3
Arden Av SW	ATLN	1976	A2
Arden Ct	ClyC	2150	D5
W Arden Rd NW	ATLN	1741	B7
Arden Rd NW	ATLN	1741	C6
	ATLN	1815	B1
Arden Wy NE	ATLN	1742	C2
Arden Wy SE	SMYR	1667	C7
Arden at Argonne NW	ATLN	1741	C6
Arden Close NW	ATLN	1741	B7
Arden Moor NW	ATLN	1741	C6
Arden Oaks Ct NW	ATLN	1741	C6
Ardis St NE	MRTA	1595	A4
Ardley Rd SW	ATLN	1888	B7
Ardmoor Dr	ClyC	2149	B7
Ardmore Cir NW	ATLN	1815	D4
Ardmore Pl NW	ATLN	1815	D4
Ardmore Rd NW	ATLN	1815	D4
Ardmore Sq NW	ATLN	1815	C4
Ardsley Ct NE	CobC	1528	D6
Ardsley Dr NE	CobC	1528	D5
Argo Dr	HPVL	2062	C2
Argo Dr SE	SMYR	1667	B6
S Argo Rd SE	CobC	1739	A6
	SMYR	1739	A6
Argo Rd SE	CobC	1739	A6
	SMYR	1739	A6
Argonne Av NE	ATLN	1816	A7
	ATLN	1891	A1
Argonne Dr	ClyC	2150	A7
	MRRW	2150	A7
Argonne Dr NW	ATLN	1741	C7
Argonne Wy NE	ATLN	1816	D3
	DKbC	1816	D3
Argus Cir NW	ATLN	1888	A2
Argyle Dr NW	ATLN	1813	D5
Argyle Dr SE	SMYR	1739	C1
Argylls Crest	FulC	1532	D3
Aristides Ln	DKbC	1980	B4
Arizona Av NE	ATLN	1892	A3
Arkose Dr SE	DKbC	1978	C2
Arkwright Dr	DKbC	1817	B6
Arkwright Pl SE	ATLN	1891	D5
Arldowne Dr	DKbC	1745	D3
Arlene Dr SE	CobC	1739	B5
Arlene Rd	CGPK	2060	D5
Arlene Wy NE	ATLN	1816	B1
Arlington Av NE	ATLN	1816	D3
	DKbC	1816	D3
Arlington Av SW	ATLN	1975	E1
Arlington Cir NW	ATLN	1889	B1
Arlington Dr NW	ATLN	1888	C3
Arlington Ln SE	SMYR	1738	D2
Arlington Pkwy NE	DKbC	1816	D3
Arlington Pl NE	ATLN	1816	D7
	CobC	1528	B7
Arlington Rd	EPNT	2060	D4
Arlington Ter SE	CobC	1596	E7
Arlington School Dr SW	ATLN	1973	E6
Armand Ct NE	ATLN	1816	C2
Armand Rd NE	ATLN	1816	C2
Armley Pt NW	GwnC	1533	A6
Armour Cir NE	ATLN	1816	A3
Armour Dr NE	ATLN	1815	E3
Armour Pl NE	ATLN	1816	A3
Armstead Pl NW	ATLN	1890	E1
Armstrong Pl SE	CobC	1813	A4
Armstrong St SE	ATLN	1891	A4
	MRTA	1595	C5
Armswood Pl	DKbC	1894	D1
Arnaud Ct	DKbC	1600	B5
Arno Ct NW	ATLN	1814	A5
Arno Dr NW	ATLN	1813	E5
Arnold Av NE	CobC	1526	B5
	DKbC	1816	E3
Arnold St	HPVL	2062	D3
Arnold St NE	ATLN	1891	B2
Around Lenox Rd NE	ATLN	1742	B5
Arpege Wy NW	ATLN	1815	A2
Arrie Wy	DKbC	1601	D5
Arrow Cir	DKbC	1744	A2
Arrow St	ATLN	1975	E4
Arrow Creek Dr	DKbC	1744	A2
Arrowhead Blvd	ClyC	2148	E7
Arrowhead Ct NE	CobC	1527	B4
Arrowhead Tr NE	CobC	1527	B5
	DKbC	1743	E7
	DKbC	1817	E1
Arrowood Dr	EPNT	1974	D7
Arrowood Dr SW	ATLN	1974	C7
Arrowwood Dr NE	CobC	1596	E3
Artesia Cir	DKbC	1818	E3
Artesia Dr	DKbC	1818	E3
Arthur St SW	ATLN	1890	C7
Arthurs Ct	DKbC	1894	C6
Arthurs Ct NE	CobC	1528	D3
Artist View Dr	DKbC	1980	C6
Artwood Rd NE	DKbC	1892	C1
Arundel Dr NW	FulC	1669	A4
Arundel Rd	CGPK	2060	E6
Asa Dr	HryC	2065	D6
Asbury Ct	DKbC	1818	B3
Asbury Ln SW	ATLN	1974	A6
Asbury Sq	DKbC	1671	A1
Asbury Commons Dr	DKbC	1600	E7
Ascot Ct	DKbC	1672	B7
	DKbC	1744	B1
	RVDL	2148	A7
Ascot Dr NE	FulC	1670	D6
Ascot Ln	FulC	1532	C1
	RSWL	1532	C1
	RVDL	2148	A6
Ascot Mnr NW	FulC	1668	E5
Ascot Ter	HryC	2065	E7
Asgard Ct	HryC	2152	B2
Asgard Ct NE	DKbC	1744	A5
Ash St	FTPK	2149	C3
N Ash St	FTPK	2149	C1
Ash St NW	GwnC	1673	B1
Ashbill Ct	ClyC	2151	C6

INDEX 6

Ashborough Cir SE — Bailey Rd

Atlanta Street Index

STREET	City	Map #	Grid
Ashborough Cir SE	CobC	1667	B1
Ashborough Ct SE	CobC	1667	B1
Ashborough Dr SE	CobC	1667	B1
Ashborough Rd SE	CobC	1667	B1
	MRTA	1667	B1
Ashborough Ter SE	CobC	1667	B1
Ashborough Wy SE	CobC	1667	B2
Ashburn Ln NE	DKbC	1743	C2
Ashburn Wk	CobC	1597	E1
Ashburn Wk NE	CobC	1598	A1
Ashburton Av	ATLN	1893	A6
	DKbC	1893	A6
Ashburton Av SE	ATLN	1893	A6
	DKbC	1893	A6
Ashburton Chase NE	CobC	1529	B1
Ashbury Cir	DKbC	1817	B5
Ashbury Ct	DKbC	1893	C2
Ashbury Dr	DKbC	1893	C3
Ashbury Ln NE	CobC	1527	B2
Ashbury Heights Ct	DKbC	1893	C2
Ashbury Heights Rd	DKbC	1893	C2
Ashbury Point Dr NE	CobC	1527	B3
Ashbury Point Ln NE	CobC	1527	B2
Ashby Cir NW	ATLN	1890	A3
Ashby Grv SW	ATLN	1890	A4
N Ashby St NW	ATLN	1815	A6
Ashby St SW	ATLN	1890	A7
Ashby Ter NW	ATLN	1890	A3
Ashdale Dr	FulC	2146	B7
Ashdowne Wy	FulC	1601	B2
Ashebark Ct NE	CobC	1529	E6
Ashebark Ln NE	CobC	1529	E6
Ashebrooke Ct NE	CobC	1596	E2
Ashebrooke Dr NE	CobC	1597	A1
Ashebrooke Pl NE	CobC	1597	A2
Ashebrooke Trc NE	CobC	1597	A2
Ashebrooke Wy NE	CobC	1597	A1
Asheforde Dr NE	CobC	1529	E6
Asheforde Ln NE	CobC	1529	E7
Asheforde Wy NE	CobC	1529	E7
Ashentree Ct	DKbC	1671	C3
Ashentree Dr	DKbC	1671	C3
Asheton Ct NE	CobC	1596	D2
Asheton Pl NE	CobC	1597	A1
Asheview Ct NE	CobC	1529	E6
Asheworth Ct NW	ATLN	1741	A5
Ashfield Dr	DKbC	1893	C2
Ashford Ct	ClyC	2064	A5
Ashford Ctr N	DKbC	1600	A6
Ashford Knls NE	DKbC	1671	B4
Ashford Ln	DKbC	1600	A6
Ashford Pkwy	DKbC	1600	A7
Ashford Pl NE	DKbC	1671	B4
Ashford Pt NE	DKbC	1671	B5
Ashford Rd NE	DKbC	1743	B2
Ashford Rdg NE	DKbC	1671	C4
Ashford Tr NE	DKbC	1671	B4
Ashford Wk	DKbC	1600	A6
Ashford Center Pkwy	DKbC	1600	A6
Ashford Club Ct NE	DKbC	1671	B6
Ashford Club Dr	DKbC	1600	A7
Ashford Dunwoody Rd	DKbC	1600	A7
Ashford Dunwoody Rd NE	DKbC	1600	A7
	DKbC	1743	B1
Ashford Gables Dr	DKbC	1599	E7
	DKbC	1600	A7
Ashford Lake Ct NE	DKbC	1671	B4
W Ashland Av NE	ATLN	1891	C3
Ashland Av NE	ATLN	1891	C3
Ashland Ct	ClyC	2147	C7
Ashland Dr NE	ATLN	1891	C3
Ashleigh Ter NE	CobC	1528	E3
Ashley Av NE	ATLN	1891	C2
Ashley Ct	ClyC	2151	C5
	DKbC	1601	A4
	RSWL	1532	B4
Ashley Ct SE	CobC	1812	C6
	SMYR	1738	B3
Ashley Ests SE	CobC	1597	C5
Ashley Ln	RSWL	1532	B4
Ashley Pl	DKbC	1819	E5
Ashley Trc	DKbC	1601	B4
Ashley Club Cir NW	GwnC	1601	D5
Ashley Creek Cir	DKbC	1819	E5
Ashley Creek Ct	DKbC	1819	E5
Ashley Forest Dr	RSWL	1532	B4
Ashley Glen Ln	FulC	1532	C4
Ashley Lake Dr NE	CobC	1596	C1
Ashley Lakes Dr NW	GwnC	1601	E5
Ashley Oaks Ct NE	DKbC	1743	E4
Ashley Run Ct NW	GwnC	1601	D5
Ashley Run Dr NW	GwnC	1601	D5
Ashleywoods Ct	DKbC	1745	C4
Ashleywoods Dr	DKbC	1745	C4
Ashling SE	CobC	1667	E5
Ashmel Ct SW	ATLN	1975	A1
Ashmel Pl SW	ATLN	1975	A1
Ashmont Ct	DKbC	1600	B5
Ashmore Dr	FTPK	2063	A7
	FTPK	2149	E1
Ashmore Hall Dr	CobC	1528	A1
Ash Rill Dr	FulC	1532	C1
Ashton Pl	AVES	1893	D1
Ashton Pl NE	CobC	1596	D5
Ashton Trc NE	DKbC	1742	E1
Ashton Bluff Dr NE	DKbC	1742	E6
Ashton Woods Ct NE	CobC	1596	D5
Ashton Woods Dr NE	CMBL	1671	C6
	CobC	1596	D5
	DKbC	1671	C6
Ashurst Dr	RSWL	1529	E3
Ashwood Av SW	ATLN	1976	C4
Ashwood Ct SE	CobC	1738	E3
Ashwood Dr SE	CobC	1738	E3
	SMYR	1739	A3
Ashwood Ln	DKbC	1745	A1
Ashwood Pkwy	DKbC	1599	E7
	DKbC	1600	A7
Ashwood Pl	DKbC	1893	C2
Ashwood Wk	DKbC	1893	C2
Ashwoody Ct NE	DKbC	1671	A2
Ashwoody Tr NE	DKbC	1671	A3
Ask Kay Dr SE	SMYR	1666	C7
Asp Dr SE	DKbC	1977	E2
Aspen Ct	DKbC	1745	A2
Aspen Ct SE	CobC	1812	C6
Aspen Dr	ClyC	2147	E4
Aspen Dr NE	DKbC	1744	C6
Aspen Rd	ClyC	2147	E3
	ClyC	2148	A4
Aspenwood Ct NE	CobC	1529	A4
Aspen Woods Ct	DKbC	1672	D1
Aspen Woods Entry	DKbC	1672	C1
Asr Rd	ClyC	2061	E7
	ClyC	2147	E1
Aston Ct	FulC	1532	E3
Astor Av	FTPK	2063	C7
Astor Av SW	ATLN	1975	E4
Astronaut Dr	DKbC	2064	E1
Astwood Ct	RSWL	1532	C5
Atcheson Ln	DKbC	1599	E6
Athas St SE	ATLN	1977	D3
Athens Av SW	ATLN	1976	B2
Atherton Cir	DKbC	1894	C5
Atherton Dr	DKbC	1894	D6
Atkins Wy SE	CobC	1738	C2
	SMYR	1738	C2
Atkinson Dr SE	ATLN	2063	A4
Atlanta Av	DCTR	1892	D2
	HPVL	2062	B3
Atlanta Av SE	ATLN	1890	E7
	ATLN	1891	A7
Atlanta Av SW	ATLN	1890	E7
E Atlanta Rd	HryC	2152	B2
S Atlanta Rd SE	ATLN	1814	B1
	CobC	1739	C5
	CobC	1814	B1
W Atlanta Rd SE	CobC	1739	C4
Atlanta Rd SE	CobC	1595	B6
	CobC	1666	B3
	CobC	1739	C4
	MRTA	1595	B6
	SMYR	1666	B3
	SMYR	1739	A1
Atlanta St	CGPK	2061	B2
	EPNT	1975	D7
	RSWL	1530	C2
Atlanta St SR-9	RSWL	1530	C2
Atlanta St SR-120	RSWL	1530	C2
S Atlanta St	RSWL	1530	C3
S Atlanta St SR-9	RSWL	1530	C3
S Atlanta St SR-120	RSWL	1530	C3
W Atlanta St SE	MRTA	1595	B5
Atlanta St SE	CobC	1595	B6
	MRTA	1595	B6
Atlanta St SE SR-5	CobC	1595	B6
	MRTA	1595	B5
Atlanta Country Club Dr SE	CobC	1597	E7
Atlanta Industrial Dr NE	MRTA	1526	C7
Atlanta Industrial Dr NW	ATLN	1813	C5
Atlanta Industrial Pkwy NW	ATLN	1813	B6
Atlanta Industrial Wy NW	ATLN	1813	C5
Atlanta South Pkwy	ClyC	2148	B2
Atlantic Av SE	CobC	1595	B7
	CobC	1666	B1
Atlantic Blvd NW	GwnC	1602	B6
Atlantic Blvd NW	NRCS	1602	B6
Atlantic Dr NW	ATLN	1815	D7
Atlantis Av NE	ATLN	1891	C3
Atoka Dr SE	CobC	1666	A5
Atridge Dr NE	CobC	1597	B5
Attaway Wk NE	DKbC	1742	E4
Atterberry Ct	DKbC	1818	D2
Atterberry Pl	DKbC	1818	D2
Attucks Blvd	ClyC	2150	C3
Atwood Dr NW	MRTA	1595	A3
Atwood Rd NE	ATLN	1742	B7
Atwood St SW	ATLN	1889	E7
Auburn Av NE	ATLN	1890	E4
Auburn Dr	ClyC	2147	B6
Aubusson Trc	FulC	1532	E4
Auden Ln NW	GwnC	1673	D4
Auden Tr	FulC	1599	D3
Auditorium Pl SE	ATLN	1890	E4
Auditorium Wy	CGPK	2061	C3
Audley Ln NW	GwnC	1533	D6
Audrey Pl NW	ATLN	1813	E4
Audubon Cir SW	ATLN	1888	E7
	ATLN	1974	E1
Audubon Dr NE	CobC	1597	D2
	DKbC	1743	C7
Augusta Av SE	ATLN	1891	A7
Augusta Dr SE	MRTA	1596	A7
Augusta Pl SE	ATLN	1891	A6
Auldon Ct SE	SMYR	1738	B2
Aurie Ct	DKbC	1978	E4
Aurie Dr	DKbC	1978	E4
Aurora Av NW	ATLN	1889	B3
Aurora Ct	DKbC	1599	E3
	DKbC	1600	A3
Aurora Ln	DKbC	1599	E3
Austell Rd SE	CobC	1666	A2
Austell Rd SE SR-5	CobC	1666	A3
Austell Rd SW	CobC	1666	A3
Austell Rd SW SR-5	CobC	1666	A3
Austell Wy NW	ATLN	1741	D6
Austin Av NE	ATLN	1891	C3
	MRTA	1595	C4
Austin Cir	DKbC	1894	C6
W Austin Ct	DKbC	1894	B5
Austin Ct SW	ATLN	1973	E5
Austin Dr	ClyC	2147	C6
	DKbC	1894	C5
Austin Dr SE	SMYR	1738	C3
Austin Pl	FTPK	2149	B2
Austin Rd	HryC	2066	E7
	HryC	2152	E1
W Austin Rd	DKbC	1894	B4
Austin Rd SW	ATLN	1974	A4
	FulC	1974	A2
Austin Glen Dr	DKbC	1600	A3
Austin Lake Cir SE	SMYR	1738	C2
Austin Lake Dr SE	SMYR	1738	C2
Austin Woods Ct SW	ATLN	1974	A3
Austin Woods Dr SW	ATLN	1974	A4
Auto Port Dr	CGPK	2061	B6
Autry St NW	NRCS	1602	D6
Autry Falls Dr	FulC	1533	A2
Autry Falls Wy	FulC	1533	B2
Autry Landing Cir	FulC	1533	A2
Autry Landing Wy	FulC	1533	A2
Autry Mill Cir	FulC	1533	B2
Autry Mill Rd	FulC	1533	C1
Autry Ridge Pt	FulC	1533	C1
Autumn Ct	HryC	2066	D7
Autumn Dr	DRVL	1672	B6
Autumn Ln NE	CobC	1598	D3
Autumn Ln SE	SMYR	1738	B3
Autumn Ln SW	ATLN	1889	B5
Autumn Pl SE	SMYR	1738	B3
Autumn Cherry Ct	DKbC	1980	C6
Autumn Glen Dr NE	FulC	1670	B1
Autumn Hill Ct	DKbC	1894	E3
Autumn Hill Dr	DKbC	1894	E3
Autumn Hill Ln	DKbC	1894	E3
Autumn Hill Pl	DKbC	1894	E3
Autumn Lake Ct	DKbC	1980	E4
Autumn Lake Ln	DKbC	1980	D4
Autumn Leaf Wy NW	GwnC	1673	D4
Autumn Ridge Tr	RSWL	1531	E5
Autumn Trace Dr NW	GwnC	1601	D6
Autumn View Apartments	MRTA	1667	C1
Autumn Woods Ct	DKbC	1894	D3
Ava Pl	DKbC	1817	E5
Avala Ct	FulC	1533	C4
Avala Park Ln NW	GwnC	1533	E7
Avalon Pl NE	ATLN	1816	D6
Avebury Ct	FulC	1532	E2
Avebury Dr	EPNT	1976	A6
Aven Rd NE	CobC	1598	E2
Avenida St SW	ATLN	1889	D7
Avensong Ln NE	CobC	1527	C3
Avenue of Redwoods	FulC	2145	D5
Avera Ln NW	GwnC	1602	B2
Avery Dr NE	ATLN	1816	A5
Avery Rd SW	ATLN	1976	B5
Avery St	DCTR	1893	A2
Avery St NE	MRTA	1595	B3
Aviation Blvd	ClyC	2062	B5
Aviation Cir NW	ATLN	1887	E1
	FulC	1887	E1
Aviation Pkwy	ClyC	2062	C7
	ClyC	2148	C1
Aviation Rd SE	MRTA	1595	D6
Aviation Wy	CMBL	1743	D1
	DKbC	1743	D1
Avignon Ct	FulC	1601	B2
Avis Ln	DKbC	1745	D6
Avon Av	ClyC	2150	D5
	DKbC	1745	B7
Avon Av SW	ATLN	1975	D1
Avon Ct NW	NRCS	1673	E1
Avon Breeze Ct	DKbC	1894	E2
Avondale Av SE	ATLN	1977	C1
N Avondale Plz	AVES	1893	D1
N Avondale Plz SR-10	AVES	1893	D1
N Avondale Plz US-278	AVES	1893	D1
S Avondale Plz	AVES	1893	E1
N Avondale Rd	AVES	1893	C1
N Avondale Rd SR-10	AVES	1893	C1
N Avondale Rd US-278	AVES	1893	C1
S Avondale Rd	AVES	1893	C1
Avonridge Ct	DKbC	1894	E3
Avonridge Dr	DKbC	1894	E3
Avonwood Cir SW	ATLN	1975	C1
Awendaw Cir	HryC	2066	E6
Awtry St NW	MRTA	1595	A3
Axson Ct NW	GwnC	1533	C7
	GwnC	1602	C1
Ayers Av NE	MRTA	1595	C5
Ayers Ct NW	GwnC	1601	C4
Aylesbury Ct NE	CobC	1529	B1
Aylesbury Lp	DKbC	1979	A5
Ayn Ct	RSWL	1532	A6
Ayr Pl SE	ATLN	1891	C7
Ayres Dr	DKbC	1894	C5
Ayrshire Cir NW	ATLN	1889	B1
Azalea Cir	DKbC	1817	D2
Azalea Cir NE	MRTA	1595	E1
Azalea Dr	ClyC	2063	E5
	DKbC	1600	E7
	HryC	2152	E6
	RSWL	1529	E5
Azalea Dr SE	CobC	1739	A5
	CobC	1812	C4
Azalea Wk	DKbC	2066	C4
Azalea Cove Ln	FulC	1533	A1
Azalia St SW	ATLN	1890	A7
Azar Pl	ClyC	2148	B1
Azimuth Ct	FulC	2146	A4
Azlee Pl NW	ATLN	1813	C7
Aztec Rd	DKbC	1672	C6
	DRVL	1672	C6
B			
Babette Ct	DKbC	1819	E7
Baby Does Ln	CobC	1668	C4
Baccurate Ct NE	CobC	1528	D2
Baccurate Dr NE	CobC	1528	D2
Baccurate Pl NE	CobC	1528	D2
Baccurate Tr NE	CobC	1528	D2
Baccurate Wy NE	CobC	1528	D2
Bach Ct	FulC	1601	C1
Bachelor Av	EPNT	2061	E2
Back St	RSWL	1530	E1
Back Tr	DKbC	1819	C2
Back Tee Ct	RSWL	1601	B1
Bacon St	CLKN	1819	A4
Baden Ct	ClyC	2150	C7
Bader Av SW	ATLN	1976	B4
Bagley Av NE	ATLN	1742	A6
Bagley Dr	DKbC	1672	B7
	DRVL	1672	B7
Bagpipe Pl	ClyC	2064	A6
Bagwell Dr SW	ATLN	1976	D6
Bailey Dr	ClyC	2151	D2
Bailey Rd	DKbC	1745	B7

INDEX 7

Bailey St | Atlanta Street Index | Beechwood Hills Ct NW

Atlanta Street Index

STREET	City	Map #	Grid
Bailey St	FulC	2059	E7
	FulC	2145	E1
Bailey St SE	DKbC	1977	D6
Bailey St SW	ATLN	1890	C4
Bailey's Cor NE	MRTA	1527	B7
Bailiff Ct NE	DKbC	1742	E1
Bainbridge Dr NW	FulC	1669	A3
Bainbridge Ln	RSWL	1531	A1
Bainbridge Tr	RSWL	1531	A1
Bainbridge Wy	RSWL	1531	A1
Bainbridge Wy SE	CobC	1740	A3
Baker Cir NW	ATLN	1889	B2
Baker Ct NW	GwnC	1601	E3
Baker Dr NW	GwnC	1673	A2
Baker Dr SW	ATLN	1976	D7
	ATLN	2062	E1
Baker Ln NE	MRTA	1595	E2
Baker Rd NW	ATLN	1888	E2
Baker St	UNCT	2145	A7
Baker St NE	ATLN	1890	E3
Baker St NW	ATLN	1890	E3
Baker Ter NW	ATLN	1889	A1
Baker-Highland Connector NE	ATLN	1891	A3
Baker Ridge Dr NW	ATLN	1888	D2
Bakers Mdws SE	CobC	1740	A5
Bakers Farm Pl SE	CobC	1740	A5
Bakers Farm Rd SE	CobC	1739	E5
Bakers Ferry Rd SW	ATLN	1887	E3
	FulC	1887	C4
Bakers Glen Dr	FulC	1599	E2
	FulC	1600	A1
Bakers Meadow Ln SE	CobC	1740	A5
Balboa Ct NE	FulC	1670	C5
Bald Eagle Wy	ClyC	2148	C5
Baldur Ct	DKbC	2065	D1
Baldwin Ct NE	CobC	1529	D6
Baldwin Ln NE	CobC	1529	D5
Baldwin Pl SW	ATLN	1890	A5
Baldwin St SW	ATLN	1890	A5
Baldwin Ter NE	CobC	1529	C6
Baldwin Wy NE	CobC	1529	D6
Baldwin Farms Dr NE	CobC	1529	D6
Baldwin Ridge Tr NE	CobC	1529	D6
Balearic Dr SE	CobC	1668	A2
Balfour Dr	DKbC	1819	C7
Ballard Rd	ClyC	2063	A6
	FTPK	2063	A6
Ball Creek Hl	FulC	1600	C1
Ball Creek Wy	FulC	1600	B1
Ballet Ct SE	SMYR	1738	E5
Ballew Ct NE	CobC	1528	A3
Ballew Dr NE	CobC	1526	D1
Ballina Dr	DKbC	1980	D6
Ball Mill Ct	DKbC	1600	C3
Ball Mill Pl	FulC	1600	B2
Ball Mill Rd	DKbC	1600	C3
Ball Park Dr	DKbC	1745	D4
Ballye Shannon Pike	UNCT	2145	C6
Ballyshannon Dr	UNCT	2145	B7
Bally Shannon Dr SE	CobC	1738	A6
Balmoral Dr	DKbC	1744	E1
Balmoral Rd NE	FulC	1670	D7
Balmoral Rd SE	SMYR	1667	B7
Balmoral Wy NE	CobC	1529	B6
Balsam Dr	DKbC	1818	C3
Balsam Pl	FTPK	2149	D5
Baltimore Pl NW	ATLN	1890	E2
Bama Ct NW	GwnC	1602	A1
S Bamby Ln NE	DKbC	1743	C2
Banberry Dr SE	ATLN	1976	E6
Banberry Rd SE	MRTA	1595	E5
Banbury Cross	AVES	1893	D3
Banbury Ct NW	GwnC	1673	D5
Bancroft Cir	DKbC	1745	D5
Bancroft Ct NE	CobC	1529	B5
Bancroft Vly	FulC	1533	C3
Bandera Dr	DKbC	1893	E7
Banford Ct NE	CobC	1598	A2
Banister Pl NE	CobC	1598	C1
E Bank Dr NE	CobC	1529	D7
W Bank Dr NE	CobC	1529	D7
Bank St SE	SMYR	1666	D7
Bankers Cir	DKbC	1672	D1
Bankers Wk	RVDL	2148	B7
Bankers Industrial Dr NW	DKbC	1672	D1
Bankhead Ct NW	ATLN	1813	A5
Bankhead Hwy SE	CobC	1812	A3
Bankhead Hwy SE SR-8	CobC	1812	A3
Bankhead Hwy SE US-78	CobC	1812	A3
Bankhead Hwy SE US-278	CobC	1812	A3
Bankhead Hwy SW	CobC	1812	A3
Bankhead Hwy SW SR-8	CobC	1812	A3
Bankhead Hwy SW US-78	CobC	1812	A3
Bankhead Hwy SW US-278	CobC	1812	A3
Banks Av SW	ATLN	1976	B5
Banks Ct	CGPK	2061	A4
Banks Wy	ClyC	2147	B5
Bankshill Row NE	DKbC	1742	E3
Bankside Dr	RSWL	1532	B1
Bankside Wy NW	GwnC	1602	E3
Bankston Rd NE	MRTA	1595	D2
Banner Rd	FulC	2059	C5
Bannister Dr	RSWL	1530	C4
Bannor Ln NW	GwnC	1602	A5
Bantry Cir	UNCT	2145	B6
Bantry Ct	UNCT	2145	B6
Banyon Brook Pt	RSWL	1532	B6
Baramore Rd NE	CobC	1527	C3
Baramore Oaks Ct NE	CobC	1527	C3
Baramore Oaks Dr NE	CobC	1527	C3
Baramore Oaks Ln NE	CobC	1527	C3
Barbara Ln	DKbC	1893	E7
	DKbC	1979	D1
	DKbC	2064	E2
Barbara Ln NE	CobC	1528	A2
Barbara Ln NW	ATLN	1741	E1
	FulC	1741	E1
Barbara Ln SE	SMYR	1667	C6
Barber Dr	HryC	2152	D4
Barber Rd SE	CobC	1666	A2
Barberrie Ln	DKbC	1892	D6
Barberry Dr NE	CobC	1528	B2
Barberry Ln	HryC	2152	E6
Barcelona Ct	FulC	2146	E5
Barcelona Dr NW	GwnC	1602	A4
Barclay Cir SE	CobC	1595	D7
	MRTA	1595	D7
	MRTA	1667	A1
Barclay Ct	DKbC	1819	E7
Barclay Dr	DKbC	1600	E7
Barclay Pl NE	ATLN	1816	D5
Barclay Wy	DKbC	1819	E7
Barcroft Wy	DKbC	1600	B3
Barfield Av SW	ATLN	1889	A5
Barfield Rd NE	FulC	1599	C7
	FulC	1670	C2
Barge Rd SW	ATLN	1974	A5
Barksdale Cir	EPNT	2061	A1
Barksdale Dr	FTPK	2063	B7
Barksdale Dr NE	ATLN	1816	A6
Barkside Ct	DKbC	1672	D7
Barkston Ct	DKbC	1671	C3
Barkston Dr	FulC	1533	A4
Barlaston Cir NE	CobC	1528	A7
Barley Ct SE	CobC	1812	A4
Barnard Pl NW	FulC	1598	D6
Barnes St NE	MRTA	1595	C5
Barnes St NW	ATLN	1815	D6
Barnesdale Dr NE	CobC	1597	A3
Barnesdale Wy NE	ATLN	1815	E4
Barnes Mill Dr NE	MRTA	1595	D3
Barnes Mill Rd NE	CobC	1595	E3
	MRTA	1595	D3
Barnes Mill Trc NE	CobC	1596	A2
Barnett Cir	HPVL	2062	D3
Barnett Dr	HPVL	2062	C3
Barnett Dr NW	ATLN	1814	B2
Barnett Rd	ClyC	2148	E2
	FTPK	2148	E2
Barnett St NE	ATLN	1816	C7
Barn Swallow Pl NE	CobC	1527	C6
Barnwell Rd	FulC	1532	D7
Barone Pl NW	ATLN	1815	C2
Baroque Cir NE	FulC	1670	C5
Barr Cir	DKbC	1745	C7
	HryC	2152	A3
Barrett Cir SE	CobC	1666	A6
Barrett Dr	FTPK	2149	E2
Barrett Dr NE	CobC	1526	C5
Barrett Dr NW	ATLN	1813	D4
Barrett Rd NW	ATLN	1813	C5
Barrett Creek Blvd NW	CobC	1526	A3
Barrett Creek Pkwy NW	CobC	1526	A3
Barrick Ln NW	GwnC	1533	B7
Barrington Cir NE	CobC	1528	B6
Barrington Ct	MRTA	1526	A5
Barrington Ct NW	ATLN	1740	D6
Barrington Dr	RSWL	1530	C3
Barrington Dr E	RSWL	1531	E1
Barrington Dr W	RSWL	1531	E1
Barrington Lp	RSWL	1531	E1
Barrington Ovlk	MRTA	1526	A6
Barrington Pl	DKbC	1894	A5
	MRTA	1526	A6
Barrington Wy	RSWL	1531	E1
Barrington Hills Dr	FulC	1599	C1
Barrington Landing Ct	RSWL	1531	E1
Barrington Oaks Cir	RSWL	1529	D4
Barrington Oaks Pl	RSWL	1529	D4
Barrington Oaks Rdg	RSWL	1529	D4
Barrington Pass NE	CobC	1528	C6
Barron Ct NW	ATLN	1740	E7
Barrow Pl SW	ATLN	1974	A7
Barrwyn Dr	ClyC	2151	E4
Barry Av SE	CobC	1666	A7
Barry Ct NE	CobC	1527	E7
Barry St	DCTR	1893	A1
Barry Lyn Dr	DRVL	1672	B2
Barston Ct	FulC	1532	E1
Barston Ln	FulC	1532	D1
Bartlett Ct	FTPK	2149	D1
Bartlett Dr	FTPK	2149	D2
Bartlett Rd	FTPK	2063	D7
	FTPK	2149	D1
Barton Dr	FTPK	2063	A7
	HPVL	2062	D2
Barton Dr NE	CobC	1597	A2
Barton Rd	MRRW	2149	E7
N Barton St NW	NRCS	1602	E5
S Barton St NW	NRCS	1602	B7
Barton Wy	DKbC	1818	A5
Barton Woods Rd NE	DKbC	1892	B1
Bartow St SW	ATLN	1975	E3
Basil Wy SW	ATLN	1887	E4
Basking Shade Ln	DKbC	2065	E1
Basque Cir SE	CobC	1739	C4
Basque Dr SE	CobC	1739	C4
Bass St SE	ATLN	1890	E6
Bass St SW	ATLN	1890	C6
Basset Ct SE	SMYR	1738	E3
Bassett Hall Pl NW	ATLN	1814	A1
Basswood Cir NE	FulC	1670	C1
Basswood Ct	FulC	2146	B7
Batavia St	EPNT	1975	E6
Bate Cir SW	ATLN	1975	D3
Bates Av NE	ATLN	1892	C4
Bates Av SE	ATLN	1892	C4
Bates Ct NE	DKbC	1743	B4
Bates St SE	SMYR	1667	B6
Batson Ct	ClyC	2147	B5
S Battery Pl NE	FulC	1670	C6
W Battery Pl NE	FulC	1670	C6
Battery Pl NE	ATLN	1891	D3
Battery Wy	EPNT	2061	D1
Battle Av SW	ATLN	1890	B4
Battle Ct SE	ATLN	1891	D5
Battle Dr NE	DKbC	1743	D4
Battlecrest Dr	DKbC	1979	A4
Battlefield Av SE	ATLN	1891	E4
Battleford Ct	DKbC	1671	C3
Battle Forrest Dr	DKbC	1979	A4
Battlement Ln	ClyC	2147	B5
Battle Overlook Dr NW	ATLN	1815	B1
Battle Ridge Dr NE	FulC	1670	C6
Battle Ridge Pl NE	FulC	1670	C6
Battleview Dr NW	ATLN	1814	E1
Bavaria Ct NE	CobC	1529	A3
Baxberry Ct	DKbC	1980	C6
Baxter Rd SW	ATLN	1976	B6
Bay Cir NW	GwnC	1602	A7
Bay St	DKbC	1818	E7
Bayard St	EPNT	1975	E7
	EPNT	2061	E1
Bayberry Dr SW	ATLN	1975	C2
Baybridge Ct	DKbC	1745	D7
Baybrook Trc SE	SMYR	1812	C1
Bayleaf Ct SE	CobC	1812	A4
Bayliss Dr NE	CobC	1598	C3
Baylor St NW	ATLN	1814	E7
Baynes Ct	DKbC	1819	C5
Baynes Hill Cir	DKbC	1819	C5
Baynes Hill Dr	DKbC	1819	C5
Baynham Dr	DKbC	1600	D4
Bayonet Ct NE	CobC	1597	B3
Bays Ferry Tr NE	CobC	1528	D4
Bays Ferry Wy NE	CobC	1528	D4
Bayshore Dr	DKbC	1673	D6
Bayside Cir	DKbC	1673	D6
Bayvale Ct NE	FulC	1599	C5
Baywood Dr SE	ATLN	1976	E6
Baywood Ln	ClyC	2147	D5
Beach Wy SW	ATLN	1889	A4
Beach Cherry Ln	DKbC	2066	B3
Beach Hill Dr	DKbC	1673	A6
Beachland Dr NE	FulC	1670	A5
Beachview Dr SE	CobC	1738	E5
Beacon Ct	DKbC	2066	B2
Beacon Dr	DRVL	1672	C2
	FulC	2146	E5
Beacon Hill Blvd NE	DKbC	1743	C7
	DKbC	1817	C1
Bea Mar Dr NE	CobC	1528	A5
Beardon Dr SE	CobC	1666	A1
Bearing Wy	FulC	2146	A5
Beatie Av SW	ATLN	1976	B2
Beaty Pl	DCTR	1892	D3
Beaty Pl NE	ATLN	1892	C3
Beaumont Av	DCTR	1817	E7
Beaumont Ln	DKbC	1600	D4
Beaupree St SW	ATLN	1976	C4
Beau Reve Pk NE	CobC	1598	D2
Beaver Rd NE	DKbC	1817	D1
Beaverbrook Dr NW	ATLN	1815	A2
Beaver Brook Ln NE	CobC	1527	E5
Beaver Creek Rd SE	SMYR	1666	D5
Beaver Creek Tr	FulC	2146	C6
Beaver Dam Ln NE	CobC	1527	D6
Beaver Falls Ct	DKbC	1980	D6
Beaver Falls Pl SW	FulC	1887	A7
Beavers Rd	ClyC	2063	D7
	FTPK	2063	D7
Beavers St NE	MRTA	1595	D4
Beaver Shop Rd NE	CobC	1527	C2
Bebout Dr NW	GwnC	1673	B4
Beck St NW	ATLN	1815	B3
Becket Dr NE	DKbC	1671	A3
Beckett Dr NE	CobC	1528	D5
Beckwith Ct SW	ATLN	1890	C4
Beckwith St SW	ATLN	1890	A4
Beckwith Tr NE	CobC	1596	E3
Becky Ln NE	DKbC	1743	A4
Bedevere Cir	DKbC	1894	C7
Bedford St NW	ATLN	1890	B1
Bedford Gardens Dr	FulC	1532	E4
Bedford Oaks Ct NE	CobC	1598	C2
Bedford Oaks Dr NE	CobC	1598	C2
Bedford Oaks Pl NE	CobC	1598	D2
Bedfordshire Ct	DKbC	1744	B7
Bedfordshire Dr	DKbC	1744	B7
Beech Ct NE	MRTA	1595	E3
Beech Dr	AVES	1893	D3
	DKbC	1893	D3
	EPNT	2060	E2
Beech Rd SE	CobC	1666	A1
Beech St NE	MRTA	1595	D3
Beech St SE	CobC	1739	C6
Beechaven Rd NE	DKbC	1816	E2
Beechcliff Dr NE	DKbC	1817	B3
Beechcrest Rd SW	FulC	1974	B1
Beecher Cir SW	ATLN	1889	A7
Beecher Ct SW	ATLN	1889	C7
Beecher Rd SW	ATLN	1889	A7
	ATLN	1975	A1
Beecher St	FTPK	2063	C7
Beecher St SW	ATLN	1889	C7
Beech Haven Dr NE	DKbC	1816	E2
Beech Haven Rd NE	DKbC	1816	E2
Beech Haven Tr SE	CobC	1739	D5
Beech Lake Ct	RSWL	1532	A5
Beech Tree Ct NE	CobC	1528	D4
Beech Valley Dr SE	SMYR	1667	C7
Beech Valley Rd NE	ATLN	1816	D5
	DKbC	1816	D5
Beech Valley Wy NE	ATLN	1816	E5
	DKbC	1816	E5
Beechview Dr SE	ATLN	1977	D1
	DKbC	1891	E7
	DKbC	1977	D1
Beechwood Av	DRVL	1672	B5
Beechwood Av SW	ATLN	1976	B1
Beechwood Blvd SW	ATLN	1975	C2
Beechwood Ct NE	CobC	1598	D1
E Beechwood Dr NW	ATLN	1740	E4
Beechwood Dr NE	CobC	1527	E6
Beechwood Dr NW	ATLN	1740	E3
Beechwood Dr SE	CobC	1668	A2
Beechwood Hills Ct NW	ATLN	1740	E3

INDEX 8

Beeler Dr SW

Atlanta Street Index

Blackhawk Tr SE

STREET	City	Map #	Grid
Beeler Dr SW	ATLN	1976	C7
Beethoven Cir	FulC	2147	B6
Beethoven Ct	FulC	2147	A7
Beggs Ct NE	MRTA	1595	D4
Belair Dr	HryC	2152	D7
Belair Ln	HryC	2152	E7
Belair Tr	HryC	2152	E7
Belair Bluff Ct SE	SMYR	1738	E7
	SMYR	1812	E1
Belaire Cir	DKbC	1672	C7
Belcourt Pkwy	RSWL	1531	D1
Beleen Ct SW	CobC	1738	A5
Belfast St SW	ATLN	1976	B2
Belford Dr NE	CobC	1527	B1
Belfort Rd SE	ATLN	2063	A2
Belgarde Pl SE	ATLN	2063	A2
Belgrade Av NE	ATLN	1891	C2
Belhaven Ln SE	ATLN	1977	B5
Belingham Dr NE	DKbC	1744	D3
Bell Av	EPNT	2061	E1
Bell Blvd	DKbC	1818	E6
Bell Dr SE	SMYR	1667	D7
Bell St	DCTR	1818	A7
Bell St NE	ATLN	1891	A3
Bell St SE	ATLN	1891	A4
	MRTA	1595	E6
Belladrum	FulC	1533	D1
Bellaire Dr NE	ATLN	1742	D3
	DKbC	1742	D3
Bellaire Ln NE	DKbC	1742	E3
Bellburn Rd	FulC	2146	C7
Belleau Ln SE	DKbC	1978	E4
Bellecour Ct SW	FulC	1973	A2
Belle Glade Dr	DKbC	1819	C4
Bellegrove Dr NE	CobC	1528	D3
Bellegrove Rdg NE	CobC	1528	C3
Belle Isle Cir NE	DKbC	1743	C7
E Belle Isle Rd NE	FulC	1670	A6
W Belle Isle Rd NE	FulC	1669	E6
Bellemeade Av NW	ATLN	1815	B4
Bellemeade Ct	ClyC	2150	D6
Bellestone Ct NE	CobC	1526	A1
Bellestone Wy NE	CobC	1526	B1
Belle Vista Ct NE	CobC	1527	D7
Bellevue Dr NE	ATLN	1816	D6
Bellewood Pk	DKbC	1599	E7
Bellewood Sq	DKbC	1599	E6
Bellfield Ct	RSWL	1531	D5
Bellflower Ct	RSWL	1531	D5
Bellgreen Wy	DKbC	1979	D1
Bell Haven Ln	ClyC	2147	B7
Bell Haven Chase Ct SE	SMYR	1812	C1
Bellingrath Av NW	ATLN	1815	A7
Bellote Dr NE	CobC	1527	E1
Bells Ferry Ln NE	MRTA	1526	A6
Bells Ferry Rd NE	CobC	1526	A6
	MRTA	1526	A6
Bells Ferry Rd NW	CobC	1526	A7
	MRTA	1526	A7
Bellview Av NW	ATLN	1888	E1
Bellville Wy NW	GwnC	1602	B1
Bellvue Rd SE	MRTA	1595	D5
Belmont Av SE	CobC	1666	E6
Belmont Av SW	ATLN	1976	B3
Belmont Cir SE	SMYR	1666	D5
Belmont Dr	DKbC	1979	A1
	RSWL	1532	B4
Belmont Pl	RSWL	1532	B6
Belmont Trc NW	FulC	1598	E7
Belmont Abbey Dr	DKbC	2066	C1
Belmont Crest Dr SE	CobC	1597	B7
Belmonte Cir SW	ATLN	1975	C1
Belmonte Ct SW	ATLN	1975	C1
Belmonte Dr SW	ATLN	1975	C1
Belmont Farms Dr	HryC	2152	A2
Belmont Glen Dr SE	CobC	1597	B7
Belmont Park Dr SE	SMYR	1666	D5
Belmont Park Ln	HryC	2152	A2
Belmore Wy	FulC	1600	A1
Beloit Pl	RSWL	1529	E4
Belridge Ct SE	SMYR	1739	B2
Belridge Dr SE	SMYR	1739	B2
Belridge Ln SE	SMYR	1739	B2
Belva Av	DKbC	1893	D5
Belvedere Av SW	ATLN	1975	A1
Belvedere Ct	FulC	1601	A3
Belvedere Dr NW	ATLN	1815	B3
Belvedere Ln	DKbC	1893	C4
Belvedere Pl NE	CobC	1598	A4
Belvedere Sq	DKbC	1894	D5
Belvedere Close NE	CobC	1598	A4
Belvoir Wy SE	DKbC	1978	A3
Ben Ln	ClyC	2150	E4
Bencal Dr SE	DKbC	1892	C7
Bench Av	FulC	2146	B6
Benchmark Ct SE	SMYR	1739	A2
Benchmark Dr	FulC	2145	E4
Ben Daniel Rd SE	CobC	1666	A7
Bend Creek Ct	DKbC	1600	B3
Bend Creek Rd	DKbC	1600	A2
Bend Creek Wy	DKbC	1600	B3
Bender St SW	ATLN	1890	C7
Benell Ct SE	CobC	1738	A4
	SMYR	1738	A4
Ben Franklin Ct NE	CobC	1528	C7
Ben Hill Av	EPNT	2060	E3
Ben Hill Ct SW	ATLN	1974	A4
Ben Hill Rd	EPNT	1974	E7
	EPNT	2059	E4
	EPNT	2061	A1
	FulC	2059	E4
	FulC	2146	A1
Ben Hill Rd SW	ATLN	1974	D5
Benita Trc NW	FulC	1669	A2
Benjamin Ct SW	ATLN	1887	E7
Benjamin Tr	ClyC	2151	C2
Benjamin E Mays Dr SW	ATLN	1888	E7
	ATLN	1974	E1
	FulC	1888	A6
Benjamin Weldon Bicker Dr SW	ATLN	1976	E3
Benmac Rd SE	SMYR	1666	C5
Benmore Bay	FulC	1532	D3
Bennett Al	FTPK	2149	B1
Bennett Dr	ClyC	2151	B7
Bennett St NW	ATLN	1815	D3
Bennette Blvd	HryC	2152	B2
Benning Pl NE	ATLN	1891	E2
Bennington Dr	DKbC	1894	A4
Bennington Dr NE	CobC	1527	D3
Benson Av SE	CobC	1666	C4
	SMYR	1666	C4
Benson Dr NE	CobC	1596	E1
E Benson St	DCTR	1892	D3
W Benson St	DCTR	1892	E3
Benson Poole Rd SE	CobC	1666	B6
	SMYR	1666	B5
Bent Brook Ct	DKbC	1601	C6
Bent Brook Dr	DKbC	1601	B6
Bentcreek Dr NE	CobC	1596	A1
Bent Creek Wy SW	ATLN	1975	A4
Benteen Av SE	ATLN	1977	B2
Benteen Wy SE	ATLN	1977	B1
Bent Hickory Dr SE	SMYR	1666	B6
Benthill Dr NE	CobC	1528	D6
Bentley Ln SE	CobC	1667	E2
Bentley Mnr NW	FulC	1668	E5
Bentley Pl	DKbC	1673	D7
Bentley Pl SE	CobC	1667	E3
Bentley Rd SE	CobC	1667	E2
	MRTA	1667	E2
Bentley Lake Rd NE	CobC	1596	A2
Benton Pl NW	ATLN	1741	A5
Benton St NE	ATLN	1890	E2
Benton Harbor Ct	DKbC	1980	E6
Benton Woods Dr NE	FulC	1670	A4
Bent Pine Ovlk NE	CobC	1596	C3
Bentwood Dr NE	CobC	1527	E5
Benwell Dr	FulC	1599	D2
Beracah Tr SW	FulC	1887	E7
Beracah Wk SW	FulC	1887	E7
	FulC	1973	E2
Berdon Ln	DKbC	2066	E1
Berean Av SE	ATLN	1891	B5
Beresford Cir	DKbC	1819	E5
Beresford Ct NW	GwnC	1533	D5
Berkele St SW	ATLN	1890	C7
Berkeley Av NW	ATLN	1815	B5
Berkeley Ct SE	SMYR	1738	E3
Berkeley Ln NE	DKbC	1743	C7
	DKbC	1817	C1
Berkeley Mw NE	DKbC	1817	C1
Berkeley Rd	AVES	1893	D2
	DKbC	1893	D3
Berkeley Run NE	FulC	1670	B4
Berkford Cir NE	DKbC	1671	B2
Berkford Ct NE	DKbC	1671	C2
Berkley Dr SE	SMYR	1738	B2
Berkley Ridge Rd	FulC	1531	A7
Berkshire Rd	FTPK	2063	D7
Berkshire Rd NE	ATLN	1816	C4
Berkshire Manor Dr	FulC	1532	D1
Bermuda Dr SE	CobC	1597	B5
Bermuda St	ClyC	2149	B6
Bernadette Ln NE	DKbC	1817	A2
Bernard Dr NE	CobC	1526	B1
Bernard Rd NW	ATLN	1813	E2
Bernard St NW	ATLN	1889	E4
Bernay Wy	FulC	1599	B2
Berne St SE	ATLN	1891	B6
Bernice St SE	ATLN	1892	C6
	DKbC	1892	C6
Bernice St SW	ATLN	1889	E6
Bernina Av NE	ATLN	1891	C2
Bernside Ct	FulC	1533	B4
Berry Ct NE	CobC	1527	A3
Berry Dr	DKbC	1979	A3
Berrybridge Wy SE	CobC	1597	C5
Berry Glen Ct	FulC	1532	E5
Berryhill Cir SE	CobC	1738	E5
	SMYR	1738	E5
Berry Hill Ct	DKbC	1894	C1
Berryhill Ct	FulC	2059	B6
Berryhill Ct SE	SMYR	1738	E5
Berry Hill Tr	DKbC	1894	C1
Berryhill Trc SE	SMYR	1738	E5
Berrypatch Ct SE	CobC	1597	A6
Berrypatch Ln SE	CobC	1597	A6
Berryton Ct NW	GwnC	1602	B1
Berryview Ct	DKbC	1980	A4
Berrywood Dr NE	CobC	1526	B3
Bert Adams Rd	CobC	1739	E2
Bertha Wy NE	CobC	1527	D7
Berwick Av NE	ATLN	1816	C6
Berwick Dr NE	FulC	1599	A4
Berwick Trc NE	CobC	1598	B1
W Berwicke Com NE	FulC	1670	C7
Beryl St SW	ATLN	1890	C7
Best Rd	CGPK	2061	B6
	CGPK	2147	B1
Best Rd SR-139	CGPK	2061	B7
Best Friend Ct NW	GwnC	1673	D2
Best Friend Rd NW	DKbC	1673	A4
	NRCS	1673	D2
Besto Dr NW	ATLN	1813	D4
Bethany Forest Dr SW	FulC	1973	B1
Bethel Dr NW	ATLN	1889	B3
Bethesda Ct	DKbC	1671	C2
Bethesda Tr	DKbC	1671	C2
Bethune Cir	ClyC	2150	C4
Betsy Av SW	ATLN	1889	B5
Bettis Ct NE	CobC	1527	B2
Betty Cir	DKbC	1893	E3
Betty Dr NE	CobC	1526	D3
Betty Ann Ct NW	ATLN	1814	B2
Between the Paces SE	CobC	1740	B3
Beutell St NW	ATLN	1890	B2
Beverly Dr	CMBL	1672	A6
Beverly Ln NE	ATLN	1742	A2
Beverly Pl NW	ATLN	1889	C1
Beverly Rd NE	ATLN	1815	E5
	CobC	1526	C2
Beverly Rd NW	ATLN	1815	B6
Beverly Hills Dr	CMBL	1672	A7
	DKbC	1672	A7
	DKbC	1744	B1
Beverly Hills Dr NE	CobC	1596	E4
Beverly Woods Ct	DKbC	1671	C3
Bevington Wy NE	CobC	1598	A2
Beya Wy	DKbC	1673	C7
Bianca Ct	DKbC	1979	A4
Bibb Blvd	DKbC	1745	E5
Bickham Wy SE	CobC	1667	D7
	CobC	1739	D1
	SMYR	1667	D7
	SMYR	1739	D1
Bicknell Dr SW	ATLN	1976	D5
Biddle Ct	DKbC	1600	B3
Big Creek Ct	RSWL	1531	E1
Bigelow Dr	ClyC	2147	E6
	RVDL	2147	E6
Biggern Av SE	CobC	1666	B7
	CobC	1738	B1
Biggers St SE	ATLN	1891	A5
Big House Rd NW	GwnC	1601	E1
Big John Tr SE	CobC	1596	B6
Biglin St SW	ATLN	1976	B1
Big Oak Bnd NE	CobC	1529	B3
Big Pine Ct	DKbC	2065	A2
Big Shanty Rd NW	CobC	1526	A1
Big Shanty Tr NW	CobC	1526	A1
Big Springs Ct	DKbC	1980	B5
Big Springs Rd	DKbC	1980	B6
Billings Av SE	ATLN	1977	C4
Billingsley Dr NE	CobC	1528	A7
Bill Joseph Wy	HryC	2065	C5
Bill Lucas Dr SE	ATLN	1890	E6
Bill Lucas Dr SW	ATLN	1890	E7
Bill Murdock Rd NE	CobC	1528	C6
Bill Thrasher Dr	DKbC	1818	B6
Billups St SW	ATLN	1976	A4
Biltmore Dr NE	DKbC	1817	A3
Biltmore Pl NW	ATLN	1890	E1
Bimini Dr	ClyC	2149	C7
Bimini Ln	ClyC	2149	C7
Binder Pl NE	ATLN	1891	E3
Bingham Ct	DKbC	1819	E4
Bingham Ln	DKbC	1819	E4
Bingham St SE	CobC	1666	B2
Binghamton Ct	DKbC	1672	B1
Binghamton Dr	DKbC	1672	B1
Birch Rd	DKbC	1818	B3
Birch St	FTPK	2149	C3
	HPVL	2062	C1
Birch St SE	SMYR	1666	C6
Birch St SW	ATLN	1975	E3
Bircham Wy	RSWL	1529	D2
Birchberry Ct SW	FulC	1973	A3
Birchberry Ter SW	FulC	1973	A3
Birchbriar Ct	DKbC	1980	C5
Birchfield Ct NE	CobC	1597	B4
Birchfield Dr NE	CobC	1597	B4
Birchfield Trc NE	CobC	1597	B4
Birch Glen Dr NW	GwnC	1673	E4
Birchmere Close SW	FulC	1973	A3
Birch Rill Dr	FulC	1532	D1
Birchton St	FulC	1532	C4
Birchwood Dr NE	ATLN	1816	A1
Birchwood Cove	DKbC	1980	D7
Bird St SE	ATLN	1976	E3
Birdie Ln SW	FulC	1973	C1
Birds Ml SE	CobC	1597	C7
	CobC	1668	C1
Birdseye Tr	FulC	2146	B5
Birkenhed Dr	FulC	1599	C3
Birkenwood Ln	DKbC	1819	E4
Birney St NE	MRTA	1595	C3
Bisbee Av SE	ATLN	1976	E2
Biscayne Blvd	ClyC	2151	C7
Biscayne Dr	ClyC	2149	B6
	FulC	2146	E3
Biscayne Dr NW	ATLN	1815	D2
Bishop Ct	DKbC	1980	B7
Bishop Dr	DKbC	1745	B7
Bishop Dr NE	MRTA	1595	C4
Bishop Pl	ClyC	2147	C6
Bishop Pl NW	ATLN	1815	B6
Bishop Rd SW	CobC	1812	B7
Bishop St NW	ATLN	1815	C6
Bishop Creek Ct NE	CobC	1529	B5
Bishop Creek Dr NE	CobC	1529	B5
Bishop Hollow Ct	DKbC	1671	B2
Bishop Hollow Run	DKbC	1671	B1
Bishop Lake Ct NE	CobC	1528	E6
Bishop Lake Rd NE	CobC	1528	E6
Bishops Green Dr NE	CobC	1528	E6
Bishopswood Pl	FulC	1533	B1
Bismark Rd NE	ATLN	1816	C3
Bison Ct	DKbC	1979	B4
Bitternut Cir	RSWL	1532	A5
Bittersweet Dr NE	CobC	1528	B2
Bittersweet Tr	FulC	1600	E2
Bixby St SE	ATLN	1892	B4
Bixby Ter SE	ATLN	1892	B4
Bixler Cir	CobC	1979	A1
Black St NE	MRTA	1595	C4
Black Bear Dr SE	CobC	1667	E1
Blackberry Ct	HryC	2152	C1
Blackberry Hl NW	GwnC	1601	E1
Blackberry Ln NE	CobC	1597	A2
Black Berry Row	ClyC	2150	D4
Blackbridle Wk SE	CobC	1597	B6
Blackburn Wy	CMBL	1671	E6
Blackfoot Ln	ClyC	2151	B6
Black Forest Tr SW	ATLN	1974	C7
Black Fox Dr NE	DKbC	1817	D1
Black Fox Tr	EPNT	1974	E6
Blackhawk Cir SE	CobC	1812	C4
Blackhawk Ct SE	CobC	1812	C4
Blackhawk Dr	DKbC	1819	D5
Blackhawk Tr SE	CobC	1812	C4

Atlanta Street Index

STREET	City	Map #	Grid
Blackjack Ct NE	CobC	1596	A1
Blackjack Dr NE	CobC	1596	A1
Black Kettle Rd	FulC	1533	E2
E Blackland Ct NE	CobC	1598	A5
W Blackland Ct NE	CobC	1597	E5
Blackland Ct NW	ATLN	1741	D4
Blackland Dr NE	CobC	1597	E5
Blackland Dr NW	ATLN	1741	E4
Blackland Rd NW	ATLN	1741	D3
Blackland Rdg SE	CobC	1597	E5
Blackland Wy SE	CobC	1597	E4
Blackmon Dr	DKbC	1818	A5
Black Oak Ct	HryC	2152	D3
Black Oak Dr NE	CobC	1526	B4
Black Oak Dr SE	ATLN	1892	A7
	DKbC	1892	A7
	DKbC	1978	A1
Blackshear Dr	DKbC	1817	E3
Black Stallion Dr NE	CobC	1529	C1
Blackstone Dr	DKbC	1818	E2
Blackwater Tr NW	FulC	1598	C7
Black Water Cove NW	FulC	1598	D6
Blackwell Ln NE	CobC	1526	C3
	MRTA	1595	B4
Blackwood Rd	DKbC	1744	C6
Blair Cir NE	DKbC	1671	B5
Blairhill Ct	DKbC	1673	C7
Blair Valley Dr NE	MRTA	1595	B3
Blair Villa Dr SE	ATLN	2063	A3
Blake Av SE	ATLN	1891	E6
Blake Ln	HryC	2152	C1
Blakeford Ct NE	CobC	1528	C5
Blakeford Wy NE	CobC	1528	C5
Blakeford Club Dr NE	CobC	1528	C5
Blakely Ct NE	CobC	1526	E3
Blakeney Ln NE	MRTA	1527	A7
Blakley Dr NE	ATLN	1816	B2
Blalock St	ClyC	2062	E6
Blalock Industrial Blvd	ClyC	2148	C2
Blanche Ct SE	MRTA	1596	A5
Blanche Dr SE	MRTA	1596	A5
Blanche St NW	ATLN	1889	C2
Blandford Pl	FulC	1601	A3
Blanton Av SW	ATLN	1973	D6
Blanton Dr	DKbC	1818	E6
Blanton Rd NW	ATLN	1741	D2
Blashfield St SE	ATLN	1977	A2
Blaylock Dr NE	CobC	1596	C1
Blayton Cir NW	ATLN	1889	C4
Blayton Ln SE	ATLN	1977	B5
Blazing Pine Knls	DKbC	1979	E7
Blazing Pine Pth	DKbC	1979	E7
Blenheim Pl	FulC	1600	D1
Bloomingdale Ct NW	GwnC	1602	C2
Blossom Ct NW	GwnC	1673	C5
Blossom Dr	ClyC	2147	D5
Blossom Ln	EPNT	2060	D1
Blossom St SW	ATLN	1976	B3
Blount Pl	EPNT	1976	A7
Blount St	EPNT	1976	A7
	EPNT	2062	A1
Bloxham Ct	DKbC	1673	B7
Blueberry Ln	HryC	2066	C7
Blueberry Tr	DKbC	1818	C2
Bluebird Ln	DKbC	1893	D4
Bluebonnet Cir	FulC	2146	C5
Bluebonnet Ct	FulC	2146	C5
Bluebonnet Tr	FulC	2146	B5
Blue Creek Ct	DKbC	2064	E2
Bluefield Dr SW	ATLN	1975	D1
Blue Granite Ct	DKbC	2064	E2
Blue Granite Wy	DKbC	2064	E2
Blue Grass Ln	DKbC	1980	A5
Blue Iris Ct NW	GwnC	1533	D7
Blue Iris Hllw NW	GwnC	1533	D7
	GwnC	1602	D1
Bluejack Ct	RSWL	1532	A5
Bluejack Ln	RSWL	1532	A5
Blue Ridge Av NE	ATLN	1891	C1
Blue Ridge Ct	HryC	2066	D7
Blueridge Dr	FTPK	2063	B6
Blue Sky Dr NE	CobC	1597	A4
Blue Sky Pl NE	CobC	1597	A4
Blue Spruce Ln NE	CobC	1529	B3
Blue Stone Rd NE	FulC	1670	A2
Blue Teal Ct NW	FulC	1669	B4
Blue Wing Ct	ClyC	2150	E6
Blue Yarrow Run NW	GwnC	1533	D7
	GwnC	1602	D1
Bluff Ct NE	CobC	1528	C1
Bluff Rd NE	CobC	1528	C1
Bluff St SW	ATLN	1890	B6
Bluff Haven Wy	DKbC	1670	E4
Bluffton Ct	DKbC	1894	C7
Bluffton Wy	DKbC	1894	C7
Bluffview Trc	RSWL	1531	C6
Bluffwind Chase	RSWL	1531	C6
Blvd Lorraine SW	ATLN	1975	B2
Blyss Av NW	ATLN	1889	D2
Blyth Ct	DKbC	1600	C6
Boardwalk NE	CobC	1526	E3
Boaz St SE	ATLN	1891	A3
Bob Bettis Rd NE	CobC	1527	B4
Bobbie Ln	AVES	1893	E3
	DKbC	1893	E3
Bobby Brown Pkwy	EPNT	2061	E2
Bobby Dodd Wy NW	ATLN	1890	D1
Bobcat Ct SE	CobC	1667	E1
Bobolink Cir SW	ATLN	1888	B6
Bobolink Ct	ClyC	2151	A7
Bobolink Dr	ClyC	2151	A7
	DKbC	1893	E5
Bobs Ct	DKbC	1894	E2
Bobs Dr SW	CobC	1812	A1
Bob White Dr SW	ATLN	1888	D7
	ATLN	1974	D1
Bob White Tr	ClyC	2148	E5
Bocage Wk NW	ATLN	1742	A5
Boca Grande Blvd	ClyC	2149	B7
Boca Grande Ct	ClyC	2149	C7
Boca Raton Ct	ClyC	2149	C7
Boca Raton Dr	ClyC	2149	C7
Bodwin Pl	DKbC	1894	C6
Bogans Lake Pth	DKbC	1600	E5
Bohler Ct NW	ATLN	1814	E1
Bohler Ln NW	ATLN	1814	E2
Bohler Mw NW	ATLN	1814	E2
Bohler Pt NW	ATLN	1814	E2
Bohler Rd NW	ATLN	1814	E1
Boise Tr SW	FulC	1887	C7
Bolan St SE	MRTA	1595	A6
Boland Dr NE	DKbC	1743	D3
Bolero Ct	DKbC	1744	E2
Bolero Dr	DKbC	1744	E2
Bolero Ln	DKbC	1744	E2
Bolero Pl	DKbC	1744	E2
Bolero Trc	DKbC	1744	E2
Bolero Wy	DKbC	1744	E2
Bolero Pass	DKbC	1744	E2
Bolfair Dr NW	ATLN	1813	A7
Boling Dr	FTPK	2063	D6
Boling Dr NE	CobC	1596	E6
Bolissa Dr	DKbC	1673	C7
W Bolling Rd NE	ATLN	1741	D5
Bolling Wy NE	ATLN	1742	A6
Bolling Brook Dr SW	ATLN	1889	A7
Bollingbrook Rd SE	CobC	1668	B2
Bolton Dr NW	ATLN	1814	D2
Bolton Pkwy	ATLN	1813	B7
Bolton Pl NW	ATLN	1813	B7
	ATLN	1814	D2
	ATLN	1888	B1
Bolton Rd NW	ATLN	1813	C5
	ATLN	1888	A1
Bomar Forest Pl	DKbC	1744	E7
Bonair St SW	ATLN	1890	B4
Bonanza Dr	DKbC	1744	C7
Bonanza Tr SE	CobC	1812	A6
Bonaparte Ct	DKbC	1745	E1
Bonaparte Dr	DKbC	1673	E7
	DKbC	1745	E1
Bonaventure Av NE	ATLN	1891	C1
Bonaventure Wy NE	CobC	1529	C5
Bond Dr	DKbC	2065	E5
Bond Dr SW	ATLN	1976	C3
Bond Lake Dr	HryC	2065	D6
Bondurant Rd SE	CobC	1739	D7
Bonecho Dr	FulC	2059	D5
Bonita Ct	ClyC	2150	D6
Bonn St SE	ATLN	1976	E4
Bonnabel Trc NE	CobC	1526	E6
Bonnell Ct	ClyC	2151	E4
Bonner Rd	EPNT	1975	A5
Bonner St	DKbC	1893	A7
Bonneville Rd	DKbC	1980	A1
Bonneville Ter NW	ATLN	1813	A7
Bonnevit Ct NE	DKbC	1743	E7
Bonnie Av	DRVL	1672	C5
Bonnie Ct NE	CobC	1527	C6
Bonnie Ln NE	ATLN	1816	D5
Bonnie Ln NW	FulC	1669	E1
Bonnie Ln SE	ATLN	2063	C4
Bonnie Wy	RSWL	1529	E5
Bonnie Brae Av SW	ATLN	1890	B7
Bonnie Dell Dr NE	MRTA	1595	E3
Bonnie Glen Ct	ClyC	2064	A7
Bonnie Glen Dr SE	CobC	1596	D7
Bonnie Glenn Ln	DKbC	1819	B1
Bonnie Glenn Cove	DKbC	1819	B1
Bonnington Ct	DKbC	1671	C3
Bonniview St SW	ATLN	1976	B4
Bonnterre Dr NE	CobC	1526	E6
	MRTA	1526	E6
Bonnybrook Dr SW	ATLN	1974	D5
Bonnybrook Wy	EPNT	1974	D6
Bonnybrook Wy SW	ATLN	1974	D5
Bonsal Rd	DKbC	2064	B3
Bontura Ct	DKbC	1819	D4
Bonview Ln NE	ATLN	1742	D7
Bonway Dr	DKbC	1893	E3
Booker Av SW	ATLN	1976	D1
Booker St	DKbC	1818	C5
Booker St NW	ATLN	1890	A4
Booker St SW	ATLN	1976	D3
Booker T Dr	ClyC	2150	C3
Booker Washington Dr NW	ATLN	1890	B3
Booth Av NW	ATLN	1815	A6
Booth Rd SE	CobC	1666	A1
Booth Rd SW	CobC	1666	A1
Booth St NW	ATLN	1815	A6
Bordeau Ct	DKbC	1599	E3
Bordeau Wk SE	SMYR	1666	A7
Bordeaux Ct SW	FulC	1973	A2
Boring Ct	DKbC	1980	C5
Boring Rd	DKbC	1980	A6
Boring Wy	DKbC	1980	B5
Boring Ridge Dr	DKbC	1980	A5
Born St NW	NRCS	1602	E5
Borning Ct	FulC	1532	E3
Bosa Nova Club Dr	DKbC	1980	D3
Bosenberry Wy	DKbC	2066	B3
Boss St NW	ATLN	1890	C1
Bostic St NW	NRCS	1602	B7
Bostic Hill Ct SE	CobC	1597	C7
Boston Com	ClyC	2148	B4
Bostwick Ct NW	GwnC	1602	C1
Bothwell Pl NE	MRTA	1595	C2
Boulder Cir	DKbC	1978	D7
Boulder Dr	RSWL	1529	D3
Boulder Rd SE	DKbC	1978	C2
Boulder Wy	EPNT	2060	E1
	RSWL	1529	D3
Bouldercliff Ct SE	DKbC	1978	B2
Bouldercliff Wy SE	DKbC	1978	B2
Boulder Creek Dr NE	CobC	1529	C3
Bouldercrest Ct	DKbC	1978	D7
Bouldercrest Dr SE	ATLN	1892	A7
	ATLN	1978	A1
	CobC	1666	A6
Bouldercrest Ln SE	DKbC	1978	C6
Bouldercrest Rd	ClyC	2151	B2
	DKbC	1978	D7
	DKbC	2064	D1
	HryC	2065	B3
Bouldercrest Rd SE	ATLN	1978	B2
	DKbC	1978	C6
Bouldercrest Wy	DKbC	2064	E3
Bouldercrest Park Rd	DKbC	2065	A3
Boulder Green Cir	DKbC	2065	A3
Boulder Hills Dr	DKbC	2064	D1
Boulder Park Dr SW	ATLN	1887	C5
	FulC	1887	C5
Boulder Pointe Ct	DKbC	2065	B3
Boulder Pointe Dr	DKbC	2065	B3
Boulder Pointe Wy	DKbC	2065	B3
Boulder Ridge Ct	DKbC	1978	D7
	DKbC	2064	D1
Boulder Ridge Pkwy	DKbC	1978	C7
Boulder Ridge Ter	DKbC	1978	D7
Boulder Springs Ct	DKbC	2065	B4
Boulder Springs Dr	DKbC	2065	A4
Boulder Springs Pt	DKbC	2065	A4
Boulder Springs Run	DKbC	2065	B4
Boulder Springs Cove	DKbC	2065	A4
Boulderview Dr SE	DKbC	1978	C4
Boulder Vista Dr	DKbC	2064	E3
Boulderwoods Dr SE	DKbC	1978	B3
Boulevard NE	ATLN	1891	B2
Boulevard SE	ATLN	1891	B4
	ATLN	1977	B2
Boulevard Dr SE	ATLN	1891	D4
Boulevard Pl NE	ATLN	1891	B2
Boulevard Granada SW	ATLN	1975	A1
Boulevard Hills Dr SE	CobC	1739	E3
Boulevard Lorraine SW	ATLN	1975	A3
N Boundary Pl NW	ATLN	1814	D1
Boundary Rd	ClyC	2063	E7
	ClyC	2149	E1
	ClyC	2150	D2
	FTPK	2063	E7
	FTPK	2064	B7
	FTPK	2149	E1
	FTPK	2150	A2
	LKCY	2150	A2
W Boundary Rd	ClyC	2149	D1
	FTPK	2149	D1
Boundary Tree Dr	HryC	2066	E6
Bounty Dr NE	CobC	1526	C4
Bourne Dr SE	SMYR	1666	B6
Bowden Dr	FTPK	2149	B4
	HryC	2066	E5
Bowden Rd	HryC	2151	E2
Bowen Av SE	ATLN	1976	E3
Bowen Cir SW	ATLN	1976	D2
Bowen Pl NW	ATLN	1815	B5
Bowen St NW	ATLN	1815	A5
Bowen Ridge Ct SE	CobC	1738	E5
Bowie Ct	DKbC	1819	D3
Bowline Cir NW	FulC	1598	D6
Bowling Green Wy	DKbC	1673	A6
Bowman Industrial Ct	DKbC	2064	B3
Boxbourne Ct SE	CobC	1596	D7
Boxelder Ln	RSWL	1532	A5
Boxwood Ct NE	DKbC	1744	D3
Boxwood Dr NE	DKbC	1744	D3
Boxwood Tr	DKbC	2066	C4
Boxwood Wk	DKbC	2066	C4
Boyce Ct SE	DKbC	1978	C5
Boyce Dr SE	DKbC	1978	C5
Boyd Av NW	ATLN	1815	A6
Boyd Dr SE	CobC	1596	B6
Boyd Rd NE	CobC	1526	D5
	MRTA	1526	D5
Boykin St SW	ATLN	1976	D1
Boylston Dr NE	FulC	1670	A1
Boyne Cir	RSWL	1531	D6
Boynton Av SE	ATLN	1976	E1
Bozeman Dr	CMBL	1671	D7
Brackenwood Cir NE	FulC	1599	C5
Brackett Rd NE	CobC	1526	D1
Bracknell Wy	FulC	1533	B1
Bradberry St SW	ATLN	1890	C5
Bradbury Dr NE	CobC	1528	D7
Bradcliff Ct NE	DKbC	1744	B4
Bradcliff Dr NE	DKbC	1744	B4
Braddock Ct	DKbC	1600	B3
Braddock St SW	ATLN	1976	B3
Bradford Sq NE	DKbC	1744	B3
Bradley Av SE	CobC	1666	A6
	DKbC	1978	A1
Bradley St NE	ATLN	1891	B4
Bradley St SE	ATLN	1891	B4
Bradmoor Ct	DKbC	1979	B4
Bradmoor Wy	DKbC	1979	B4
Brady Av NW	ATLN	1815	B7
Braeburn Cir SE	ATLN	1892	B7
	DKbC	1892	B6
Braeburn Dr SE	ATLN	1891	E6
Braemar Av SW	ATLN	1888	B7
	ATLN	1974	B1
Braemore Dr NW	FulC	1669	E2
Braesridge Wy	FulC	1532	E1
Brafferton Pl	DKbC	1894	D2
Brafferton Wy	DKbC	1601	A7
Braffington Ct	DKbC	1601	B4
Bragg St	DKbC	1743	C2
Braithwood Ct NE	DKbC	1744	D2
Braithwood Rd NE	DKbC	1744	C3
Bramante Cir SW	FulC	1973	A3
Bramble Ct NE	CobC	1528	E3
Bramble Rd NE	DKbC	1817	B2
Bramblewood Dr NE	DKbC	1743	A6
Bramlet Ct	DKbC	1745	D6
Bramwell Dr	DKbC	1819	E3
Bramwell Ln	DKbC	1819	E4
Branch Av NE	ATLN	1816	A1
Branch Bnd NE	DKbC	1743	E6
Branch Dr NW	GwnC	1673	E6
Branch Dr SW	ATLN	1887	E4
Branch Valley Ct	RSWL	1531	D4
Branch Valley Dr	RSWL	1531	D4

STREET	City	Map #	Grid
Branch Valley Wy	RSWL	1531	D4
Branch View Dr NE	CobC	1527	A6
Branch Water Ct	DKbC	1599	E5
Branchwind Close	RSWL	1531	D5
Branchwood Dr	EPNT	1974	D7
Brandeis Ct	DKbC	2066	B1
Brandeis Wy	DKbC	2066	B1
Brandenberry Ct	DKbC	1979	A3
Brandenberry Dr	DKbC	1978	E3
Brandon Cir SE	MRTA	1596	B7
Brandon Pl NE	FulC	1598	E4
Brandon Rd	CGPK	2060	E6
Brandon Hall Dr	FulC	1531	D7
Brandon Mill Rd	FulC	1599	C2
Brandon Mill Rd NW	FulC	1598	E5
Brandon Park Pl NW	ATLN	1815	B2
Brandon Ridge Dr NE	FulC	1598	E7
Brandonshire Rd	FulC	1601	B4
Brandons Valley Ct	ClyC	2151	A3
Brandy Sta SE	CobC	1740	A4
Brandy Station Ct SE	CobC	1740	A3
Brandy Turk Wy	DKbC	1601	B6
Brandywine Cir	FulC	1531	A4
Brandywine Ct	DKbC	1600	C5
Brandywine Rd	DKbC	1744	C2
Brandywine St SW	ATLN	1976	A4
Brandywine Tr NW	GwnC	1602	A4
Branford Ct NE	CobC	1528	B3
Branham St NE	ATLN	1892	C4
Brannen Rd SE	ATLN	1978	B2
	DKbC	1978	B2
Brannon Hill Rd	DKbC	1819	C5
Bransford Rd NE	FulC	1670	B4
Brantford Dr	DKbC	1745	E7
Brantley Pl SW	ATLN	1889	D5
Brantley Rd	FulC	1599	D1
Brantley St NE	ATLN	1891	D3
Brantley St NW	ATLN	1814	A3
Brassy Ct	FulC	1532	D6
Braswell Rd NE	CobC	1527	D7
Bratton St NW	ATLN	1815	D3
Braves Dr	FTPK	2062	D7
	FTPK	2148	D1
Brawley Cir NE	DKbC	1671	B2
Brawley Dr NE	DKbC	1671	B2
Brawley Wy NE	DKbC	1671	B2
Brayward Chase	RSWL	1531	E6
Breakwater Cir NW	FulC	1598	C6
Break Water Pt	ClyC	2064	D5
Breakwater Rdg NW	FulC	1598	D6
Bream Ct NE	CobC	1598	A2
Breckenridge Ct	ClyC	2151	C7
Breckenridge Ct NE	DKbC	1744	C6
Breckenridge Dr NE	DKbC	1744	C6
Breckenridge Run	ClyC	2151	C7
Breckenridge Wy NE	DKbC	1744	B6
Breckenridge Close	FulC	1532	E1
Breech Block Dr	RSWL	1532	A4
Breezewood Ct	HryC	2152	C4
Breezy Ln NE	DKbC	1817	B2
Bremond St	EPNT	2061	B1
Brenda Dr	ATLN	2059	E2
	DKbC	1894	E7
Brenda Dr SE	SMYR	1667	D6
Brendon Ct	DKbC	1600	E5
Brendon Dr	DKbC	1600	E5
Breneau Ct	DKbC	2066	E1
Brengare Dr	DKbC	1817	E5
Brenmar Wy	DKbC	1745	B1
Brennan Ln SW	ATLN	1889	B6
Brenston Blvd	ClyC	2150	D4
Brenston Ct	ClyC	2150	E4
Brenston Dr	ClyC	2150	D4
Brenston Ln	ClyC	2150	E4
Brenston Wy	ClyC	2150	E4
Brent Ct SW	CobC	1738	A6
Brentford Pl	DKbC	1979	A2
Brenton Dr NE	DKbC	1671	A4
Brenton Wy NE	DKbC	1671	A4
Brentwood Ct	DKbC	1979	A1
	RSWL	1530	D2
Brentwood Ct NE	MRTA	1527	A7
Brentwood Dr NE	ATLN	1742	A7
	MRTA	1527	A7
Brentwood Dr SE	SMYR	1738	D3
Brentwood Ln NE	MRTA	1527	A7
Brentwood Pl SE	MRTA	1596	B7
Brentwood Rd	ClyC	2147	E2
	DKbC	1979	B1
Brentwood Ter NE	ATLN	1742	A7
Brentwood Wy	FulC	1599	D2
Brentwood Wy NE	MRTA	1527	A7
Brentwood Cove	DKbC	2064	E1
Brer Rabbit Rd	DKbC	1819	E2
Bressler Cir	DKbC	1980	C1
Breton Cir NE	DKbC	1670	E6
Breton Ct NE	DKbC	1670	E6
Bretton Woods Rd	DKbC	1819	C7
Brevard Av SW	ATLN	1976	D6
Brewer Blvd SW	ATLN	1976	A2
Brewer Dr SW	ATLN	1887	D4
Brewster St SW	ATLN	1975	E2
Brian Ct	ClyC	2149	C6
Brian Dr	DKbC	1894	B4
Brian Ln	ClyC	2149	C6
Brian Wy	DKbC	1818	D3
Brianwood Ct	DKbC	1817	E1
Brianwood Rd	DKbC	1817	E1
Brianwood Tr	DKbC	1817	E1
Briar Ct	EPNT	2060	D1
Briar Ln NE	CobC	1529	B3
Briar Chase Ct	RVDL	2148	A7
Briarcliff Cir NE	DKbC	1743	C6
Briarcliff Coms NE	DKbC	1744	D4
Briarcliff Ct NE	ATLN	1816	D7
Briarcliff Ln NE	DKbC	1744	C4
Briarcliff Pl NE	ATLN	1891	D1
Briarcliff Rd NE	ATLN	1816	E7
	DKbC	1743	B7
	DKbC	1744	E5
	DKbC	1816	E7
	DKbC	1817	A4
Briarcliff Rd NE SR-42	ATLN	1816	E7
	DKbC	1816	E7
Briarcliff Ter NE	ATLN	1816	D7
Briarcliff Wy NE	DKbC	1744	D4
Briarcliff Cove NE	DKbC	1744	D4
Briarcliff Gables Cir NE	DKbC	1743	B7
Briarcrest Ct NE	CobC	1528	E4
Briarcrest Tr NE	DKbC	1744	D4
Briardale Ln NE	DKbC	1817	A6
Briar Gate Ct NW	CobC	1526	A1
Briar Gate Ln NW	CobC	1526	A1
Briarglade Wy	DKbC	1745	D1
Briarglen Ct	DKbC	1745	C2
Briarglen Dr	DKbC	1745	C1
Briar Glen Ln SW	ATLN	1974	B5
Briargreen Ct	DKbC	1745	C2
Briar Hill Ct	ClyC	2148	B5
Briar Hill Ln	ClyC	2148	B5
Briarhill Ln NE	DKbC	1816	E1
Briar Hills Dr NE	DKbC	1817	A5
Briaridge Cir	DKbC	1745	C1
Briarlake Cir	DKbC	1744	D6
Briarlake Ct NE	DKbC	1744	B3
Briarlake Rd	DKbC	1744	C6
Briarlake Rd NE	DKbC	1744	B5
Briarlake Trc NE	DKbC	1744	B5
Briarlake Woods Wy NE	DKbC	1744	B5
Briarleaf Dr	DKbC	1980	C5
Briarleigh Wy	DKbC	1601	A4
Briarleigh Close	DKbC	1601	A4
Briarlyn Ct NE	DKbC	1744	A6
Briarmill Rd NE	DKbC	1743	D6
Briarmoor Rd NE	DKbC	1744	D3
Briaroaks Tr NE	DKbC	1817	B1
Briar Park Ct NE	DKbC	1817	A4
Briar Pond Wy NE	MRTA	1527	A6
Briar Ridge Wy SW	ATLN	1974	B5
Briar Trail Ct SW	ATLN	1974	B5
Briarvale Ct SE	DKbC	1978	B4
Briar Villa Pl	FulC	1599	D2
Briar Vista Ter NE	DKbC	1816	E3
Briar Vista Wy NE	DKbC	1817	A3
Briarwillow Dr NE	DKbC	1744	A5
Briarwood Blf NE	DKbC	1743	A5
Briarwood Blvd	EPNT	2060	D1
Briarwood Ct	ClyC	2147	D7
Briarwood Ct NE	CobC	1597	C3
	DKbC	1743	B6
Briarwood Dr NE	DKbC	1816	D6
Briarwood Dr SE	CobC	1667	B3
Briarwood Rd	HryC	2152	E2
Briarwood Rd NE	DKbC	1743	A4
Briarwood Wy NE	DKbC	1743	B5
Briarwood Hills Dr NE	DKbC	1743	A4
Briarwood Industrial Ct NE	DKbC	1743	B6
Brice Dr	UNCT	2145	B6
Brickey Ln NE	CobC	1597	B5
Brickleberry Ln NE	CobC	1596	B1
Brickle Ridge Ln SE	CobC	1812	C4
Brick Plant Rd NW	ATLN	1813	C3
Brickstone Dr NW	FulC	1668	E4
Bridal Pth NE	ATLN	1816	C5
Bridge Av	FTPK	2149	B1
Bridge Ct NW	GwnC	1533	D6
Bridge Ln SE	SMYR	1738	D3
W Bridge Pl NE	CobC	1527	E4
Bridgeboro Wy NW	GwnC	1602	C2
Bridgegate Ct	FulC	1600	E1
Bridgegate Ct NE	CobC	1596	E2
Bridgegate Dr NE	CobC	1596	E2
Bridgegate Trc NE	CobC	1596	E1
Bridgegate Cove NE	CobC	1596	E1
Bridge Mill Ct NW	GwnC	1602	E2
Bridge Mill Dr SE	CobC	1667	E3
Bridgeport Dr NE	DKbC	1743	C7
Bridgeport Dr NW	ATLN	1813	D5
Bridgeport Ln NW	GwnC	1533	D6
Bridgeport Wy NW	GwnC	1533	D6
Bridges Av SW	ATLN	1975	D1
Bridges Creek Tr NE	FulC	1670	B1
Bridgestone Cir NE	MRTA	1526	A5
Bridgestone Ct NE	MRTA	1526	A6
Bridgestone Dr NE	MRTA	1526	A6
Bridge View Dr NW	MRTA	1526	A5
Bridgewater Dr NW	FulC	1669	C1
Bridgewater St SW	ATLN	1976	B4
Bridgewood Dr SW	CobC	1812	A6
Bridgewood Valley Rd NW	FulC	1598	D7
	FulC	1669	D1
Bridle Blf	DKbC	1894	E3
Bridle Ln NE	CobC	1598	C5
Bridle Pth NE	CobC	1598	C5
Bridle Tr SE	CobC	1597	C7
Bridle Path Ct	DKbC	1600	D7
	DKbC	1745	E6
Bridlewood Cir	DKbC	1818	B6
Bridlewood Dr SE	CobC	1739	D7
Bridlewood Ln SE	CobC	1739	D7
Brier Ct	RSWL	1532	A3
Brier Mill Ct	FulC	1533	B1
Briers Dr	DKbC	1819	E2
Briers Pl	DKbC	1819	E2
Briers Wy	DKbC	1819	E2
Briers North Dr	DKbC	1601	B7
Brierwood Pl	DKbC	1601	B7
Brigham Dr	FulC	1601	A4
Bright Ct	DKbC	1980	C3
Brighthampton Dr SE	CobC	1739	D7
S Brighton Ct NW	FulC	1669	C4
Brighton Pl NE	CobC	1528	C7
Brighton Rd NE	ATLN	1815	E3
Bright Water Cove	FulC	1533	A1
Brightwood Ln SE	CobC	1597	B7
Brightwood Ln SW	FulC	1973	B1
Brindle Rd	FulC	2145	B4
Brinkley Ln NE	FulC	1670	A7
Brinson Wy NW	GwnC	1533	C7
Brintons Ml NE	CobC	1528	E5
Brinwick Dr	ClyC	2151	E3
Brisbaine Mnr	FulC	1533	C4
Brisbane Ct NE	CobC	1528	C3
Brisbane Dr NE	CobC	1528	C3
Bristol Dr NE	DKbC	1743	C7
Bristol Ln NE	CobC	1526	B4
Bristol Oaks Dr	RSWL	1529	E2
Britley Ter	FulC	2147	A3
Britney Forest Dr	FulC	2147	A3
Britt Av NW	NRCS	1602	B7
Britt Rd	DKbC	1673	D7
Britt Rd NW	DKbC	1673	E7
Brittain Dr NW	ATLN	1890	D1
Brittany Ln NE	CobC	1529	A4
Brittany Tr	FulC	2147	A3
Brittany Wy NE	ATLN	1742	D7
Brittingham Ct	FulC	1533	A2
Britts Gate Ln	DKbC	1745	D3
Brittwood Wy NW	GwnC	1673	E7
Brixham Ct NE	FulC	1599	A5
Brixham Wy	FulC	1533	B4
Brixton Cir	DKbC	1819	E2
Brixworth Pl NE	DKbC	1742	E6
Broad Av	EPNT	1975	C6
Broad St	CMBL	1671	E5
	DKbC	1818	D7
Broad St NE	FulC	1670	A4
Broad St NW	ATLN	1890	E4
Broad St SE	CobC	1666	D4
Broad St SW	ATLN	1890	D4
Broadgreen Dr NW	GwnC	1533	D7
Broadland Ct NW	ATLN	1741	D2
N Broadland Rd NW	ATLN	1741	C2
Broadland Rd NW	ATLN	1741	C2
Broadleaf Av	FulC	2146	C5
Broad Leaf Ct	FulC	1533	B1
Broadleaf Wk	DKbC	2066	C4
Broadleaf Wy	ClyC	2147	D4
Broad Oak Ct	DKbC	1979	D7
Broad River Ct	DKbC	2065	A1
Broad River Pl	DKbC	2065	A1
Broadview Ct	DKbC	1894	B7
Broadwell St SW	ATLN	1976	B4
Brocken Wy	DKbC	1745	C6
Brockett Pl	DKbC	1819	C2
Brockett Rd	DKbC	1745	D6
	DKbC	1819	C1
Brockett Tr	DKbC	1819	B1
Brockett Wk	DKbC	1745	D5
Brockett Wy	DKbC	1819	B2
Brockett Creek Ct	DKbC	1745	D6
E Brockett Creek Ct	DKbC	1745	D6
W Brockett Creek Ct	DKbC	1745	D6
Brockett Creek Dr	DKbC	1745	D6
Brockett Oaks	DKbC	1745	D7
Brockham Wy	FulC	1532	D1
Brockton Gln NE	DKbC	1743	C7
Brockton Pl	DKbC	1819	B7
Brockton Close	CobC	1598	B5
Brogdon Ct	CMBL	1672	A5
Broken Arrow Ct SE	CobC	1738	B6
Bromack Dr SE	ATLN	1976	E6
Bromley Rd	AVES	1893	D3
Brompton Ct	DKbC	1600	B4
Bronco Ct NE	CobC	1529	C1
Bronner Bros Wy SW	ATLN	1890	B6
Bronx St NW	ATLN	1889	E3
Bronze Leaf Ct	DKbC	1894	E4
Brook Av NE	MRTA	1595	D1
Brook Av NW	ATLN	1814	A7
Brook Ct	ClyC	2151	C5
Brook Dr	DKbC	1818	D3
Brook Dr NE	FulC	1599	A6
Brook Wy SE	CobC	1812	A3
Brook Wy SW	ATLN	1888	A4
Brookcliff Cir NE	CobC	1528	A7
Brookcliff Ct NE	CobC	1528	A7
Brookcliff Dr NE	CobC	1527	E7
Brookcliff Ln NE	CobC	1528	A7
Brookcliff Lndg NE	CobC	1527	E6
Brookcliff Pl	CobC	1528	A7
Brookcliff Trc NE	CobC	1597	D4
Brookcliff Wy NE	DKbC	1744	C3
Brookcrest Cir	DKbC	1894	B5
Brookcrest Ct NE	CobC	1596	E5
Brookcrest Dr NE	CobC	1596	E4
	CobC	1597	A5
Brook Ct Av	DKbC	1673	B5
Brookdale Dr	EPNT	1975	E6
	FTPK	2149	B3
Brookdale Dr NE	DKbC	1744	C4
Brookdale Dr NW	ATLN	1815	C1
Brookdale Dr SW	ATLN	1976	B6
Brookdale Ln SW	CobC	1812	A3
Brookdale Pl	DKbC	1818	D4
Brooke Farm Ct	DKbC	1600	E4
Brooke Farm Dr	DKbC	1600	E4
Brooke Farm Tr	DKbC	1600	E4
Brooke Greene NE	DKbC	1742	D2
Brookelake Dr	DKbC	1601	A4
Brooke Ridge Cir	DKbC	1601	A2
Brooke Ridge Dr	DKbC	1601	A4
Brookfield Dr NE	FulC	1670	B7
Brookfield Ln	DKbC	1894	A5
Brook Forest Dr NE	DKbC	1816	E2
Brookforest Dr NE	DKbC	1816	E2
Brook Forest Trc	DKbC	2066	C1
Brookgate Cross	ClyC	2064	D5
Brookgate Ct	ClyC	2064	D5
Brookgate Dr	ClyC	2064	D5
Brookgate Wy	ClyC	2064	D5

Atlanta Street Index

STREET	City	Map #	Grid
Carlow Ct	DKbC	1980	D2
Carlow Ct SE	CobC	1812	E3
Carlo Woods Dr SW	FulC	1887	A7
Carlton Dr	DKbC	1671	E4
Carlton Dr NE	ATLN	1741	E2
Carlton Pl NE	DKbC	1743	C2
Carlton Rdg NE	ATLN	1742	C3
Carluke Ct NE	CobC	1527	B1
E Carlyle Ct NE	CobC	1528	D5
S Carlyle Ct NE	CobC	1528	D5
W Carlyle Ct NE	CobC	1528	D5
Carlyle Dr NE	CobC	1528	D4
Carlyle Lk	DKbC	1817	D4
Carlyle St NW	NRCS	1602	E6
Carmain Dr NE	ATLN	1742	C2
Carmel Av NE	ATLN	1891	D2
Carmel Dr	EPNT	2060	C6
Carmel Rd	CMBL	1671	C5
Carmen Ct	ClyC	2150	C5
Carmichael St	EPNT	1975	D7
Carmon on Wesley NW	ATLN	1741	B7
Carnaby Ct	DKbC	1600	B4
Carnegie Av	EPNT	1975	D7
Carnegie Wy NW	ATLN	1890	E3
Carnes Dr SE	CobC	1595	A7
Carnwath Ct	FulC	1532	E1
Carobet Ter	FulC	2146	E6
Carol Ct	EPNT	2060	E3
Carol Dr NE	CobC	1527	D2
Carol Ln NE	DKbC	1817	A5
Carol Ln NW	FulC	1669	C6
Carol Wy NW	FulC	1669	C6
Carol B Mathews Ln	RSWL	1531	B6
Carole Dr	DKbC	1672	D4
Caroline St NE	ATLN	1891	D3
Caroll Dr SW	CobC	1812	A1
Carolwood Ln NE	FulC	1670	B7
Carolyn Ct	ClyC	2151	A7
Carolyn Dr NE	DKbC	1817	B2
Carolyn Dr SE	SMYR	1667	D7
Carolyn St NE	CobC	1528	C2
	MRTA	1595	E3
Carolyn St NW	ATLN	1814	D4
Carolyn St SW	ATLN	1973	D5
Caron Cir NW	ATLN	1888	C1
Carondelett Cove SW	FulC	1887	B6
Carousel Ct NE	CobC	1527	D1
Carpenter Ct	ClyC	2064	A6
Carpenter Dr NE	FulC	1670	A3
Carr St NW	ATLN	1814	E7
Car Rental Rd	CGPK	2061	B6
Carriage Cir	HryC	2152	C7
Carriage Ct	FulC	2146	D5
	HryC	2152	C7
	UNCT	2146	A7
Carriage Dr	ClyC	2150	C6
Carriage Dr NE	FulC	1599	A7
	FulC	1670	B1
Carriage Ln	FulC	2146	D5
Carriage Pth SE	CobC	1738	D5
Carriage Tr	DKbC	1894	E2
Carriage Trc	HryC	2152	C7
Carriage Trc NE	CobC	1597	A5
Carriage Wy	CGPK	2060	E3
	EPNT	2060	E3
Carriage Wy NE	CobC	1528	D1
Carriage Wy NW	ATLN	1741	B2
Carriage Wy SE	CobC	1738	D5
Carriage Chase Rd	FulC	2146	A4
Carriage Cove	UNCT	2145	E7
Carriage Gate Tr SW	FulC	1973	B3
Carriage House Ct	EPNT	2060	B5
Carriage Lakes Dr NE	CobC	1529	B1
Carriage Place Ct	DKbC	1818	B5
Carriage Station Cir	RSWL	1531	A1
Carriage Wy Ln	RSWL	1532	A6
Carrington Dr	DKbC	2064	E1
	FulC	1532	E2
Carrington Wy NE	FulC	1599	D5
Carrington Wy SE	CobC	1596	D7
Carroll Av SW	ATLN	1973	C5
Carroll Cir	CMBL	1672	A6
Carroll Dr NW	ATLN	1814	C4
Carroll St SE	ATLN	1891	B5
Carroll Manor Dr	FulC	1530	E5
Carrollton Ct NE	CobC	1526	B2
Carrollwood Ct	DKbC	1894	D3
Carrollwood Dr	DKbC	1894	D4
Carrollwood Wy	DKbC	1894	E4
Carruth Dr SE	CobC	1595	A7
	CobC	1666	B1
Carryback Dr NE	CobC	1598	B5
Carson Ct	ClyC	2150	C7
Carson Dr SE	CobC	1739	B3
Carson Ln SE	CobC	1739	B3
Carson Pass SW	ATLN	1973	B6
Cartecay Dr NE	DKbC	1743	A4
Carter Av SE	ATLN	1892	D5
	DKbC	1892	D6
Carter Cir	EPNT	1975	C4
Carter Dr NE	ATLN	1742	C1
Carter Rd	DKbC	1893	C4
N Carter Rd	DKbC	1893	C2
Carter St NW	ATLN	1890	B4
Carter Center Entrance	ATLN	1891	E1
Carteret Pl	DKbC	1894	C3
Carter Pond Rd	CGPK	2147	A2
Carthage Rd	DKbC	1745	C6
Cartier Ct	RSWL	1531	E6
Cartwright Ct	DKbC	1744	C7
Cartwright Dr	DKbC	1744	C7
Cartwright Dr SE	CobC	1813	B2
Cartwright Pl SE	CobC	1813	B2
Caruso Ct	FulC	1601	C1
Carver Cir	DKbC	1672	B2
	DRVL	1672	A2
Carver Cir NW	ATLN	1889	B3
Carver Dr	DKbC	1672	A3
	DRVL	1672	A3
N Carver Dr	DRVL	1672	A2
Carver Dr NW	ATLN	1889	A3
Carver Rd	ClyC	2150	C3
Casa Ct	CLKN	1819	A4
	DKbC	1819	A4
Casa Dr	CLKN	1819	A3
	DKbC	1819	A3
Casa Linda Dr	DKbC	1979	E1
Casa Loma Dr	DKbC	1980	D6
Casa Verde Dr	FulC	2059	C5
Casa Woods Ln	CLKN	1819	A3
	DKbC	1819	A3
Cascade Av SW	ATLN	1889	D7
	ATLN	1975	B1
Cascade Cir SW	ATLN	1975	C1
Cascade Dr	FTPK	2063	C6
Cascade Ovlk SW	FulC	1887	A6
Cascade Pkwy SW	FulC	1974	B1
Cascade Pl SW	ATLN	1889	D7
Cascade Rd SW	ATLN	1974	B1
	FulC	1887	C7
	FulC	1973	E1
	FulC	1974	B1
Cascade Ter SW	ATLN	1889	C7
Cascade Falls Ct SW	ATLN	1974	B2
Cascade Falls Dr SW	ATLN	1974	B2
Cascade Knolls Dr SW	FulC	1887	C7
Cascade Manor Dr	DKbC	1980	A5
Cascade Point Dr SW	FulC	1887	B7
Casey Dr SE	CobC	1666	A4
Casey's Cove	DKbC	2065	A1
Cash Ct NW	GwnC	1602	B6
Casher Ct	DKbC	1978	E3
Casher Dr	DKbC	1978	E3
Cash Memorial Blvd	FTPK	2149	A3
Cason Dr NE	CobC	1526	B5
Casplan Ct SW	ATLN	1976	B3
Casplan St SW	ATLN	1976	B3
Cassanova St SE	ATLN	1977	B2
Casson St NE	ATLN	1892	B3
Castaway Ct	DKbC	1673	B7
	DKbC	1745	B1
Castaway Ln	DKbC	1673	B7
	DKbC	1745	B1
Casteel Rd NE	CobC	1528	A4
Castellum Close	DKbC	2066	C3
Castile Dr	ClyC	2150	D7
Castle Ct	ClyC	2147	C7
E Castle Ct	DKbC	1818	E1
W Castle Ct	DKbC	1818	E2
Castle Ln NE	CobC	1528	C4
Castlebar Ct SE	CobC	1738	A5
Castleberry St SW	ATLN	1890	D5
Castlebrooke Wy NE	CobC	1527	A2
Castle Falls Dr NE	DKbC	1817	B4
Castlegate Ct	ClyC	2147	B6
Castle Gate Ct NE	CobC	1527	E3
Castlegate Dr	ClyC	2147	B6
N Castlegate Dr	ClyC	2147	B4
Castlegate Dr NW	ATLN	1741	B3
Castlegate Ter	DKbC	1893	B7
Castlehill Ct	DKbC	1745	A4
Castlehill Wy	DKbC	1745	A4
Castle Lake Dr SE	CobC	1812	C6
Castlemain Dr SE	CobC	1812	E4
Castle Pines Ct	DKbC	1745	E2
Castleridge Ct	DKbC	1745	B4
Castleridge Dr	DKbC	1745	A4
Castleridge Dr NE	FulC	1670	A4
Castle Rock Wy	DKbC	1819	B1
Castleton Dr NW	FulC	1598	E6
Castleton Ln	ClyC	2149	C6
Castleton Wy	ClyC	2149	C6
Castleton Wy NE	CobC	1528	A6
Castletree Ct	DKbC	1819	C4
Castleway Dr NE	DKbC	1744	B6
Castleway Ln NE	DKbC	1744	B6
Castlewood Dr	ClyC	2150	D6
Castlewood Dr NW	ATLN	1741	B7
Castlewood Dr SE	CobC	1596	C7
Castlewood St	EPNT	1974	E5
Catafalque Dr	ATLN	1890	A5
Catalina Cir	EPNT	2060	C6
Catalina Ct	ClyC	2149	B7
Catalina Dr	CMBL	1671	E6
	DKbC	1893	C5
Catalpa Ct	DKbC	2066	B4
Catalpa Ln	DKbC	2066	B4
Catalpa Pk	DKbC	2066	B4
Catalpa Wy	DKbC	2066	B4
Catamaran Ct NE	CobC	1527	D3
Cat Cay Ct	FulC	1600	B1
Cates Av NE	DKbC	1670	E7
Cates Ridge Rd NW	FulC	1668	E6
Catherine St	DKbC	1893	B4
	FTPK	2063	B7
Catherine St SW	ATLN	1976	B1
Catina Ct NE	FulC	1599	B5
Cativo Dr SW	ATLN	1888	E6
Catkin Ct NE	CobC	1527	C1
Cato St NW	ATLN	1814	B7
Catskill Ct NE	CobC	1529	D4
Cat Tail Lp	ClyC	2064	D5
Cauthen Ct	HryC	2066	D7
Cavalier Dr	DKbC	1979	B3
Cavalier Dr SE	CobC	1738	C7
	CobC	1812	C1
Cavalier Wy	DKbC	1979	B3
Cavan Dr	DKbC	1819	E3
Cavan Wy SW	CobC	1738	A6
Cavanaugh Av SE	ATLN	1892	A7
	DKbC	1892	A7
	DKbC	1978	A1
Cave Rd NW	ATLN	1740	D2
Cavendish Ct	DKbC	1819	E2
W Cavendish Ct	FulC	1533	B3
Cave Spring Ct	HryC	2066	C7
Cay Ct	FulC	2145	E3
Cecil Dr NE	CobC	1596	E5
Cecile Av SE	ATLN	1892	A7
Cecilia Dr SE	DKbC	1978	B2
Cedar Av	EPNT	1976	A7
Cedar Av NW	ATLN	1889	A1
Cedar Brk SE	CobC	1667	B3
Cedar Brk W	CobC	1667	D1
Cedar Cir	DKbC	1819	C1
	FTPK	2149	C5
Cedar Cr N	CobC	1667	B3
Cedar Cr S	CobC	1667	E1
Cedar Ct SE	CobC	1668	A2
Cedar Dr NE	CobC	1527	B4
Cedar Hllw	FulC	1530	E6
Cedar Ln	HryC	2152	E6
E Cedar Ln SW	ATLN	1975	B3
W Cedar Ln SW	ATLN	1975	B3
Cedar Run	FulC	1530	E5
Cedar St	DKbC	1818	D6
Cedar St NW	GwnC	1673	B1
Cedar Trc	RSWL	1530	B2
Cedar Wy SE	CobC	1666	A6
Cedar Bluff Ct NE	CobC	1596	A2
Cedar Bluff Dr NE	CobC	1528	B2
Cedar Bluff Tr NE	CobC	1596	A2
Cedar Bluff Wy NE	CobC	1596	A2
Cedarbrook Ct SE	DKbC	1891	E7
	DKbC	1977	E1
Cedar Brook Dr	DKbC	1818	D5
Cedarbrook Dr NE	CobC	1526	B2
Cedar Canyon Ct NE	DKbC	1744	C6
Cedar Canyon Ct SE	CobC	1667	B3
Cedar Canyon Dr NE	DKbC	1744	C7
Cedar Canyon Dr SE	CobC	1667	B3
Cedar Canyon Pl SE	CobC	1667	E1
Cedar Canyon Rd SE	CobC	1667	E1
	MRTA	1667	E1
Cedar Canyon Sq SE	CobC	1667	B3
Cedar Chase	DKbC	1600	E4
Cedar Chase Cir NE	ATLN	1816	C2
Cedar Chase Dr NE	ATLN	1816	C2
Cedar Chase Ln NE	ATLN	1816	C2
Cedar Cliff Ct SE	SMYR	1739	B3
Cedar Cliff Dr SE	CobC	1739	B3
	SMYR	1739	B3
Cedar Corners Pl NW	GwnC	1602	C2
Cedar Corners Tr NW	GwnC	1602	C3
Cedar Cove	RSWL	1530	B3
Cedar Creek Ct	RSWL	1530	B2
Cedar Creek Ct SE	CobC	1667	B3
Cedar Creek Dr	ClyC	2147	D5
	DKbC	1818	D3
Cedar Creek Ln	ClyC	2147	D5
Cedar Creek Pkwy	DKbC	1818	D3
Cedar Forest Ct	DKbC	1819	E3
Cedar Forks Ct NE	CobC	1527	E4
Cedar Forks Dr NE	CobC	1527	E4
Cedar Forks Tr NE	CobC	1527	D5
Cedar Forks Trc NE	CobC	1527	E4
Cedar Grove Dr NE	CobC	1527	B4
Cedar Grove Pl	DKbC	2064	E3
Cedar Grove Rd	DKbC	2064	A3
Cedar Hill Wy NE	CobC	1596	E2
Cedar Hills Ct NE	DKbC	1744	B4
Cedarhurst Dr	DKbC	1600	B5
Cedar Hurst Tr	FulC	2146	A7
Cedar Island Dr SW	ATLN	1888	B6
Cedar Knoll Cir	RSWL	1531	B4
Cedar Knoll Ct	RSWL	1531	B4
Cedar Knoll Dr	DKbC	1745	D7
	RSWL	1531	B4
Cedar Knoll Wy	ClyC	2147	E2
Cedar Lake Ct	DKbC	2064	C4
Cedar Lake Dr	DKbC	2064	D3
Cedar Lake Cove	DKbC	2064	D4
Cedar Park Dr	DKbC	1819	E2
Cedar Post Ct	DKbC	1818	B2
Cedar Ridge Ct SE	SMYR	1739	B3
Cedar Ridge Dr SE	SMYR	1739	B3
Cedar Shoals Dr	ClyC	2148	A3
Cedar Trace Ct	DKbC	2065	C1
Cedar Trace Dr	DKbC	2065	C1
Cedar Trace Ln	DKbC	2065	C2
Cedar Tree Ln	ClyC	2150	E5
Cedar Valley Ct	DKbC	2064	E3
Cedar Valley Ct SE	SMYR	1739	A2
Cedar Valley Dr SE	SMYR	1739	A2
Cedar Valley Ln	DKbC	2064	E4
Cedar Valley Pl	DKbC	2064	E4
Cedar Valley Wy	DKbC	2064	E3
Cedar Walk Ln	DKbC	2064	D4
Cedar Wood Ct	FulC	2146	C5
Cedar Wood Ct NE	CobC	1596	D5
Cedar Wood Dr	FulC	2146	C5
Celebration Ct SW	FulC	1973	D1
Celebration Dr SW	ATLN	1973	D1
	FulC	1973	D1
Celeste Dr SE	ATLN	2062	E4
Celia Wy	DKbC	1893	D4
Celina Ct	ClyC	2150	D7
Celtic Cir	DKbC	1819	D3
Celtic Ct	DKbC	1819	D3
Cemetery Av	DKbC	1745	A7
Cemetery Dr	DKbC	1818	C5
Cemetery Rd NE	CobC	1596	D1
N Cemetery St NW	NRCS	1602	E6
S Cemetery St NW	NRCS	1602	E6
Cemetery St SE	MRTA	1595	A6
Centennial Dr	HryC	2152	C3
Centennial Sq NW	GwnC	1602	C3
Centennial Trc	RSWL	1531	E4
Centennial Olympic Park Dr NW	ATLN	1890	D4
Centennial Olympic Park Dr SW	ATLN	1890	D4
Center Av	EPNT	2061	C1
Center Dr	DKbC	1600	A5
Center St	AVES	1893	D1
	DKbC	1893	D1
Center St NW	ATLN	1813	E6
	ATLN	1890	D2
Center St SE	CobC	1740	A7
Center Cross Pass NE	MRTA	1527	B6
Center Hill Av NW	ATLN	1814	A7

INDEX 15

Chestnut Ridge Dr — E Clinton Ct NE

Atlanta Street Index

STREET	City	Map #	Grid
Chestnut Ridge Dr	DKbC	1600	B6
Chestnut Ridge Wy NE	CobC	1528	D3
Chestnut Rose Ln NW	FulC	1669	C3
Chestnut Springs Blvd NE	CobC	1527	C6
Chestnut Springs Tr NE	CobC	1527	D6
Chestwick Ct	FulC	1600	E3
Chestwood Ln SW	CobC	1812	A6
Cheswich Ct SE	CobC	1597	B7
Chevaux Ct NW	FulC	1669	E4
Chevelle Ln SE	ATLN	1893	A4
	DCTR	1893	A4
Cheviot Gln	EPNT	1974	D6
Chevoit Dr	DKbC	1819	B7
Chevron Dr	FulC	1600	C2
Chevron Dr NE	FulC	1600	C2
Chevron Wy	FulC	1600	B2
Chevy Chase Ln	DKbC	1980	B1
Chewning Dr	DKbC	1818	D1
Chewning Wy	DCTR	1892	C1
Chicadee Ct NE	CobC	1527	D7
Chicago Av NW	ATLN	1889	B2
Chicamauga Av NW	ATLN	1889	E4
Chicamauga Av SW	ATLN	1889	E4
Chicamauga Pl SW	ATLN	1889	E4
Chicapoo Dr NE	CobC	1526	C3
Chicasaw Dr NE	MRTA	1595	B3
Chickadee Ct	RVDL	2148	A7
Chickadee Ct SW	ATLN	1888	E6
Chickering Pkwy	RSWL	1529	D1
Chickering Lake Ct	RSWL	1529	D1
Chickering Lake Dr	RSWL	1529	D1
Chicopee Dr	DKbC	1672	C2
	DRVL	1672	C2
Chicopee Dr NE	MRTA	1595	B3
Chicory Ct	DKbC	2066	E1
Childerlee Ln NE	DKbC	1743	B7
Childers Ct NE	DKbC	1742	E7
Childers Pl NE	DKbC	1742	D6
Childers Rd NE	CobC	1529	A1
	DKbC	1742	E7
Childress Dr SW	ATLN	1974	C3
Childs Dr NW	ATLN	1889	D3
Chilton Dr NW	ATLN	1888	E2
Chimney Blf	FulC	1532	C6
Chimney Hts NE	CobC	1528	E1
Chimney Ln NE	CobC	1528	E1
Chimney Lake Dr NE	CobC	1528	B2
Chimney Mill Ct	DKbC	2066	C3
Chimney Mill Tr	DKbC	2066	C3
Chimney Oaks Ct SE	CobC	1738	C7
	SMYR	1738	C7
Chimney Oaks Dr SE	CobC	1738	B7
Chimney Ridge Ct	DKbC	2066	C3
Chimney Ridge Dr	DKbC	2066	C2
Chimney Ridge Wy	DKbC	2066	C2
Chimney Smoke Dr	HryC	2152	E7
Chimney Springs Ct NE	CobC	1529	A4
Chimney Springs Dr NE	CobC	1529	B5
Chimney Stone Ct	DKbC	2066	C3
Chimney Sweep Ln NE	CobC	1529	B4
Chimney Swift Cir NE	CobC	1527	D6
Chinaberry Ln	RVDL	2148	A7
Chinaberry Wy SW	ATLN	1974	D5
Chinkapin Cir SW	FulC	1974	B1
Chinkapin Ln	RSWL	1532	A5
Chinquapin Ct NE	CobC	1527	C1
Chipley Ct	RSWL	1529	E2
Chipley Ct NE	CobC	1596	B2
Chipley St NE	ATLN	1891	E3
Chipmunk Tr SE	CobC	1667	E1
Chippewa Ct NE	DKbC	1671	A3
Chippewa Dr	ClyC	2151	A6
Chippewa Pl NE	DKbC	1671	A3
Chipwood Pth NW	GwnC	1673	E7
Chisholm Tr	ClyC	2147	D4
Chisolm Ct	DKbC	1745	B6
Chivers St NW	ATLN	1813	D7
Chondra Dr NE	CobC	1527	C6
Chowning Wy	DKbC	1671	E1
Christie Ct SW	CobC	1666	A7
Christina St NW	ATLN	1889	D2
Christine Ct	DKbC	1894	E6
Christine Dr NE	CobC	1526	A1
Christman St SW	ATLN	1890	C6
Christmas Ln NE	DKbC	1817	C2
Christopher Ct	DKbC	1601	B5
Christopher Ter	ClyC	2151	D6
Christopher Wy SE	CobC	1812	A2
Christophers Ct NE	CobC	1527	D2
Christophers Wk NW	ATLN	1814	E2
Chriswell Ct NE	CobC	1527	D3
Chrysler Av SE	SMYR	1666	D5
Chrysler Cir NE	DKbC	1743	D5
Chrysler Ct NE	DKbC	1743	E6
Chrysler Dr NE	DKbC	1743	E6
Chrysler Ter NE	DKbC	1743	E6
Chukar Tr	DKbC	1980	C4
Chumley Cir NE	CobC	1526	D1
Church Dr	DRVL	1672	B4
N Church Ln SE	CobC	1739	D6
Church Rd	HryC	2152	D2
Church Rd SE	CobC	1738	A1
	CobC	1739	C7
	MRTA	1596	A6
	SMYR	1738	C1
Church Rd SW	CobC	1738	A1
Church St	CLKN	1819	A4
	ClyC	2063	D5
	DCTR	1818	A6
	DKbC	1745	E4
	DKbC	1818	E5
	EPNT	1975	C7
	EPNT	2061	C1
	FulC	2145	E1
	LKCY	2150	A3
	UNCT	2145	B6
Church St SR-139	EPNT	1975	D6
Church St US-29	EPNT	1975	D6
Church St NE	MRTA	1595	A3
Church St NE SR-5	MRTA	1595	A3
Church St NW	ATLN	1813	E3
Church St SE	SMYR	1666	C7
	SMYR	1738	C1
Churchill Dr	DKbC	1600	D1
Churchill Wy NE	CobC	1528	B7
Churchill Downs Rd NE	FulC	1670	D6
Church St Ext NW	CobC	1595	A1
	MRTA	1595	A1
Churchwell Ct	DKbC	1745	B2
Churchwell Ln	DKbC	1745	B3
Cimarron Ct	DKbC	1819	D3
Cimarron Ct SE	SMYR	1739	B2
Cimarron Dr	DKbC	1819	D2
Cimarron Pkwy	FulC	1599	A3
Cinderella Ct	DKbC	1818	D4
Cinderella Wy	DKbC	1818	C4
Cindy Dr	DKbC	1894	A7
Cindy Dr SW	CobC	1595	A7
Cindy Ln SE	SMYR	1738	C2
Cindy Wy	ClyC	2151	C6
Cinnamon Ct	ClyC	2150	E6
Cinnamon Teal Ct NE	CobC	1597	D1
Circassian Ct	FulC	1533	E1
Circle Av	FTPK	2150	C2
Circle Dr	LKCY	2149	E3
N Circle Dr	HryC	2066	E6
N Circle Dr NW	ATLN	1814	A6
S Circle Dr	HryC	2066	E6
W Circle Dr	HryC	2066	D6
Circle 75 Pkwy SE	CobC	1667	E7
	CobC	1668	A5
	SMYR	1667	E7
Circle 85 St	ClyC	2148	C1
Circle Oaks Dr SE	CobC	1740	A2
Circlewood Rd NE	DKbC	1744	A4
Citadel Cir NE	CobC	1529	A7
Citadel Dr NE	DKbC	1816	E2
Citadella Ct	FulC	1532	E5
Citation Ct	HryC	2152	A2
Citation Dr	DKbC	1980	B4
Citrus Ct	DKbC	1979	E5
Cityheights Dr NE	ATLN	1891	B7
Cityline Av NE	ATLN	1891	A2
Cityscape Plz NE	ATLN	1891	B7
Cityview Ct NE	ATLN	1891	A1
City View Dr	FTPK	2063	A7
	FTPK	2149	A1
Civic Club Pl	DKbC	1893	D5
Civitania Rd SE	CobC	1738	B7
	CobC	1812	B1
	SMYR	1738	B7
Clackum Rd NE	CobC	1527	E6
E Claiborne Ct NE	CobC	1526	B2
W Claiborne Ct NE	CobC	1526	B1
Claiborne Ct NE	CobC	1527	C5
Clairborne Ct	DKbC	1600	D3
Claire Dr	HPVL	2062	C3
Claire Dr NE	ATLN	1892	B2
Claire Dr SE	ATLN	1976	E4
Claire Dr SW	ATLN	1976	B3
Claire Ter	DKbC	1893	B6
Clairemont Av	DCTR	1817	E7
	DKbC	1817	E7
Clairemont Av SR-155	DCTR	1817	E7
Clairemont Av SR-155	DKbC	1817	E7
Clairemont Av US-23	DCTR	1817	E7
	DKbC	1817	E7
Claire Rose Ln NW	FulC	1669	C3
Clairmeade Wy NE	DKbC	1743	D4
Clairmeade Valley Rd NE	DKbC	1743	D4
Clairmont Cir	DKbC	1743	C5
	DKbC	1817	E5
Clairmont Ct NE	DKbC	1743	C5
Clairmont Lk	DKbC	1817	D4
Clairmont Ln NE	DKbC	1817	D1
Clairmont Pl NE	DKbC	1743	B5
Clairmont Rd	DKbC	1817	D4
Clairmont Rd SR-155	DKbC	1817	D4
Clairmont Rd US-23	DKbC	1817	D4
Clairmont Rd NE	CMBL	1671	D6
	CMBL	1743	D1
	DKbC	1743	C6
	DKbC	1817	D1
Clairmont Rd NE SR-155	DKbC	1743	C6
	DKbC	1817	D1
Clairmont Rd NE US-23	DKbC	1743	C6
	DKbC	1817	D1
Clairmont Run	DKbC	1817	D6
Clairmont Ter NE	DKbC	1743	C4
Clairmont Wy NE	DKbC	1743	C5
Clairmont North NE	DKbC	1743	C4
Clairview Dr	CMBL	1672	A6
Clairwood Ter	CMBL	1671	D7
Clanton Ter	DKbC	1978	E3
Claremont St NW	ATLN	1815	A3
Clarendale Dr NW	ATLN	1740	E6
Clarendon Av	AVES	1893	D2
	DKbC	1893	C3
N Clarendon Av	AVES	1818	D7
	DKbC	1818	D7
Clarendon Dr NE	CobC	1598	B1
Clarendon Pl	AVES	1893	D2
	ClyC	2151	D6
Claridge Ct	DKbC	1672	C1
Claridge Dr NE	FulC	1670	C5
Claridge Sq	DKbC	1601	B4
Clarion Av	DCTR	1892	D1
Clarissa Dr NW	ATLN	1814	B5
Clark Dr	DKbC	2066	A4
	HryC	2152	A1
N Clark Dr	EPNT	1975	B6
S Clark Dr	EPNT	1975	B7
	EPNT	2061	B1
Clark St	CLKN	1819	B3
	DKbC	2064	E3
Clark St NW	ATLN	1813	E7
Clarkdell Dr	HryC	2152	B4
Clarke Dr	DKbC	1672	D1
Clarke Ln	DKbC	1894	E6
Clarke St SE	ATLN	1890	E5
Clark Howell Hwy	ClyC	2062	B7
	ClyC	2148	B1
Clarkston Industrial Blvd	CLKN	1819	A2
Claron Av	DKbC	2064	C3
Clary Trc NE	CobC	1529	B2
Clary Hill Ct NE	CobC	1529	B2
Clary Hill Dr NE	CobC	1529	A2
Clary Hill Pl NE	CobC	1529	B2
Clary Lakes Ct NE	CobC	1529	A2
Clary Lakes Dr NE	CobC	1529	B2
Classic Wy	FulC	1600	C1
Classic Cove	FulC	1600	C1
Clate Ct	ClyC	2150	D5
Clate Ln	ClyC	2150	D5
Claude St NW	ATLN	1813	D3
Claudel Ct SW	FulC	1973	A3
Clay Dr	DRVL	1672	B3
	FulC	1531	C7
	FulC	1600	B1
Clay Dr SE	CobC	1666	A1
Clay Pl	HPVL	2062	A3
Clay Rd SE	CobC	1666	B4
Clay St NE	ATLN	1892	A4
Clay St SE	ATLN	1892	A5
Clay Brooke Ct SE	SMYR	1739	A7
Clay Brooke Dr SE	SMYR	1739	A6
Clay Brooke Ln SE	SMYR	1739	A7
Clayhill	DKbC	1819	C2
Claymore Dr SE	MRTA	1595	D5
E Clayton Dr	ClyC	2150	E3
Clayton Crossing Ln	ClyC	2151	D1
Clayton Crossing Wy	ClyC	2151	D1
Clayton State Blvd	MRRW	2150	A5
Clearbrook Ct NE	CobC	1597	A3
Clearbrook Dr	MRRW	2149	D7
Clearbrook Dr NE	CobC	1597	A3
Clearbrook Dr SW	ATLN	1974	C1
Clearbrook Wy NE	CobC	1597	A3
Clear Creek Ct	RSWL	1531	D4
Clear Creek Ter	RSWL	1531	D4
Clearlake Ct NW	GwnC	1601	D6
Clear Lake Ter	RSWL	1531	C4
Clear Spring Ct NE	CobC	1596	D4
Clearstream Ln SW	CobC	1812	A5
Clearstream Wy SW	CobC	1812	A6
Clearview Av	DRVL	1672	C5
Clearview Dr	ClyC	2151	C5
Clearview Dr NE	DKbC	1742	E6
Clearview Pkwy	DRVL	1672	C5
Clearview Pl	DRVL	1672	C5
Clearview St SE	CobC	1666	B3
Clearvue Ter SW	ATLN	1889	C7
Clearwater Dr	FulC	2145	E4
Clearwater Dr SE	CobC	1596	B5
Clearwater Rd SW	ATLN	1974	B7
	ATLN	2060	B1
Cleavemark Dr	CLKN	1819	C3
Cleburne Av NE	ATLN	1891	D2
Cleburne Ter NE	ATLN	1891	D1
Clement Dr SW	ATLN	1887	C4
Clement Wy SW	ATLN	1887	C4
Clementstone Dr NE	FulC	1670	D4
Clemmons Dr	ClyC	2064	E7
	ClyC	2150	D1
Clemont Dr NE	ATLN	1816	C7
Clemson Dr	DKbC	1672	A5
Clermont Av	EPNT	1975	D5
Clermont Ct	EPNT	1975	D4
Cleveland Av	EPNT	1975	E7
E Cleveland Av	ATLN	1976	A7
	EPNT	1976	A7
Cleveland Av SE	ATLN	1976	E7
	ATLN	1977	A7
	ATLN	2063	C1
Cleveland Av SW	ATLN	1976	C7
	EPNT	1976	C7
Cleveland Cir SW	ATLN	1976	C6
Cleveland St SE	ATLN	1891	D5
Clevemont Ct	DKbC	2065	E4
Clevemont Rd	DKbC	2065	E4
Clevemont Wy	DKbC	2065	E4
Cliff Ovlk	FulC	1599	B1
Cliffchase Close	RSWL	1531	C6
Cliffcove Ct	RSWL	1531	C6
Cliff Creek Ct SE	SMYR	1739	B3
Cliffcreek Trc	FulC	1530	B7
Cliff Crest Dr SE	SMYR	1739	B3
Clifford Av NE	ATLN	1892	C3
Cliffridge Ct SE	CobC	1668	B1
Cliffs	FulC	1530	B7
Cliffside Cross	FulC	1530	B7
Cliff Side Ct SE	SMYR	1739	B3
Cliffside Ct SE	CobC	1598	A7
Clifftop Ct	RSWL	1531	C6
N Cliff Valley Wy NE	DKbC	1743	A5
Cliff Valley Wy NE	DKbC	1743	B7
Cliffway Dr	DKbC	1743	D2
Cliffwood Dr SE	CobC	1738	E2
	SMYR	1738	E2
Clifton Cir SE	SMYR	1666	D7
	SMYR	1738	D1
E Clifton Rd NE	DKbC	1817	B7
Clifton Rd NE	ATLN	1892	A2
	DKbC	1817	B7
Clifton Rd SE	ATLN	1892	B7
	SMYR	1666	D7
	SMYR	1738	D1
Clifton St NE	ATLN	1892	A4
Clifton St SE	ATLN	1892	A6
Clifton Ter NE	ATLN	1892	A1
Clifton Wy NE	DKbC	1817	B5
Clifton Wy SE	ATLN	1892	A6
Clifton Church Rd SE	DKbC	1978	D5
Clifton Downs Dr SE	DKbC	1978	B3
Clifton Downs Tr SE	DKbC	1978	B3
Clifton Farm Dr	DKbC	1979	B6
Clifton Run Pl SE	DKbC	1978	B3
Clifton Run Trc SE	DKbC	1978	B3
Clifton Springs Ct	DKbC	1979	A5
Clifton Springs Mnr	DKbC	1979	A6
Clifton Springs Rd	DKbC	1978	E4
Clifton Springs Wy	DKbC	1978	E4
Cliftwood Dr NE	FulC	1669	E3
Climax Pl SW	ATLN	1976	C4
Climax St SE	ATLN	1977	A1
Clinchfield Tr NW	GwnC	1533	C7
	GwnC	1602	B1
Cline Dr SE	CobC	1738	A3
E Clinton Ct NE	CobC	1528	D5

INDEX 18

Crab Orchard Ln NW — Danbridge Wy

Atlanta Street Index

Street	City	Map #	Grid
Crab Orchard Ln NW	GwnC	1602	A3
Crabtree Ct NE	CobC	1597	B4
Crabtree Dr	RSWL	1531	D1
Crabtree Dr E	RSWL	1531	D1
Crabtree Dr W	RSWL	1531	D2
Craggy Ln SE	CobC	1740	B3
Craig Ct NE	CobC	1527	E6
Craig Dr	ClyC	2064	C7
Craig Pl NW	ATLN	1889	D4
Craighead Dr NE	FulC	1670	D6
Craighill Ct NW	GwnC	1673	E6
Craigie Av	AVES	1893	B1
	DKbC	1893	B1
Cranberry Pl	RSWL	1531	E1
Cranborne Chase NE	CobC	1528	C2
Cranbourne Ct	DKbC	1600	D3
Cranbrooke Dr	DKbC	1979	A1
Crandall Ct	DKbC	1818	C4
Crane Rd NE	ATLN	1742	C6
Cranfill Rd SE	CobC	1666	B3
Cranford Dr	CLKN	1819	B3
Cranford Dr SW	ATLN	1974	A2
Cranton Ct NE	DKbC	1671	C2
Cravenridge Dr NE	DKbC	1743	B1
Cravey Dr NE	DKbC	1744	C3
Cravey Ln NE	DKbC	1744	C2
Cravey Tr NE	DKbC	1744	C2
Cravey Cove NE	DKbC	1744	D4
Cravey Forest Ln NE	DKbC	1744	C2
Crawford Cir NE	CobC	1526	C1
Creat Tr SE	SMYR	1739	B2
Creatwood Cir SE	SMYR	1739	B1
Creatwood Pl SE	SMYR	1739	B1
Creatwood Tr SE	CobC	1739	B2
	SMYR	1739	B2
Creek Ct	DKbC	1894	D3
S Creek Ct	DKbC	1894	C1
Creek Ct NE	CobC	1528	C1
	CobC	1529	B2
Creek Dr NE	CobC	1528	C1
Creekbank Wy SE	SMYR	1738	E6
Creekbank Cove	DKbC	1980	C3
Creek Brook Dr NW	GwnC	1533	C6
Creek Cove Ln	DKbC	2066	A6
Creekdale Ct	DKbC	1819	A5
Creekdale Dr	DKbC	1818	E3
Creekland Trc NE	CobC	1529	C4
Creekland Vw NE	CobC	1529	B4
Creekmont Ct	RSWL	1531	D3
Creekmont Wy	RSWL	1531	D2
Creek Park Dr NE	CobC	1528	B2
Creek Park Rd	DKbC	1817	E2
Creek Pond Cove	DKbC	1893	D6
Creek Shoals Ct	DKbC	2066	B2
Creek Shoals Ln	DKbC	2066	B2
Creekside Ct	DKbC	1893	D7
	RSWL	1531	E3
Creekside Ct NW	GwnC	1533	A6
Creekside Ct SE	CobC	1597	D5
	CobC	1738	E6
	SMYR	1667	D6
	SMYR	1738	E6
Creekside Dr	ClyC	2151	C5
Creekside Dr NW	GwnC	1533	A6
Creekside Pl SE	SMYR	1738	E6
Creekside Trc	RSWL	1532	A3
Creekside Trc SE	SMYR	1738	E6
Creekside Wy	RSWL	1531	B1
Creek Station Ln	DKbC	1894	C1
Creekstone Ct	DKbC	1819	D6
Creekstone Ct NE	CobC	1529	B4
	CobC	1597	D2
Creekstone Dr NW	GwnC	1602	B3
Creekstone Ln SE	SMYR	1738	E6
Creekstone Pl NW	GwnC	1602	B3
Creekstone Wy NE	CobC	1529	B4
	CobC	1597	C2
Creek Valley Ct SW	ATLN	1973	C6
Creek Valley Dr SE	CobC	1738	B2
	SMYR	1738	B2
Creekview Cir	DKbC	1819	A6
	FulC	2146	A3
	RVDL	2147	E7
Creekview Ct	DKbC	1819	A6
	RVDL	2147	E7
E Creekview Ct	ClyC	2151	A5
W Creekview Ct	ClyC	2151	A5
Creek View Ct NE	CobC	1529	D2
Creekview Dr	DKbC	1819	B6
Creekview Dr NE	CobC	1597	C4
Creek View Mnr NE	DKbC	1670	D5
Creekview Pl	DKbC	1819	A6
Creekview Tr SE	SMYR	1738	E6
Creekway Cross SE	SMYR	1738	E6
Creekway Ct	CobC	1526	A4
Creekway Dr	CobC	1526	A4
	DKbC	1980	B6
Creekway Ln	CobC	1526	A4
	DKbC	1980	B6
Creekwood Cross E	RSWL	1531	D3
Creekwood Cross W	RSWL	1531	D3
Creekwood Ct NE	CobC	1597	B2
Creekwood Dr NE	CobC	1597	B3
Creekwood Ter	DKbC	1893	B3
Creekwood Tr NE	CobC	1596	E3
Creek Wood Close NE	ATLN	1742	B1
	FulC	1742	B1
Creel Dr	ClyC	2147	C6
Creighton Av	DKbC	1818	E7
Creighton Rd SW	ATLN	1974	A4
Crepe Myrtle Cir SE	SMYR	1738	D2
Crescendo Dr NW	ATLN	1888	D1
Crescent Av NE	ATLN	1815	D7
Crescent Cir	DKbC	1600	E7
Crescent Cir SW	MRTA	1595	A5
Crescent Dr NE	CobC	1527	A1
Crescent Dr NW	GwnC	1673	E3
Crescent Wk	DKbC	1818	D1
Crescent Center Pkwy	DKbC	1745	A6
Crescent Centre Blvd	DKbC	1745	A6
	DKbC	1819	A1
Crescent Ct Dr	DCTR	1817	E6
Crescent Ridge Dr	RSWL	1532	B1
Crescent Ridge Tr SE	SMYR	1738	C6
Crescentwood Ln	DKbC	1893	E3
Cresent Hill Ln	RSWL	1532	C1
Cresson Dr SW	CobC	1666	A5
Cress Wy Dr	DKbC	2065	E1
Cress Wy Run	DKbC	2065	E1
Crest Wy	UNCT	2145	C6
Cresta Ct	RSWL	1530	E1
Cresta Dr	DKbC	1892	E7
	DKbC	1978	E1
Crest Brook Ln	RSWL	1530	B1
Crestcliff Ct	DKbC	1745	B5
Crestcliff Dr	DKbC	1745	B4
Crestdale Cir SE	DKbC	1978	A3
Cresthaven Approach SE	SMYR	1812	D1
Cresthill Av NE	ATLN	1816	B7
Crestknoll Cir	DKbC	1980	A2
Crest Knoll Dr SW	CobC	1738	A6
Crestknoll Wy	DKbC	1980	A2
Crestlane Dr SE	CobC	1739	C1
Crestline Ct NE	DKbC	1743	E6
Crestline Dr NE	DKbC	1743	E6
	DKbC	1744	A6
Crestline Pkwy NE	FulC	1670	D1
Crestline Ter NW	GwnC	1602	A6
Crest Ln Dr SE	CobC	1739	D3
Crestmont Ln SW	ATLN	1888	C7
	ATLN	1974	C1
Crestmoore Dr	DKbC	1893	D7
Crest Oaks Pl NE	DKbC	1744	A7
Creston Dr	DRVL	1672	C4
Creston Wy	ClyC	2150	D5
Crest Park Ln NE	CobC	1529	C6
Crestridge Ct	DKbC	1819	E7
Crestridge Dr	ClyC	2147	D3
Crestridge Dr NE	ATLN	1816	C7
Crestridge Dr SE	MRTA	1596	A6
Crestridge Ln	DKbC	1819	E7
Crestridge Pl NE	DKbC	1743	E6
Crestvale Pl NE	DKbC	1743	E7
Crest Valley Dr NW	FulC	1668	E7
Crest Valley Rd NW	FulC	1669	B5
Crestview Av	DKbC	1892	D6
	DKbC	1893	A6
Crestview Cir	RSWL	1530	D1
Crestview Ct	DKbC	2065	E4
Crestview Dr SE	SMYR	1738	D2
Crestview Ln	ClyC	2149	C6
Crestway Av NE	MRTA	1595	D1
Crestwicke Trc NE	FulC	1670	D7
Crestwicke Pointe NE	FulC	1670	D7
Crestwood Cir	FulC	2146	D5
Crestwood Dr SE	DKbC	1891	E7
Crestwood Ln SE	CobC	1739	E3
Crestwood Rd SE	SMYR	1666	D7
Crew St SW	ATLN	1890	E7
	ATLN	1976	E1
Crider Rd SE	CobC	1666	A3
Crimson Rose Ln NE	CobC	1527	D2
Crique Wy	RSWL	1531	C1
Cristie Dr	ClyC	2150	E5
Crockett Ct	DKbC	1818	B4
Crockett Dr SE	CobC	1596	D6
Croesus Av NW	ATLN	1889	B3
Croft Ct	FulC	1533	C3
Croft Pl NW	ATLN	1888	A1
Croft St NW	CobC	1595	A2
Crogman St SE	ATLN	1976	E3
Crompton Ct N	FulC	1601	B3
Cromwell Ct	FulC	1533	A3
Cromwell Rd NE	FulC	1669	E1
Crooked Creek Ct	ClyC	2150	E7
Crooked Creek Ct SE	CobC	1812	D2
Crooked Creek Ln	ClyC	2151	C6
Crooked Creek Rd NW	GwnC	1602	B4
Crooked Tree Ct NE	CobC	1528	B3
Crosby Dr NW	ATLN	1888	A1
Cross Ln	DKbC	1980	E1
Cross Rd SE	ATLN	2063	A1
Cross St NW	ATLN	1889	A1
Crossbridge Al	FulC	1532	E1
Cross Creek Pkwy NW	ATLN	1814	E2
Cross Gate Ct NE	CobC	1597	C4
Cross Gate Ct NW	FulC	1669	E4
Cross Gate Dr NE	CobC	1597	C4
Cross Gate Dr NW	FulC	1669	D4
N Crossing Cir NE	DKbC	1817	C1
Crossing Dr	DKbC	1743	B2
N Crossing Dr NE	DKbC	1817	C1
Crossing Pk NW	GwnC	1602	C5
N Crossing Wy	DKbC	1817	E3
Crossings Ct	DKbC	1894	C3
Crossings Wy	DKbC	1894	C3
Crossing Valley Ln NW	FulC	1668	E4
S Cross Keys Dr NE	DKbC	1743	A2
Cross Keys Dr NE	DKbC	1743	A2
Cross Roads Ct NW	FulC	1669	A5
Cross Roads Ln NW	FulC	1669	A5
Cross Roads Mnr NW	FulC	1669	A5
Crosstree Ln NW	FulC	1598	C6
Crossway Dr NE	DKbC	1743	B2
Crosswind Rd	CGPK	2061	B6
Crosswycke Forest Cir NE	DKbC	1742	E3
Crosswycke Forest Ct NE	DKbC	1742	E3
Crosswycke Forest Dr NE	DKbC	1742	E1
Crow Ct	ClyC	2151	B6
Crowe Dr SE	CobC	1739	B7
Crown Rd SE	ATLN	2062	D4
Crown Rd SE SR-3	ATLN	2062	D4
Crown Rd SE US-19	ATLN	2062	D4
Crown Rd SE US-41	ATLN	2062	D4
Crown Ter NE	MRTA	1526	E7
Crown Mill Ct NE	CobC	1596	E3
Crown Point Ct	DKbC	1894	A7
Crown Point Pl	DKbC	1894	A7
Crown Pointe Pkwy	DKbC	1599	E7
	DKbC	1670	E1
Croydon Ln	FulC	1533	E1
Cruise Ct	RSWL	1531	C4
Crumley St SE	ATLN	1890	E6
Crumley St SW	ATLN	1890	C6
Crystal Ln	ClyC	2147	C3
Crystal Green Ct	FulC	2146	D6
Crystal Lake Rd	ClyC	2147	E3
	ClyC	2148	A3
Culberson St SW	ATLN	1890	A6
Cullen Copse	FulC	1532	D3
Cullingworth Dr	FulC	1533	E1
Culpepper St NW	ATLN	1815	A6
Culver Dr	ClyC	2150	E7
Cumberland Blvd SE	CobC	1667	E7
	CobC	1668	B6
	CobC	1739	D1
	SMYR	1667	E7
Cumberland Cir NE	ATLN	1816	B5
Cumberland Cross SE	SMYR	1667	D7
	SMYR	1739	D1
Cumberland Ct	CMBL	1672	A7
Cumberland Ct SE	CobC	1739	D1
Cumberland Dr	ClyC	2151	D7
	CMBL	1672	A6
Cumberland Dr SE	CobC	1739	C2
	SMYR	1739	C2
Cumberland Pkwy SE	CobC	1739	E2
	SMYR	1739	C5
Cumberland Pl NE	ATLN	1816	B5
Cumberland Pl SE	CobC	1739	C2
Cumberland Rd	EPNT	2060	C3
Cumberland Rd NE	ATLN	1816	D5
Cumberland Sq SE	SMYR	1667	E7
Cumberland Wy SE	SMYR	1667	D7
Cumberland Club Cir SE	CobC	1739	D1
Cumberland Club Dr SE	CobC	1739	E2
Cumberland Gate SE	SMYR	1667	D7
	SMYR	1739	D1
Cumberland Glen Ln SE	CobC	1667	D5
	SMYR	1667	D5
Cumberland Mall SE	CobC	1667	E7
	CobC	1739	E1
Cumberland Point Dr SE	MRTA	1667	C3
Cumberland Valley Dr SE	SMYR	1667	B7
Cumberland Valley Pl SE	SMYR	1667	B7
Cumming Dr SW	ATLN	1975	E3
Cummings Dr SW	ATLN	1975	B2
Cummings St SE	ATLN	1891	C5
Cunningham Pl SW	ATLN	1890	A5
Cupit Close	FulC	1532	D3
Curlew Ct NW	FulC	1669	B4
Curling Stone Pl	FulC	1532	E3
Curran St NW	ATLN	1815	C7
Currie Ct	FTPK	2063	B6
Currie Dr	FTPK	2063	B6
Currier Pl NE	ATLN	1891	A2
Currier St NE	ATLN	1890	E2
	ATLN	1891	A2
Currin Ct	RSWL	1532	A6
Curry Ct NE	CobC	1598	D1
Curtis Dr	FTPK	2063	D7
Curtis Dr NE	DKbC	1742	E5
	DKbC	1743	A6
Cushman Cir SW	ATLN	1888	C4
Custer Av SE	ATLN	1977	D2
	DKbC	1977	D2
Custer St	HPVL	2062	A3
Custer St NE	MRTA	1595	C3
Custis Ct	DKbC	1599	E7
Cuthbert St NE	MRTA	1595	B3
Cutler Rdg SE	SMYR	1739	B3
Cutstone Ct	ClyC	2147	D5
Cutwater Tr NW	FulC	1598	D6
Cynthia Ct NE	CobC	1527	E2
Cynthia Dr NE	DKbC	1743	B1
Cynthia Ln	FTPK	2149	A4
Cypress Av	ClyC	2150	C3
Cypress Ct	FTPK	2149	C4
Cypress Dr	FTPK	2149	C4
Cypress St NE	ATLN	1815	E7
	ATLN	1890	E1
Cypress Pointe Dr	UNCT	2145	A7
Cypress Pointe St	FulC	1532	D6

D

Street	City	Map #	Grid
N D Av	FTPK	2064	B7
D & B Dr SE	MRTA	1667	D2
Dabney Rd SE	CobC	1739	C4
Dabney Ter	EPNT	1975	A7
Daffodil Dr NE	CobC	1527	E7
Daffodil Ln NW	GwnC	1601	E1
Dahlgreen St SE	ATLN	1891	E5
Dahlia Av NW	ATLN	1889	A3
Dairy Wy NW	GwnC	1532	E7
Daisy Dr	DKbC	1894	B6
Dale Dr NE	ATLN	1742	C6
	CobC	1596	E5
Dale Dr SE	ATLN	1977	C3
Dale Ln SW	ATLN	1974	B5
Dale Pl	DKbC	1893	C7
Dale Rd	ClyC	2151	B7
Dale Creek Dr NW	ATLN	1888	D2
Dalerose Av	DKbC	1893	C1
Daleview Dr SE	ATLN	1976	E4
Dalewood Dr NE	DKbC	1817	A2
Daley Ct	ClyC	2150	D6
Dalhouise Ln	DKbC	2066	C1
Dalhousie Pl NE	CobC	1529	B6
Dallas St NE	ATLN	1891	B2
Dalmer Rd NE	FulC	1670	A7
	FulC	1742	B1
Dalney St NW	ATLN	1815	D7
Dalon Rd NE	DKbC	1816	E4
Dalrymple Rd NE	FulC	1598	E4
Dalton St SE	ATLN	1977	A1
Daltree Ct NE	CobC	1597	B4
Dalvigney St NW	ATLN	1890	B1
Damar Rd NE	MRTA	1595	C2
Dameron Cir SW	ATLN	1888	B5
Damon Ct	DKbC	1600	B5
Damon Pl	DKbC	1600	C5
Dan Dr	ClyC	2150	D5
Dan Pl SE	CobC	1738	B1
	SMYR	1738	B1
Danbridge Wy	RSWL	1531	E5

INDEX 19

Danbury Ct — Atlanta Street Index — Dewey Av

STREET	City	Map #	Grid
Danbury Ct	ClyC	2150	C5
Danbury Ct NW	GwnC	1673	E4
Danbury Dr NW	GwnC	1673	E4
Danbury Ln	DKbC	1819	C7
Danbury Ln NW	FulC	1669	D7
	GwnC	1673	E4
Danby Ct	DKbC	1745	B2
Danbyshire Ct NE	DKbC	1744	D3
Dancing Fox Rd	DKbC	1892	D6
Dandelion Cir NE	CobC	1598	B4
Danforth Ct NE	CobC	1528	C6
Danforth Dr NE	CobC	1528	C6
Danforth Ln	DKbC	1818	B1
Danforth Rd SW	FulC	1887	B7
	FulC	1973	C1
Daniel Av	ATLN	1892	E7
	DKbC	1892	E7
Daniel Av NE	ATLN	1892	E4
	DCTR	1892	E4
Daniel Av SE	ATLN	1892	E5
	DKbC	1892	E5
Daniel Dr SE	CobC	1666	D4
	SMYR	1666	D4
Daniel Rd SW	ATLN	1973	E6
Daniel St SE	ATLN	1891	B4
	CobC	1739	B4
	SMYR	1739	B4
Daniel Green Ct SE	SMYR	1739	B4
Daniel Green Tr SE	CobC	1739	B4
	SMYR	1739	B4
Daniell Dr SE	CobC	1738	E2
	SMYR	1738	E2
Danielle Ct NE	CobC	1527	D2
Dan Johnson Rd NE	DKbC	1817	A7
Danner Dr	HryC	2152	A2
Danner St SE	ATLN	1977	D1
Danrich Dr	DKbC	1894	C6
Danrich Pl	DKbC	1894	C6
Dansford Ct NE	CobC	1528	D7
Danube Rd NE	ATLN	1742	B2
Danvers Wk SE	SMYR	1739	A2
Dara Dr NE	CobC	1526	E1
Darbytown Ct SE	CobC	1740	A4
Dargan Pl SW	ATLN	1890	A5
Darlington Cir NE	ATLN	1742	B7
Darlington Rd NE	ATLN	1742	B7
Darlington Oak Dr	DRVL	1672	E3
Darnell Rd SE	CobC	1666	B2
Daron Ct	DKbC	2066	C3
Darrah Ct SW	ATLN	2060	A1
Darrah Dr SW	ATLN	1974	A7
	ATLN	2060	A1
Darrah Wy SW	ATLN	2060	A1
Darrell Dr NE	CobC	1526	B5
Dartford Dr	DKbC	1600	E5
Dartington Wy	FulC	1533	B1
Dartmoor Cir NE	FulC	1599	A5
Dartmoor Dr NE	CobC	1598	A4
Dartmouth Av	AVES	1893	C1
Dartmouth Dr SW	ATLN	1887	E3
Dartmouth Wy NE	CobC	1528	C7
Darwen Ct	DKbC	1819	E1
Darwen Ln	DKbC	1819	E1
Darwin Rd SE	CobC	1666	C3
Data Dr NW	GwnC	1602	C2
Dauphine St	EPNT	1975	D5
Davage St SW	ATLN	1976	D2
Davana Dr	DKbC	2066	A4
Davantry Ct	DKbC	1600	E5
Davantry Dr	DKbC	1600	E5
Davenport St SE	SMYR	1667	B6
Daventry Wy NE	DKbC	1742	E1
David Cir	DKbC	1893	E4
David Dr	ClyC	2063	C5
David Pl SE	SMYR	1738	E5
David Rd	DKbC	1672	E7
	DKbC	1673	A7
Davidson Av NE	ATLN	1742	D1
Davidson Rd NE	CobC	1598	C3
Davie Cir SE	CobC	1667	B6
Da Vinci Blvd	DKbC	1979	E3
Da Vinci Cres	DKbC	1979	E3
Da Vinci Ct	DKbC	1979	E3
Davinci Ct NW	GwnC	1602	E1
Davis Av	EPNT	1975	D6
Davis Cir NW	ATLN	1815	A4
Davis Cir SW	MRTA	1595	A7
Davis Ct	CGPK	2061	A4
Davis Dr	FTPK	2149	A2
Davis Dr NW	FulC	1669	A7
Davis Dr SE	CobC	1666	E6
	SMYR	1666	E6
Davis Ln SE	MRTA	1667	B3
Davis Pl NW	ATLN	1815	A4
Davis Pl SW	MRTA	1595	A7
Davis Rd NE	CobC	1527	E1
Davis Rd SE	CobC	1666	E5
	SMYR	1666	E5
E Davis St	DCTR	1892	E3
W Davis St	DCTR	1892	E3
Davis St NW	ATLN	1815	A4
Davis St SE	SMYR	1666	E7
Dawes Av SE	ATLN	1893	A6
	DKbC	1893	A6
Dawn Ct	DKbC	1979	A2
Dawn Dr	DKbC	1979	A1
Dawn View Ln NW	ATLN	1741	A7
Dawson Blvd NW	DKbC	1673	B4
Day Tr N	DKbC	2066	C2
Day Tr S	DKbC	2066	C2
Dayna Dr	ClyC	2148	A5
Dayron Cir NE	CobC	1527	D5
Dayron Ct NE	CobC	1527	D5
Dayron Trc NE	CobC	1527	D5
Daytona Ct	ClyC	2149	B6
Day Trail Ct	DKbC	2066	C2
Deacon Ln	DKbC	1672	A3
Dean Cir SE	MRTA	1596	B5
Dean Dr NW	ATLN	1815	A2
Dean Ovlk NW	ATLN	1815	A2
Deann Dr	ClyC	2150	D4
Deans Wy	ClyC	2150	B6
Dearborn Plz	HPVL	2062	C3
Dearborn St SE	ATLN	1892	B5
	DKbC	1892	B5
De Arc Pl NW	ATLN	1815	C2
Dearing Ct SE	CobC	1812	C6
Dearing St	FTPK	2149	C2
Dearwood Dr SW	ATLN	1976	C7
	ATLN	2062	E1
Dease Dr	ClyC	2151	A5
Deauville Ct NW	ATLN	1814	B5
Debbie Sue Ln	ClyC	2150	B7
Debden Pl	DKbC	1819	E2
Debelle Ct	CLKN	1819	B4
	DKbC	1819	B4
Debelle St	CLKN	1819	B4
Deborah Dr NE	DKbC	1744	B6
Deborah Dr NW	GwnC	1673	B1
Debra Dr NE	CobC	1526	C4
Debra Dr SE	CobC	1739	A2
Debra Ln NE	CobC	1527	C2
Decatur Av	DKbC	1818	D6
N Decatur Ln	DKbC	1818	B5
Decatur Rd	ClyC	2151	A3
N Decatur Rd	DCTR	1817	E6
	DKbC	1817	E6
	DKbC	1819	A6
N Decatur Rd NE	DKbC	1816	E6
	DKbC	1817	C6
Decatur St SE	ATLN	1890	E4
	ATLN	1891	A4
Deckner Av SW	ATLN	1976	C2
Declair Dr NE	DKbC	1817	A2
Declaire Ct NW	FulC	1669	D3
Declaire Wy NE	CobC	1598	B4
Dedee Ct	DKbC	1745	C4
Deep Creek Dr NE	CobC	1596	D4
Deep Shoals Cir	DKbC	1979	A3
Deep Woods Wy NE	CobC	1527	D4
Deer Creek Tr SE	CobC	1666	A5
Deere St	HryC	2152	B4
Deerfield Cir	DKbC	1744	B7
Deerfield Ct	ClyC	2150	D5
	FulC	2146	D4
Deerfield Ln	FulC	2146	D4
Deerfield Tr	FulC	2146	D4
Deerfield Tr SE	CobC	1812	A3
E Deerhollow Wy NW	GwnC	1601	E3
W Deerhollow Wy NW	GwnC	1601	E3
Deering Rd NW	ATLN	1815	C5
Deering Tr NE	CobC	1529	D7
Deerings Dr NW	GwnC	1601	E2
Deerings Hllw NW	GwnC	1601	E3
Deerings Ln NW	GwnC	1601	E3
Deer Park Rd NE	DKbC	1817	D1
Deer Pass Wy	DKbC	1980	D1
Deer Pause Ln	DKbC	2065	E1
Deer Run Rd	HryC	2066	D7
	HryC	2152	D1
Deer Springs Ct	DKbC	1979	A7
Deer Springs Pkwy	DKbC	1979	A7
Deer Springs Rd	DKbC	1978	E7
	DKbC	2065	A1
Deer Springs Tr	DKbC	1978	E7
Deerview Tr NE	CobC	1527	A2
Deerwood Cir SE	SMYR	1738	A4
Deerwood Ct SE	SMYR	1738	A4
Deerwood Dr	DKbC	1893	B4
Deerwood Pkwy SE	SMYR	1738	A4
Deerwood Tr NE	CobC	1527	E4
Defoor Av NW	ATLN	1814	E3
Defoor Cir NW	ATLN	1815	A4
Defoor Pl NW	ATLN	1815	A4
Defoor Hills Rd NW	ATLN	1814	D2
Defoors Cross NW	ATLN	1814	D3
Defoors Ct NW	ATLN	1814	D3
Defoors Dr NW	ATLN	1815	A3
Defoors Lndg NW	ATLN	1815	A4
Defoors Wk NW	ATLN	1814	D4
Defoors Ferry Rd NW	ATLN	1814	D2
Defoors Mill Cir NW	ATLN	1814	D3
Defoors Mill Ct NW	ATLN	1814	D3
Defoors Mill Dr NW	ATLN	1814	D3
Defoors Mill Pl NW	ATLN	1814	D3
Defoors Mill Wy NW	ATLN	1814	D3
Defoor Village Ct NW	ATLN	1814	E3
Degress Av NE	ATLN	1891	D3
Deidra Dr SE	CobC	1812	B3
Dejarnette Dr	EPNT	2060	E1
DeKalb Av NE	ATLN	1891	C4
	DCTR	1892	B3
	DKbC	1892	B3
DeKalb Dr	DKbC	1892	E6
N DeKalb Dr	DKbC	1672	D4
	DRVL	1672	D4
DeKalb Pl	ATLN	1892	C2
DeKalb Industrial Wy	DKbC	1818	B5
DeKalb Technology Pkwy	DKbC	1672	C7
Delachaise Wy NW	NRCS	1602	E4
Delacoure Dr NE	CobC	1526	B3
Delamere Ln	ClyC	2151	D6
Deland Rd	DKbC	1745	D3
Delano Dr	DKbC	1893	B5
Delano Dr NE	ATLN	1892	B4
Delano Rd	FulC	2059	E7
	FulC	2145	E1
Delaware Av NE	ATLN	1892	B2
Delaware Av SE	ATLN	1891	D7
Delbridge St NW	ATLN	1890	B3
Delcourt Dr	DKbC	1818	C2
Deleher Ct SE	CobC	1978	C4
De Leon Ct	DKbC	1818	E3
De Leon Dr	DKbC	1818	E3
De Leon Ln	DKbC	1818	E3
De Leon St NE	ATLN	1816	C7
Delevan St SW	ATLN	1976	C1
Delford Ct SE	SMYR	1739	A6
Delford Wy SE	SMYR	1739	A7
Delft Wy	FulC	1532	E4
Delia Ct	DKbC	1818	E1
Delia Dr	DKbC	1818	E2
Delk Rd SE	CobC	1667	B2
	MRTA	1667	D2
Delk Rd SE SR-280	CobC	1667	B2
	MRTA	1667	B2
Delk St SE	MRTA	1595	B6
Delk Industrial Blvd SE	MRTA	1667	C1
Dell Av SE	SMYR	1738	D1
Della St SE	CobC	1668	A1
Dellfield Ct	DKbC	1600	D3
Dellinger Ct NE	CobC	1528	A7
Dellinger Dr NE	CobC	1527	E7
Dellrose Ct	DKbC	1601	B4
Dellrose Dr	DKbC	1601	A4
Dellwood Cir	LKCY	2150	A3
Dellwood Dr NW	ATLN	1815	D1
Dellwood Pl	DKbC	1893	C7
Delmar Av SE	ATLN	1891	B7
Delmar Ct SE	ATLN	1891	C7
Delmar Ln NW	ATLN	1888	C4
Del Monico Dr	DKbC	1893	D5
Delmont Dr NE	ATLN	1741	D4
Delmont Ter	RSWL	1530	E1
Delmoor Ct NW	ATLN	1888	C3
Delmoor Dr NW	ATLN	1888	C3
Delores Wy	FTPK	2149	D1
Delowe Dr	EPNT	1975	B6
	EPNT	2061	B1
Delowe Dr SW	ATLN	1975	A2
Delowe Pl SW	ATLN	1975	B4
Delowe-Stanton Access Rd	ATLN	1975	B4
	EPNT	1975	B4
Delphine Dr	DKbC	1892	D7
Delphine Wy	DKbC	1892	D7
Del Ray Ct	DKbC	1979	E1
Delray Dr NW	ATLN	1813	D5
Del Rio Ter	DKbC	1894	B4
Delta Blvd	FulC	2062	A4
Delta Cir NE	MRTA	1595	D3
Delta Cir SE	CobC	1812	B7
Delta Ct SE	CobC	1887	B1
Delta Dr	EPNT	2061	E2
Delta Pl NE	ATLN	1891	C4
	MRTA	1595	D3
Delverton Ct	DKbC	1601	A6
Delverton Dr	DKbC	1601	A6
Demere Dr	ClyC	2150	C7
Demetra Dr SE	CobC	1738	B7
Demorest Av NE	ATLN	1815	E1
Denards Mill Rd SE	CobC	1597	C7
Dencrest Ct SE	SMYR	1739	A1
Denham St	RVDL	2148	B7
Denise Dr	DKbC	1894	E5
Denison Dr	DKbC	1819	C3
Denmead Ml SE	CobC	1668	C1
Denmead St NW	MRTA	1595	C7
Dennington Ct SE	SMYR	1738	A4
Dennis Dr	DKbC	1894	B4
	FTPK	2063	C7
	HryC	2152	C6
Dennis St	FTPK	2063	C7
Denny Dr	ClyC	2147	B3
Densley Dr	DKbC	1817	E5
Denson Blvd	ClyC	2150	C4
Denton Cir NW	GwnC	1602	B1
Denton Pl NE	CobC	1529	B1
Denton Walk Ct NE	CobC	1529	B6
Denville Tr SW	ATLN	1974	A2
DePauw Wy	DKbC	2066	D1
Depot St NW	MRTA	1595	C6
Derby Dr SW	ATLN	1975	B4
Derby Ln SE	SMYR	1738	C5
Derby Country Dr	HryC	2151	E3
Derbyshire Ct NW	NRCS	1673	E1
Deren Wy NE	DKbC	1744	D5
Dering Cir NE	DKbC	1743	D3
Dering Ct NE	DKbC	1743	E3
Derrick Jones Rd	ClyC	2148	A2
Derrill Dr	DKbC	1893	E6
Derringer Wy	DKbC	1894	B5
Derry Av SW	ATLN	1889	C5
Derry St	FTPK	2063	C7
	FTPK	2149	C1
Derry Brooke Wk SE	SMYR	1739	A7
Derrydown Wy	DCTR	1893	B2
	DKbC	1893	B2
Desert Cir	EPNT	2060	B4
Desert Dr	EPNT	2060	C4
N Desert Dr	EPNT	2060	B2
Deshler St SW	ATLN	1975	E4
Desmond Dr	DKbC	1817	D5
Desoto Av SW	ATLN	1976	B2
Desoto St NW	ATLN	1890	A3
Desoto Falls Ct SW	ATLN	1974	C2
Despoilation Al	DKbC	1744	A2
Destiny Dr SE	CobC	1812	B5
Detroit Av NW	ATLN	1889	B2
Detroit Ct NW	ATLN	1889	C2
Deverell St	FulC	1533	B4
Devereux Ct	DKbC	1600	B6
N Devereux Ct NW	FulC	1669	A4
Devilla Ct	FulC	2146	B6
Devilla Trc	FulC	2146	B6
Devin Cir NE	DKbC	1670	E7
Devoe Ct NE	CobC	1528	B5
Devon Ln	AVES	1893	D2
Devonash Ln	DKbC	1600	A7
Devon Chase Rd	FulC	2146	A4
Devonshire Av	DCTR	1892	D2
Devonshire Ct	DKbC	1600	B7
Devonshire Ct NW	GwnC	1673	D5
Devonshire Pl NW	ATLN	1741	A6
Devonshire Rd	DKbC	1600	B7
Devonshire Wy	DKbC	1600	B7
Devonwood Ct	DKbC	1819	D1
Devonwood Dr NE	FulC	1598	D5
Dewberry Cir NE	MRTA	1596	A3
Dewberry Ln	EPNT	1975	B5
Dewberry Tr NE	MRTA	1596	A4
Dewdrop Ct	FulC	1533	D1
Dewey Av	EPNT	1974	E5

INDEX 20

Dewey Ln SE

Atlanta Street Index

Dunning St SE

STREET	City	Map #	Grid
Dewey Ln SE	CobC	1666	A6
Dewey St SW	ATLN	1890	C7
Dewfield Ct	FulC	1533	D2
Dewpoint Ln	FulC	1533	E1
Dial Dr	DKbC	1819	B6
Dial Wy	DKbC	1819	B6
Diamond Av SE	DKbC	1978	A2
Diamond Cir	DKbC	2066	C1
Diamond Head Cir	DKbC	1818	B1
Diamond Head Ct	DKbC	1818	B1
Diamond Head Dr	DKbC	1818	C1
Diana Dr SW	ATLN	1976	B7
	ATLN	2062	B1
N Diane Ct SE	SMYR	1738	D4
S Diane Ct SE	SMYR	1738	D4
Diane Dr NW	GwnC	1673	A2
Diane Dr SE	CobC	1666	A7
Diann Ct	FulC	2059	B6
Diann Dr	FulC	2059	B6
Dianne Ct SE	DKbC	1978	B2
Dickerson Dr SE	CobC	1813	A3
Dickerson Rd SE	CobC	1597	E4
Dickey Dr	DKbC	1817	B6
Dickson Ct NE	CobC	1526	A7
Dickson Dr	MRTA	1526	B6
Dickson Pl NE	ATLN	1816	A7
Dickson Rd NE	CobC	1526	A7
	MRTA	1526	B6
Dickson St NE	DKbC	1670	E7
	DKbC	1742	E1
Dietz Av SW	ATLN	1975	E3
Dilbeck Pl NE	ATLN	1742	A1
Dill Av SW	ATLN	1976	A2
Dillard Cross	DKbC	1745	E5
Dillard Rd	DKbC	1745	E5
Dillard Wy	DKbC	1745	E6
Dillon St NW	ATLN	1815	A7
Dimmock St SW	ATLN	1890	A7
	ATLN	1976	A1
Dink Ln SE	CobC	1666	B4
Dior Dr NE	CobC	1527	B6
Discovery Blvd SE	CobC	1812	D6
Discovery Pl SE	CobC	1812	C7
Dividend Dr SE	MRTA	1667	D2
Division St NW	ATLN	1890	A2
Division St SW	ATLN	1976	A2
E Dixie Av SE	MRTA	1595	B6
W Dixie Av SE	MRTA	1595	A6
W Dixie Av SE SR-5	MRTA	1595	B6
Dixie Av NE	ATLN	1891	C3
Dixie Av SE	CobC	1666	D3
	SMYR	1666	D4
Dixie St SE	ATLN	1892	A4
Dixie Hills Cir NW	ATLN	1889	C3
Dixie Industrial Dr	LKCY	2149	E3
Dixie Lake Rd	UNCT	2145	A6
Dixie Lee Ln	DKbC	1819	E6
Dixon St	DKbC	1818	E6
Dixon Lake Dr SE	SMYR	1739	A6
Doane St SW	ATLN	1890	D7
Dobbins Pl SE	CobC	1667	A2
Dobbs Cir NW	ATLN	1814	E1
Dobbs Cross	CobC	1598	A1
Dobbs Dr	RSWL	1530	D2
Dobbs Dr SE	DKbC	1977	E5
Dobbs St NE	MRTA	1595	A4
Dobbs St NW	ATLN	1889	D1
	MRTA	1595	C6
Dobbs Wy	EPNT	2061	B1
Dock Ct NW	GwnC	1533	E5
Docs Creek Ct NW	NRCS	1602	D5
Dodd Av SW	ATLN	1890	D7
Dodd St SE	MRTA	1595	D5
Dodge St SE	SMYR	1666	D5
Dodson Dr	ATLN	1974	E6
	EPNT	1974	E6
	EPNT	2060	D1
Dodson Dr SW	ATLN	1974	E3
Dodson Rd	UNCT	2145	A5
Dodson Ter	EPNT	2060	E2
Dodson Ter SW	ATLN	1974	D4
Dodson Drive Connector	CGPK	2060	E1
	EPNT	2060	E1
Dodson Lee Dr	EPNT	1974	D7
	EPNT	2060	D1
Doerun Ct NW	GwnC	1533	C6
Doeskin Ct SE	SMYR	1738	B4
Doeskin Ln SE	SMYR	1738	A4
Doeskin Tr SE	SMYR	1738	B4
Dogleg Ct	RSWL	1601	B1
Dogwood Cir NW	NRCS	1602	D5
Dogwood Cir SE	CobC	1738	E2
	SMYR	1738	E2
Dogwood Ct SW	ATLN	1888	E5
Dogwood Dr	EPNT	1974	D7
	EPNT	2060	D2
	HPVL	2062	B3
Dogwood Dr SR-3	HPVL	2062	B3
Dogwood Dr US-19	HPVL	2062	B3
Dogwood Dr US-41	HPVL	2062	B3
N Dogwood Dr NE	CobC	1526	D5
Dogwood Dr NE	MRTA	1596	B4
Dogwood Dr NW	ATLN	1813	C7
Dogwood Dr SW	ATLN	1889	A4
Dogwood Ln	ClyC	2147	E4
Dogwood Ln NE	DKbC	1743	E6
Dogwood Ln NW	GwnC	1673	D6
Dogwood Pl	DKbC	1980	E7
Dogwood Pl NE	MRTA	1595	E1
Dogwood Rd	RSWL	1531	A3
Dogwood St	CGPK	2061	D2
Dogwood Ter NE	CobC	1527	A1
	DKbC	1743	A3
Dogwood Tr	DKbC	1980	E7
Dogwood Tr SE	CobC	1598	A6
Dogwood Trc	DKbC	1980	E7
Dogwood Wy	DCTR	1817	D6
Dogwood Farm Rd	DKbC	1980	E7
	DKbC	2066	E1
Dogwood Farms Dr	DKbC	1980	E7
	DKbC	2066	E1
Dogwood Forest Dr NE	CobC	1597	B1
Dogwood Lake Ct	RSWL	1532	A5
Dogwood Point Ln NW	GwnC	1673	D6
Dogwood Valley Ct NE	CobC	1597	B1
Dogwood Valley Dr NE	FulC	1670	B5
Dogwood Walk Ln NW	NRCS	1602	D5
Dollar Mill Ct SW	ATLN	1887	D5
Dollar Mill Rd SW	ATLN	1887	D5
Dollar Mill Wy SW	ATLN	1887	D6
Dolphin Dr SW	ATLN	1975	A1
Dominion Wy	FulC	1532	D4
Donald Dr NE	CobC	1527	B6
Donald Lee Hollowell Pkwy NW	ATLN	1813	B5
D L Hollowell Pkwy NW SR-8	ATLN	1813	B5
D L Hollowell Pkwy NW US-78	ATLN	1813	B5
D L Hollowell Pkwy NW US-278	ATLN	1813	B5
Donaldson Ct NE	DKbC	1671	B5
Donaldson Dr	CMBL	1671	C5
Donaldson Dr NE	DKbC	1671	B5
Donavan Ct	DKbC	1980	B5
Donavan Wy	DKbC	1980	B5
Doncaster Ct SE	CobC	1738	B6
Doncaster Dr NE	ATLN	1815	E5
Donegal SE	CobC	1667	E5
Donegal Ct	DKbC	1745	C3
Donegal Dr	UNCT	2145	B6
Don Griffith Dr	DCTR	1892	E1
Don Hastings Dr	ClyC	2148	E6
Don Juan Cir	CMBL	1671	E7
Don Juan Ln	DKbC	1893	B7
Donna Ct	ClyC	2065	A5
Donna Pl	DKbC	1892	D7
Donnalee St SE	DKbC	1892	C6
Donna Lynn Dr SE	SMYR	1667	A7
Donnas Cove Dr SE	CobC	1666	C4
	SMYR	1666	C4
Donnebrook Ln SE	ATLN	2063	B2
Donnelly Av SW	ATLN	1889	E6
Donzi Ln SE	DKbC	1977	E2
Dooley Dr	DKbC	1817	D5
N Doolin Dr	RSWL	1531	D6
S Doolin Dr	RSWL	1531	E6
Dora Dr SE	CobC	1738	A3
Dora St SW	ATLN	1890	B5
Dorado Cir SE	CobC	1597	E7
Doral Cir	DRVL	1672	C4
Doral Cir SE	CobC	1598	A6
Doral Ct	DRVL	1672	C3
Doral Ct SW	ATLN	1973	C6
Doral Dr	DRVL	1672	C4
Doral Dr SW	ATLN	1973	C6
Doral Park Dr	ATLN	2063	C4
Doran Av SE	MRTA	1595	B5
Doranne Ct SE	SMYR	1667	C6
Dorby Close NE	DKbC	1742	E2
Dorby Park Dr NE	DKbC	1742	E3
Dorchester Av NW	ATLN	1814	D4
Dorchester Dr	ClyC	2151	C6
Doreen Ct NE	DKbC	1744	B4
Doris Dr	DKbC	1978	E2
Dorita Ct	ClyC	2150	D7
Doroco Dr	DKbC	1745	B1
Dorothy Dr	DKbC	1893	C4
Dorothy Dr NE	CobC	1527	B1
Dorothy St SE	ATLN	1976	E3
Dorr Av SE	ATLN	1891	E6
Dorsey Av	EPNT	1975	A7
Dorsey Dr	FTPK	2149	B4
Dorsey Rd	HPVL	2062	C2
Dorsey Rd NE	CobC	1526	D5
	MRTA	1526	D5
Dorsey St SW	ATLN	1975	E2
Doster Dr SW	ATLN	1887	D4
Dot Dr	FulC	2145	D5
Dot St NE	MRTA	1595	E3
Dotson Ct	ClyC	2147	B5
Double Bridge Rd	ClyC	2151	A4
Doug Davis Dr	HPVL	2062	B3
E Dougherty St	DCTR	1892	D3
W Dougherty St	DCTR	1892	E2
Douglas Dr	EPNT	1975	A7
Douglas Dr SE	CobC	1738	A7
	CobC	1812	A1
Douglas St SE	ATLN	1892	C4
	DKbC	1892	C5
Douglas St SW	ATLN	1889	E4
Dove Ct	MRRW	2149	D7
Dove Dr SW	FulC	1973	A4
Dove Wy	DKbC	1818	D2
Dove Field Ct NW	GwnC	1601	E1
Dover Blvd SW	ATLN	1888	A4
Dover Ct SW	ATLN	1888	A4
Dover Rd NW	ATLN	1741	B7
Dover Cliff Wy	FulC	1533	B3
Dover Hill Pl NE	DKbC	1743	D4
Dovers Al SW	ATLN	1889	E7
	ATLN	1975	E1
Dovershire Dr NW	GwnC	1533	C6
Dovershire Trc NW	GwnC	1533	C6
Dove Valley Rd	DKbC	1894	B3
Dove Valley Wy	DKbC	1894	A3
Dowdell Dr	CMBL	1671	E6
Dowman Dr NE	DKbC	1817	B6
Downey Dr	ClyC	2147	B6
Downing Ct NE	CobC	1598	A2
Downing Ln	DKbC	1744	C7
Downing Ln NE	DKbC	1670	E4
Downing Ln NW	GwnC	1673	D5
Downing St	FulC	1533	A5
Downs Dr SW	ATLN	1975	B2
Downshire Cir	DKbC	1744	C6
Downshire Ln	DKbC	1744	C7
Downwood Cir NW	ATLN	1740	E6
Doyal Mills Ct	DKbC	1819	D5
Doyle Av SE	CobC	1812	A6
Doyle St	DKbC	1745	E1
Doyle St SE	ATLN	1892	B4
Dozier Dr NE	CobC	1526	C3
Drawbridge Dr	RVDL	2147	E7
Drawbridge Rd SE	SMYR	1739	A3
Draycott Pl NW	ATLN	1740	E7
Drayton Woods Ct	DKbC	1819	E1
Drayton Woods Dr	DKbC	1745	E7
	DKbC	1819	E1
Dr Ben Reid Dr	DKbC	1819	C7
Dresden Ct	DKbC	1743	E2
Dresden Dr NE	DKbC	1742	E3
	DKbC	1743	A3
	DKbC	1744	B2
Dresden Tr	EPNT	2060	D3
Dresden Wy	DKbC	1744	A2
Dresden Square Dr	DKbC	1744	B2
Drew Dr NW	ATLN	1814	B5
Drew Pl NW	ATLN	1814	C5
Drewry St NE	ATLN	1816	C7
Drewsbury Ct SE	SMYR	1667	C7
	SMYR	1739	C1
Drewsbury Pl SE	SMYR	1667	C7
E Drew Valley Rd NE	DKbC	1743	C4
Drew Valley Rd NE	DKbC	1743	B4
Drexel Av	DCTR	1892	D2
Drexel Ct NE	CobC	1529	B7
Drexel Ln	EPNT	2060	B4
Driftwood Pl	DCTR	1893	A3
Driftwood Ter	DCTR	1893	A3
Driftwood Tr SE	CobC	1812	B3
Driskell Av SW	CobC	1812	A1
Driver Cir	FulC	1532	D6
Driver Cir Ct	FulC	1532	D6
Drivers Cir	FulC	1532	D6
Drogheda Ln NE	MRTA	1527	A6
Drucilla Pl SE	CobC	1738	A2
	SMYR	1738	A2
Druid Cir NE	ATLN	1891	C3
Druid Lk	DKbC	1818	B3
Druid Pl NE	ATLN	1891	D2
Druid Wk	DKbC	1818	B3
Druid Chase	DKbC	1742	E7
N Druid Hills Cir	DKbC	1818	B3
W Druid Hills Dr NE	DKbC	1742	E7
N Druid Hills Rd	DKbC	1817	E3
N Druid Hills Rd NE	DKbC	1742	E4
	DKbC	1817	D2
N Druid Hills Rd NE SR-42	DKbC	1742	E7
	DKbC	1817	A1
Druid Hills Reserve Dr NE	DKbC	1743	B6
Druid Knoll Dr NE	DKbC	1742	E6
Druid Oaks NE	DKbC	1817	C1
Druid Valley Dr NE	DKbC	1817	A1
N Druid Woods Ct	DKbC	1818	B3
Drumflower Ct	DKbC	1894	D4
Drummen Ct NE	FulC	1599	B6
Drummond Pt SE	CobC	1739	E6
Drummond St SW	ATLN	1890	B4
Drury Ct	DRVL	1672	C6
Dry Creek Rd NE	CobC	1528	C1
Duberry Ct NE	DKbC	1670	E5
Dublin Dr	DKbC	1979	E1
Dublin Dr SW	FulC	1973	A5
Duchess Dr NE	CobC	1526	C5
Dudley Ct NW	FulC	1741	D1
Dudley Dr	HryC	2152	B1
Dudley Ln NW	ATLN	1741	E1
	FulC	1669	D7
	FulC	1741	E1
Duesenberg Dr	DKbC	1745	D7
Duffey Dr	MRRW	2150	A7
Duffield Dr NW	ATLN	1888	D2
Duke Dr NE	CobC	1526	C5
Duke Rd	DKbC	1743	C2
Dukehart Ct	DKbC	1894	D1
Duke of Gloucester	EPNT	2060	C3
Duke of Windsor	EPNT	2060	D2
Dumbarton Ct NW	ATLN	1741	A4
Dumbarton Rd NW	ATLN	1741	A3
Dumont Trc	RSWL	1529	E4
Dunaire Ct SW	CobC	1738	A6
Dunbar Dr	DKbC	1671	E1
Dunbar St SW	ATLN	1976	C1
Dunbar Tr SE	CobC	1739	B5
Dunbarton Trc NE	DKbC	1742	E1
Dunbery Chase SE	CobC	1597	B6
Dunbritan Ln	FulC	2147	A5
Dunbrooke Ln	DKbC	1599	E3
	DKbC	1600	A3
Duncan Dr	DKbC	1743	C2
Duncan Pl	DKbC	1979	C7
Duncan St	ClyC	2148	C2
Duncannon Ct	DKbC	1671	C3
Duncourtney Dr NE	FulC	1599	A4
Dundee Rd SE	SMYR	1667	C7
Dunedin Dr SW	FulC	2059	B4
Dunes Wy	FulC	1532	D7
Dunhaven Ct	DKbC	1672	A1
Dunhaven Rd	DKbC	1672	A1
Dunhill Ct NE	FulC	1598	E4
Dunhill Dr SE	CobC	1668	B1
Dunhill Ter NE	FulC	1599	A4
Dunkerrin Ln	DKbC	1601	A7
Dunlap Av	EPNT	2061	C2
Dunlap Ct NE	DKbC	1671	B7
Dunlieth Ct	DKbC	1819	C4
Dunmoor Dr	ClyC	2149	B7
Dunmore Rd	DKbC	1980	D6
Dunmore Rd NE	CobC	1598	A2
Dunmoreland Ct	FulC	2146	E2
Dunmoreland Ter	FulC	2146	D2
Dunn Av SE	CobC	1666	B1
Dunn Rd	ClyC	2064	D6
Dunn Rd SW	FulC	2145	E1
Dunn St SE	CobC	1738	E2
	SMYR	1666	E7
	SMYR	1738	E1
Dunn St SW	ATLN	1890	B6
Dunnally Ct	FulC	1533	B1
Dunning St SE	ATLN	1890	E7
	ATLN	1976	E1

INDEX 22

Elm St — Fairview Rd

Atlanta Street Index

STREET / City	Map #	Grid
Elm St		
DKbC	1671	E3
EPNT	2061	D2
HPVL	2062	C4
RSWL	1530	C3
Elm St NW		
ATLN	1890	B3
Elm St SW		
ATLN	1890	B4
Elmdale Dr		
DKbC	1745	E6
Elmhurst Cir SE		
DKbC	1978	A1
Elmira Pl NE		
ATLN	1891	E3
El Monte Ct		
FulC	2146	B6
Elmscourt Dr		
DKbC	1819	C4
Elmside Village Ln NW		
GwnC	1601	E4
GwnC	1602	A4
Elmtree Dr SW		
ATLN	1888	B7
Elmwood Cir SE		
CobC	1813	C2
Elmwood Ct		
FulC	2146	C5
Elmwood Dr NE		
ATLN	1816	B6
Elmwood Dr SE		
CobC	1813	C2
SMYR	1667	B7
Elmwood Rd NW		
ATLN	1889	D2
Eloise Ct SE		
ATLN	1891	C6
Eloise St SE		
ATLN	1891	C7
Elon Wy		
DKbC	1818	A1
El Paso Rd SW		
ATLN	1973	C5
Elrod St NW		
GwnC	1673	A2
Elsinore St		
EPNT	1976	A6
Elsmere Ln		
ClyC	2147	D6
Elvira St SE		
ATLN	1977	A2
Elysian Wy NW		
ATLN	1815	A2
Embarcadero Ln		
CGPK	2147	A1
Embassy Ct NE		
ATLN	1742	D7
Embassy Ct NW		
FulC	1669	E3
Embassy Dr		
CGPK	2061	A7
Embassy Row NE		
FulC	1599	D6
Ember Dr		
DKbC	1979	D3
Ember St NE		
CobC	1526	E1
Embers Dr SE		
CobC	1668	A2
Embry Cir		
DKbC	1672	E7
DKbC	1744	E1
N Embry Cir		
DKbC	1672	D7
Embry Ct		
DKbC	1744	E1
Embry Ln NE		
CobC	1526	D1
Embry Downs Ct		
DKbC	1673	A7
Embry Hills Dr		
DKbC	1672	E7
DKbC	1744	E1
EMC Pkwy NE		
CobC	1595	B1
EMC Pkwy NW		
CobC	1595	B1
Emerald Av SE		
DKbC	1978	A2
Emerald Av SW		
ATLN	1889	C5
Emerald Ct SW		
ATLN	1888	D4
Emerald Pt		
DKbC	1980	C7
DKbC	2066	C1
Emerald Rdg NE		
MRTA	1527	A7
Emerald Castle Dr		
DKbC	1980	C2
Emerald Falls Ct		
DKbC	1980	C1
Emerald Falls Dr		
DKbC	1980	C1
Emerald Glen Dr NE		
MRTA	1527	A7
Emerald Green Ct		
FulC	2146	E6
Emerald Lake Ct		
DKbC	1980	D2
Emerald Lake Dr		
DKbC	1980	C2
Emerald North Cir		
DKbC	1980	C1
Emerald North Dr		
DKbC	1980	C1
Emerald Pointe Cir		
FulC	2146	E6
NE Emerald Ridge Ct		
DKbC	1743	D3
Emerald Springs Ct		
DKbC	1980	C1
Emerald Springs Dr		
DKbC	1980	C1
Emerson Av		
DCTR	1892	D1
Emerson Av SE		
ATLN	1891	C7
Emerson Ct NE		
CobC	1528	D6
Emerson St NE		
CobC	1528	D6
Emerson St SE		
ATLN	1891	D6
Emerson Bridge Ct NE		
CobC	1528	D6
Emerson Bridge Dr NE		
CobC	1528	D6
Emery Pl NE		
ATLN	1892	C3
Emery St NW		
ATLN	1815	B3
Emily Cir		
ClyC	2151	B3
Emily Pl NW		
ATLN	1889	C1
Emma Ln NE		
ATLN	1742	A3
Emmerose Dr SE		
CobC	1738	C2
Emory Cir NE		
DKbC	1817	C6
Emory Dr NE		
CobC	1528	C1
DKbC	1817	C6
Emory Ln NE		
CobC	1596	D3
Emory Ln SE		
SMYR	1667	B7
N Emory Pl NE		
DKbC	1817	A5
Emory Rd NE		
DKbC	1817	A5
Emory Oaks Wy		
DKbC	1817	D5
Emory Parc Pl		
DKbC	1817	D3
Emory Parc Wy		
DKbC	1817	D4
Emory Place Dr NE		
DKbC	1817	C1
Emory Ridge Dr NE		
DKbC	1743	C7
Emperor Wy		
DKbC	1745	A3
Empire Av		
EPNT	1975	C5
Empire Blvd SW		
ATLN	2062	D2
Empire Rd NE		
DKbC	1817	B3
Empire Wy SW		
ATLN	2062	D3
Empire Forest Dr		
DKbC	1745	A4
Emporia Ct		
DKbC	1894	D7
Emrose Dr		
DKbC	1819	A1
Enchanted Forest Dr		
ClyC	2063	E5
Enclave Cir		
FulC	1670	B5
Enclave Pl		
DKbC	2064	C3
Enclave Wk		
RSWL	1530	C3
W End Av SW		
ATLN	1890	B5
W End Pl SW		
ATLN	1890	A6
Endden Ct NW		
GwnC	1602	A1
Enfield Pt NE		
CobC	1597	A4
Engineering Dr NW		
GwnC	1602	C3
Engineers Dr SE		
CobC	1596	D6
Engle Rd NW		
ATLN	1888	D2
Englewood Av SE		
ATLN	1977	A1
Englewood Dr		
EPNT	1975	A7
English Av NW		
ATLN	1890	B1
English Cir SW		
SMYR	1666	C6
English Dr SW		
ATLN	1888	A5
English Ln		
CGPK	2061	B2
EPNT	2061	B2
English St NW		
ATLN	1815	A5
English Ivy Ct SE		
CobC	1739	D6
English Oak Dr		
DRVL	1672	E3
English Valley Dr		
DKbC	2066	E3
Ennisbrook Dr SE		
CobC	1738	A1
SMYR	1738	A1
Ennisbrook Wy SE		
SMYR	1738	B1
Enoch Dr		
ClyC	2063	C5
Enon Ct SW		
FulC	1973	A4
Enon Rd SW		
FulC	1973	A5
Enon Mill Ct		
FulC	1973	A4
Enon Mill Dr SW		
FulC	1973	A4
Enon Mill Ln		
FulC	1973	A4
Enon Pines Dr SW		
FulC	1973	A4
Enota Pl SW		
ATLN	1889	E5
Ensign Ct		
DKbC	1671	D4
Ensign Dr		
CMBL	1671	D4
DKbC	1671	D4
Ensley St NE		
ATLN	1891	C2
Enterprise Blvd SW		
FulC	1887	A4
Enterprise Ct SE		
DKbC	1978	C6
Enterprise Dr NW		
GwnC	1673	D4
Enterprise Wy SE		
MRTA	1667	C3
S Entrance Dr		
MRRW	2150	A5
Epping Forest Dr NE		
DKbC	1671	A6
Eppington Dr NW		
ATLN	1741	D1
FulC	1741	D1
Epworth St SW		
ATLN	1975	E2
Equestrian Ct		
DKbC	1600	D7
Equestrian Wy		
DKbC	1600	D7
Equifax Wy NW		
ATLN	1815	E5
Equitable Pl NE		
ATLN	1890	E4
Eric St SE		
ATLN	1977	A2
Ericson St SE		
ATLN	1891	E4
Erie Av		
DCTR	1817	E7
Erie Pl		
LKCY	2149	E3
Erin Av SW		
ATLN	1976	B2
Erin Rd SW		
FulC	1973	A6
Ernest Dr		
FTPK	2063	C7
FTPK	2149	C1
Ernest W Barrett Pkwy NW		
CobC	1526	A3
N Errol Ct NW		
FulC	1669	C4
Errol Pl NW		
FulC	1669	C3
Erskine Rd		
DKbC	1819	C2
Ervin Cir		
FTPK	2063	D6
Esprit Ct SW		
FulC	1973	A3
Esquire Ct NW		
GwnC	1673	D5
Esquire Pl		
RVDL	2147	E7
Esquire Pl NW		
GwnC	1673	D5
Essex Av SE		
CobC	1740	B2
Essex Av SW		
ATLN	1975	A2
Essex Pl		
HryC	2065	D7
Essie Av SE		
ATLN	1891	D7
Estate Wy NE		
FulC	1670	D7
Estates Ln SE		
CobC	1739	D3
Estelle Ct SE		
SMYR	1666	C6
Estelle St		
HPVL	2062	B3
Esten St SE		
ATLN	1891	D4
Ester Dr SW		
ATLN	1887	E4
Estes Dr		
FulC	2146	A3
Estes Dr SW		
ATLN	1976	A4
Estoria St SE		
ATLN	1891	C5
Ethan Dr NE		
CobC	1528	D1
Ethan Allen Dr		
FulC	2060	A7
Ethel Ln		
DKbC	1892	D7
DKbC	1978	D1
HryC	2152	B3
Ethel St NW		
ATLN	1815	B6
Etheridge Dr NW		
ATLN	1813	E6
Etheridge St NW		
ATLN	1890	A1
Eton Ct NE		
DKbC	1670	E6
Eton Ct NW		
NRCS	1602	D5
Eton Ct SE		
CobC	1812	A1
Etowah Dr NE		
DKbC	1743	A3
MRTA	1595	B3
Etowah Rdg		
HryC	2152	B6
Eubanks Av		
EPNT	2061	E2
Eubanks Dr		
LKCY	2149	D2
Euclade Ct NE		
DKbC	1817	A3
Euclid Av NE		
ATLN	1891	D2
Euclid Ter NE		
ATLN	1891	E2
Eugene Gunby Rd		
CobC	1668	C3
N Eugenia Pl NW		
ATLN	1814	B7
S Eugenia Pl NW		
ATLN	1889	B1
Eugenia St SW		
ATLN	1890	D5
Euhrlee St SW		
ATLN	1890	B4
Eula Cir		
DRVL	1672	B3
Eula Ct		
DRVL	1672	B3
Eulalia Rd NE		
ATLN	1742	C4
Eureka Dr NE		
ATLN	1816	A2
Eva Dr NW		
ATLN	1814	A6
Eva Lee Ct NE		
CobC	1527	E2
Evangeline Rd		
DKbC	1894	C3
Evans Dr		
ClyC	2147	D6
ClyC	2151	B7
DCTR	1892	E2
FTPK	2149	C1
HryC	2152	D7
UNCT	2145	B5
Evans Dr SW		
ATLN	1975	E3
ATLN	1976	A3
Evans Rd		
DKbC	1673	C7
DKbC	1745	A2
Evans St		
ClyC	2062	E6
DCTR	1892	D4
Evans St SE		
ATLN	1891	C7
Evans St SW		
ATLN	1890	B6
Evans Dale Cir		
DKbC	1745	B2
Evans Dale Dr		
DKbC	1745	B2
Evans Oaks Ct		
DKbC	1745	B1
Evans Ridge Cir		
DKbC	1745	A2
Evans Ridge Dr		
DKbC	1745	A1
Evans Ridge Tr		
DKbC	1745	A2
Evanston Cir NE		
MRTA	1527	A5
Evanston Ct NE		
MRTA	1527	A6
Evanston Ln NE		
MRTA	1527	A6
Evans Woods Dr		
DKbC	1745	B2
Evelyn Dr		
FTPK	2063	D6
N Evelyn Pl NW		
ATLN	1889	C1
S Evelyn Pl NW		
ATLN	1889	C1
Evelyn St		
DKbC	1744	E5
Evelyn St SE		
SMYR	1738	D1
Evelyn Wy NW		
ATLN	1889	C1
Evening Star Dr SE		
CobC	1666	A5
Everett Pl SW		
ATLN	1976	C2
Evergreen Dr		
FTPK	2063	A6
Evergreen Dr NE		
DKbC	1670	D6
Evergreen Dr SE		
CobC	1666	B6
Evergreen Ln NW		
ATLN	1815	C3
Evergreen Ter		
FTPK	2063	A6
Evergreen Tr SE		
SMYR	1666	B6
Everhart St SW		
ATLN	1976	B2
Eves Cir		
RSWL	1531	D5
Eves Pl		
RSWL	1531	D6
Eves Rd		
RSWL	1531	E5
RSWL	1532	A4
Ewing Dr		
FTPK	2149	C2
Ewing Dr NE		
DKbC	1743	B4
Ewing Pl SW		
ATLN	1889	E7
Ewing St NW		
NRCS	1602	D6
Ewing St SW		
ATLN	1973	E5
Exchange Av		
DKbC	1818	D6
Exchange Pl		
MRRW	2149	E7
E Exchange Pl		
DKbC	1745	B5
W Exchange Pl		
DKbC	1745	A6
Exchange Tr		
DKbC	1979	E4
Executive Dr		
DKbC	1819	E3
Executive Park Dr NE		
DKbC	1743	A7
DKbC	1817	A1
Executive Park Ln NE		
DKbC	1743	B7
DKbC	1817	B1
Executive Park East NE		
DKbC	1743	A7
DKbC	1817	A1
Executive Park North NE		
DKbC	1816	C3
Executive Park South NE		
DKbC	1816	E1
DKbC	1817	A1
Executive Park West NE		
DKbC	1817	A1
Exerter Ct NE		
CobC	1529	A3
Exeter Cir NW		
NRCS	1602	D5
Exeter Ct NE		
CobC	1529	B6
Exeter Rd		
AVES	1893	C1
Exeter Close NW		
ATLN	1741	C2
Exmoor Dr NE		
CobC	1598	A4
Exodus Ct NE		
CobC	1529	C4
Ezra Church Dr NW		
ATLN	1889	D3
Ezzard St SE		
ATLN	1891	B4
F		
N F Av		
FTPK	2150	B1
Fabin St NW		
ATLN	1813	D3
Fair Dr		
HryC	2065	E5
Fair Dr SW		
ATLN	1976	C4
Fair Ln		
DKbC	1979	A1
W Fair St SW		
ATLN	1889	E4
Fair St SE		
CobC	1595	B7
Fair St SW		
ATLN	1889	E4
Fairbanks St SW		
ATLN	1976	B2
Fairbrook Cir NE		
CobC	1598	B4
Fairbrook Wy NE		
CobC	1598	B4
Fairburn Av		
UNCT	2145	A5
Fairburn Av SW		
ATLN	1973	D5
Fairburn Cir NW		
ATLN	1888	A1
Fairburn Pl NW		
ATLN	1888	A1
Fairburn Rd NW		
ATLN	1813	A7
Fairburn Rd SW		
ATLN	1888	A5
ATLN	1973	E7
ATLN	2059	E2
FulC	1888	A5
FulC	1974	A1
Fairfax Av		
EPNT	1975	D6
Fairfax Ct SE		
CobC	1740	A3
Fairfield E		
DKbC	1600	B3
Fairfield N		
DKbC	1600	A4
Fairfield W		
DKbC	1600	B3
Fairfield Ct		
ClyC	2150	C6
Fairfield Ct NE		
CobC	1597	E2
Fairfield Dr		
AVES	1893	C1
ClyC	2150	D5
HryC	2152	C1
Fairfield Dr NE		
CobC	1597	E1
Fairfield Dr SE		
CobC	1598	A3
Fairfield Pl NW		
ATLN	1889	A3
Fairfield Plz		
AVES	1893	C1
Fairfield Rd NW		
ATLN	1741	B3
Fairfield St		
DCTR	1817	D7
Fairfield St SE		
SMYR	1666	C5
Fairfield Trc NE		
CobC	1597	E2
Fairgreen Dr NE		
CobC	1597	E3
Fairgreen Ln NE		
CobC	1597	E3
Fairgreen Ter NE		
CobC	1597	E3
S Fairground St SE		
CobC	1595	C5
MRTA	1595	C5
Fairground St NE		
MRTA	1595	C4
Fairgrove Ct NW		
GwnC	1601	E3
Fairhaven Cir NE		
ATLN	1815	E3
Fair Haven Wy SE		
SMYR	1667	B5
Fairhill Ln NE		
DKbC	1743	A4
Fairlake Dr		
DKbC	1979	D3
Fairlane Cir NW		
ATLN	1888	B2
Fairlane Ct NW		
ATLN	1888	B2
Fairlane Dr		
ClyC	2150	E7
DKbC	1672	B7
DRVL	1672	B7
Fairlane Dr NW		
ATLN	1888	A2
Fairlane Dr SE		
ATLN	1977	A7
Fairlane Dr SW		
MRTA	1595	A6
Fairlee Dr		
DKbC	1893	B5
Fairley Hall Ct NW		
GwnC	1533	A6
Fairlie St NW		
ATLN	1890	E3
Fairlock Ln NW		
ATLN	1888	A2
Fairly Wy SW		
ATLN	1973	D2
Fairmont Av NW		
ATLN	1815	A6
Fairmont Rd SE		
CobC	1739	B7
Fairmont St NW		
NRCS	1602	E7
Fair Oaks Av SE		
CobC	1666	B2
Fair Oaks Ct		
DKbC	1743	E7
Fair Oaks Mnr NW		
FulC	1669	B3
Fair Oaks Pl		
DKbC	1744	B7
Fair Oaks Rd		
DKbC	1743	E7
Fairport Wy NE		
CobC	1527	C4
Fairview Av		
DCTR	1817	E7
Fairview Av NE		
MRTA	1596	A3
Fairview Blf		
FulC	1532	C6
Fairview Dr NE		
CobC	1526	D3
Fairview Pt		
HryC	2065	D5
Fairview Rd		
HryC	2065	E6

INDEX 23

Fairview Rd — W Fontainbleau Ct

Atlanta Street Index

STREET / City / Map # Grid

Fairview Rd
HryC 2151 E1
HryC 2152 B2
N Fairview Rd
DKbC 2065 D5
Fairview Rd NE
ATLN 1891 E1
ATLN 1892 A1
Fairview St
DCTR 1818 B7
Fairview Springs Rd
HryC 2065 E5
Fairville Ct NE
CobC 1529 B6
Fairway Cir NE
DKbC 1743 A5
Fairway Cir SW
ATLN 1973 B6
Fairway Ct NE
CobC 1597 E3
Fairway Ct SW
ATLN 1973 C6
Fairway Dr
CGPK 2060 E3
Fairway Dr SE
CobC 1666 B1
Fairway Ests NE
DKbC 1742 E5
Fairway Gdns NE
DKbC 1742 E5
Fairway Hill Dr SE
DKbC 1892 B6
Fairway Ridge Dr
FulC 1532 D6
Fairway Village Dr
RSWL 1532 A1
Fairway Villas Dr
FulC 1533 B3
Fairwood Ln NE
DKbC 1743 D6
Faith Av SE
ATLN 1891 D5
Faith Cove
ClyC 2147 B4
Fala Pl NE
DKbC 1671 B7
DKbC 1743 A1
N Falcon Blf
FulC 1532 C6
S Falcon Blf
FulC 1532 D6
Falcon Ct
ClyC 2064 A6
Falcon Dr
ClyC 2148 D1
FTPK 2148 D1
Falcon Dr SW
ATLN 1888 E7
Falcon Chase Ln NE
FulC 1670 C5
Falcon Glen Ct
RSWL 1532 C5
Falcon Glen Rd
FulC 1532 C5
RSWL 1532 C5
Falkirk Pl NE
DKbC 1745 A3
Fall Creek Dr NE
CobC 1597 A3
Fall Creek Trc
RSWL 1531 E4
Falling Brook Dr NE
CobC 1528 C4
Falling Ridge Ct SE
SMYR 1667 D6
Falling Rocks Ct
RSWL 1531 E5
Falling Valley Ct SE
SMYR 1667 D6
Falling Water Dr SE
SMYR 1667 D6
Falling Water Pt
FulC 2146 D4
Falls Bay Ct
FulC 1533 B2
Falls Lake Dr
FulC 1533 B2
Falls Landing Ct
FulC 1533 A2
Falls Landing Dr
FulC 1533 A2
Falls Point Cir
FulC 1533 B2
Falls Point Tr
FulC 1533 B2
Falls Ridge Dr
FulC 1533 B1
Falls Ridge Cove
FulC 1533 B1
Falls Watch Cir
FulC 1533 B1
Fall View Dr
ClyC 2149 B4
FTPK 2149 B4
Fallview Ter
EPNT 1976 A6
Fama Dr NE
DKbC 1817 D1
Fantasy Ln
DKbC 1818 C4
Faraday Ct
DKbC 1818 C2
Faraday Pl
DKbC 1818 C2

Faragut Wy
DKbC 2066 D1
Farewell Ln
FulC 1532 C3
Fargo Pl SE
DKbC 1978 D5
Farleigh Trc NE
CobC 1596 C3
Farley Ct
EPNT 1975 A5
Farley Ml SE
CobC 1597 C7
Farley St
EPNT 1975 A5
Farm Ct
ClyC 2151 C5
RSWL 1530 A2
Farm Dr
FTPK 2148 D1
Farm Ln SE
SMYR 1666 C5
Farm Pth
RSWL 1530 A2
Farm Rd SE
CobC 1598 A5
Farm Trc
RSWL 1530 A2
Farmbrook Ln
ClyC 2151 C5
FulC 1533 E2
Farm Brook Ln NE
DKbC 1742 E2
Farmbrooke Ct
FulC 1601 A3
Farm Cove Ct
RSWL 1530 A2
Farmcrest Pt SE
CobC 1813 A3
Farm Dale
RSWL 1530 A2
Farm Hill Cir
RSWL 1530 A2
Farmington Ct SE
CobC 1740 A5
Farmington Dr SE
CobC 1740 A5
Farmington Ln NE
DKbC 1742 E2
Farmington Ln SE
CobC 1740 A5
Farmington Pl SE
CobC 1740 B5
Farmlake Ct SE
CobC 1813 A4
Farmlake Dr SE
CobC 1813 A4
Farm Land Ct
DKbC 1980 B6
Farm Overlook Dr
HryC 2151 E3
Farmstead Cir SE
SMYR 1667 D7
Farmstead Rd SE
SMYR 1667 D7
Farm Track
RSWL 1529 E2
Farmwood Wy SE
CobC 1812 E4
Farn Dr
ClyC 2150 D2
Farnell Ct
DKbC 1817 D5
Farnham Ct
DKbC 1894 B4
Farnworth Ln
RSWL 1531 A1
Faron Ct
DKbC 2066 C3
Faronview Rd
DKbC 1673 C7
Farrar Ct
DKbC 1819 A7
Farrier Wk SE
CobC 1597 B6
Farrington Av SE
ATLN 1977 A1
Farrington Pl SE
ATLN 1891 A7
ATLN 1977 B1
E Farris Av
EPNT 2061 C1
W Farris Av
EPNT 2061 B1
Farris Cir
FTPK 2063 B7
Farris Dr
DKbC 1893 D6
Farthingale Ct
CobC 1596 B2
Faulkner Rd NE
ATLN 1816 C3
Fauna Ct
FulC 1530 C7
Faunsworth Dr NE
FulC 1598 E5
Favor Dr
FTPK 2149 B2
Fawn Ct NE
CobC 1597 E2
Fawn Ln SE
CobC 1738 A5
SMYR 1738 A5
Fawn Pl NE
CobC 1596 C2

Fawn Run NE
CobC 1597 E2
Fawn Tr NE
CobC 1527 A1
Fawn Tr SE
CobC 1738 B7
CobC 1812 C1
Fawn Wy NE
CobC 1597 D2
Fawndale Wy
FulC 1601 B2
Fay Ct
ClyC 2151 C6
Fay Dr
ClyC 2151 C6
Fay St SE
DKbC 1892 C7
E Fayetteville Cir
ClyC 2147 D6
Fayetteville Ct SE
DKbC 1892 C7
E Fayetteville Dr
ClyC 2147 D6
Fayetteville Rd
DCTR 1892 E4
E Fayetteville Rd
ClyC 2147 D5
RVDL 2147 D5
W Fayetteville Rd
CGPK 2147 C2
ClyC 2147 C6
W Fayetteville Rd SR-314
CGPK 2147 C2
ClyC 2147 C6
Fayetteville Rd NE
ATLN 1892 D4
DCTR 1892 D4
Fayetteville Rd SE
ATLN 1892 C7
ATLN 1978 B1
DKbC 1892 C7
DKbC 1977 E5
Fearn Cir NE
DKbC 1743 B4
Feather Sound Ct
FulC 1532 D2
Featherstone Rd
FulC 1533 A4
Federal Dr NW
ATLN 1889 C4
Federal Rd
RSWL 1529 E2
Federal Ter SE
ATLN 1977 B2
Fedora Wy NW
ATLN 1888 A2
Feld Av
DCTR 1892 D2
Felder Av NE
ATLN 1891 E2
Feldwood Pl
FulC 2145 E3
Feldwood Rd
FulC 2145 E5
UNCT 2145 E5
Feldwood Pines St
FulC 2146 A4
Felker Ward St NW
ATLN 1813 E3
Fellowship Ct
DKbC 1745 E5
Fellowship Pl
DKbC 1745 D5
Fellowship Rd
DKbC 1745 E5
Felton Dr
EPNT 1976 A7
Felton Dr NE
ATLN 1891 A2
Felton Ln SE
CobC 1812 B7
Fenbrook Ct
FulC 1533 E3
Fenhurst Pl
DKbC 1601 A6
Fennel Cir SW
ATLN 1887 E4
Fennel Wy SW
ATLN 1887 E4
Fenway Cir
DKbC 1893 B4
Fenwick Pl NE
FulC 1599 C3
Fenwood St SW
ATLN 1889 E4
Fenwood Tr
RSWL 1529 E2
Fenwood Tr NE
CobC 1596 B2
Ferguson Ct
FTPK 2149 C1
Ferguson St NE
ATLN 1891 E2
Feridan St NE
ATLN 1892 C3
Fern Av SE
ATLN 1890 E7
ATLN 1976 E1
Fern Ct
CobC 1596 E7
Fern Dr
DKbC 1744 E7
DKbC 1818 E1
Fern St SE
CobC 1596 E7

Fernbank Dr SW
ATLN 1973 B6
Fern Brooks Dr SW
FulC 1887 C7
Ferncliff Dr NE
CobC 1526 E1
Ferncliff Pl NE
ATLN 1742 C5
Ferncliff Rd NE
ATLN 1742 C6
Fern Creek Ln NE
DKbC 1817 C1
Ferndale Dr
DCTR 1817 E6
DKbC 1817 E6
Fernie Ct NE
CobC 1529 B6
Fernleaf Cir NW
ATLN 1814 D2
Fernleaf Ct NW
ATLN 1814 D2
Fernleaf Ln
DKbC 1818 A4
Fernleaf Ln NE
CobC 1597 A5
Fernley Rd
SMYR 1667 C6
Fernly Park Dr
FulC 1533 E1
Ferno Dr NW
ATLN 1813 D5
Fern Park Ct NW
GwnC 1533 D7
Fern Valley Ct
EPNT 1974 E6
Fern Valley Dr
EPNT 1974 D6
Fernvalley Rd NE
CobC 1526 B2
Fernway Ct NE
DKbC 1670 E3
Fernway Ct NW
GwnC 1601 E2
Fernwood Cir NE
DKbC 1743 A3
Fernwood Dr
EPNT 1975 C5
Fernwood Rd NW
ATLN 1815 B4
Ferrell Av
DKbC 1818 E6
Ferris St SW
ATLN 1889 B6
W Ferry Ct NE
FulC 1670 D4
E Ferry Dr NE
FulC 1670 D4
W Ferry Dr NE
FulC 1670 D4
Ferry Dr NE
CobC 1526 B5
FulC 1669 E1
Ferry Ln SW
ATLN 1887 E3
Ferry Lndg NW
FulC 1668 E1
Ferry Heights Dr SW
ATLN 1887 E3
Ferryman Ct
FulC 1532 E1
Ferst Dr NW
ATLN 1815 D7
ATLN 1890 D1
Field Pkwy NW
MRTA 1526 A7
Field Rd NW
ATLN 1813 D7
Field St SE
ATLN 1891 C4
Field Creek Ct NE
CobC 1528 B3
Fieldcrest Dr
ClyC 2150 D6
Fielder Av NW
ATLN 1815 A7
Fielder Rd
ClyC 2151 A7
Fielding Ct SW
ATLN 1888 D5
Fielding Dr NE
DKbC 1744 E4
Fielding Ln NW
GwnC 1533 B6
Fielding Ln SW
ATLN 1888 D5
Fielding Wy NE
CobC 1597 E1
Fielding Park Ct NE
DKbC 1670 E5
Fieldsborn Ct NE
FulC 1599 C3
Fieldsborn Wy NE
FulC 1599 C4
Fields Pond Ct NE
CobC 1529 C5
Fields Pond Dr NE
CobC 1529 C5
Fields Pond Gln NE
CobC 1529 C5
Fields Pond Ln NE
CobC 1529 B3
Fields Pond Close NE
CobC 1529 C5
Fields Pond Cove NE
CobC 1529 C5

Fieldstone Pth NE
CobC 1529 A3
Fieldstone Trc
DKbC 2066 A3
Fieldway Rd
ClyC 2151 D3
Fieldwood Dr SE
SMYR 1739 A1
Fifth Green Ct
FulC 1530 B6
Filbert Ln
ClyC 2147 B5
Fillmore Rd SE
ATLN 2063 C3
Financial Dr NW
GwnC 1673 E2
Finch Dr SE
ATLN 1976 E5
Finch Tr NE
ATLN 1891 A2
Finch Forest Tr NW
FulC 1668 E6
Finchley Ct NW
FulC 1598 E6
Finesse Dr
DKbC 1980 A1
Finistere Ct NE
DKbC 1671 A7
Finley Av NW
ATLN 1890 A1
Finley Dr
FTPK 2149 C1
Finley St NE
ATLN 1891 E3
Fir St NE
ATLN 1892 A3
Fireside Ct SE
CobC 1596 E6
Firestone Dr SE
CobC 1598 A6
Firth Ln
DKbC 1601 A6
Fishburne Dr
DKbC 1817 B6
Fisher Av NW
ATLN 1814 A2
Fisher Rd SE
ATLN 1977 C2
Fisher Tr NE
DKbC 1743 D6
Fitzgerald Ct
DKbC 1818 B7
Fitzgerald St SE
ATLN 1891 B4
Fitzpatrick Ter NW
GwnC 1533 B6
Fitzpatrick Trc NW
GwnC 1533 B7
Fitzpatrick Wy NW
GwnC 1533 A5
Flagler Av NE
ATLN 1816 A4
Flagler Cir SE
SMYR 1666 D7
Flagstone Ct SW
ATLN 1887 E5
Flagstone Dr SE
DKbC 1978 C3
Flagstone Dr SW
ATLN 1887 E5
Flagstone Ln SE
CobC 1596 D7
Flagstone Trc
DKbC 2065 E3
Flair Knoll Ct NE
DKbC 1744 B3
Flair Knoll Dr NE
DKbC 1744 B3
Flairview Ct
ClyC 2149 C6
Flakes Mill Rd
DKbC 1980 C7
DKbC 2066 C1
HryC 2152 B1
Flakes Mill Manor Ln
DKbC 2066 C3
Flakes Mill Manor Wy
DKbC 2066 B3
Flamingo Dr
DKbC 1818 D2
EPNT 2060 D2
Flamingo Dr SW
ATLN 1888 E6
ATLN 1975 A1
Flamingo Wy
MRRW 2149 D6
Flankers Rd
FTPK 2149 E2
LKCY 2149 E2
Flat Rock Rd
HryC 2152 E7
Flat Shoals Av SE
ATLN 1891 D4
Flat Shoals Pkwy
DKbC 1979 E5
Flat Shoals Pkwy SR-155
DKbC 1979 E5
Flat Shoals Rd
ClyC 2147 E4
DKbC 1978 E3
DKbC 1979 A3
FulC 2145 D6
FulC 2146 D6
UNCT 2145 D6

Flat Shoals Rd SR-155
DKbC 1979 C4
Flat Shoals Rd SE
ATLN 1892 A7
ATLN 1978 C1
DKbC 1978 C1
W Flat Shoals Ter
DKbC 1978 D2
Flat Shoals Wy SE
ATLN 1892 A7
Fleet St SW
ATLN 1976 B4
Fleetwood Cir SW
ATLN 1889 A6
Fleetwood Ct SW
ATLN 1889 A6
Fleetwood Dr SE
DKbC 1977 E6
Fleming Rd
ClyC 2150 C7
Fleming St SE
SMYR 1666 D6
Flemington Rd NE
DKbC 1744 A5
Flemish Ct
ClyC 2147 B2
Fletcher St SW
ATLN 1976 C1
Fleur Dr SE
CobC 1666 A5
Fleur de Lis Ct
DKbC 1601 C5
Fleur de Lis Dr
ClyC 2149 C7
Fleur de Lis Pl
DKbC 1601 B5
Fleur de Lis Wy
DKbC 1601 C5
Flightway Dr
CMBL 1671 D7
Flindt Ct
DKbC 1672 B7
Flint Av
DKbC 2066 A2
Flint Ter
DKbC 2066 A2
Flintlock Rd NW
ATLN 1740 D2
Flintlock Tr
HryC 2152 C6
Flintridge Dr
DKbC 1819 D6
Flint Ridge Dr SW
CobC 1738 A6
Flintshire Ct
DKbC 1672 A1
Flintwood Dr NE
CobC 1596 E3
Flintwood Dr SE
DKbC 1978 C3
Flippen Tr NW
GwnC 1533 B7
GwnC 1602 B1
Flora Av NE
ATLN 1891 E4
Flora Dr NE
CobC 1527 D1
Florence Pl NW
ATLN 1889 D1
Florence St NW
CobC 1595 A2
MRTA 1595 A2
Florida Av NW
GwnC 1673 A1
Florida Av SE
ATLN 1891 D6
Florida Av SW
ATLN 1889 A4
Floss Flower Ct
RSWL 1531 C4
Flowerland Dr NE
DKbC 1671 C4
Flowers Dr
CGPK 2061 A2
DKbC 1745 B5
Flowers Pl NW
ATLN 1890 A3
Flowers Rd
DRVL 1672 B4
Flowers Rd S
DKbC 1744 D2
Flowerwood Tr
DKbC 2064 D1
Floyd Dr SE
CobC 1666 B7
SMYR 1666 B7
Flynn St NW
ATLN 1815 C7
Flyway Ct NE
CobC 1529 C7
Flyway Dr NE
CobC 1529 C6
Foal Dr
RSWL 1532 A6
Foliage Ct
RSWL 1601 B1
Folkstone Rd NE
DKbC 1743 B5
Folly Pl NW
GwnC 1533 B6
Fontainbleau Ct
DKbC 1601 B5
W Fontainbleau Ct
DKbC 1601 B4

INDEX 24
Fontaine Av SW — Galangale Wy

Atlanta Street Index

STREET	City	Map #	Grid
Fontaine Av SW	ATLN	1975	A2
Fontaine Cir	DKbC	1979	A1
Fontaine Rd SE	CobC	1738	A7
Fontaine Rd SW	CobC	1738	A7
Fontainebleau Dr	DKbC	1601	B5
W Fontainebleau Dr	DKbC	1601	B4
Fontainebleau Wy	DKbC	1601	C4
Fontana Ct	DKbC	1745	E1
Foote St NE	ATLN	1892	A3
Foothill Tr NE	CobC	1527	B2
Foot Path Ln NE	MRTA	1595	C2
Foot Path Wy	MRTA	1595	C2
Ford Pl	DKbC	1818	D5
Ford St NW	ATLN	1814	C4
Ford St SE	DKbC	1978	A2
Fordham Ct NE	ATLN	1816	D5
Forest Av	FTPK	2149	C1
N Forest Av NE	MRTA	1595	B4
Forest Av NE	MRTA	1595	B4
Forest Ct	DKbC	1894	D5
Forest Dr	RVDL	2148	B7
N Forest Dr NE	CobC	1529	C4
Forest Dr SE	CobC	1738	E2
	SMYR	1738	E2
Forest Ln SE	CobC	1667	E2
Forest Pkwy	ClyC	2148	D1
	ClyC	2150	A3
	FTPK	2148	D1
	FTPK	2149	B1
	LKCY	2149	E2
Forest Pkwy SR-331	ClyC	2148	E2
	FTPK	2148	E2
	LKCY	2149	B1
Forest Pl	RSWL	1531	E1
Forest St	RSWL	1530	C2
Forest Tr	EPNT	1974	D6
N Forest Tr	DKbC	1671	E1
Foresta Ct	DKbC	1671	C4
Forest Breeze Cove	RSWL	1532	A3
Forest Brook Ct NE	CobC	1598	C1
Forest Brook Pkwy NE	CobC	1598	D1
Forest Crossing Dr SW	FulC	1973	B1
Forest Crossing Wy	FulC	2145	A3
Forestdale Dr NE	FulC	1670	B6
Forest Downs Cir	FulC	2145	A3
Forest Downs Ln	FulC	2145	A3
Forestgate Ct	FulC	1530	E7
Forest Glen Cir	DKbC	1818	E7
Forest Glen Wy	DKbC	1818	E7
Forest Green Ct NE	CobC	1527	D4
Forest Green Dr NE	CobC	1527	D4
	DKbC	1743	D6
Forest Haven Dr	ClyC	2148	C7
Forest Haven Ln	ClyC	2148	D7
Forest Heights Rd	DKbC	1819	E3
Forest Highlands Dr NE	CobC	1528	A1
Foresthill Ct	LKCY	2149	C3
Forest Hills Dr NE	FulC	1670	B6
Forest Hills Dr NW	GwnC	1602	A3
Forest Hills Ln NW	GwnC	1602	A3
Forest Hills Pl NW	GwnC	1602	D4
Forest Hills Wy NW	GwnC	1602	D4
Forest Lakes Av SE	ATLN	1892	C5
Forest Mist Dr SE	SMYR	1738	D4
Forestmont Ct NE	CobC	1529	C4
Forest Overlook Dr SW	FulC	1973	A1
Forest Overlook Tr SW	FulC	1973	A1
Forest Pond Cir NE	CobC	1598	D2
Forest Pond Ct NE	CobC	1598	D2
Forest Pond Dr NE	CobC	1598	D2
Forest Ridge Cir NE	FulC	1669	E5
Forest Ridge Ct	FulC	1530	D5
Forest Ridge Dr SE	CobC	1596	C7
	CobC	1667	C1
Forest Ridge Rd SE	DKbC	1978	D6
Forest Springs Ct	DKbC	1600	C4
Forest Springs Dr	DKbC	1600	C4
Forest Valley Ct NE	FulC	1670	A6
Forest Valley Dr SE	ATLN	2063	C4
Forest Valley Rd NE	FulC	1670	B6
Forest View Cir SE	SMYR	1812	C1
Forest View Ct SE	SMYR	1738	C7
Forest View Tr SE	SMYR	1812	C1
Forestwood Dr	FulC	1669	E2
Forestwood Ln NE	FulC	1669	E2
N Fork Rd	DKbC	1819	E5
S Fork St	DKbC	1819	E6
Fork Creek Tr	DKbC	1818	B2
Fork Creek Church Rd	DKbC	2065	B2
Forkner Dr	DCTR	1818	A6
Formwalt St SW	ATLN	1890	D6
Forrest Av	HPVL	2062	B4
E Forrest Av	EPNT	1975	D7
W Forrest Av	EPNT	1975	C6
Forrest Av NW	ATLN	1813	E3
Forrest Blvd	DKbC	1893	C2
Forrest Cir SE	ATLN	2063	C1
Forrest Ct	DKbC	1672	A4
Forrest Dr SE	ATLN	2063	C1
Forrest Pl NE	FulC	1669	E2
Forrest Pl NW	ATLN	1813	E2
Forrest Rd	FulC	2145	D5
Forrest St NW	ATLN	1815	B5
Forrest Ter SE	ATLN	2063	C1
Forrest Tr	DKbC	1671	E2
Forrest Tr NW	ATLN	1815	B4
Forrest Wy NE	ATLN	1816	A1
Forrest Wy NW	ATLN	1815	B5
Forrestal Dr	DKbC	1671	E3
Forrest Hill Dr	ATLN	2062	D2
	HPVL	2062	D2
Forrest Hills Dr SW	ATLN	1976	C7
	ATLN	2062	D1
Forrest Lake Dr NW	ATLN	1669	E7
	FulC	1669	E7
Forrest Park Rd SE	ATLN	1977	C5
	ATLN	2063	C1
Forrest Ridge Dr NW	ATLN	1888	D2
Forrest View Ter	FulC	1532	D1
Forshaw Dr	HryC	2152	C4
Forsyth St NW	ATLN	1890	D4
Forsyth St SW	ATLN	1890	D4
Fort Dr SE	CobC	1739	C6
Fort St NE	ATLN	1891	A3
	MRTA	1595	B4
Fort St SE	ATLN	1891	A5
Fort Fisher Wy NW	GwnC	1533	B5
Fortingale Rd	CMBL	1671	C5
Fortner St	EPNT	2061	E3
Fortress Av SW	ATLN	1890	D7
	ATLN	1976	D1
Fortune Pl NE	ATLN	1891	B3
Fortune St NE	ATLN	1891	B3
Fort Valley Dr	EPNT	1975	C4
Fort Valley Dr SW	ATLN	1975	C3
	EPNT	1975	C3
Foster Pl NW	ATLN	1814	E7
Foster St	FTPK	2063	D6
Foster St NW	ATLN	1815	A6
Foster St SE	SMYR	1667	A7
Foster Ridge Ct NE	DKbC	1744	C3
Foster Ridge Rd NE	DKbC	1744	B3
Founders Wy SE	MRTA	1595	E6
Founders Cove	FulC	1532	E1
Foundry St NW	ATLN	1890	D3
Fountain Dr NE	CobC	1598	A4
Fountain Dr SW	ATLN	1890	A4
Fountain Oaks Ln NE	FulC	1669	E6
Fountain Oaks Wy NE	FulC	1669	E6
Four Oaks Ct	DKbC	1601	C6
Four Oaks Dr	DKbC	1601	C6
Fourth Fairway Dr	RSWL	1532	B7
	RSWL	1601	B1
Fouts Rd	RSWL	1532	A5
Fowler Cir NE	MRTA	1595	B3
Fowler Ct	DCTR	1892	E1
Fowler Dr NE	CobC	1526	D1
Fowler St NE	ATLN	1892	C3
Fowler St NW	ATLN	1815	D5
	ATLN	1890	D3
Fox Dr NE	CobC	1526	C4
Fox Gln NE	CobC	1598	B4
Fox Ln SE	CobC	1667	E1
Fox Run	ClyC	2151	E5
Fox St NW	ATLN	1890	B1
Foxboro Ln	DKbC	1601	B6
Foxbrush Cir	FulC	1533	A2
Fox Chapel Dr SE	CobC	1739	B5
Fox Chase Ct	RVDL	2148	A7
Fox Chase Ln	RVDL	2148	A7
Foxcliff Ct SE	SMYR	1738	C4
Fox Cove Ct	FulC	1533	E2
Foxcreek Ct	DKbC	1601	A5
Foxcroft Cir SE	CobC	1597	A7
Foxcroft Ct	FTPK	2149	D5
	MRRW	2149	D5
Foxcroft Dr	MRRW	2149	D5
Foxcroft Rd NW	ATLN	1741	A4
Foxcroft Tr SE	CobC	1597	A7
	CobC	1668	A1
Foxfield Ln SE	CobC	1739	E7
Foxfield Tr	ClyC	2151	E5
Foxfield Trc SE	CobC	1739	D7
Foxford Ct	DKbC	1673	C7
Foxford Dr	DKbC	1673	C6
Fox Glen Ct NE	DKbC	1671	B4
Foxglove Ct	DKbC	1745	D6
Foxglove Rd	DKbC	1745	C6
Fox Grape Ln	FulC	1532	C4
Fox Hall Ln N	FulC	2146	D7
Foxhall Ln SE	DKbC	1978	A3
Foxhall Wy SE	DKbC	1978	B3
Fox Hill Ct NW	GwnC	1533	C6
Fox Hill Dr NW	GwnC	1533	C5
Fox Hills Cir SE	CobC	1597	D5
Fox Hills Dr	DKbC	1818	B4
Fox Hills Dr SE	CobC	1597	C5
Fox Hollow Ct	DKbC	1601	A5
Fox Hollow Ct NE	CobC	1597	C2
Fox Hollow Dr NE	CobC	1597	C3
Fox Hollow Pkwy NE	CobC	1597	C2
Fox Hollow Trc NE	CobC	1597	C2
Fox Hollow Wy NE	CobC	1597	C2
Fox Hollow Close NE	CobC	1597	C3
Fox Hound Pkwy NE	CobC	1529	B4
Fox Hound Chase NE	CobC	1529	B5
Fox Hunt Ln	EPNT	2060	B5
Fox Hunter Dr	FulC	1533	D2
Foxlair Dr	FulC	2146	B7
Foxlair Tr	FulC	2146	B7
Fox Ln Dr	FulC	2147	A4
Foxmoor Cir	FulC	1533	A2
Fox Ridge Cir	FulC	1533	E2
Foxridge Ct SE	CobC	1597	B5
Foxridge Rd NW	FulC	1669	C3
Fox Run Ln SE	CobC	1598	B5
Fox Tail Ct	DKbC	1980	E7
Fox Tail Ct NE	CobC	1528	B1
Fox Tail Ln	DKbC	1980	E7
Fox Trail Dr	FulC	2147	A4
Fox Trot Cir	GwnC	1673	E5
Foxwood Ct	DKbC	1601	A5
Foxwood Tr SE	CobC	1738	A1
Foxworth Dr	FulC	1533	A2
Foxworth Chase	FulC	1533	A2
Fradon Ct	FulC	2059	D7
Framons Ct	DKbC	1600	B6
Frances Av NE	MRTA	1595	A3
Frances St	DKbC	1818	D6
Francine Ct	DKbC	1818	E2
Francine Dr	DKbC	1818	D3
Francis Av NW	ATLN	1814	C4
Francis Av SE	ATLN	1977	B1
Francis Dr SE	SMYR	1666	D6
Francis Pl NW	ATLN	1889	D1
Francis Rd	DKbC	1979	C5
Francis St	EPNT	2061	C2
Francis St NE	DKbC	1670	E7
Francis St NW	ATLN	1815	D6
Francyne Ct NE	FulC	1670	C2
Frank Ln SE	CobC	1666	A4
	SMYR	1666	B4
Frank St SW	ATLN	1890	A5
Frankie Ln	DKbC	2065	A4
Frankie Ln NE	CobC	1527	E2
Franklin Cir NE	DKbC	1817	A3
Franklin Ct	DCTR	1892	E2
Franklin Ct SE	MRTA	1596	B7
	MRTA	1667	B1
Franklin Dr SE	CobC	1667	B2
	MRTA	1667	B1
Franklin Ln NE	FulC	1599	B5
Franklin Pl NE	FulC	1670	A7
Franklin Rd NE	FulC	1670	A7
Franklin Rd SE	MRTA	1596	A6
	MRTA	1667	B2
Franklin St	AVES	1893	C1
Franklin Wy SE	MRTA	1667	C2
Franklin Pond NE	FulC	1670	A6
Frank Neely Rd NW	GwnC	1601	E1
Franks Ct	DKbC	1745	C7
Franks Dr	DKbC	1745	D7
Franks St SW	CobC	1595	A7
Fraser Rd NE	CobC	1526	D3
Fraser St SE	ATLN	1890	E7
	SMYR	1666	D7
Frasier Cir SE	MRTA	1595	C5
Frasier St SE	MRTA	1595	B5
Fraternity Row	DKbC	1817	B5
Frazier Ct	DKbC	1818	D1
Frazier Rd	DKbC	1744	C7
	DKbC	1818	D1
Frazier St	RSWL	1530	C1
Frazier Park Dr	DKbC	1744	D7
Frazier Woods Rd	DKbC	1744	D7
Freda Ct	DKbC	1980	B4
Fredell Cir	EPNT	1976	A7
Fredell Pl	EPNT	1976	A7
Frederica St NE	ATLN	1891	D1
Frederick Ct SW	FulC	1887	C2
Frederick Dr SW	FulC	1887	B2
Fredericksburg Dr	CGPK	2060	E6
Fredrick Rd NE	CobC	1527	E2
Freedom Ln	RSWL	1530	D1
E Freedom Pkwy NE	ATLN	1891	D2
E Freedom Pkwy NE SR-42 CONN	ATLN	1891	D2
Freedom Pkwy NE	ATLN	1891	E1
Freedom Pkwy NE SR-10	ATLN	1891	B3
Freedom Vly	DKbC	1894	B5
Freeman Cir NW	NRCS	1602	E5
Freeman Ct	CGPK	2061	B3
Freeman Pkwy SE	SMYR	1813	B3
Freeman Rd NE	CobC	1528	E2
Freeman St	DCTR	1893	B2
Freemans Wk	DKbC	1819	C7
Fremont St SE	ATLN	1977	A5
Freydale Rd SE	CobC	1596	D6
Freyer Dr NE	MRTA	1595	B3
Freys Gin Ct SE	MRTA	1595	E5
Freys Gin Rd SE	MRTA	1595	E5
Freywood Dr SE	CobC	1596	C6
Friar Ct	ClyC	2147	B5
Friar Tuck Rd NE	ATLN	1816	A4
Friar Tuck Wy	DKbC	1672	E4
Front St	ClyC	2151	B3
Frontac Wy NW	ATLN	1742	A4
Frontage Rd	CGPK	2060	D4
	ClyC	2062	D7
	ClyC	2148	D1
	DKbC	1672	E5
	EPNT	2060	B3
	FTPK	2148	D1
Frontenac Ct NE	DKbC	1671	A7
Frontier Ct	ClyC	2151	C3
	DKbC	1744	A2
Frontier Tr	DKbC	1744	A2
Front Royal Ct	DKbC	1600	E6
Fruithurst Ln NW	GwnC	1602	A2
Fuller Rd NE	DKbC	1742	E2
Fulton Av	EPNT	1975	D7
N Fulton Av	HPVL	2062	C2
S Fulton Av	HPVL	2062	B3
Fulton Blvd SW	ATLN	1976	A4
Fulton Br SE	ATLN	1977	C3
N Fulton Dr NE	ATLN	1742	A7
S Fulton Pkwy	FulC	2145	D1
Fulton St SE	ATLN	1890	E6
Fulton St SW	ATLN	1890	C6
Fulton Ter SE	ATLN	1891	C5
Fulton Industrial Blvd NW	ATLN	1813	A7
	FulC	1813	A7
Fulton Ind Blvd NW SR-70	ATLN	1813	A7
	FulC	1813	A7
Fulton Industrial Blvd SW	ATLN	1887	C3
	FulC	1887	C3
Fulton Ind Blvd SW SR-70	ATLN	1887	C3
	FulC	1887	C3
Fulton Industrial Cir SW	FulC	1887	C2
Fulton St Ext	ATLN	1890	E5
Funston Av SE	ATLN	1977	B2
Future St SE	CobC	1666	A5
G			
N G Av	FTPK	2150	B1
Gaberonne Ct NE	ATLN	1816	D1
Gabi Ln NE	DKbC	1743	C7
Gable Rd NE	MRTA	1596	B4
Gables Dr NE	DKbC	1742	E5
Gables Ln	FulC	1599	D4
Gables Wy NE	DKbC	1743	C7
Gablewood Ct	DKbC	1818	E2
Gablewood Dr NE	CobC	1527	E5
Gaidrew	FulC	1533	D1
Gail Dr NE	DKbC	1742	E6
Gailsmill Cir	DKbC	2066	E3
Gainer Rd SW	ATLN	1976	B6
Gainsborough Dr	DKbC	1671	C3
Gaitskell Ln	FulC	1533	E1
Galahad Ct	DKbC	2066	D3
Galahad Dr NE	DKbC	1744	B5
Galangale Wy	DKbC	1673	C7

STREET	City	Map #	Grid
Galangale Wy	DKbC	1745	C1
Galaxy Ct	DKbC	1980	A3
Galewood Cir NE	MRTA	1527	A6
Galilee Ct	DKbC	1745	C7
Gallahad Ct	RVDL	2147	E7
Gallant Cir SE	CobC	1812	A6
Gallant Ct SE	CobC	1812	A6
Gallant Ln SE	CobC	1812	A6
Gallant Chase SE	CobC	1812	A6
Gallant Fox Ln NE	CobC	1527	E6
Gallatree Ln NW	GwnC	1533	B5
Galleria Dr SE	CobC	1668	A7
Galleria Ln SE	CobC	1668	A7
	SMYR	1667	D7
Galleria Pkwy SE	CobC	1668	A7
Gallery Ct	DKbC	1600	A4
Galway Dr	RSWL	1531	D6
Galway Ln	DKbC	1893	E7
	DKbC	1979	E1
Gambrell Dr NE	DKbC	1817	C6
Gambrell Rd SE	CobC	1738	A6
Gammon Av SE	ATLN	1976	E2
Ganges Ct	FulC	1532	D5
Gann Rd SE	SMYR	1738	D4
Gann Rd SW	CobC	1666	A1
Gant Pl NE	CobC	1597	A5
Gant Quarters Cir NE	CobC	1597	A5
Gant Quarters Ct NE	CobC	1597	A5
Gant Quarters Dr NE	CobC	1597	A5
Gant Quarters Ln NE	CobC	1597	A5
Gant Quarters Ter NE	CobC	1597	A5
Gant Quarters Wy NE	CobC	1597	A5
Garber Dr NE	FulC	1670	B3
Garden Cir	DKbC	1892	D7
Garden Cir NE	CobC	1526	E6
	MRTA	1526	E6
Garden Ct	ClyC	2150	C6
	EPNT	2060	C5
S Garden Ct NE	DKbC	1743	C3
Garden Ct NE	FulC	1670	D2
Garden Ct NW	GwnC	1602	A2
Garden Ln	DCTR	1817	D7
N Garden Ln NW	ATLN	1815	D5
Garden Ln NW	ATLN	1815	D5
Garden Pl	ClyC	2150	E5
E Garden Wk	ClyC	2148	C5
Gardengate Wy SE	CobC	1596	C6
Gardenia Cir NE	CobC	1598	C3
Gardenia Dr NW	ATLN	1889	D4
Gardenia Ln	DKbC	1818	B4
Gardenia Ln NE	CobC	1598	C3
Gardenia St NW	ATLN	1889	E4
Garden Ln Cir NE	CobC	1528	A7
Garden Ln Dr NE	CobC	1528	B7
Garden Mill Ln	DKbC	2065	E2
Garden Mill Ter	DKbC	2065	E2
Garden Park Dr SE	CobC	1739	B4
Garden Ridge Dr	ClyC	2148	A4
Gardenside Cir SE	CobC	1596	D7
Gardenside Ct NE	DKbC	1743	C3
Garden Springs Dr	ClyC	2148	A5
Garden View Dr NE	ATLN	1742	D5
	DKbC	1742	D5
Garden Walk Blvd	ClyC	2147	E4
Garden Wood Ct	ClyC	2148	A5
Garden Wood Dr	ClyC	2147	E5
Gardner Rd	FTPK	2149	E2
Gardner St SW	ATLN	1890	C7
Garfield Ct	DKbC	1819	C4
Garfield Dr	DKbC	1819	C4
Garfield Wy SE	ATLN	2063	C3
Garibaldi St SW	ATLN	1890	D6
	ATLN	1976	D1
Garland Av	DCTR	1892	E3
Garland Ct	ClyC	2147	B6
Garland St SW	ATLN	1976	D3
Garmon Dr NW	ATLN	1741	A1
W Garmon Rd NW	ATLN	1668	E7
	FulC	1668	E7
Garmon Rd NW	ATLN	1740	E2
	FulC	1741	A1
Garmon Ferry Rd NW	ATLN	1740	E2
Garnaby Ln NW	GwnC	1533	D7
Garnet Wy	FulC	2146	D7
Garnett St SW	ATLN	1890	D4
Garr Cir SW	FulC	1887	C6
Garraux Pl NW	ATLN	1740	C5
Garraux Rd NW	ATLN	1740	B4
Garraux St NW	ATLN	1815	A5
Garraux Woods Rd NW	ATLN	1740	C4
Garrett Cir	DRVL	1672	B3
Garrett Ct	DKbC	2065	D2
Garrick Wy NE	CobC	1529	C7
Garrison Dr SE	MRTA	1595	B6
Garrison Dr SW	ATLN	1974	A2
	FulC	1974	A2
Garrison Rd SE	CobC	1595	A6
	MRTA	1595	A6
Garrison Plantation Dr SE	CobC	1595	A7
Garson Dr NE	ATLN	1816	B2
Gartrell St SE	ATLN	1891	A4
Gary Av NW	ATLN	1889	E1
Gary Ct NW	ATLN	1889	A2
Gary Rd NW	ATLN	1889	A1
Gaskill St SE	ATLN	1891	B5
Gaskin Wk NE	CobC	1598	B1
Gas Light Cir NE	CobC	1529	B1
Gaspero St NE	ATLN	1891	B3
Gaston St SW	ATLN	1889	D7
E Gate Ct	DKbC	1600	D6
Gatehouse Dr	DKbC	1894	A1
Gatehurst Ct SE	CobC	1739	C2
Gateside Cts SE	CobC	1598	A5
Gateside Ln SE	CobC	1598	B5
Gateside Pl SE	CobC	1598	A5
Gateside Trc SE	CobC	1598	A5
Gatestone Wy	GwnC	1673	A1
Gateswalk Dr SE	CobC	1739	D4
Gateswalk Wy SE	CobC	1739	D4
Gateview Cir NE	MRTA	1527	A7
Gateview Dr NE	MRTA	1527	A7
Gateview Wy NE	MRTA	1527	A7
Gateway Dr NW	GwnC	1601	E7
Gatewood Ct NW	ATLN	1741	A5
Gatewood Dr NE	CobC	1597	B5
N Gatewood Rd NE	DKbC	1817	B5
Gatewood Rd NE	DKbC	1817	C5
Gathering Pkwy SW	FulC	1973	C1
Gatsby Pl	FulC	1532	C4
Gault St SE	ATLN	1977	B1
Gavinwood Pl	DKbC	1818	B3
Gay Dr	DKbC	1979	D1
Gaylemont Cir	DKbC	1818	A4
Gayles Ct SE	ATLN	2063	B1
Gaylor Cir SE	CobC	1739	A6
Gaylor Dr SE	CobC	1739	A5
Gaylor St SE	CobC	1739	A5
	SMYR	1739	A5
Geary Dr NW	ATLN	1815	D5
Geddy Wy	FulC	1532	C4
Gelding Ct	RSWL	1532	A6
Gelding Ct NE	CobC	1527	D4
Gelding Ln NE	CobC	1527	E3
Gemstone Ct	FulC	2146	E6
Gemstone Pl	FulC	2146	D6
Gemstone Ter NE	CobC	1529	A4
Gena Dr	DKbC	1979	C1
Generals Rd	CobC	1666	C1
General Truman St NW	ATLN	1814	C3
Genessee Av SW	ATLN	1976	B2
Geneva St	ClyC	2062	E6
	DCTR	1817	E6
Genny Ln	ClyC	2147	E7
	RVDL	2148	A7
Gentilly Pl	DRVL	1672	B3
Gentry Gate	FulC	1533	A2
Gentrys Wk	DKbC	1671	E3
George St NW	ATLN	1813	E2
George St SE	ATLN	1891	A5
George Howell Wy	DKbC	1818	E6
George Luther Dr	DKbC	1819	B7
George McMillan Dr SE	CobC	1666	C3
Georgetown Blf NE	CobC	1528	A1
Georgetown Ct	DKbC	1671	B2
Georgetown Pl NE	CobC	1527	D1
Georgetown Sq	DKbC	1671	C2
Georgetown Wy	DKbC	1671	C1
Georgetown Chase	RSWL	1530	D3
Georgetown Park Dr NW	NRCS	1602	C6
George Washington Dr	ClyC	2065	C7
	ClyC	2151	C1
George Wythe Pl NW	ATLN	1814	A2
Georgia Av	EPNT	2061	D1
	FTPK	2149	B1
	HPVL	2062	B3
Georgia Av NE	DKbC	1670	E7
Georgia Av NW	GwnC	1673	A1
Georgia Av SE	ATLN	1890	E6
Georgia Dome Dr NW	ATLN	1890	C4
Georgian Ct NE	CobC	1596	E6
Georgian Dr E	DKbC	1743	D2
Georgian Dr W	DKbC	1743	D2
Georgian Ter	DKbC	1743	C2
Georgian Ter NE	CobC	1596	E5
Georgiana Dr NE	DKbC	1817	C1
Georgian Manor Ct	FulC	1532	C4
Georgian Manor Dr	FulC	1532	C4
Georgian Woods Cir	DKbC	1980	D6
Geraldine Ct NW	GwnC	1601	D4
Geraldine Dr SE	CobC	1738	A3
Geraldine Dr SW	CobC	1738	A3
Gerizm Ct SE	CobC	1812	C5
Gerry Ln NE	FulC	1670	B3
Gertrude Pl NW	ATLN	1814	C7
Gettysburg Ln SE	CobC	1596	E7
Gettysburg Pl	FulC	1531	A6
Gibbons Dr	DKbC	1818	E5
Gibbons Ln	DKbC	1818	E5
Gibbs St	CobC	1595	C7
Giben Rd SW	ATLN	1976	C3
Gibson St SE	ATLN	1891	D5
Gideons Dr SW	ATLN	1889	E4
Gifford Dr	DKbC	1818	E5
Gifford St	DKbC	1818	E5
Gift Av SE	ATLN	1891	D6
Gilbert Pl	FTPK	2063	B6
Gilbert Rd SE	ATLN	2063	A3
	ClyC	2063	A3
Gilbert St SE	ATLN	1891	D7
	ATLN	1977	D1
	SMYR	1666	E6
Gilbert Tr NE	ATLN	1891	A2
Gilbert Wy SE	ATLN	2062	E4
Gilford Wy	FulC	1601	B4
Gilgal Wy	ClyC	2151	B2
Gillem Dr	EPNT	1975	C4
Gillette Av SW	ATLN	1890	B7
Gilmer St SE	ATLN	1890	E4
Gilmore Rd SE	CobC	1739	C4
Gilston Ct	DKbC	1894	B5
Gin Row SE	MRTA	1596	B7
Ginn St NW	CobC	1595	A1
	MRTA	1595	A1
Givens Av NW	ATLN	1814	A4
Glace Rd	FulC	2146	C7
E Glade Ct	DKbC	1894	D6
Glade Rd	FTPK	2063	B6
Glade Springs Dr NE	DKbC	1744	C7
Gladesworth Ln	DKbC	1894	D6
Glade Wood Run	UNCT	2145	A5
Glad Morning Ct	FulC	2059	B5
Glad Morning Dr	FulC	2059	B5
Gladney Dr	DKbC	1745	B1
Gladstone Dr SW	CobC	1666	A5
Gladstone Rd NW	ATLN	1815	B3
Glandor Ct SE	CobC	1812	E2
Glandor Dr SE	CobC	1812	E3
Glasgow Dr	DKbC	1894	C5
Glasgow Rd NE	CobC	1528	D7
Glass St NW	ATLN	1890	A1
Glaze Dr	DKbC	1601	C5
Glen Ct	HryC	2152	C1
Glen Wy NE	DKbC	1742	E3
	DKbC	1743	C1
Glen Acres Ct	DKbC	1894	C6
Glenairy Ct NE	FulC	1670	C2
Glenairy Dr NE	FulC	1670	B2
Glenald Wy NW	ATLN	1814	E2
Glen Arbor Ct NE	DKbC	1671	B4
Glen Arden Dr NW	ATLN	1741	C6
Glen Arden Pl NW	ATLN	1741	C5
Glen Arden Wy NE	ATLN	1816	C7
	CobC	1596	D3
Glenbonnie Ct	DKbC	1601	A7
Glenbonnie Dr	DKbC	1601	A6
Glenbriar Dr NE	DKbC	1744	C4
Glenbrook Dr NW	ATLN	1815	A2
Glenbrooke Tr	DKbC	1601	A4
Glencastle Dr NW	FulC	1669	C4
Glenco Dr	DKbC	1893	E6
Glencourtney Dr NE	FulC	1599	A5
Glen Cove	DKbC	1818	E7
Glencove Av SE	DKbC	1892	B5
Glen Cove Dr	DKbC	1818	E7
Glencrest Dr NE	MRTA	1596	A4
Glen Crossing Dr	FulC	1532	E6
Glenda Dr	CGPK	2060	D6
Glenda Ln NE	CobC	1527	E7
Glenda Wy	DRVL	1672	C2
Glendale Av	DCTR	1893	A1
Glendale Av NE	ATLN	1892	A3
Glendale Cir SE	SMYR	1666	C6
Glendale Ct	DKbC	1979	D1
	EPNT	2060	D1
Glendale Dr	DKbC	1893	D7
	DKbC	1979	D1
	EPNT	1975	E6
Glendale Dr NE	CobC	1526	E1
Glendale Pl SE	SMYR	1666	C6
Glendale Rd	DKbC	1818	E5
Glendale Ter NE	ATLN	1816	A7
Glendalough Pl SW	ATLN	1889	D6
Glendeven Ct NW	ATLN	1814	E2
Glen Devon Dr NW	ATLN	1741	B3
Glen Eagles Cir SE	CobC	1597	E7
Gleneagles Ct	DKbC	1745	C3
Gleneagles Dr	DKbC	1745	C4
Gleneagles Ln	DKbC	1745	B3
Glen Echo Dr	DKbC	1894	B6
Glen Echo Dr SW	ATLN	1974	C3
Glen Echo Wy NE	MRTA	1527	B7
Glen Errol Rd NW	FulC	1669	C3
Glen Eves Dr	RSWL	1531	E5
Glenfair Rd	DKbC	1894	C7
	DKbC	1980	C1
Glen Falls Dr	DKbC	1894	B7
Glen Ferry Dr	FulC	1532	E6
Glenferry Tr NW	FulC	1598	E7
Glenforest Rd NE	FulC	1670	B3
Glen Forest Wy	DKbC	1894	A4
Glengary Ct NE	ATLN	1742	C2
Glengary Dr NE	ATLN	1742	C1
Glengary Wy NE	ATLN	1742	C2
Glengate Av	FulC	1599	B7
Glengate Pl	FulC	1599	B7
Glengate Cove	FulC	1599	B7
Glen Haven Cir	DKbC	1894	E6
Glen Haven Dr	ClyC	2147	E3
	DKbC	1894	E5
Glenhill Pl	DKbC	1893	B6
Glen Hollow Cir	DKbC	1979	D5
Glen Hollow Dr	DKbC	1979	D5
Glen Hollow Ln	DKbC	1979	D5
Glen Holly Dr	RSWL	1531	E5
Glenhurst Dr SE	SMYR	1739	A3
Glen Iris Dr NE	ATLN	1891	B2
Glen Ivy Dr	RSWL	1531	E5
Glen Lake Dr NW	FulC	1669	D3
Glenlake Pkwy NE	FulC	1599	C6
Glenlake Commons Dr	DCTR	1818	A6
Glenleaf Dr NW	GwnC	1602	A5
Glenleigh Dr SW	CobC	1738	A6
Glenloch Ct	HryC	2152	C5
Glenloch Ln	HryC	2152	C5
Glenloch Pkwy	HryC	2152	C5
Glenloch Pt	HryC	2152	C5
Glenmar Dr	DKbC	1894	A7
Glen Meadow Ct NE	FulC	1599	D6
Glen Meadow Dr NW	GwnC	1602	A2
Glen Meadow Ln NW	GwnC	1602	A1
Glenmont Ct	FulC	1601	B2
Glen Moor Rd	ClyC	2151	C1
Glen Moore Rd	RSWL	1532	B1
Glen Mora Ct	DKbC	1894	B7
Glen Mora Dr	DKbC	1894	B7
Glenn Av NW	ATLN	1815	A3
Glenn Cir	DCTR	1818	A7
Glenn Ct	DCTR	1818	B6
Glenn Dr	FTPK	2149	B3
Glenn Pl	ClyC	2064	A6
Glenn Rd	DKbC	1894	A4
Glenn St	DCTR	1893	B1
Glenn St SE	ATLN	1890	E6
	CobC	1666	B7
Glenn St SW	ATLN	1890	C6
Glenncrest Ct NE	DKbC	1671	B4
Glenndale Av	DCTR	1818	A7
Glennhurst Ln SW	FulC	1887	C7
Glen Oaks Ct NE	DKbC	1744	A6
Glen Oaks Dr NW	FulC	1669	C3
Glen Oaks Ln NE	FulC	1670	B1
Glenover Cir NE	MRTA	1527	A6
Glenover Wy NE	MRTA	1526	E6
Glen Pointe Wy SE	CobC	1739	B5
Glen Raven Ct	DKbC	1894	E5
Glenrich Ct	DKbC	1600	A3

INDEX 26

Glenrich Dr — Greenwillow Dr

Atlanta Street Index

STREET	City	Map #	Grid
Glenrich Dr	DKbC	1600	A3
Glenridge Coms NE	FulC	1670	B1
Glenridge Ct NE	CobC	1527	C5
Glenridge Dr NE	CobC	1527	C5
	FulC	1599	B7
	FulC	1670	C3
Glenridge Close Cir NE	FulC	1599	B6
Glenridge Close Dr NE	FulC	1599	B7
	FulC	1670	C1
Glenridge Perimeter Connector	FulC	1670	C3
Glenridge Point Pkwy NE	FulC	1670	C3
Glenridge Stratford Dr NE	FulC	1670	B4
Glen River Wy	FulC	1532	E6
Glenrock Dr	DKbC	1979	E2
Glenrock Dr NW	ATLN	1813	E5
Glenrose Cir SW	ATLN	2062	D1
Glenrose Ct	RSWL	1531	E2
Glenrose Ct SW	ATLN	2062	D1
Glenrose Dr	DKbC	1745	A3
Glenrose Dr SE	SMYR	1666	D7
Glenrose Hl	DKbC	1745	A3
Glenrose Pt	DKbC	1745	A3
Glenrose Tr	DKbC	1745	A3
Glenroy Dr SE	SMYR	1667	B7
Glenroy Pl SE	SMYR	1667	C7
Glen Royal Ct	RSWL	1532	B7
Glen Royal Dr	RSWL	1532	B7
Glensford Dr	DKbC	1894	A6
Glenshire Ct	ClyC	2148	A6
	RVDL	2148	A6
Glenshire Pl	DKbC	1600	A7
Glenvale Pl	DKbC	1893	E6
Glenvalley Dr	DKbC	1893	B6
Glenverness Dr NE	CobC	1598	D1
Glenview Cir SW	ATLN	1974	A4
Glenview Dr SW	ATLN	1974	B3
Glenway Dr	ATLN	1976	B7
	EPNT	1976	B7
Glenwood Av	ATLN	1890	E5
Glenwood Av SE	ATLN	1890	E5
	ATLN	1892	A6
	ATLN	1893	A6
	DKbC	1892	C6
Glenwood Av SE SR-260	ATLN	1891	E6
	ATLN	1892	C6
	DKbC	1892	A6
	DKbC	1893	A6
Glenwood Ct SE	CobC	1668	A2
Glenwood Dr NE	ATLN	1815	E2
Glenwood Pkwy	DKbC	1894	B6
Glenwood Pl SE	ATLN	1891	D6
Glenwood Rd	DKbC	1893	B6
	DKbC	1894	B6
Glenwood Rd SR-260	DKbC	1893	B6
Glenwood Av Ext N	ATLN	1891	B6
Glenwood Downs Dr	DKbC	1894	C7
Glenwood Downs Ln	DKbC	1894	C7
Glenwyck Pl	DKbC	1745	C7
Global Gateway Connector	CGPK	2061	A6
Glochester Pl NW	NRCS	1602	E7
E Glochester Rd NW	NRCS	1602	E7
Gloucester Dr	DKbC	1745	B7
N Gloucester Pl	DKbC	1671	E3
Gloucester Wy	DKbC	1745	C7
Glouchester Ct	ClyC	2149	B4
Glover Av SE	CobC	1595	B7
Glover St SE	MRTA	1595	B6
Glynbrook Dr	DKbC	1745	E6
Glynda Dr NE	CobC	1527	E5
Glynn Dr SE	DKbC	1978	A2
Glynn Oaks Dr	DKbC	1819	A4
Gober Av SE	CobC	1666	C4
	SMYR	1666	C4
Gober Ter SE	SMYR	1666	C4
Godby Pl	CGPK	2146	D2
	FulC	2146	D2
Godby Rd	CGPK	2146	E2
	ClyC	2147	A2
	FulC	2146	D2
Goddard St SE	ATLN	1977	C4
Godfrey Dr NW	ATLN	1888	E3
Gold Ct	HryC	2152	C2
Gold Dr SW	ATLN	1974	C2
Gold Creek Ct	FulC	1530	C7
Golden Dr	EPNT	2060	C1
Golden Dawn Dr SW	ATLN	1974	C5
Golden Gate Dr NW	ATLN	1815	D4
Golden Leaf Grv NW	GwnC	1602	D1
Golden Leaf Tr NW	GwnC	1602	D1
Golden Meadow Ct	RVDL	2147	E6
Golden Meadow Dr	RVDL	2147	E6
Goldie Dr SE	MRTA	1596	A5
Goldleaf Ct	ClyC	2152	A4
Goldleaf Ter	ClyC	2151	E5
Goldleaf Wy	ClyC	2152	A4
Goldmill Ct	DKbC	2066	B7
Goldmill Rd	DKbC	2066	B7
Goldrush Cir NE	FulC	1670	C3
Goldsboro Rd NE	ATLN	1891	E2
Golf Cir NE	ATLN	1816	A4
Golf Club Ln SE	CobC	1739	E2
Golf View Dr	CGPK	2060	E4
Golf View Dr NW	ATLN	1815	D3
Golf View Rd NW	ATLN	1815	C3
Goodchild Ct	DKbC	1600	E5
Goodfellows Ct	DKbC	1745	E2
Goodfellows Rd	DKbC	1745	E2
Goodrum Ln NE	CobC	1526	C4
Goodson St	UNCT	2145	A7
Goodwin Pl NE	DKbC	1742	E6
Goodwin Rd NE	ATLN	1742	D6
	DKbC	1742	D6
Goodwood Blvd SE	SMYR	1667	E7
	SMYR	1739	C1
Goose Creek Wy NW	GwnC	1533	B5
Goose Creek Cove NW	GwnC	1533	B5
Gordon Av NE	ATLN	1892	B3
Gordon Cir	HPVL	2062	B1
N Gordon Cir	HPVL	2062	B1
S Gordon Cir	HPVL	2062	B1
Gordon Cir SE	SMYR	1667	B6
Gordon Mnr	ATLN	1892	B3
Gordon Pl SW	ATLN	1890	A6
Gordon St	ATLN	1892	D4
	DCTR	1892	D4
S Gordon St SW	ATLN	1889	C6
Gordon Ter SW	ATLN	1889	C5
Gordy Pkwy NE	CobC	1528	A1
Gorham Close	FulC	1532	E3
Goss Ct	CGPK	2061	B4
Goswell Rd SE	SMYR	1738	D5
Gotham Wy NE	ATLN	1816	B3
Gothic Elm Ct	DKbC	1980	C5
Gould St SE	ATLN	1977	A3
Goulding Pl	RSWL	1530	C1
Governors Ct NE	CobC	1526	C2
Governors Dr	FTPK	2149	A2
Governors Lake Dr NW	GwnC	1601	C7
Governors Lake Pkwy NW	GwnC	1601	E7
Grace Ct SE	SMYR	1738	C3
Grace Dr	FTPK	2063	D7
Grace St SE	ATLN	1892	A7
Grace Arbor Ct NE	DKbC	1817	D1
Graceland Cir	MRRW	2149	E6
Graceland Ct	MRRW	2149	E6
Grace Marie Ln	HryC	2065	C5
Grace Meadows Ln SE	SMYR	1738	C3
Gracewood Av SE	ATLN	1891	D7
Gracewood Dr NE	CobC	1527	E2
Gracewood Park Dr	ClyC	2065	A5
Grady Pl	HPVL	2062	C2
Grady Pl SW	ATLN	1889	E6
Grady St SE	SMYR	1666	D6
Graham Cir SE	DKbC	1892	B7
	DKbC	1978	B1
Graham St SW	ATLN	1976	B2
Gramercy Cir	DKbC	1671	D4
Gramercy Ct	DKbC	1600	D4
Gramercy Dr NE	CobC	1598	C4
Gramling Cir	MRTA	1595	A6
W Gramling St SW	MRTA	1595	A6
Gramling St SE	MRTA	1595	A6
Gran Ct	RSWL	1531	C1
Granada Dr	ClyC	2149	B7
	FulC	2059	E7
Granada Ln	FulC	2059	E6
Granada Pl	EPNT	2060	D1
Granade Dr	FTPK	2149	B2
Granby Av	DKbC	1818	E6
Granby Wy NE	CobC	1529	A6
Granby Hill Pl	RSWL	1532	B6
Gran Crique Dr	RSWL	1531	B1
N Grand Av NW	ATLN	1814	B7
S Grand Av NW	ATLN	1889	A1
Grand Av SW	ATLN	1976	C7
	ATLN	2062	C1
Gran de Ct	FulC	2146	C6
Grande Wy	ClyC	2149	C7
Grand Forest Ct NW	GwnC	1602	A3
Grand Forest Dr NW	GwnC	1602	B2
Grand Manor Ct NE	CobC	1596	D6
Grand Manor Dr NE	CobC	1596	D6
Grand Pines Ct	DKbC	1980	C4
Grand Pines Dr	DKbC	1980	C4
Grand Prix Ct NE	DKbC	1744	B6
Grand Prix Dr NE	DKbC	1744	B6
Grandview Av NE	ATLN	1742	A7
Grandview Av NW	ATLN	1813	E3
Grandview Cir SE	DKbC	1892	C7
Grand View Dr SE	SMYR	1738	E7
	SMYR	1812	D1
Grandvista Approach NE	CobC	1529	A6
Grange Ct SE	ATLN	1977	C4
Grange Dr SE	ATLN	1977	C4
Granger Ct	DKbC	1671	C4
Granger Dr	DKbC	1671	C4
Granite Ridge Pl	FulC	1599	D1
Granite Springs Ln	GwnC	1532	E7
Grant Cir SE	ATLN	1977	A1
Grant Dr NE	DKbC	1743	B3
Grant Dr SW	ATLN	1973	D4
Grant Pl SW	ATLN	1973	D4
Grant Rd	ClyC	2064	C5
	ClyC	2065	A6
	ClyC	2150	E1
Grant Rd SW	ATLN	1973	E4
Grant St SE	ATLN	1891	A5
	ATLN	1977	A1
Grant St SW	ATLN	1976	C4
Grant Ter SE	ATLN	1891	A7
	ATLN	1977	A1
Grant Wy	EPNT	2060	C2
Grant Wy SE	ATLN	1977	A1
Grant Estates Dr	EPNT	2060	C2
Grantland Dr	DKbC	1745	C5
Grantley Ct	FulC	1530	C7
Grant Park Pl SE	ATLN	1891	A7
Grant Valley Rd NW	ATLN	1741	E5
Granville Ct NE	FulC	1599	C7
Grape St NE	ATLN	1891	B3
Grape St SE	ATLN	1976	E2
Grapevine Run	FulC	1600	B2
Grassnut Ct	RSWL	1531	C5
Grass Valley Rd SW	ATLN	1974	C5
Graves Ln NW	GwnC	1673	D5
Graves Rd NW	GwnC	1673	D5
Graves St NW	ATLN	1890	C3
Graves Mill Ct NW	GwnC	1673	D6
Graves Mill Dr NW	GwnC	1673	D6
Gray Rd SE	CobC	1666	A7
	CobC	1738	A1
Gray St NE	MRTA	1595	A2
Gray St NW	ATLN	1890	C2
Graymont Dr SW	ATLN	1975	D1
Grayson Ct NE	CobC	1528	E7
Grayson Pl	DKbC	1818	C7
Gray Squirrel Cross NE	CobC	1528	D7
Graywall Ct	EPNT	1975	A6
Graywall St	EPNT	1975	A6
Graywood Cir SE	CobC	1813	A3
Graywood Dr SE	CobC	1813	A3
Graywood Trc NW	GwnC	1533	A6
Graywood Willow Ln SE	CobC	1813	A3
Great Oaks Brch	HryC	2152	C6
Green Av SE	ATLN	1892	E5
	DKbC	1892	E5
Green St	DCTR	1892	E3
	RSWL	1530	C1
Green St NW	ATLN	1815	B5
Green St SE	MRTA	1595	B5
Green Acres Rd SE	SMYR	1666	C5
Greenbank Ter NW	GwnC	1533	A7
Greenbower Ln	FulC	2146	D7
Greenbriar Cir	DKbC	1818	D3
Greenbriar Ln	HryC	2152	E6
N Greenbriar Pkwy NE	MRTA	1596	C3
Greenbriar Pkwy NE	CobC	1596	C3
	MRTA	1596	C3
Greenbriar Pkwy SW	ATLN	1974	C6
Greenbriar Pl	ATLN	1974	D5
	DKbC	1818	D4
	EPNT	1974	D5
Greenbriar Rd NE	FulC	1670	B3
Greenbriar Tr SW	ATLN	1973	B4
Greenbrook Tr NE	DKbC	1744	C5
Greenbrook Wy NE	DKbC	1744	D5
Greenbush Pl NE	DKbC	1744	C4
Greencastle Wy NE	CobC	1528	B3
Greencastle Chase NE	CobC	1528	B3
Greencliff Dr NE	DKbC	1744	D5
Greencove Av NE	ATLN	1816	C7
Greencove Ln SE	ATLN	1892	A6
Greencrest Ct NE	CobC	1597	B4
Greencrest Dr NE	DKbC	1744	D4
Green Cup Ct SW	FulC	1887	C7
Green Cup Ln SW	FulC	1887	B7
Greendale Dr NW	ATLN	1740	E6
Greendale Dr SE	ATLN	1977	A4
Green Elm Wy	RSWL	1531	E4
Green Falls Pt	FulC	1600	D2
Greenfield Av SE	ATLN	1890	E7
Greenfield Ct NE	CobC	1597	A3
Greenfield Dr NE	CobC	1597	B3
Greenfield St NW	ATLN	1815	B7
Greenfield Trc NE	CobC	1597	A3
Green Forest Dr SE	SMYR	1738	C3
Greenforest Ln SE	SMYR	1738	D3
Green Forest Pkwy SE	SMYR	1738	C4
Green Forrest Dr	DKbC	1893	E7
	DKbC	1979	D1
Greenglade Rd NE	DKbC	1743	D5
Green Glen Wy NW	FulC	1669	D3
Greenhaven Dr SE	ATLN	1892	C6
Green Hawk Ct	DKbC	1980	D1
Green Hawk Tr	DKbC	1980	D1
Greenhill Dr	CMBL	1671	D4
	DKbC	1671	D4
Green Hill Pl NE	FulC	1670	A5
Green Hill Rd NE	FulC	1670	A5
Greenhill Wy	FTPK	2063	A6
Greenhouse Pkwy	RSWL	1532	C7
Green Industrial Wy	DKbC	1671	E4
Greenland Dr NE	ATLN	1816	C6
Greenland Rd NE	FulC	1670	B5
Greenland Trc NE	FulC	1670	A5
Greenlaurel Dr NE	FulC	1670	A5
Greenleaf Cir SW	ATLN	1973	B7
Greenleaf Dr NE	CobC	1598	D2
Greenleaf Ln	FTPK	2063	A6
Greenleaf Rd SE	DKbC	1891	E7
Green Marsh Ct	DKbC	1979	C7
	DKbC	2065	C1
Green Meadow Dr NE	CobC	1526	E3
Green Meadow Ln NE	CobC	1527	A3
Green Meadow Wy	ClyC	2151	B5
Green Meadows Ln NE	DKbC	1743	A3
Green Mountain Tr	FulC	2060	A6
Green Oak Ct NW	FulC	1669	E5
Green Oak Dr	DRVL	1672	E3
Green Oak Rdg NE	CobC	1598	C4
Greenoaks Cir	DKbC	1744	D4
Green Park Ct NW	FulC	1669	C4
Greenpine Dr NE	FulC	1670	C5
Green Pointe Pkwy NW	GwnC	1601	D6
Green Pointe Wy NE	CobC	1598	B4
Greenridge Cir	DKbC	1819	B6
Green Ridge Dr NE	CobC	1528	E6
Green Ridge Rd SE	CobC	1666	C4
	SMYR	1666	C4
Green River Ct NE	CobC	1598	C4
Greenrock Ct	DKbC	1745	C2
Greenrock Tr	DKbC	1745	C2
Greensferry Av SW	ATLN	1890	B5
Greenspan Ct	DKbC	1980	C4
Greenspring Rd	CGPK	2060	E7
Greenstone Ct	DKbC	1980	D2
Greensward Dr NE	DKbC	1744	C5
Green Trail Dr	FulC	2146	D6
Greentree Ct	FulC	2059	B6
Greentree Dr	DKbC	1894	B7
	DKbC	1980	B1
Greentree Dr SE	CobC	1667	E1
Greentree Ln	CobC	2059	B6
Greentree Tr	FulC	2059	A6
Greentree Farms Dr	DKbC	1980	B4
Greenvale Dr	DKbC	1980	E5
Greenvale Wy	DKbC	1980	E5
Green Valley Dr	FulC	2060	C1
Green Valley Dr SE	SMYR	1738	C4
Greenview Av NE	ATLN	1742	B6
Greenview Dr NE	CobC	1597	D2
Greenville Trc	DKbC	1980	A2
Greenville Wy	DKbC	1980	A3
Greenvine Pl	RSWL	1531	C3
Greenvine Trc	RSWL	1531	C3
Greenway	FulC	1530	D6
Greenway Dr	DKbC	1980	D2
Greenwich St SW	ATLN	1889	E5
	ATLN	1890	A5
Greenwick St	ATLN	1889	D5
Greenwillow Dr	ClyC	2063	E6

INDEX 27

Greenwillow Dr NE — Atlanta Street Index — Hardee St NE

Atlanta Street Index

STREET	City	Map #	Grid
Greenwillow Dr NE	DKbC	1744	C5
Greenwillow Wy	ClyC	2064	A6
Green Wing Wy	ClyC	2150	E6
Greenwood Av	DCTR	1892	E2
Greenwood Av NE	ATLN	1891	B1
Greenwood Cir	DCTR	1892	E2
	EPNT	1974	E6
Greenwood Dr NW	GwnC	1673	E4
Greenwood Ln	ClyC	2147	E5
Greenwood Ln SW	FulC	1887	B6
Greenwood Pl	DCTR	1892	E2
Greenwood Tr SE	CobC	1597	A7
Greenwood Wy	FTPK	2149	C4
Greenwood Close NE	DKbC	1670	D6
Gregg St SW	ATLN	1890	C5
Gregory Rd	DKbC	1894	E7
Gregory L Davis Plz NE	ATLN	1891	D2
Grenoble Ct	DKbC	1601	C4
Grenock Cir NE	FulC	1599	B4
Gresham Av NE	MRTA	1595	E4
Gresham Av SE	ATLN	1891	E7
	DKbC	1891	E7
	DKbC	1977	E1
Gresham Rd NE	MRTA	1595	E4
Gresham Rd SE	DKbC	1978	D4
Gresham St	UNCT	2145	A7
Gresham Park Dr NE	MRTA	1596	A3
Gress Av SE	ATLN	1891	B7
Gretna Ct	ClyC	2152	A5
Gretna Green Dr	DKbC	1894	C5
Gretna Green Wy	DKbC	1894	C5
Grey St SW	ATLN	1976	D7
Greyfield Ct NE	CobC	1528	A3
Greyfield Dr SE	CobC	1668	A1
Greyfield Ln	FulC	1530	E5
Greyfield Pl NW	FulC	1669	D3
Greyfield Pl SE	CobC	1668	A1
Greyfield Trc SE	CobC	1668	A1
Greyhurst Wy SE	SMYR	1738	A4
Greylock Pl	DKbC	1818	A6
Greypointe Cove	DKbC	1980	A5
Greyson Dr NE	CobC	1527	C6
Greyson Rdg NE	CobC	1527	D7
Grey Squirrel Ct SE	CobC	1667	C2
Greystone Cir	DKbC	1745	A1
Greystone Ct E	DKbC	1819	C4
Greystone Ct NE	CobC	1529	D6
Greystone Ct W	DKbC	1819	C4
Greystone Ln	DKbC	1745	A2
Greystone Pk NE	ATLN	1816	B4
Greystone Rd NW	ATLN	1815	C4
Greystone Tr NE	CobC	1597	B3
Greystone Trc NE	CobC	1597	B3
Greystone Wy	DKbC	1979	A1
Greystone Cove N	DKbC	1745	A1
Greystone Cove S	DKbC	1745	A2
Griff Ln N	HryC	2066	A6
Griff Ln S	HryC	2066	A6
Griffin Cir	DCTR	1892	E3

STREET	City	Map #	Grid
Griffin St NW	ATLN	1890	B1
Griffin Ter SE	CobC	1738	B2
Griggs Al NW	ATLN	1890	C3
Griggs St SW	MRTA	1595	A5
Grimes Dr	HPVL	2062	A1
Grimes Pl	RSWL	1530	E1
Grimes Bridge Lndg	RSWL	1530	E3
Grimes Bridge Rd	RSWL	1530	E2
Grist Mill Dr NE	CobC	1596	B1
Grist Mill Rd NE	CobC	1596	E2
Grist Stone Ct NE	DKbC	1817	C6
Grizzard Ct NW	GwnC	1602	B2
Grizzard Tr NW	GwnC	1602	B2
Grogan St SE	MRTA	1595	B6
Grogans Lndg	FulC	1599	C1
Grogans Ferry Rd	FulC	1530	C7
Grogans Lake Dr	FulC	1599	C1
Grogans Lake Pt	FulC	1599	B1
Groover Dr SE	CobC	1739	C7
Groover Rd NE	CobC	1527	B7
Grosvenor Pl NW	FulC	1669	E3
Ground Pine Dr NE	CobC	1528	B1
Grove Av	EPNT	1975	B6
Grove Cir	HPVL	2062	C1
Grove Ct	LKCY	2149	D3
Grove Pkwy SE	CobC	1597	A7
Grove Pl	DKbC	1818	B7
	RSWL	1530	D2
Grove St	DCTR	1893	B1
Grove St NE	DKbC	1743	A2
Grove Wy	RSWL	1530	C2
Grove Gate Ln SE	CobC	1740	A2
Grove Hill Ct NW	GwnC	1602	A2
Grovehurst Dr	FulC	1533	A1
Grovehurst Dr NE	CobC	1528	E7
Grovehurst Wy NE	CobC	1528	E7
Groveland Av NW	ATLN	1815	C5
Grovemont Ct	DKbC	1818	B7
Grovenor Wy	ClyC	2147	E6
Grove Park Ct	DKbC	1744	A7
Grove Park Ln SE	CobC	1597	A7
Grove Park Pl NW	ATLN	1814	D7
Grove Park Wy	DKbC	1744	A7
Grove Park Wy NE	CobC	1527	C4
Grover St SE	MRTA	1595	C5
Grove St Ext	DKbC	1893	B1
Guffin Ln NE	CobC	1526	D5
	MRTA	1526	D5
Guildhall Grv	FulC	1532	C2
Guildhall Pl	FulC	1532	C3
Guilford Cir NE	CobC	1596	C3
Guilford Ct	DKbC	2066	B1
Guilford Ln	FulC	2146	E5
Guilford Forest Dr SW	FulC	1973	A1
Guilford Forest Ln SW	FulC	1973	B1
Guinevere Dr NE	DKbC	1744	C5
Guinevere Wy NE	DKbC	1744	C5
Guinn St SW	CobC	1666	A3

STREET	City	Map #	Grid
Gulfstream Ln NE	CobC	1528	B7
Gullatt Dr	UNCT	2145	A6
Gum Ct	ClyC	2150	E4
Gunby Rd SE	CobC	1597	C7
	CobC	1668	C1
Gunby St NE	ATLN	1891	B4
Gun Club Rd NW	ATLN	1814	A5
Gunlock Trc	RSWL	1532	B4
Gunners Wk NW	GwnC	1673	E7
Gunnin Rd NW	GwnC	1533	A7
	GwnC	1602	A1
Gunnison Ct	DKbC	1819	D3
Gunpowder Ln NE	CobC	1597	B3
Gunstock Ln NW	GwnC	1673	E7
Gunston Cove Rd SW	FulC	2059	C2
Gunter Dr	FTPK	2063	D5
Gunter St NE	MRTA	1595	D4
Gus Pl	DKbC	1979	D4
Guthridge Ct NW	GwnC	1602	D4
	NRCS	1602	D4
Guthrie St SE	SMYR	1666	D7
Guy Wy	DKbC	1893	D5
Guynelle Dr NE	CobC	1526	C1
Guyton Ct NW	GwnC	1533	C7
Gwendoline Dr	FulC	2146	A2
Gwendon Ct	DKbC	1979	B4
Gwendon Ter	DKbC	1979	B4
Gwinn Dr NW	GwnC	1673	C2
Gwinnett Station Cir NW	GwnC	1673	C4
Gym Rd SE	CobC	1667	A2
Gypsum Ct SE	DKbC	1977	D2
H			
N H Av	FTPK	2150	A1
Haas Av SE	ATLN	1891	E5
Haberfield Ct NE	DKbC	1743	C3
Habershal Dr NW	ATLN	1814	C6
Habersham Ct	HryC	2065	D5
Habersham Ct NW	ATLN	1741	E6
Habersham Dr	DKbC	1979	A1
Habersham Rd NE	ATLN	1742	A4
Habersham Rd NW	ATLN	1741	D6
	ATLN	1815	D1
Habersham Wy NW	ATLN	1741	D7
Habersham at Northlake	DKbC	1745	A4
Habersham Cove NW	ATLN	1741	E4
Habersham Valley Rd NW	ATLN	1741	E4
Habersham Waters Ct	FulC	1600	E1
Habersham Waters Rd	FulC	1531	E7
	FulC	1600	E1
Habitat Cir	DKbC	1978	E2
Habitat Pl	DKbC	1979	A3
Hacienda Ct NE	CobC	1526	E2
Hackberry Ct	RSWL	1532	A5
Hackberry Ln	RSWL	1532	A5
Hackney Dr	ClyC	2151	D6
Hackney Dr SE	CobC	1597	B6
Hadden Hall Rd NW	ATLN	1741	B4
Haddenham Ln SE	CobC	1738	A3
	SMYR	1738	A3
Hadfield Ct NE	CobC	1528	D5

STREET	City	Map #	Grid
Hadfield Dr NE	CobC	1528	D5
Hadleigh Ct SE	CobC	1597	A7
Hadley Ct	FulC	1599	B1
Hadlock St SW	ATLN	1975	C3
Hagger Ct	EPNT	2060	C2
Hagger Wy	EPNT	2060	C2
Haggerty Pt	ATLN	1892	B3
Hagman Ln	DKbC	2063	E2
S Hairston Rd	DKbC	1980	E2
Halah Cir NE	FulC	1670	C2
Halbro Dr NE	CobC	1527	B6
Haldane Dr SW	ATLN	1888	D5
Hale Rd	FTPK	2149	A1
Hale St NE	ATLN	1891	C3
Haley St SE	MRTA	1595	C5
Half Penny Pl	FulC	1599	D4
Halifax Ct	DKbC	1819	A1
Hall Ct	FulC	1533	A1
Hall Dr SE	CobC	1666	B7
Hall Pl NW	ATLN	1814	E7
Hall St NW	ATLN	1814	A7
Hall St SE	ATLN	1891	D6
Hall St SW	ATLN	1890	A7
Hallbrook Dr NW	GwnC	1533	D6
Hallcrest Dr NE	DKbC	1670	E6
Hallford Ct	DKbC	1600	D4
Hallford Dr	DKbC	1600	D3
Hallman St NE	ATLN	1892	B4
Hallmark Ct SE	DKbC	1978	D4
Hallmark Dr SE	CobC	1668	B1
Halsey Av SE	CobC	1666	C3
Halsey Dr NE	MRTA	1595	E4
Halstead Ct	RSWL	1532	C5
Halston Ct NE	CobC	1596	C2
Ham Dr	CMBL	1671	D7
Hambledon Bnd	FulC	1532	C3
Hambledon Wk	FulC	1532	C3
Hambrick Ct	DKbC	1819	E2
Hambrick Pl	DKbC	1819	E2
Hambrick Rd	DKbC	1819	E2
Hambrick Sq	DKbC	1819	E5
Hambrick Wy	DKbC	1819	E2
Hamby Dr NE	CobC	1526	D3
Hamby Rd SE	MRTA	1596	B5
Hamby St SE	SMYR	1666	E7
Hamden Trc SW	FulC	1973	B1
Hamden Forest Dr SW	FulC	1973	B1
Hamden Forest Tr SW	FulC	1973	B1
E Hamilton Av	EPNT	2061	D1
W Hamilton Av	EPNT	2061	C1
Hamilton Av SE	ATLN	1977	B1
Hamilton Blvd SW	ATLN	2062	E3
Hamilton Ct	ATLN	2062	E2
Hamilton Ct NE	MRTA	1596	B4
Hamilton Pl	DKbC	1744	D7
Hamilton Pl SE	CobC	1596	B6
Hamilton Rd	DKbC	1893	D4

STREET	City	Map #	Grid
Hamilton Sq	DKbC	1744	C7
Hamilton St	HPVL	2062	A3
Hamilton Trc NE	MRTA	1596	B4
Hamlin Cir	CMBL	1671	D6
Hamlin Rd	CMBL	1671	D5
Hammack Cir	MRRW	2149	E7
Hammack Dr	MRRW	2149	E7
Hammarskjold Dr	EPNT	2060	B5
Hammerstone Ct NW	GwnC	1601	E1
Hammett Dr	DKbC	1819	C7
Hammock Pl SE	ATLN	1890	E6
Hammond Ct	ClyC	2150	C4
Hammond Dr NE	DKbC	1670	C2
	FulC	1669	E2
Hammond Dr NW	FulC	1669	E2
Hammond St SW	ATLN	1890	B5
Hampshire Av	DCTR	1892	D2
Hampshire Ct	AVES	1893	C3
Hampshire Dr NW	DKbC	1673	E7
Hampshire Pl	DKbC	1894	B5
Hampton Av	ATLN	1892	D6
	DKbC	1892	D6
Hampton Cir NE	CobC	1598	C2
Hampton Ct	FulC	2146	D5
E Hampton Ct	FulC	2146	D4
Hampton Ct NW	GwnC	1602	E2
Hampton Dr	FulC	1599	D2
N Hampton Dr NE	FulC	1598	E7
	FulC	1669	E1
Hampton Ln	DCTR	1892	B1
Hampton Pl	DKbC	1980	C5
N Hampton Rdg NW	GwnC	1602	E2
Hampton St NW	ATLN	1815	C7
	ATLN	1890	C1
Hampton Ter NE	ATLN	1892	B3
Hampton Wk SE	CobC	1597	E5
Hampton Wy NE	ATLN	1816	D3
	DKbC	1816	D3
Hampton Bluff Ct	RSWL	1529	E4
Hampton Bluff Wy	RSWL	1529	E4
Hampton Chase NE	CobC	1529	A7
Hampton Farms Ct NE	CobC	1598	B4
Hampton Farms Dr NE	CobC	1598	C4
Hampton Glen Ct	DKbC	1817	E1
Hampton Green Wy	DKbC	1673	B7
Hampton Hall Dr NE	DKbC	1670	E6
Hampton Hall Wy NE	DKbC	1671	A6
Hampton Lake Dr NE	CobC	1598	B1
Hampton Park Ct	CobC	1527	D3
Hampton Park Dr NE	CobC	1527	D3
Hampton Park Wy NE	CobC	1527	D3
Hampton Woods Dr NE	CobC	1597	E1
Hancock Cir	DKbC	1673	C5
Hancock Dr NE	DKbC	1816	E6
E Hancock St	DCTR	1893	A2
W Hancock St	DCTR	1892	E2
Handley Av SW	ATLN	1889	B6
Handley Blvd	ClyC	2150	B4
	LKCY	2150	B4
E Handy Dr NW	ATLN	1888	D1

STREET	City	Map #	Grid
W Handy Dr NW	ATLN	1888	D1
Handy Dr NW	ATLN	1888	D2
Hanes Dr	DKbC	1894	D7
	FTPK	2063	B7
Haney Plz SW	ATLN	1975	E2
Hanford Dr SW	ATLN	1976	B6
Hanfred Ct	DKbC	1745	E5
Hanfred Ln	DKbC	1745	E5
Hank Aaron Dr SW	ATLN	1890	E7
	ATLN	1976	E1
Hannaford Dr	RSWL	1529	D1
Hannah Ln	DKbC	1745	B5
Hannah Rd	DKbC	1745	D3
	FulC	2146	A1
Hannah St SE	ATLN	1977	A2
Hannover Park Rd	FulC	1530	D5
Hanover Ct	DKbC	1672	D4
Hanover Ln SE	MRTA	1596	B7
Hanover St SE	ATLN	1891	D4
Hanover West Ct NW	ATLN	1814	E1
Hanover West Dr NW	ATLN	1814	D2
Hanover West Ln NW	ATLN	1814	E2
Hanover West Ter NW	ATLN	1814	E1
Hansell St NE	MRTA	1595	A4
Hansell St NW	MRTA	1595	A4
Hansell St SE	ATLN	1891	B6
Hanson Dr SE	CobC	1739	C6
	SMYR	1739	C6
Hapeville Rd SW	ATLN	1976	D7
	ATLN	2062	D1
Happy Hollow Ct	FulC	2059	C6
Happy Hollow Rd	DKbC	1601	B5
Happy Hollow Rd SE	CobC	1666	E5
	SMYR	1666	E5
Happy Valley Tr SE	DKbC	1891	E7
Hapsburg Ct	DKbC	1980	D7
Haralson Av NE	ATLN	1891	D3
Haralson Rd	DKbC	1818	D2
Harber Valley Dr	DRVL	1672	B3
Harbin Rd SW	ATLN	1974	D2
Harbin Village Ct	ClyC	2150	D6
Harbin Woods Dr	MRRW	2150	B6
N Harbor Ct NW	FulC	1598	C6
N Harbor Dr NW	FulC	1598	C7
Harbor Lndg	RSWL	1531	C4
Harbor Lake Ct NE	MRTA	1526	A6
Harbor Pointe Pkwy	FulC	1599	B2
Harbor View Ct	DKbC	1980	B6
Harbor Woods Rd	DKbC	1980	B6
Harbour Gate Cir	FulC	1533	B2
Harbour Oaks Rd	DKbC	1745	D7
	DKbC	1819	E1
Harcourt Dr	DKbC	1818	C2
Harcourt Pl SE	CobC	1596	D7
Hardage St	CLKN	1819	B3
Hardee Av	CMBL	1671	D7
	CMBL	1743	D1
	EPNT	1975	E4
W Hardee Av	DKbC	1743	D2
Hardee Av SW	ATLN	1975	E4
Hardee Cir NE	ATLN	1892	A3
Hardee St NE	ATLN	1891	E4

INDEX 29

Hendon Rd SE — Hitching Post Ln NE

Atlanta Street Index

STREET	City	Map #	Grid
Hendon Rd SE	ATLN	2063	C3
Hendreson Chase Ct	DKbC	1745	A2
Hendrix Av	EPNT	1975	D7
Hendrix Av SW	ATLN	1890	D7
Hendrix Dr	FTPK	2063	B6
	FTPK	2149	B1
Henley Park Ct	DKbC	1673	B7
Henley Park Dr	DKbC	1673	B7
Henrico Rd	DKbC	2063	E1
Henry Ct	ClyC	2151	D5
Henry Dr SW	MRTA	1595	A5
Henry St SE	CobC	1595	B7
Henry Aaron Av SW	ATLN	1889	B5
Henry C Walker Ct	EPNT	2061	D1
Henry Ford II Av	ATLN	2062	C4
	HPVL	2062	C4
Henry Thomas Dr SE	ATLN	1977	D4
Hensley Dr	DKbC	1600	C5
Hepplewhite Dr	FulC	1532	E3
Herbert Dr SE	MRTA	1596	B5
Herbert St SE	CobC	1666	C4
Hercules Wy	CobC	1667	A2
Hercules Wy SE	CobC	1667	A2
Heritage Blf	DKbC	1817	E4
Heritage Ct	RSWL	1530	C4
Heritage Ct NW	ATLN	1740	E4
Heritage Ct SE	CobC	1667	E6
Heritage Dr NE	DKbC	1744	A5
Heritage Hls	DKbC	1817	E4
Heritage Hts	DKbC	1817	E4
Heritage Pl	ClyC	2150	B7
	DKbC	1817	E4
Heritage Run	ClyC	2150	B7
Heritage Sq	DKbC	1817	E4
Heritage Tr	RSWL	1530	C4
Heritage Wy NE	FulC	1599	B7
Heritage Wy SE	CobC	1812	A4
Heritage Glen Ct NE	CobC	1529	A7
Heritage Glen Dr NE	CobC	1529	A7
Heritage Trace Ct NE	CobC	1529	C5
Heritage Trace Dr NE	CobC	1529	C4
Heritage Trace Ln NE	CobC	1529	B4
Heritage Trace Vw NE	CobC	1529	C4
Heritage Two	DKbC	1817	E4
Heritage Valley Rd SW	ATLN	1974	A3
Herman St SE	ATLN	1892	E5
Hermance Dr NE	DKbC	1671	B7
	DKbC	1743	A1
Hermer Cir NW	ATLN	1888	D3
Hermitage Pl	DKbC	1744	C7
Hermosa Dr	DKbC	1978	E4
Herndon Blvd	ClyC	2150	B3
Herndon Dr	DKbC	1818	E6
Herndon Dr NE	CobC	1527	B4
Herndon Ln NE	MRTA	1527	A6
Herndon St NW	ATLN	1815	A7
Herodian Cir SE	CobC	1667	E6
	SMYR	1667	E6
Herodian Wy SE	CobC	1667	E6
	SMYR	1667	E6
Heron Cir	ClyC	2064	D5
Herring Rd SW	ATLN	1889	A7
	ATLN	1975	A1
Herrington Dr NE	ATLN	1742	A2
Herringwood Ct	DKbC	1979	E7
Herschel Rd	CGPK	2060	E3
Herschel Park Dr	CGPK	2060	E5
Hershey Dr NE	CobC	1596	E1
Hershey Ln	DKbC	1745	A2
Hertford Cir	DKbC	1817	C7
Hess Dr	AVES	1893	E3
Hesters Ct	DKbC	1819	C5
Heterodox View Rd	CobC	1597	A4
Hewlett Rd	FulC	1600	B1
Hezekiah Wy	HryC	2065	D6
Hialeah Ct NE	CobC	1528	B7
Hiawassee Dr NE	CobC	1526	D4
Hiawassee Dr SW	ATLN	1888	C6
Hibernia Av	DCTR	1892	D2
Hickman Dr NW	ATLN	1888	C4
Hickory Cir SE	CobC	1739	A2
	SMYR	1739	A2
Hickory Ct	ClyC	2149	B6
Hickory Ct NE	CobC	1528	C1
Hickory Dr	ClyC	2149	B6
Hickory Ln	DRVL	1672	C2
Hickory Ln SE	SMYR	1666	B6
Hickory Pl SE	SMYR	1739	A3
Hickory Rd	CMBL	1671	C7
	CMBL	1743	C1
Hickory St	DCTR	1818	B7
Hickory Tr SE	CobC	1812	C4
Hickory Acres Dr SE	SMYR	1666	B6
Hickory Bend Ct	ClyC	2148	A3
Hickory Bend Rd	ClyC	2148	A3
Hickory Bluff Dr NE	CobC	1528	C1
Hickory Glen Ln SW	FulC	1974	B1
Hickory Hill Dr SE	SMYR	1666	E6
Hickory Mill Dr SE	SMYR	1738	B5
Hickory Springs Dr NW	GwnC	1673	E2
Hickory Walk Ln	DKbC	2066	C4
Hickory Wood Ln	DRVL	1672	C2
Hicks Dr SE	CobC	1666	B1
Hidden Ct	FulC	2059	C6
Hidden Ct SE	CobC	1812	A5
Hidden Acres Dr	DKbC	1673	B7
Hidden Branches Cir	DKbC	1599	E5
Hidden Branches Ct	DKbC	1599	E6
Hidden Branches Dr	DKbC	1599	E6
Hidden Branches Ln	DKbC	1599	E5
Hidden Branches Close	DKbC	1599	E5
Hidden Brook Cir	ClyC	2147	E4
Hidden Brook Ct	FulC	2146	B7
Hidden Brook Tr	ClyC	2147	E4
	FulC	2146	A7
Hidden Cove Cir NW	GwnC	1602	B5
Hidden Falls Ln NW	FulC	1598	E5
Hidden Forest Ct SE	DKbC	1978	C4
Hidden Glade Ct SW	ATLN	1974	B5
Hidden Glen Dr SE	MRTA	1667	B2
Hidden Hills Ct NE	CobC	1526	C3
Hidden Hills Dr NE	CobC	1526	C3
Hidden Hollow Ct NE	CobC	1597	C2
Hidden Hollow Dr NE	CobC	1597	C1
Hidden Lake Ct NE	CobC	1598	B4
Hidden Oak Ct SW	FulC	1973	B3
Hidden Ridge Ln	DKbC	1599	E5
Hidden Springs Ct NE	CobC	1529	A3
Hidden Springs Pth SE	CobC	1738	E4
Hidden Springs Tr SE	CobC	1738	E4
Hidden Springs Wk SE	CobC	1738	D4
Hidden Trail Rd SE	SMYR	1738	B1
Hidden Valley Dr	FulC	2059	C6
Hidden Valley Rd	DKbC	1894	E5
Hideaway Dr	DKbC	1819	D1
Higgins Dr	ClyC	2148	A6
Higgins St SW	ATLN	1976	A1
High Dr	FTPK	2149	B2
High Tr	CobC	1668	B3
High Branch Wy	RSWL	1529	E6
High Bridge Chase	FulC	1533	C4
Highbrook Ct NE	CobC	1526	C2
Highbrook Dr NE	FulC	1670	A6
Highbury Tr SW	ATLN	2062	D1
Highcourt Rd NW	FulC	1741	B1
High Creek Dr	RSWL	1531	B1
High Creek Trc	RSWL	1531	B1
High Ct Pl	DKbC	1894	B6
High Falls Cir	FulC	1533	A1
High Falls Ct SW	ATLN	1974	C2
High Falls Pointe	FulC	1533	A2
Highfield Wy NE	CobC	1528	E2
Highgate Ct SW	FulC	1973	B3
Highgate Dr SE	SMYR	1738	A3
High Green Ct NE	CobC	1597	D2
High Green Dr NE	CobC	1597	D2
Highgreen Pl NE	CobC	1597	D2
High Green Pt NE	CobC	1597	D2
Highgrove Ct	ClyC	2147	D4
Highgrove Dr	ClyC	2147	D4
Highgrove Pt NE	FulC	1670	D7
High Grove Wy	DKbC	1670	E5
Highgrove Wy	ClyC	2147	D5
High Haven Ct NE	DKbC	1817	C1
N Highland Av NE	ATLN	1816	D6
Highland Av NE	ATLN	1891	B3
Highland Av SE	SMYR	1667	A6
Highland Cir	FTPK	2149	C4
Highland Ct	DKbC	1894	E5
Highland Ct NE	CobC	1598	C3
Highland Dr NE	ATLN	1742	B5
	MRTA	1526	D7
Highland Dr SE	SMYR	1667	C7
	SMYR	1739	B1
Highland Pl	DKbC	1894	E6
Highland Pl SE	SMYR	1738	B3
Highland Rd	DKbC	1894	E6
Highland St	FTPK	2149	C4
Highland Ter	HryC	2152	C2
Highland Ter NE	ATLN	1816	C6
Highland Vw NE	ATLN	1816	C7
Highland Bluff Dr SE	CobC	1668	B6
Highland Club Dr NE	CobC	1598	C3
Highland Lake Dr	FulC	2059	A5
Highland Lake Trc	FulC	2059	A5
Highland Lake Vw	FulC	2059	A5
Highland Oaks Ct SE	SMYR	1738	C7
Highland Oaks Ln SE	SMYR	1738	C7
Highland Oaks Run SE	SMYR	1738	C7
Highland Oaks Wy SE	SMYR	1738	C7
Highland Parc Pl SE	MRTA	1667	D1
Highland Park Ln NE	ATLN	1816	B6
Highland Park Tr	FulC	1530	E7
Highlands Ct	FulC	1533	A1
	RSWL	1529	E4
Highlands Dr	UNCT	2145	C6
Highlands Ovlk	RSWL	1530	A4
Highlands Pkwy SE	SMYR	1738	E7
	SMYR	1813	A1
Highlands Trc	RSWL	1529	E4
Highland Square Dr NE	DKbC	1817	A5
Highlands Ridge Rd SE	SMYR	1738	E6
Highlands View Dr SE	SMYR	1813	A1
Highland Trace Apartment Homes	MRTA	1596	C7
	MRTA	1667	C1
Highland Valley Ct NW	FulC	1669	C3
High Meadow Ct	DKbC	1894	E4
High Meadow Dr	DKbC	1894	E4
High Meadow Dr NE	CobC	1597	C4
High Meadow Dr NW	GwnC	1533	B7
High Meadow Pl	DKbC	1894	E4
Highoak Ct NW	CobC	1526	A3
Highoak Dr NW	CobC	1526	A3
Highpoint Ct	LKCY	2149	C3
High Point Dr NE	ATLN	1816	D5
High Point Ln NE	FulC	1670	B7
High Point Ln SW	FulC	2059	C4
High Point Pl NE	ATLN	1816	D5
Highpoint Rd	UNCT	2145	A5
Highpoint Rd NE	FulC	1670	B6
High Point Tr SW	FulC	2059	B4
High Point Wk NE	FulC	1670	B6
Highridge Ct	RSWL	1532	A2
High Shoals Dr NW	GwnC	1602	C1
High Tarn	FulC	1531	A7
Hightower Ct NW	ATLN	1888	E3
Hightower Pl NW	ATLN	1813	D6
Hightower Rd	RSWL	1529	E2
Hightower Rd NW	ATLN	1813	E7
	ATLN	1888	E1
	ATLN	1889	A3
Hightower Rd NW SR-280	ATLN	1888	E1
	ATLN	1889	A3
Hightower Tr	FulC	1530	C6
Highview Dr SE	CobC	1812	B4
	SMYR	1738	B3
High View Rd	ClyC	2150	C7
Highview Rd SW	ATLN	1889	A7
Highview Ter SE	SMYR	1738	D3
Highwood Dr SW	ATLN	1974	A5
E Hilda Cir	DKbC	1894	C4
W Hilda Cir	DKbC	1894	C4
Hilderbrand Dr NE	FulC	1669	E2
Hildon Cir	CMBL	1671	C6
Hildon Rd	CMBL	1671	C6
Hill Blvd	DKbC	1818	E5
Hill Ct NE	CobC	1529	B1
Hill Ct SE	MRTA	1595	D5
Hill Ln	HryC	2152	C1
N Hill Pkwy	DKbC	1671	E3
Hill Rd NE	CobC	1527	B4
Hill St	CLKN	1819	B3
	FTPK	2149	B1
	RSWL	1530	C2
E Hill St	DCTR	1892	E3
W Hill St	CLKN	1819	A3
	DCTR	1892	E3
Hill St NW	ATLN	1813	E7
Hill St SE	ATLN	1891	A7
	ATLN	1977	A1
	CobC	1595	A7
	CobC	1739	C6
	SMYR	1666	E6
Hill Acres Rd SW	ATLN	1974	A4
Hillandale Dr	FulC	2146	D5
Hillandale Dr NW	GwnC	1602	A5
Hillary Gln	DKbC	2066	C3
Hillbrook Wy	DKbC	1818	C1
Hillburn Dr SE	ATLN	1892	B7
	ATLN	1978	B1
	DKbC	1892	B7
Hill Creek Ct NE	CobC	1529	B4
Hill Creek Wy NE	CobC	1529	C3
Hillcrest Av	DCTR	1818	B7
	DKbC	1892	E7
Hillcrest Av NE	ATLN	1892	C4
Hillcrest Ct NE	CobC	1529	C2
Hillcrest Dr	EPNT	1975	B6
	RSWL	1530	B4
	UNCT	2145	A4
Hillcrest Dr SE	ATLN	1977	E4
	CobC	1739	D3
	CobC	1812	A7
	DKbC	1977	E4
Hillcrest Dr SW	CobC	1812	A6
Hillcrest Wy SE	CobC	1738	B7
Hillcrest Chase Dr SE	CobC	1812	A7
Hillcrest Chase Ln SE	CobC	1812	A7
Hillcrest Chase Ter SE	CobC	1812	A7
Hilldale Dr	DCTR	1893	A2
Hillhaven Dr NE	CobC	1527	A7
Hilliard St NE	ATLN	1891	A3
Hilliard St SE	ATLN	1891	A4
Hill Industrial Blvd	FTPK	2149	A1
Hillingdon Ct SE	CobC	1597	B5
Hillmont Av	DKbC	1893	B1
Hill Park Ct	DKbC	1817	E3
Hill Park Ct NE	CobC	1528	B2
Hillpine Dr NE	ATLN	1816	B5
Hillpine Ln NE	ATLN	1816	C6
Hillpine Rd	FTPK	2063	C7
Hillpine Ter NE	ATLN	1816	C5
Hills Av NW	ATLN	1814	D3
Hills Av SW	ATLN	1890	C5
N Hills Dr	DKbC	1818	A3
N Hills Dr NE	ATLN	1742	B7
Hills Pl NW	ATLN	1814	E3
Hillsborough Ln	DKbC	1894	B5
Hillsdale Ct SE	CobC	1668	A2
Hillsdale Dr	DKbC	1893	D6
Hillsdale Dr SE	ATLN	1976	E6
Hillsdale Pkwy SE	SMYR	1667	C5
Hillsdale St SE	SMYR	1666	D7
Hillshire Pl NE	DKbC	1817	B3
Hillside Av	DKbC	1892	E6
Hillside Av NW	MRTA	1595	A3
Hillside Av SE	ATLN	1976	E4
Hillside Ct	HryC	2066	E7
Hillside Dr	ClyC	2148	C3
	RSWL	1531	C3
Hillside Dr NW	ATLN	1741	C2
	GwnC	1673	B1
Hillside Dr SE	CobC	1666	E5
	SMYR	1666	E5
Hillside Dr SW	ATLN	1976	C2
Hillside Ln	RSWL	1531	C3
Hillside Rd SE	SMYR	1666	C7
Hillside St NE	CobC	1527	B1
Hillside Village Dr SE	ATLN	1892	C6
Hillsleigh Rd	FulC	1533	B4
Hills Ln Dr SE	CobC	1739	C3
Hillsman Ln NE	CobC	1528	E2
Hillstone Ct NE	DKbC	1670	E6
Hillswick Ct NE	FulC	1599	A4
Hilltop Cir NE	CobC	1526	D1
Hilltop Cir NW	ATLN	1890	B3
Hilltop Dr	ClyC	2149	A6
	CMBL	1744	A1
	CobC	1527	E7
	DKbC	1744	A1
Hilltop Dr NE	CobC	1526	D1
Hilltop Dr SW	ATLN	1976	D4
Hilltop Ln	ClyC	2151	D6
Hilltop Pl SW	ATLN	1976	D4
Hillview Av NE	DKbC	1670	C7
	DKbC	1742	D2
Hillwood Ct SE	DKbC	1891	E7
Hillwood Dr NE	CobC	1597	E2
Hillwood Dr NW	ATLN	1815	C1
Hillwood Pt NE	CobC	1597	E2
Hillwood Ter NE	DKbC	1743	A2
Hillyer Av	DKbC	1893	B1
Hillyer Pl	DCTR	1893	A1
Hilo Ct	DKbC	1818	B1
Hilton Ct	DKbC	1894	C7
	DKbC	1980	C1
Hilton Dr	DKbC	1894	C7
	DKbC	1980	C1
Hilton Dr NE	CobC	1527	E7
Hipp St SW	ATLN	1976	D3
Hirsch St NW	ATLN	1815	B7
Hitchcock Mill Run NE	CobC	1596	E3
Hitching Post Ct SE	CobC	1597	D6
Hitching Post Ln NE	CobC	1529	C5

INDEX 32
James River Pl NE
Atlanta Street Index
Kelso Dr SW

STREET	City	Map #	Grid
James River Pl NE	ATLN	1742	A4
Jamestown Ct	DKbC	1672	D4
Jamestown Ct SE	SMYR	1739	B1
N Jamestown Rd	DKbC	1817	D3
Jamestown Wy	DKbC	1979	B3
James Wendell George Pkwy	ATLN	1815	D7
	ATLN	1976	C3
James Wendell George Pkwy I-75	ATLN	1815	D7
	ATLN	1976	C3
James Wendell George Pkwy I-85	ATLN	1815	D7
	ATLN	1976	C3
James W George Pkwy SR-401	ATLN	1815	D7
James W George Pkwy SR-403	ATLN	1815	D7
James Wendell George Pkwy NE	ATLN	1890	E2
James Wendell George Pkwy NW	ATLN	1890	E2
James Wendell George Pkwy SE	ATLN	1891	A4
Jamison Ct	DKbC	1819	B4
Jamison Pl	CLKN	1819	B4
	DKbC	1819	B4
Jamount Ct NE	CobC	1596	E1
Janann Wy	FulC	1601	D2
Jane Ct SE	SMYR	1739	C1
Jane Rd NW	GwnC	1673	B1
Janellen Dr NE	DKbC	1744	C4
Jane Lyle Rd SE	CobC	1739	C2
	SMYR	1739	C2
Jane Marie Ln	DKbC	1894	C3
Janes Ln NE	DKbC	1816	E3
Janet Ln	DKbC	1894	D7
Jan Hill Ln NE	DKbC	1817	C1
Janice Cir	CMBL	1672	A7
	CMBL	1744	A1
	DKbC	1744	A1
Janice Ct	CMBL	1744	A1
Janice Dr	CGPK	2060	D5
	EPNT	2060	D5
	FulC	2060	D7
	FulC	2146	D1
Janie Ct	DKbC	1745	A1
Janis Dr NE	CobC	1526	B4
Janjolin Dr	DKbC	2064	C3
Janjolin Wy	DKbC	2064	C3
Janmar Dr	DKbC	1894	B4
Jarrod Pl SE	SMYR	1739	A3
Jasmine Ct NE	DKbC	1744	C2
Jason Ct SW	CobC	1666	B6
Jasper St SW	ATLN	1889	E4
Jay Ln SE	SMYR	1739	C1
Jay Pl SE	ATLN	1976	E5
Jay Bird Al NW	GwnC	1602	B3
Jaynes Valley Dr	DKbC	1979	A5
Jeannine Ct	DKbC	1745	E6
Jefferson Av	EPNT	1975	E6
	FTPK	2149	B5
Jefferson Av SW	ATLN	1976	B6
Jefferson Cir NE	FulC	1599	C5
Jefferson Dr	FulC	1599	C2
Jefferson Pl	DCTR	1892	E2
Jefferson St	CGPK	2061	C3
Jefferson St	CMBL	1743	D1
	DKbC	1743	D1
Jefferson St NW	ATLN	1889	D1
Jefferson Ter	EPNT	1975	E6
Jefferson Hill Pl NE	ATLN	1741	E2
Jefferson Square Ct	DKbC	1818	C6
Jeffery Ct	ClyC	2147	C7
Jeffrey Dr	ClyC	2065	A5
	FulC	2145	D1
Jeffrey Pl SE	CobC	1738	A3
	SMYR	1738	A3
Jenay Ct	DKbC	1979	A2
Jenkins St SW	ATLN	1976	E3
Jennifer Ct NE	CobC	1528	E3
Jennifer Ln SW	CobC	1666	A7
Jennings Wy NW	GwnC	1673	E4
Jenny Mill Ct NE	CobC	1596	E2
Jenny Wren Ln SW	ATLN	1888	E7
Jeptha St SW	ATLN	1890	B4
Jericho Ct	DKbC	1745	C7
Jericho Rd	DKbC	1745	C7
Jeri Lynn Ct	DKbC	1673	D7
Jeri Lynn Dr	DKbC	1673	E7
Jernigan Dr SE	ATLN	1977	B5
Jernigan Pl SE	ATLN	1977	B5
Jerome Rd	FulC	2146	E3
Jerri Ct	ClyC	2147	E7
Jerry Wy NW	GwnC	1673	C4
Jersey Rd	EPNT	2060	E1
Jerusalem Ct	DKbC	1745	C7
Jesse Norman Wy	DRVL	1672	C5
Jessica Av	DKbC	1892	D7
Jessica Pl NE	CobC	1528	E3
Jessica Run	DKbC	2066	A1
Jesup Av	EPNT	1975	B5
Jet Rd	CGPK	2061	B6
Jetal Pl NW	ATLN	1889	C2
Jett Dr	DKbC	1672	D4
Jett Pl NW	ATLN	1741	C1
Jett Rd NW	ATLN	1741	C1
	FulC	1669	C7
	FulC	1741	C1
Jett St NW	ATLN	1890	B2
Jett Ferry Ct	FulC	1600	E3
Jett Ferry Mnr	FulC	1601	A2
Jett Ferry Rd	DKbC	1600	E4
	FulC	1601	A2
Jett Forest Ct NW	FulC	1669	A6
Jett Forest Tr NW	FulC	1669	A5
Jettridge Dr NW	ATLN	1669	C7
	ATLN	1741	C1
Jewel St	EPNT	1976	A7
Jewel Ter	ClyC	2063	E5
Jewell Dr NE	CobC	1526	D3
JG Glover Ct	ClyC	2150	D3
Jim Harbuck Cir	DKbC	1744	C6
Jimmy Carter Blvd NW	GwnC	1602	C7
	NRCS	1602	C7
Jimmy Carter Blvd NW SR-140	GwnC	1602	C7
	NRCS	1602	C7
Jimmys Ln	HryC	2066	E5
Jo Ann Dr SE	CobC	1596	D6
Joanne Ct	ClyC	2063	D5
Joan of Arc Pl	ClyC	2147	B2
Joberry Ct	DKbC	1600	A5
Jobeth Av SE	ATLN	1892	A7
Jody Ln NE	DKbC	1817	C2
Joel Ct	DKbC	1601	C5
Joel Ln	DKbC	1601	C5
Joel Pl	DKbC	1601	C5
Joe Louis Dr NW	ATLN	1889	B3
John St NW	ATLN	1890	B2
John Alden Ct	DKbC	1894	D1
John Alden Rd	DKbC	1894	D1
John Arnold Cir	ClyC	2063	E5
John Calvin Av	CGPK	2061	D3
John Carrol Dr	DKbC	2066	B1
John Dodgen Wy NE	CobC	1528	C5
John Freeman Wy	EPNT	2062	A1
John Glenn Dr	DKbC	1672	A4
John Hopkins Ct	DKbC	2066	C1
Johnnys Ln	DRVL	1672	C2
John Robert Dr	MRRW	2149	E7
Johns Rd	DKbC	1819	A1
Johns Creek Ct	FulC	1533	E4
Johnson Av	ATLN	1892	D6
	DKbC	1892	D6
Johnson Av SW	ATLN	1975	E4
E Johnson Cir	DKbC	1672	A3
W Johnson Cir	DKbC	1671	E3
Johnson Ct	DCTR	1892	E2
Johnson Dr NW	DRVL	1672	E2
	GwnC	1672	E2
Johnson Rd	ClyC	2148	E5
Johnson Rd NE	ATLN	1816	E5
	ATLN	1817	A4
	DKbC	1743	E4
	DKbC	1744	A3
	DKbC	1817	A4
Johnson Rd NW	ATLN	1814	C6
Johnson Ferry Ct NE	CobC	1528	D4
Johnson Ferry Dr NE	CobC	1528	D4
Johnson Ferry Pkwy NE	FulC	1670	D4
Johnson Ferry Pl NE	CobC	1598	A1
Johnson Ferry Rd NE	CMBL	1671	B6
	CobC	1528	E6
	CobC	1598	B3
	DKbC	1671	A6
	FulC	1669	E1
	FulC	1670	D4
Johnson Ferry Rd NW	FulC	1598	C6
	FulC	1669	E1
Johnston Pl	DCTR	1892	D3
John Wesley Av	CGPK	2061	B4
John Wesley Ct	DKbC	1894	E7
John Wesley Dr	DKbC	1894	E7
John Wesley Dobbs Av NE	ATLN	1890	E3
Joiner Ct	DKbC	1818	A4
Jointer Av	DKbC	1818	E6
Jolly Av	CLKN	1819	A3
Jolly Av S	CLKN	1819	B5
	DKbC	1819	B5
Jolly Rd	FulC	2146	E2
Jolly Green Ct	ClyC	2064	A6
Jolly Green Dr	ClyC	2064	A6
Jolyn Pl NE	FulC	1742	A1
Jomarc Wy NE	CobC	1527	D6
Jonathon Ln NE	DKbC	1743	A5
Jones Av NW	ATLN	1814	B7
	ATLN	1890	D2
Jones Cir	CGPK	2147	B2
Jones Ct	LKCY	2149	D3
Jones Dr	RSWL	1530	C4
Jones Rd	ClyC	2151	B2
	FTPK	2149	A2
Jones Rd NW	ATLN	1813	C7
Jones St	EPNT	1975	C7
	EPNT	2061	C1
Jones St NW	NRCS	1602	B7
Jonesboro Rd	FTPK	2063	C5
	FTPK	2149	D2
	LKCY	2149	D2
	MRRW	2149	E7
Jonesboro Rd SR-54	FTPK	2063	C5
	FTPK	2149	D2
	LKCY	2149	D2
	MRRW	2149	E7
Jonesboro Rd SR-160	FTPK	2149	D1
Jonesboro Rd SE	ATLN	1976	E2
	ATLN	2063	B3
Jonesboro Rd SE SR-54	ATLN	1976	E2
	ATLN	2063	B3
Jonesboro St	ClyC	2151	A2
Jones Bridge Cir NW	GwnC	1533	B6
Jones Bridge Rd	FulC	1532	E2
E Jones Bridge Rd NW	GwnC	1533	D6
W Jones Bridge Rd NW	GwnC	1533	C6
	GwnC	1602	C1
Jones Bridge Wy	FulC	1532	E1
Jones Chapel Ct NW	GwnC	1601	D3
Jones Ferry Ln	FulC	1532	E1
Jones Mill Ct NW	GwnC	1601	E6
Jones Mill Rd NW	DKbC	1601	D5
	GwnC	1602	A6
	GwnC	1673	A1
Jones Mill Spur NW	GwnC	1601	D6
Jonquil Dr SE	SMYR	1667	B7
Joppa Ln	DKbC	1745	C6
Jordan St NW	CobC	1595	A2
Jordan St SE	ATLN	1977	A4
Jordan Ter NE	DKbC	1743	D4
Jordan Lake Dr NE	CobC	1528	E3
Joseph Av SE	ATLN	1891	E6
Joseph Ct	DKbC	1978	D1
Joseph Wy NW	GwnC	1673	E4
Joseph E Lowery Blvd NW	ATLN	1815	A7
	ATLN	1890	A2
Joseph E Lowery Blvd SW	ATLN	1890	A6
Josephine Av SE	DKbC	1892	B7
Josephine Ct NE	CobC	1527	C6
Josephine Dr	CGPK	2146	D1
Josephine Rd NW	GwnC	1673	B1
Josephine St NE	ATLN	1891	D3
Joseph Skinner Dr	RSWL	1530	C2
Joshua Cross	DKbC	1819	E2
Joy Ln	DKbC	1894	A4
Joy Ln SE	CobC	1812	B7
Joyce Av	DKbC	1893	B6
Joyce Dr	FTPK	2149	B3
Joyce St SW	ATLN	1890	A5
Joyce Paris Dr	DCTR	1893	B2
Joy Lake Rd	ClyC	2150	B3
	LKCY	2150	A3
Joyland Pl SW	ATLN	1976	D2
Joyland St SW	ATLN	1976	D3
Joyner Av SE	CobC	1666	B3
Joyous Vw	ClyC	2152	A5
JT Alexander Av	CGPK	2061	B3
Juanita St	DKbC	1892	D7
	DKbC	1978	D1
Jubilant Dr	ClyC	2151	E4
Judith Wy NE	ATLN	1742	D7
Judson Av	EPNT	1974	E5
Judson Wy	FulC	1533	E4
Judson Walk Ct	FulC	1533	E3
Judy Cir SE	CobC	1666	A4
Judy Dr SW	CobC	1666	A4
Judy Ln SW	ATLN	1976	D6
Judylyn Dr	DKbC	1818	D5
Julian St	DKbC	1893	B5
Julian St NW	ATLN	1890	B2
Juliana Ct	HryC	2152	C1
Juliana Dr	HryC	2066	C7
	HryC	2152	C1
Junction Av NE	ATLN	1815	E2
June Dr	DKbC	1894	C4
June Apple Ct	DKbC	1980	C5
June Apple Dr	DKbC	1980	C5
Juneau Ct	DKbC	1819	A2
Juneberry Ct	DKbC	1980	E7
Juniper Cir	FTPK	2149	C5
Juniper Dr	FTPK	2149	D1
Juniper St NE	ATLN	1815	E7
	ATLN	1890	E1
Juniper St NE SR-8	ATLN	1890	E1
Juniper St NE US-29	ATLN	1890	E1
Juniper St NE US-78	ATLN	1890	E1
Juniper St NE US-278	ATLN	1890	E1
Juniper St SE	CobC	1812	C6
K			
N K Av	FTPK	2150	A1
Kacoonis Dr	ClyC	2062	E5
Kadleston Wy NE	DKbC	1671	B6
Kahanna Dr	DKbC	1818	C1
Kakki Ct NE	CobC	1527	E6
Kalah Pl SE	CobC	1597	D7
Kalb St SE	ATLN	1891	C5
Kammeyer Ln	DKbC	1744	B1
Kandell Cove	FulC	1599	B2
Kanuga St NE	ATLN	1816	B7
Karen Ct	ClyC	2148	A7
Karen Ct SE	SMYR	1738	B5
Karen Ln NE	CobC	1527	E2
Karen Rd	CGPK	2060	D5
Karla Cir	ClyC	2063	E7
Karla Ct	RSWL	1531	E1
Karland Dr NW	ATLN	1741	E5
Karls Gate Dr NE	CobC	1529	B7
Kasandra Dr SE	MRTA	1595	E5
E Kasselryne Ct	DKbC	1745	D3
W Kasselryne Ct	DKbC	1745	D3
Kate Dr	FTPK	2149	A2
Katherine Rd	ClyC	2151	C5
Katherine Valley Rd	DKbC	1893	C7
Katherine Village Dr	ClyC	2151	C3
Katherwood Dr SW	ATLN	1976	A3
Kathie Ct	ClyC	2150	E6
	RSWL	1531	E1
Kathie Ln	ClyC	2150	E6
Kathleen Dr SE	MRTA	1595	E6
Kathryn Av	DCTR	1817	D7
Kathryn Cir	FTPK	2149	D1
Kathryn Cir SW	ATLN	1974	A7
	ATLN	2060	A1
Kathryn Ct	EPNT	1974	E7
Kathryn Ct SW	ATLN	1973	E7
Kathryn Dr NE	CobC	1526	A1
Kathryn Dr SW	ATLN	1973	E7
Kathryn Ln NE	CobC	1526	B1
Kathryn Wy NE	CobC	1528	E2
Kathy Ln SE	CobC	1739	A2
Katie Ln	ClyC	2150	E7
Katie Kerr Dr	DCTR	1893	C3
	DKbC	1893	B1
Katomarick Dr SE	ATLN	2063	C2
Katrina Ct	DKbC	1894	D3
Katrina Dr SE	CobC	1812	B2
Kay Ln NE	ATLN	1817	A4
	DKbC	1817	A4
Kay St	FTPK	2149	B3
Kayanne Ct	DKbC	1745	B3
Kaybrook Rd	DKbC	1979	C2
Kayla Ct	FulC	2146	D6
Kayron Dr NE	FulC	1670	B3
Keats Dr SW	ATLN	1888	D5
Keenan Ct E	FulC	2146	C7
Keenan Ct W	FulC	2146	C7
Keenan Ln	FulC	2146	C7
Keenan Rd	FulC	2146	C7
Keheley Dr	DKbC	1892	E7
Kelden Cir	FulC	2059	E7
Kelden Ct	FulC	2059	E7
Kelden Rdg NE	CobC	1598	C1
Kellerman Kreek NE	CobC	1598	D2
Kelley Chapel Rd	DKbC	1980	D3
Kellogg Cir	DKbC	1671	C1
Kellogg Springs Dr	DKbC	1671	C1
Kelly Ct SE	CobC	1738	A6
Kelly Dr NE	CobC	1526	C1
Kelly Ln NE	CobC	1527	C1
Kelly St	DKbC	1818	D6
Kelly St NW	NRCS	1602	D7
Kelly St SE	ATLN	1891	A5
Kelly Lake Ct	DKbC	1979	B2
Kelly Lake Dr	DKbC	1979	B2
Kelly Lake Rd	DKbC	1979	B2
Kellys Ct	ClyC	2151	C3
Kelso Dr SW	ATLN	1889	A5

INDEX 33

Kelso at Peyton Dr SW — Kissing Tree Ln SE

Atlanta Street Index

Street	City	Map #	Grid
Kelso at Peyton Dr SW	ATLN	1889	B5
Kelson Dr NW	FulC	1668	E4
Kelton Dr	MRTA	1596	B4
Kelton Woods Dr	GwnC	1673	E5
Kempton Pl NE	CobC	1598	A3
Kenbrook Dr NW	FulC	1669	C5
Kenbrook Wy NW	FulC	1669	C5
Kendall Ct NE	FulC	1670	B6
Kendall St NE	ATLN	1891	C3
Kendall Cove	DKbC	1673	C7
Kendall Knoll Ct	SMYR	1812	C1
Kendall Knoll Wy SE	SMYR	1812	C1
Kendrick Av SE	ATLN	1891	A7
Kendrick Rd NE	DKbC	1742	E2
Kenelworth Dr	EPNT	2060	B4
Kenilworth Dr SW	ATLN	1975	E2
Kenland Rd SE	CobC	1738	B2
	SMYR	1738	B2
Kenley Ct NE	CobC	1596	D5
Kenlock Pl NE	ATLN	1816	A1
Kenmare Cir	UNCT	2145	B6
Kenmare Cir SE	CobC	1738	A6
Kenmare Hall NE	ATLN	1742	D5
Kenmore St SW	ATLN	1889	C7
	ATLN	1975	D1
Kennard Ln	DKbC	1979	D1
Kennedy Ct NW	ATLN	1889	A1
Kennedy Dr	ClyC	2148	D3
Kennedy Rd	ClyC	2148	D2
Kennedy St NW	ATLN	1890	B2
Kenner Dr SW	ATLN	1888	A3
Kennersly Close	DKbC	1744	E7
Kennesaw Av NE	ATLN	1891	B1
	MRTA	1595	A4
Kennesaw Av NW	MRTA	1595	A3
Kennesaw Dr	FTPK	2063	B6
Kennesaw Dr NW	ATLN	1889	D2
Kennesaw Dr SE	SMYR	1666	C5
Kennesaw Pl	FTPK	2063	C6
Kennesaw Wy SE	SMYR	1666	C5
Kennestone Cir NE	CobC	1595	B1
	MRTA	1595	B1
Kennestone Cir NW	CobC	1526	A7
	MRTA	1595	A1
Kennestone Dr NE	MRTA	1595	B2
Kenneth St NE	CobC	1526	C3
Kenneth St SE	ATLN	1890	E6
Kenney Ct	EPNT	1975	A5
Kenninghall Ct SE	SMYR	1738	E4
Kenninghall Dr SE	SMYR	1738	E3
Kenninghall Ln SE	SMYR	1738	E3
Kennington Ct NE	DKbC	1670	E6
Kennolia Dr SW	ATLN	1889	C7
Kenny Rd SW	ATLN	1973	B6
	FulC	1973	B6
Kennys Al SW	ATLN	1890	E4
Kenora Dr SW	ATLN	1887	D3
Kenridge Cir	DKbC	1819	D6
Kenridge Pkwy	DKbC	1894	B2
Kensington Ct	DKbC	1894	B2
	FulC	1533	A3
Kensington Rd	AVES	1893	D1
	DKbC	1893	E1
Kensington St NE	ATLN	1891	D4
Kensington Parc Cir	DKbC	1819	A7
Kensington Parc Dr	DKbC	1819	A7
Kensington Parc Wy	DKbC	1819	A7
Kensingwood Trc	DKbC	1894	B2
Kent Ln	ClyC	2149	A4
Kent Rd	CGPK	2060	D7
	FulC	2060	D7
	FulC	2146	D1
Kent St SE	ATLN	1891	A6
Kenton Pl SE	DKbC	1977	E7
Kentucky Av NE	ATLN	1816	D7
Kentucky Ct	EPNT	2061	A1
Kentucky St	DKbC	1818	C6
Kenview Rd NE	MRTA	1595	E3
Kenville Ln	DKbC	2065	D1
Kenway Cir SE	SMYR	1738	D4
Kenway Ct SE	SMYR	1738	D5
Kenway Dr SE	ATLN	2063	A4
Kenway Pl SE	SMYR	1738	D4
Kenwood Av NW	ATLN	1815	C5
Kenwood Pl SE	CobC	1739	B7
Kenwood Rd SE	CobC	1739	B7
	SMYR	1739	B7
Kenwyck Ct NE	CobC	1528	E5
Kenyon Rd	FTPK	2149	D3
	LKCY	2149	D3
Kenyon St SE	ATLN	1891	C4
Kerr Dr	DKbC	1980	B5
Kerries Ct	ClyC	2151	C3
Kerry Cir NW	ATLN	1814	B6
Kerry Ct NE	CobC	1526	E3
Kerry Dr NW	ATLN	1814	C5
Kerry Dr SW	FulC	1973	A5
Kerry Pl NW	ATLN	1814	C6
Kerry Creek Dr NE	CobC	1527	C2
Kessler Ridge Dr NE	CobC	1528	E5
Keswick Ct	CMBL	1671	C6
Keswick Dr	CMBL	1671	C6
Keswick Dr SE	CobC	1740	A4
Keswick Wy	FulC	1533	B1
Ketchem Dr NE	CobC	1526	C4
Kettering Ct	FulC	1533	A3
Kettering Dr NE	CobC	1529	A1
Kettering Pl	FulC	1533	A3
Kevin Ct	FulC	2059	D7
Kevin Ct NW	ATLN	1888	C3
Key Ct SW	ATLN	1974	C2
Key Dr NE	MRTA	1595	D5
Key Dr SW	ATLN	1974	C2
Key Rd	HryC	2066	E6
Key Rd SE	ATLN	1977	E5
	DKbC	1977	E5
Key St NE	CobC	1527	A1
Keymar Ct	FulC	1601	B3
Keys Cross NE	DKbC	1743	B5
Keys Lake Dr NE	DKbC	1742	E6
Keystone Dr	DKbC	1978	C1
Key West Ln	EPNT	2060	C6
Key West St	ClyC	2149	B6
Khalil Dr	DKbC	1892	D6
Kibbys Ct	ClyC	2151	C3
Kilarney Ct	DKbC	1979	E1
Kilarney Rd	DKbC	1893	E7
	DKbC	1979	E1
Kilburn Dr NE	ATLN	1816	B3
Kilby Pl NW	ATLN	1741	A5
E Kildare Av NW	ATLN	1888	C2
W Kildare Av NW	ATLN	1888	C2
Kildare Av NW	ATLN	1888	C2
S Kilgo Cir NE	DKbC	1817	B6
Kilgore Dr SE	CobC	1812	A1
Kilkenny Dr	UNCT	2145	B6
Killarney SE	CobC	1667	E5
Killarney Ct	UNCT	2145	B6
Killarney Dr	UNCT	2145	B6
Killian St SE	ATLN	1891	B6
Killingsworth Trc NW	GwnC	1533	D6
Kilmory Close	FulC	1600	E3
Kilrain Ct	RSWL	1531	D6
Kilrush Ct SE	CobC	1812	E2
Kilrush Dr SE	CobC	1812	E3
Kilt Ct	DKbC	1601	A6
Kim Ct	DKbC	1673	A6
Kim Pl	DKbC	1600	E5
Kimamy Ct	FulC	1533	E2
Kimball Rd SW	ATLN	1973	C6
Kimball Wy SE	ATLN	1890	E4
N Kimberly Ct	DKbC	1745	B1
	RSWL	1531	E1
S Kimberly Ct	RSWL	1531	E1
Kimberly Ct SW	ATLN	1888	E5
N Kimberly Dr	DKbC	1745	B1
Kimberly Ln NE	DKbC	1816	E5
W Kimberly Rd SW	ATLN	1973	D4
Kimberly Rd SW	ATLN	1973	E1
	FulC	1973	E1
Kimberly Wy SW	ATLN	1973	D2
Kimberly Creek Pl	FulC	2146	D7
Kimberly Forest Ct	FulC	2146	D7
Kimberly Forest Wy	FulC	2146	D7
Kimberly Mill Ln	FulC	2146	C7
Kimberly Mill Rd	FulC	2146	C6
Kimberlyn Ct	ClyC	2151	D6
Kimberly Village Ln SE	CobC	1667	E4
Kimblewick Cove	DKbC	1600	B4
Kimbrough Ct	FulC	1601	A4
Kimlie Ct	DKbC	1894	D4
	RSWL	1531	E1
Kimlie Ln	DKbC	1894	D4
Kimlie Cove	DKbC	1894	D4
Kimmeridge Dr	EPNT	1975	B7
	EPNT	2061	B1
Kincaid Rd NE	CobC	1526	E5
Kincaid Cove NE	CobC	1526	E5
King Av	DRVL	1672	C4
King Rd	ClyC	2062	E5
	ClyC	2147	E7
	RVDL	2147	E7
King Rd	RVDL	2148	A7
King Rd NW	ATLN	1741	C3
King St	RSWL	1530	B3
King St SE	ATLN	1891	A5
	SMYR	1666	E7
King Alfred Dr SW	ATLN	1973	E4
King Arms Wy	FulC	1532	D4
King Arnold St	HPVL	2062	C3
King Arthur Cir NE	DKbC	1744	D3
King Arthur Ct NE	DKbC	1744	E3
King Arthur Ct SE	CobC	1739	A4
King Arthur Ln	DKbC	2066	D3
King Arthur Rd SW	ATLN	1973	E4
King Arthurs Ct NE	CobC	1527	D6
King Bird Ct NE	CobC	1527	D6
King Carter Ct	ClyC	2151	C1
King Charles Rd SW	ATLN	1973	E4
King David Dr	HryC	2065	D7
King Edward Tr SW	ATLN	1973	E4
Kingfisher Ct	DKbC	1980	A6
Kingfisher Dr	DKbC	1980	A6
Kingfisher Dr NE	CobC	1527	D7
King Fisher Pt	ClyC	2064	D5
King George Ln SW	ATLN	1973	E4
King George Wy	ClyC	2149	C7
King Henry Rd SW	ATLN	1973	E4
King Industrial Dr NE	MRTA	1595	B1
King James Dr	ClyC	2149	C7
King James Dr SW	ATLN	1973	E4
King James Pl NE	ATLN	1741	E2
Kinglet Ct NE	CobC	1527	D7
Kinglet Ln NE	CobC	1527	D6
King Richard Rd	CobC	1598	B5
Kings Br NE	DKbC	1743	C6
Kings Cir NE	ATLN	1816	A2
Kings Cswy	DKbC	2066	C3
Kings Ct NE	ATLN	1816	C6
	CobC	1597	E4
	DKbC	1744	E4
Kings Ct SE	MRTA	1595	B6
Kings Hwy	DCTR	1892	E2
Kings Ln	RSWL	1531	C2
Kings Pl	DKbC	2066	C3
Kings Rd NE	MRTA	1526	D6
Kings Row NE	CobC	1597	E4
Kings Wk NE	ATLN	1892	B1
Kings Wy	ClyC	2147	C7
Kings Wy NE	CobC	1598	A4
Kings Wy NW	ATLN	1741	B4
Kings Abbot Wy NW	GwnC	1533	C5
Kings Arms Ct NE	DKbC	1744	E3
Kings Arms Dr NE	DKbC	1744	E4
Kings Arms Pt NE	DKbC	1744	E4
King Saul Dr	ClyC	2151	B1
Kings Bay Cir	DKbC	1979	B5
Kings Bay Ct	DKbC	1979	B5
Kings Bay Dr	DKbC	1979	B5
Kingsbere Ct NE	CobC	1528	C2
Kingsbere Trc NE	CobC	1528	C1
Kingsboro Rd NE	ATLN	1742	C5
Kingsbridge Rd NW	GwnC	1673	E7
Kingsbrook Blvd	DKbC	1980	C7
Kingsbrooke Ct	DKbC	1980	A3
Kingsbrooke Wy	DKbC	1980	A3
Kingsburgh Ct NE	CobC	1527	E1
Kings Chase NE	CobC	1598	A4
Kingscliff Dr NE	DKbC	1744	D4
Kingscliff Wy NE	DKbC	1744	D4
Kings Cove	DKbC	2066	C3
Kings Cross Rd	FulC	1533	A3
Kingsdale Dr SW	ATLN	1974	C1
Kings Down Cir	DKbC	1600	B7
Kings Down Ct	DKbC	1600	C7
Kings Down Rd	DKbC	1600	B7
Kings Down Wy	DKbC	1600	B7
Kingsfield Ct	DKbC	1672	A1
Kingsgate Ct	DKbC	1672	A1
Kingsgate Dr	DKbC	1672	A1
	DKbC	1819	E1
Kingsglen Ct	DKbC	1601	A5
Kings Glen Dr	DKbC	1979	D7
Kings Glen Tr	DKbC	1979	D7
Kings Grant Dr NW	ATLN	1813	D7
Kingship Dr	DKbC	2066	C3
Kingshouse Coms	FulC	1532	D3
Kings Lake Ct NE	DKbC	1744	E3
Kings Lake Dr NE	CobC	1598	A4
Kingsland Ct	DKbC	1601	B5
Kingsland Ct SE	CobC	1740	A3
Kingsland Dr	DKbC	1601	A5
Kingsley Cir	FulC	1533	A1
Kingsley Cir NE	DKbC	1816	E1
Kingsley Dr NE	CobC	1528	C4
Kingsley Ln NE	CobC	1528	C4
Kingsley Park Ct	GwnC	1533	E7
Kingsley Park Ln	GwnC	1533	E7
Kings Mill Ct	RSWL	1530	D3
King Smith Rd SE	ATLN	2063	B1
Kings Paddock Ct NW	GwnC	1533	D7
Kings Park Cir	DKbC	1980	A3
Kings Park Wy	DKbC	1980	B3
Kings Peak Dr	FulC	1532	E4
E Kings Point Cir	DKbC	1601	A7
Kings Point Ct	DKbC	1601	A7
Kings Point Dr	DKbC	1601	A7
Kingsport Dr NE	FulC	1669	E3
King Springs Rd SE	CobC	1738	E2
	SMYR	1738	E2
King Springs Village Pkwy SE	SMYR	1738	E4
Kings Tavern Pl NW	ATLN	1814	D1
W Kingston Ct NE	FulC	1670	D5
Kingston Ct NW	GwnC	1602	A6
Kingston Ct SE	MRTA	1667	C1
W Kingston Dr NE	FulC	1670	D5
Kingston Dr NE	FulC	1670	D5
Kingston Rd	MRRW	2149	D6
Kingston Rd NW	ATLN	1813	C7
Kingston Ter	EPNT	1974	D7
Kingston Crossing Cir	FulC	1533	E3
Kingstone Rd	AVES	1893	D1
Kingston Manor Ct NE	FulC	1670	D5
Kingstown Ct	DKbC	1817	E3
Kings Troop Rd	DKbC	1894	D1
Kings Valley Dr NE	CobC	1529	B2
Kingsview Cir SE	CobC	1738	E3
Kingsview Dr SE	CobC	1738	E3
	SMYR	1738	E3
Kingswood Cir	ClyC	2147	D2
Kingswood Dr	DKbC	1819	B7
Kingswood Dr NE	CobC	1526	C5
	CobC	1529	B2
Kingswood Gln	DKbC	1979	E7
Kingswood Ln NW	ATLN	1741	C7
Kingswood Pl	DKbC	1979	E7
Kingswood Run	DKbC	1979	E7
Kingswood Tr	DKbC	1979	E7
Kings Woods Dr	CobC	1526	C5
King Valley Rd SE	CobC	1738	D5
	SMYR	1738	D5
King William Dr	ClyC	2149	C7
Kinjac Dr NE	CobC	1527	B2
Kinley Ln	HryC	2152	D6
Kinloch St NW	ATLN	1741	B2
Kinnard Dr NW	GwnC	1601	D4
Kinridge Ct NE	CobC	1527	C5
Kinridge Rd NE	CobC	1527	B5
Kinridge Tr NE	CobC	1527	C5
Kinross Ct	RSWL	1532	B1
Kinross Rd	RSWL	1532	B2
Kinsella Ct	FulC	1599	D3
Kinsey Ct NE	ATLN	1816	A2
Kinsmon Dr NE	CobC	1529	A6
Kinsmon Ln NE	CobC	1529	A6
Kinsmon Pl NE	CobC	1529	B5
Kinsmon Wy NE	CobC	1529	A6
Kinsmon Cove NE	CobC	1529	A6
Kinvarra Cir SW	CobC	1738	A5
Kiowa Ct	ClyC	2151	B6
	DKbC	1819	E6
Kiowa Dr NE	MRTA	1595	B2
Kipling Cir SE	ATLN	1977	D5
Kipling Dr NE	MRTA	1596	B4
Kipling Dr NW	ATLN	1815	A3
Kipling St SE	ATLN	1977	D4
Kirk Dr	ClyC	2147	E3
Kirk Rd	DCTR	1893	A3
Kirk Crossing Dr	DCTR	1893	A3
Kirkland Dr NE	DKbC	1744	A6
Kirkpatrick Wy	ATLN	1892	B2
Kirksford Dr	DKbC	1894	C6
Kirkton Knls	FulC	1532	D3
Kirkwood Av SE	ATLN	1891	B4
Kirkwood Ct	DKbC	1980	A4
Kirkwood Ln SE	CobC	1738	E6
Kirkwood Rd NE	ATLN	1892	B3
Kissing Tree Ln SE	SMYR	1666	D5

Atlanta Street Index

INDEX 37

Lone Oak Av SW

Atlanta Street Index

Mallory Dr NE

STREET	City	Map #	Grid
Lone Oak Av SW	ATLN	2062	D1
Lonesome Pine Ln SE	CobC	1739	E3
Lone Star Tr	DKbC	1745	C2
Lonetia St SE	ATLN	1977	B1
Long Cir	RSWL	1530	C1
Long Dr	DKbC	1893	C7
Long Dr SW	CobC	1666	A6
Long St	EPNT	1975	E7
	EPNT	2061	E1
Long Wy	DKbC	1893	C7
Long Acres Dr NW	FulC	1598	E7
Long Beach Cir	FulC	1531	A5
Long Branch Ct NE	DKbC	1671	B2
Longchamps Dr NE	FulC	1670	D7
Longcourt Cir SE	CobC	1739	D7
Longcourt Dr SE	CobC	1739	D6
Longcourt Trc SE	CobC	1739	D7
Longcourt Wy SE	CobC	1739	C7
Longcourte Dr NW	ATLN	1740	D6
Longdale Dr	DKbC	1978	C1
Longfellow Tr NE	CobC	1528	C3
Long Grove Ct NE	CobC	1528	E3
Long Grove Ct NW	FulC	1669	D2
Long Grove Dr NE	CobC	1528	E3
Long Grove Dr NW	FulC	1669	D2
Longino Dr	UNCT	2145	A6
Long Island Ct NW	FulC	1669	E1
Long Island Dr NE	FulC	1669	E6
	FulC	1670	A6
Long Island Dr NW	FulC	1598	E7
	FulC	1669	D4
Long Island Pl NW	FulC	1598	D7
	FulC	1669	E1
Long Island Ter NE	FulC	1669	E6
Long Island Wy NW	FulC	1669	D5
Long Lake Ct NE	CobC	1529	C3
Long Lake Dr NE	CobC	1529	C3
Long Lake Ter NE	CobC	1529	C3
Longleaf Ct SW	FulC	1973	A4
Longleaf Dr	DKbC	1894	A5
	FTPK	2149	C5
	RSWL	1530	A3
Longleaf Dr NE	ATLN	1742	B4
Longleaf Dr SE	CobC	1666	B6
Longley Av NW	ATLN	1815	A7
Longmeadow Dr	DKbC	1818	D6
Longmeadow Ln	FulC	2146	D2
Longmire Ext	DKbC	1672	C4
	DRVL	1672	C4
Longmire Wy	DRVL	1672	C4
Long Pines Ct	DKbC	1745	E6
Longplace Ct SE	CobC	1739	D7
Longshore Dr	DKbC	1894	B3
Longs Peak Dr	FulC	1532	E4
Longstreet Cir SW	ATLN	1975	D2
Longview Dr	CMBL	1671	E4
	DKbC	1671	D3
	EPNT	1975	E7
	EPNT	2061	E1
Longview Dr NW	NRCS	1602	D5
Longview Wy	DKbC	1671	D2
Longwater Cove	RSWL	1529	E5
Longwood Ct NW	ATLN	1815	B2
Longwood Dr NW	ATLN	1815	B2
Longwood Trc	DKbC	1816	E1
Lonsdale Ct	FulC	1533	A3
Lookout Av NW	ATLN	1814	A6
Lookout Dr	FTPK	2063	B6
Lookout Pl NE	ATLN	1742	A7
Lookout Pt	HryC	2152	C7
Loomis Av SE	ATLN	1891	B5
Loop Rd	ClyC	2062	A7
	ClyC	2147	E1
Loraine St NE	DKbC	1742	E4
Lord N Lady Ln	FulC	1532	D4
Lorell Ter NE	FulC	1670	B2
Loren Dr	DKbC	1894	B4
Lorenzo Dr SW	ATLN	1975	E2
Lori Ct	ClyC	2063	E7
Lori Ln	DKbC	1673	B6
Lori Ann Wy	ClyC	2147	E2
Loridan Cir NE	ATLN	1742	C1
Loridan Wy SE	CobC	1740	A2
Loridans Dr NE	ATLN	1742	B1
Loring Ct	DKbC	1979	B1
Loring Dr NW	ATLN	1815	D5
Loring St SE	ATLN	1891	D6
Lorraine Pl	FTPK	2149	D2
Lorrie Dr NE	CobC	1527	A3
Los Angeles Av NE	ATLN	1816	C7
Lost Forest Ct NW	FulC	1598	E6
Lost Forest Dr NW	FulC	1598	E6
Lost Mill Trc NE	CobC	1528	B6
Lost Mine Tr	DKbC	1672	B1
Lott Av SE	MRTA	1596	A5
Lotus Av NW	ATLN	1814	A7
Louden Dr NE	DKbC	1744	E5
Loudermilk Dr NW	CobC	1595	B2
	MRTA	1595	B2
Louise Cir SE	CobC	1667	B6
Louise Pl NW	ATLN	1814	B7
Louise St	HPVL	2062	C3
Louise Ter SW	FulC	1887	A7
Louis XIV Ln	ClyC	2147	A2
Louvre Ct SW	FulC	1973	A2
Love St SE	SMYR	1666	E7
	SMYR	1738	E1
Love St SW	ATLN	1890	D7
Lovejoy St	DKbC	1819	A4
Lovejoy St NW	ATLN	1890	D2
Lovejoy St SE	MRTA	1595	A6
Loveland Ter	CMBL	1671	C5
Loveless Av NW	ATLN	1889	E1
Loveless Dr	DKbC	2064	E3
Loveless Pl	DKbC	2064	E4
Lovell Dr SW	ATLN	1974	C4
Lovely Ln	DKbC	1745	A7
Lovena Rd SE	MRTA	1596	A6
Lovette Ln NE	ATLN	1742	C3
Lovridge Dr SW	ATLN	1973	C5
Lowe Al SW	ATLN	1890	C5
Lowe Ct NE	CobC	1526	B1
Lowe St	CGPK	2061	C2
Lowe St NW	ATLN	1814	A3
Lowe Tr NE	CobC	1526	B1
Lowe Wy NE	CobC	1526	B1
Lower Alabama St SW	ATLN	1890	E4
Lowergate Dr NE	DKbC	1817	C6
Lower Roswell Rd NE	CobC	1529	E7
	CobC	1598	B3
	MRTA	1596	B5
Lower Roswell Rd SE	CobC	1596	D6
	MRTA	1596	A5
Lowndes Av SW	ATLN	1890	B7
Lowndes St	CGPK	2061	B2
	EPNT	2061	B2
Lowrance Dr	DKbC	1818	D5
Lowry St NE	ATLN	1891	E3
Loyola Ct	DKbC	2066	C1
Loyola Wy	DKbC	2066	C1
Lucerne Ln SE	CobC	1739	C4
Lucerne St	DCTR	1817	D6
Lucia Dr SE	CobC	1738	A2
Lucile Av SE	MRTA	1595	E6
Lucile Av SW	ATLN	1889	E5
Lucile Ln	EPNT	2060	D2
Luckie Ln NE	DKbC	1817	C5
Luckie St NW	ATLN	1890	D3
Lucky Dr NE	CobC	1596	D5
Lucky Dr SE	CobC	1596	D6
Lucy St SE	ATLN	1891	A4
Ludovie Ln	DKbC	1744	D6
Lu Jan Dr	CMBL	1672	A6
Luke Dr	ClyC	2150	E4
Lullingstone Dr SE	CobC	1596	D7
Lullingstone Wy SE	CobC	1596	D7
Lullwater Ct	RSWL	1530	A3
Lullwater Dr SE	CobC	1812	B3
Lullwater Pkwy NE	ATLN	1817	A7
	DKbC	1817	A7
Lullwater Pl NE	ATLN	1891	E1
Lullwater Rd NE	ATLN	1817	A7
	DKbC	1817	A7
Lullwater Estate Rd NE	ATLN	1892	A1
Lullwood Ct NE	CobC	1526	E2
Lullwood Tr	DKbC	1978	E1
Lumby Dr	DKbC	1979	D4
Lumby Ln	HryC	2152	E3
Lumpkin St	EPNT	1975	C6
Lunsford Dr	ClyC	2065	A6
Luray Ct	DKbC	1600	E7
Luray Dr	DKbC	1600	E7
Lusk Dr SE	SMYR	1738	D1
Luther Cir	EPNT	1975	A7
Luther Dr	EPNT	1975	B7
Luther St SE	ATLN	1977	C4
Luxembourg Cir	DKbC	1980	E6
Luxembourg Dr	DKbC	1980	E6
Luxuria Ct	DKbC	1745	C3
Lydia Dr SE	ATLN	1976	E6
Lyle Av	CGPK	2061	B2
	EPNT	1975	D7
	EPNT	2061	D1
Lyle Dr SE	CobC	1596	C7
Lyle Pl NW	ATLN	1815	D6
Lyle Rd	CGPK	2061	A2
	EPNT	2061	A2
Lyle Ter	CGPK	2061	A2
	EPNT	2061	A2
Lynboro Ct	DKbC	1600	A3
Lynburn Dr	DKbC	1745	E4
Lynch Av NW	ATLN	1815	C7
Lynchburg Pl NE	MRTA	1527	A7
Lynda Pl	DKbC	1979	C1
Lyndale Cir	FTPK	2149	B3
Lyndale Dr SE	ATLN	1891	D7
	DKbC	1891	D7
Lynfield Dr SW	ATLN	1888	B7
Lynford Dr SW	ATLN	1975	D1
Lynhurst Cir SW	ATLN	1888	C5
Lynhurst Dr NE	CobC	1528	D1
Lynhurst Dr SW	ATLN	1888	C5
	ATLN	1974	C1
Lynhurst Rd SE	SMYR	1738	B3
Lynmoor Dr NE	DKbC	1742	E5
Lynn Cir SW	ATLN	1888	C6
Lynn Ct	ClyC	2150	E5
Lynn Dr SW	ATLN	1888	C6
Lynn Ln	DKbC	1893	E6
Lynn Dale Ln	ClyC	2150	B7
Lynnhaven Dr SW	ATLN	1976	C2
Lynnhaven Ln SE	SMYR	1738	E2
Lynn Iris Dr	DKbC	1893	A6
Lynnray Dr	DKbC	1673	C7
Lynnray Ln	DKbC	1673	D7
Lynns Wy	DKbC	1894	D7
Lynn Valley Rd SW	ATLN	1888	D6
Lynview Ct E	DKbC	1980	B5
Lynview Ct W	DKbC	1980	A5
Lynway Ln SW	ATLN	1974	D1
Lynwood Ct	ClyC	2149	C6
	RSWL	1530	A1
Lynwood Dr	ClyC	2149	C6
	RSWL	1530	A1
Lynwood Dr NE	DKbC	1670	E7
Lynwood Pl	ClyC	2149	C7
Lynwood St SE	ATLN	1891	C7
Lynwyn Ln SE	DKbC	1977	D2
Lyon Av SW	FulC	1973	A3
Lyon Ct SW	FulC	1973	A3
Lyric Ct SE	ATLN	2062	E4
Lyric Ln SE	ATLN	2062	E4
Lyric Wy NW	ATLN	1888	E1
Lytham Ct	DKbC	1600	D4
Lytle Av SE	ATLN	1891	D6
M			
N M Av	FTPK	2149	E1
Mableton Pkwy SE	CobC	1812	A6
Mableton Pkwy SE SR-139	CobC	1812	A6
Mabros Industrial Pkwy	ClyC	2064	C6
Mabry Ln NE	DKbC	1742	E2
Mabry Rd NE	CobC	1528	E1
	DKbC	1670	E7
	DKbC	1742	E1
	FulC	1599	B5
MacArthur Blvd NW	ATLN	1814	C3
Macaw St NW	ATLN	1813	D3
MacBaine Ln	DKbC	1601	B6
Macby Av NE	CobC	1527	C3
Macby Ct NE	CobC	1527	C2
Macby Dr NE	CobC	1527	B2
Macby Wk NE	CobC	1527	C2
Macedonia Rd SE	ATLN	2063	A2
Macintosh Tr	ATLN	1973	D2
Mack Dr NW	ATLN	1814	B6
MacKenzie Dr NE	ATLN	1891	B3
Mackinac Dr	FulC	1532	C4
Mackinaw Pl SE	SMYR	1739	B2
MacKlone St NE	ATLN	1891	E4
MacLaren Cir	DKbC	1601	A6
MacLaren Dr	CLKN	1819	B4
	DKbC	1819	B4
Maco St NW	ATLN	1813	D3
Macon Dr SW	ATLN	1976	D5
	ATLN	2062	E1
Macon Hwy	ClyC	2151	A7
Macon Hwy SR-42	ClyC	2151	A7
Macon Hwy US-23	ClyC	2151	A7
Macon Pl SE	ATLN	2062	E1
Macon Ter SW	ATLN	1976	E4
Maddox Dr NE	ATLN	1816	A5
Maddox Rd	ClyC	2150	C5
Madera Ct	FulC	1599	D1
Madison Av	DCTR	1892	D3
Madison Av NE	DKbC	1670	E7
Madison Coms	DKbC	1672	B1
Madison Dr	DKbC	1671	A1
E Madison Dr	DKbC	1601	B7
W Madison Dr	DKbC	1601	B7
Madison St	CGPK	2061	D2
	FTPK	2149	B3
Madison St SE	SMYR	1667	B7
Madison Place Ln	DKbC	1672	B1
Madora Pl	DKbC	1978	C1
Madrid Cir NW	GwnC	1602	A4
Madrona St NW	ATLN	1889	C2
Mae Av NE	DKbC	1670	E7
Maediris Dr	DCTR	1817	D6
Magbee Dr SE	SMYR	1738	D2
Magill Pk NE	ATLN	1816	A7
Magna Carta Dr NW	ATLN	1888	D1
Magnolia Av SE	CobC	1812	C6
Magnolia Cir SE	CobC	1598	B6
Magnolia Dr SE	SMYR	1738	D3
Magnolia Grv	FulC	1532	C1
Magnolia Ln	ClyC	2063	C5
	MRRW	2149	E6
W Magnolia Ln NE	MRTA	1595	B2
Magnolia Pl	RSWL	1530	B2
Magnolia Pth	DKbC	1980	E7
Magnolia St	EPNT	2061	D2
	RSWL	1530	B2
Magnolia St NW	ATLN	1890	B3
	NRCS	1602	E7
Magnolia Wk	RSWL	1530	B2
Magnolia Wy	MRRW	2149	E6
	RSWL	1530	B2
Magnolia Wy SE	SMYR	1666	B7
Magnolia Bluff Dr	FulC	1601	C2
Magnolia Mill Ct NW	GwnC	1602	A1
Magnolia Park Dr NW	GwnC	1673	D5
Magnolia Park Ln NW	GwnC	1673	C5
Magnolia Springs Ct NE	DKbC	1744	E4
Magnolia View Ct NW	GwnC	1673	C5
Magnolia View Pl NW	GwnC	1673	C5
Magnolia Walk Cir	DKbC	1600	B3
Magnolia Walk Ct NW	GwnC	1673	C5
Magnolia Walk Ln	FulC	2146	B5
Maid Ln NW	ATLN	1814	C2
Maiden Ln NE	ATLN	1891	C1
Mailing Av SE	ATLN	1977	A1
Main Dr	FTPK	2148	D1
Main St	ATLN	1975	D6
	CGPK	2061	C3
	ClyC	2147	E3
	DKbC	1745	E4
	EPNT	1975	D6
	EPNT	2061	C3
	FTPK	2062	E7
	FTPK	2149	A1
	UNCT	2145	A7
Main St SR-139	ATLN	1975	D6
	CGPK	2061	C3
	EPNT	1975	D6
	EPNT	2061	C3
Main St SR-154	ATLN	1975	D6
	EPNT	1975	D6
Main St US-29	ATLN	1975	D6
	CGPK	2061	C3
	EPNT	1975	D6
	EPNT	2061	C3
E Main St	CGPK	2061	C2
	EPNT	2061	C2
N Main St NW	ATLN	1813	E4
W Main St NW	ATLN	1813	E2
Main St NW	ATLN	1813	E3
Main St SE	CobC	1739	B5
	SMYR	1739	B5
E Main Entrance SE	MRTA	1595	E6
W Main Entrance SE	MRTA	1595	E6
Mainsail Ct NE	CobC	1527	C3
Mainsail Dr NE	CobC	1527	C3
Mainstream Cir NW	GwnC	1533	C6
Maison Pl NW	ATLN	1815	C2
Majestic Cir	AVES	1893	E2
Majestic Dr SW	ATLN	1887	E3
Majestic Oaks Wy SW	FulC	1887	D7
Majesty Ln	ClyC	2149	C7
Major Ct	RSWL	1532	B7
Malabar Dr NE	DKbC	1743	E4
Maldo Dr NW	ATLN	1813	D4
Malfre Ln	DKbC	1600	B5
Malibu Ct	LKCY	2149	D5
Malibu Dr	LKCY	2149	D5
Mallard Cir	ClyC	2064	A7
Mallard St NW	ATLN	1814	C4
Mallard Lake Dr NE	CobC	1529	C6
Mallard Lake Pl	FulC	1532	D3
Mallory Dr NE	MRTA	1595	D2

INDEX 39

May Apple Ct — Metropolitan Pkwy SW

Atlanta Street Index

STREET	City	Map #	Grid
May Apple Ct	DKbC	1980	D5
Mayapple Ct NW	GwnC	1602	A1
Mayes Dr SE	CobC	1596	B6
Mayfair Dr NE	DKbC	1816	E1
Mayfair Pl NE	ATLN	1742	B4
Mayfair Rd NE	ATLN	1742	B4
Mayfield Dr	DKbC	1818	E3
Mayflower Av SW	ATLN	1889	D7
Mayflower Dr NE	CobC	1526	D1
Mayflower Rd	CGPK	2060	E7
May Jo Ct SE	CobC	1596	C6
Mayland Av SW	ATLN	1890	B7
	ATLN	1976	C1
Mayland Cir SW	ATLN	1976	C1
Maynard Ct NW	ATLN	1813	B6
Maynard Rd NW	ATLN	1813	B5
Maynard Ter SE	ATLN	1892	A6
Mayo Pl SW	ATLN	1974	B5
Mays Cross SW	ATLN	1887	E7
Mays Ct	DKbC	1744	D7
Mays Ct SW	ATLN	1887	E7
Mayson Av NE	ATLN	1892	A4
Mayson St NE	ATLN	1816	A3
Mayson Turner Rd NW	ATLN	1889	E2
May's Ridge Ct	ClyC	2151	D5
Maywood Ct NE	CobC	1528	B7
Maywood Pl NW	ATLN	1889	B1
McAfee Pl	DKbC	1892	E7
McAfee Rd	DKbC	1892	D7
McAfee St NW	ATLN	1890	D2
McAllister St SW	ATLN	1889	D6
McAlpin Ter	EPNT	1974	D6
McArthur Dr NE	MRTA	1595	B4
McBride Ct	RSWL	1530	A4
McBurnett Rd NE	CobC	1596	D3
McCall Dr	DKbC	1672	E5
McCall Pl	DKbC	1672	E5
McCallie Blvd NW	ATLN	1814	B5
McCarthy St	ATLN	1890	B3
McCauley Rd SE	SMYR	1738	D2
McClatchey Cir NE	ATLN	1742	B2
McClave Dr	DRVL	1672	B6
McClean St	DCTR	1893	A4
McClelen Wy	DKbC	1818	A5
McClelland Av	EPNT	1975	D4
McClure Av NW	ATLN	1889	E3
McClure Rd	CobC	1595	A1
McCoba Dr SE	SMYR	1667	B6
McConnell Dr	DKbC	1817	D3
McCoy Av	EPNT	1974	E7
McCoy Dr	EPNT	1974	E7
McCoy Pl	EPNT	1974	E7
McCoy Rd SE	ATLN	2063	A3
McCoy St NE	ATLN	1816	C5
McCree Dr	CGPK	2061	A4
McCully Ct NE	DKbC	1744	E5
McCully Dr NE	DKbC	1744	D5
McCurdy Wy	DKbC	1818	A5
McDaniel St	DKbC	1671	E3
McDaniel St SW	ATLN	1890	C6
	ATLN	1976	C1
McDonald Ct SW	MRTA	1595	A5
McDonald Dr SE	ATLN	1976	C3
McDonald St	CGPK	2061	B3
McDonald St SE	ATLN	1891	B5
McDonald St SW	MRTA	1595	A5
McDonough Blvd SE	ATLN	1976	E1
McDonough Blvd SE SR-42 SPUR	ATLN	1976	E2
McDonough Blvd SE SR-54	ATLN	1976	E1
McDonough Dr NW	GwnC	1673	D4
N McDonough St	DCTR	1892	E1
S McDonough St	DCTR	1892	E2
McDougall Dr SW	FulC	1887	A4
McEachern Wy NW	GwnC	1602	A4
McElroy Rd	DKbC	1672	D4
	DRVL	1672	D3
McFerrin Cir	ClyC	2148	D7
McGaw Dr	CMBL	1671	C6
McGee St SW	ATLN	1975	E3
McGee Wy	EPNT	1975	C7
McGill Ct	DKbC	2066	C2
McGill Dr	DKbC	2066	C2
McGill Ln	DKbC	2066	C2
McGill Pl NE	ATLN	1891	A2
McGill Wy	DKbC	2066	C2
McGillicuty Dr	UNCT	2145	B7
McGill Park Av NE	ATLN	1891	A3
McGlynn Ct	DKbC	1979	B4
McGlynn Dr	DKbC	1979	B5
McGruder St NE	ATLN	1891	B3
McHenry Av	DKbC	1818	E6
McInnes Cir SE	CobC	1666	B3
McIntosh Av NE	MRTA	1595	B4
McIntyre Pl SW	ATLN	1975	E3
McJenkin Dr NE	DKbC	1743	C5
McKay Dr SE	ATLN	1977	C4
McKenzie Ct	DKbC	1819	A2
McKenzie Ct SW	ATLN	1888	D7
McKenzie Dr	DKbC	1893	E5
	EPNT	2061	A1
McKinley Av	UNCT	2145	A7
McKinley Rd NW	ATLN	1815	B3
McKinley Wy	DKbC	1979	B1
McKinnon Dr	DKbC	1893	B3
E McKinnon Dr	DKbC	1893	B3
McKoy St	DCTR	1892	E4
McLain Ln	DKbC	1894	E6
McLendon Av NE	ATLN	1891	E2
McLendon Cir NW	ATLN	1813	C7
McLendon Dr	DKbC	1818	E4
McLinden Av SE	SMYR	1738	D1
McLynn Av NE	ATLN	1816	D6
	DKbC	1816	D6
McMillan St NW	ATLN	1815	C7
McMullin Ter	EPNT	1975	C4
McMurray Dr SW	ATLN	1974	C4
McNair Ln SW	ATLN	1975	D3
McNeal Dr SE	CobC	1666	A6
McNeel Al NW	MRTA	1595	C6
McPherson Av SE	ATLN	1891	E5
McPherson Dr	EPNT	1975	E4
McPherson Dr NE	CobC	1529	C2
McPherson Pl SE	ATLN	1891	E5
McPherson Rd NE	CobC	1529	B1
McWilliams Av SE	ATLN	1892	A6
McWilliams Rd SE	ATLN	1977	B6
Mead Rd	DCTR	1892	D3
Mead St SE	ATLN	1891	B7
Meade Cir SE	CobC	1597	A7
Meador Av SE	ATLN	1977	A5
Meador Wy SE	ATLN	1976	E5
Meadow Ct	DKbC	1672	B7
N Meadow Ct NE	CobC	1528	D1
S Meadow Ct NE	CobC	1528	D2
Meadow Dr	FTPK	2063	D6
Meadow Dr NE	CobC	1528	C2
Meadow Ln	ClyC	2151	C5
	DKbC	1893	C7
Meadow Ln NE	CobC	1528	D2
	CobC	1598	C3
Meadow Pl NE	MRTA	1595	D3
Meadow Rd	HPVL	2062	C3
Meadow Rdg NE	CobC	1527	A3
Meadow Tr	DKbC	1980	E5
Meadow Wy	MRRW	2150	A6
Meadoway Ct	ClyC	2151	C5
Meadowbrook Dr NE	ATLN	1742	A1
	FulC	1742	A1
Meadowbrook Dr SE	CobC	1596	B6
Meadowbrook Ln	ClyC	2150	A7
	MRRW	2150	A7
Meadowbrook Ln NE	MRTA	1595	B2
Meadowbrook Ln SE	CobC	1596	B6
Meadow Chase Dr NE	CobC	1528	C6
Meadowcliff Dr NE	DKbC	1743	E5
Meadowcreek Ct	DKbC	1600	B4
Meadowcreek Dr	DKbC	1600	B4
Meadow Creek Dr NW	GwnC	1601	D4
Meadowcreek Ln	DKbC	1600	B4
Meadowdale Av NE	ATLN	1816	E4
Meadowdale Ct NW	GwnC	1533	C6
Meadowglades Dr	DKbC	1894	C6
Meadow Glen Cir	ClyC	2151	C1
Meadowglenn Village Ln	DKbC	1673	C5
Meadow Green Cir NW	GwnC	1601	E4
Meadow Green Ct NW	GwnC	1601	D3
Meadow Grove Wy SE	CobC	1596	E7
Meadowind Ct NE	CobC	1528	B4
Meadowind Ln NE	CobC	1528	B4
Meadow Lake Dr	DKbC	1600	D5
Meadow Lake Ln	DKbC	1600	D5
Meadow Lake Rd	FulC	2146	D4
Meadowland Trc	FulC	1532	D1
Meadowlane Cir SW	ATLN	1974	B5
Meadowlane Dr SW	ATLN	1974	B5
Meadowlane Pl SW	ATLN	1974	A5
Meadowlark Dr	DKbC	1894	A4
	EPNT	1975	A7
	EPNT	2060	E1
	RVDL	2148	A7
Meadow Lark Ln	EPNT	2060	E1
Meadowlawn Dr SE	CobC	1667	E1
Meadow Ln Rd	DKbC	1599	E7
	DKbC	1600	A7
Meadow Mere E	DKbC	1672	B7
Meadow Mere W	DKbC	1672	B7
Meadow Mere Dr	DKbC	1672	C7
Meadowood Ct	RSWL	1530	D2
Meadowood Dr	RSWL	1530	D2
Meadowood Dr NE	CobC	1528	A5
Meadowood Ln	DKbC	1672	B7
	DKbC	1744	B1
Meadow Park Dr SW	ATLN	1976	D6
Meadow Park Ln SW	ATLN	1976	D6
Meadow Ridge Ct	ClyC	2151	C5
Meadowridge Dr SW	ATLN	2060	A1
Meadow Rue Dr NW	GwnC	1601	E4
Meadow Rue Ln NW	GwnC	1601	E4
Meadow Run Ct NW	GwnC	1601	E3
Meadowsweet Trc	RSWL	1531	E4
Meadowvale Dr NE	DKbC	1743	E5
Meadow Valley Dr NE	FulC	1669	E7
	FulC	1741	E1
Meadowview Ct	ClyC	2151	C5
Meadowview Dr NE	CobC	1527	A6
Meadowview Dr SE	DKbC	1978	D4
Meadowview Ln SE	DKbC	1978	D4
Meadowview Rd	ClyC	2151	C5
Meadow Wood Ct NE	CobC	1596	C1
Means Dr	DKbC	1817	B5
Means St NW	ATLN	1890	C1
Mecaslin St NW	ATLN	1815	C5
Mechanicsville Rd NW	GwnC	1602	B7
	GwnC	1673	B1
Mechelle Ln NE	CobC	1526	B2
Mecklinburg Pl	DKbC	1894	B5
Medfield Tr NE	DKbC	1743	D5
Medford Pl SE	CobC	1666	C4
N Medical Dr NW	MRTA	1595	A2
S Medical Dr NW	MRTA	1595	A2
Medical Wy	ClyC	2148	D7
	RVDL	2148	D7
Medinah Ct	DKbC	1745	A1
Medley Rdg	DKbC	1818	D2
Medlin St SE	SMYR	1666	E7
	SMYR	1738	D1
Medlock Cir NW	GwnC	1533	E7
Medlock Rd	DCTR	1818	A6
	DKbC	1818	A6
Medlock Bridge Rd NW	GwnC	1533	E7
	GwnC	1602	E1
Medlock Bridge Rd NW SR-141	GwnC	1533	E7
Medlock Corners Dr NW	GwnC	1602	E3
Medway Ct	FulC	2146	B7
Meeting Ln NE	FulC	1670	A4
Meharris Pl NE	CobC	1529	A5
Meissen Ct	FulC	1532	D4
Melandre Dr	ClyC	2150	C7
Melanie Ct	DKbC	1893	C5
	FulC	2145	E4
Melanie Dr	FulC	2145	E4
Melanie Ln	FulC	2145	D4
Melanie Tr	FulC	2145	E4
Melanie Wy	FulC	2145	E5
Melanie Woods Dr	FulC	2145	E4
Melante Dr NE	ATLN	1816	D2
Melba Ct NE	CobC	1527	B3
Melbenan Dr SW	FulC	1974	B1
Melbourne Ct	DKbC	1819	E1
Meldon Av SE	ATLN	1976	E3
Meldon Av SW	ATLN	1976	D3
Meldrum St NW	ATLN	1890	B2
Melford Pl	AVES	1893	D1
Melinda Ct NE	DKbC	1744	A4
Melinda Dr NE	DKbC	1744	A4
Melinda Wy SE	CobC	1738	A2
Melissa Ct NE	CobC	1528	A5
Melissa Belle Ct	HryC	2065	C6
Mell Av	CLKN	1819	A4
	DKbC	1819	A4
Mell Av NE	ATLN	1892	A3
Mell Av NW	ATLN	1813	B5
Mell Ct SE	SMYR	1666	D5
Mell Pl	CLKN	1819	A4
	DKbC	1819	A4
Mellrich Av NE	ATLN	1892	D3
Mellview Av SW	ATLN	1976	C2
Mellville Av	DKbC	1893	A7
Mellwood Pl SW	ATLN	1974	A6
Melody Ln	DKbC	1892	E7
	RSWL	1530	E2
Melrose Av	DCTR	1892	D2
Melrose Av SE	DKbC	1977	E5
Melrose Dr	ClyC	2149	B5
	DKbC	1819	C3
	FTPK	2149	B5
Melrose Dr NE	CobC	1527	C1
Melrose Dr SW	ATLN	1976	A3
Melvin Dr SW	ATLN	1973	E3
Memorial Dr	AVES	1893	D3
	AVES	1894	A2
	DKbC	1819	B7
	DKbC	1893	D3
Memorial Dr SR-10	DKbC	1819	D5
	DKbC	1894	A1
Memorial Dr SR-154	AVES	1893	D3
	AVES	1894	A2
	DKbC	1893	D3
Memorial Dr SE	ATLN	1890	E5
	ATLN	1891	C5
	ATLN	1893	A5
	DKbC	1892	A5
	DKbC	1893	A5
Memorial Dr SE SR-154	ATLN	1890	E5
	ATLN	1891	C5
	ATLN	1893	A5
	DKbC	1892	A5
	DKbC	1893	A5
Memorial Dr SW	ATLN	1890	D5
Memorial Dr SW SR-154	ATLN	1890	E5
Memorial Pl SE	SMYR	1666	E7
Memorial Ter SE	ATLN	1891	E5
Memorial College Av	DKbC	1819	C5
Memory Ln	CobC	1598	A1
Memory Ln SE	CobC	1739	A1
	SMYR	1739	A1
Mendel Ct SE	CobC	1739	B5
Mendel Ct SW	FulC	1887	B4
Mendel Dr SW	ATLN	1887	B4
	FulC	1887	B4
Mendell Cir NE	DKbC	1670	E7
Mendenhall St	CMBL	1671	D5
Menlo Dr	DKbC	1745	C1
Menlo Dr NW	ATLN	1815	A6
Menlo Wy	ClyC	2151	A7
	DKbC	1745	D1
Menlo Park Dr	ClyC	2151	A7
Mentelle Dr NE	ATLN	1816	A7
Mercedes Ct NE	DKbC	1744	B6
Mercedes Dr NE	DKbC	1744	B6
Mercer Av	CGPK	2061	B2
	EPNT	2061	E2
Mercer Rd	DKbC	1894	E5
Mercer Rd SE	CobC	1739	B3
Mercer St SE	ATLN	1891	B6
Mercer Wy	DKbC	1894	E5
Mercer University Dr	DKbC	1744	D1
Mercury Dr NW	ATLN	1813	A7
Meredith Dr NW	ATLN	1815	C3
Meredith Wk	DKbC	2065	A1
Merganser Ln	FulC	1532	D3
Meridian St SE	ATLN	1891	E4
Meridian Marks Rd NE	FulC	1670	D4
Merk Rd SW	FulC	2059	A1
Merle Cir	DKbC	1893	B7
Merlendale Ct NW	FulC	1669	E7
Merlendale Dr NW	FulC	1669	D6
Merlin Av SE	ATLN	1891	D4
Merrick Dr NE	ATLN	1742	D6
Merrifield Ln NE	MRTA	1527	B7
Merrill Av	DCTR	1817	D7
Merrill Av SW	ATLN	1889	E7
Merrilyn Dr SE	ATLN	1977	A4
Merrimac Ct NE	DKbC	1743	C7
Merriman Ln NE	DKbC	1816	E1
Merritt Dr	RSWL	1532	B7
Merritt Rd NE	CobC	1595	E2
	MRTA	1595	E2
Merritt St SE	MRTA	1595	C5
Merritts Av NE	ATLN	1891	A2
Merritts Av NW	ATLN	1890	D2
Merriweather Woods	FulC	1533	A3
Merry Ln NE	DKbC	1817	C2
Mershon Tr NW	GwnC	1602	C2
Merton Rd NE	ATLN	1816	D4
Mesa Clfs NE	DKbC	1817	B2
Mesa Dr SE	DKbC	1978	D5
Mesa Verde Dr	FulC	2146	B6
Messina Wy NE	FulC	1599	B5
Metcalf Rd	FTPK	2149	D2
	LKCY	2149	D2
Metric Pl NW	GwnC	1602	D1
Metropolitan Av SE	ATLN	1891	E5
Metropolitan Pkwy SW	ATLN	1890	C7
	ATLN	1976	C3
	ATLN	2062	B1

INDEX 40

Metropolitan Pkwy SW — Atlanta Street Index — Moonlight Forest Ct

STREET	City	Map #	Grid
Metropolitan Pkwy SW SR-3	ATLN	1890	C7
	ATLN	1976	C3
	ATLN	2062	B1
Metropolitan Pkwy SW US-19	ATLN	1890	C7
	ATLN	1976	C3
	ATLN	2062	B1
Metropolitan Pkwy SW US-41	ATLN	1890	C7
	ATLN	1976	C3
	ATLN	2062	B1
Metropolitan Pl SE	ATLN	1891	E5
Meuse Wy	FulC	1532	C5
Miami Cir NE	ATLN	1742	C7
	ATLN	1816	B1
Micah Ct	DKbC	2065	A1
Michael Dr	FulC	2146	D6
Michael Ln	DKbC	1818	D3
Michael Pl SW	ATLN	1975	E3
Michael St NE	DKbC	1817	B5
Michael Wy NE	CobC	1528	D7
Michael James Dr	ATLN	1974	D5
Michelle Cir NW	FulC	1669	E3
Michigan Av	DCTR	1817	E7
Michigan Av NW	ATLN	1890	A3
Middle St SW	ATLN	1890	C7
Middlebrooks Dr	FTPK	2149	B2
Middleburg Dr	FulC	2146	C5
Middlebury Ct NE	CobC	1529	A7
Middlebury Ln NW	FulC	1669	C5
Middleham Ct	DKbC	1745	E2
Middle Plantation Rd NW	ATLN	1814	A1
Middlesex Av NE	ATLN	1816	C6
Middleton Ct SE	SMYR	1667	C5
Middleton Rd NW	ATLN	1888	C4
Middleton St SW	ATLN	1976	D3
Middlewich Ln NW	GwnC	1602	E1
Midlawn Dr	DKbC	1893	D4
Midsummer Ct NE	CobC	1597	A1
Midtown Pl NE	ATLN	1816	B7
Midvale Cir	DKbC	1745	B4
Midvale Ct	DKbC	1745	B4
Midvale Dr NE	ATLN	1742	A1
Midvale Ln	DKbC	1745	A3
Midvale Rd	DKbC	1745	A3
Midvale Rd NE	DKbC	1745	A3
Midvale Cove	DKbC	1745	A4
Midvale Forest Ct	DKbC	1745	B3
Midvale Forest Dr	DKbC	1745	A3
Midview Dr	DKbC	1893	E4
Midway Rd	DCTR	1893	A3
	DKbC	1893	C4
Midway St SE	ATLN	1977	C6
Midway Pointe	HryC	2066	D6
Mifflin Pl NE	ATLN	1816	C5
Mikal Pl	DKbC	1892	D6
Milam Av SW	ATLN	1976	C5
Milam Cir	DKbC	1818	E4
Milam Dr	HryC	2066	D7
Milan Dr	ClyC	2148	B1
Milano Dr SW	FulC	1887	A6
Mildred Pl NW	ATLN	1814	B7
Mildred Pl SE	SMYR	1667	B7
Mildred St SW	ATLN	1890	B4
Mile Post Dr	DKbC	1599	E7
Miles Cir	EPNT	1976	A7
Miles Ln NE	DKbC	1817	D2
Milesford Ct	RSWL	1532	C5
Milky Wy	HryC	2152	B4
Mill Cir	FulC	1533	C3
Mill Ct	ClyC	2150	E7
	DRVL	1672	B3
N Mill Ct NW	FulC	1598	D6
Mill Ct NE	CobC	1596	B1
Mill Dr NE	CobC	1596	B1
Mill Ovlk NE	DKbC	1670	E6
N Mill Rd NW	FulC	1598	D6
Mill St	ClyC	2151	C5
	RSWL	1530	C3
Mill St NW	MRTA	1595	A4
Mill Wk NW	ATLN	1741	B6
Mill Acres Dr SW	ATLN	1974	E2
Millbank Pl	RSWL	1532	C1
Mill Bridge Ct NE	CobC	1528	C6
Mill Bridge Dr NE	CobC	1528	C6
Millbrook Cir	RSWL	1530	D1
Mill Brook Dr	DKbC	1600	B6
Millbrook Dr NW	ATLN	1669	C7
Millbrook Trc NE	CobC	1596	E5
Millbrook Farm Ct NE	CobC	1597	A6
Millbrook Farm Rd NE	CobC	1597	A5
Mill Chase Cir SE	CobC	1597	A7
Mill Creek Bnd NE	DKbC	1817	C6
Mill Creek Ct	DKbC	1671	C4
Mill Creek Mnr NE	DKbC	1670	E6
Mill Creek Pl	RSWL	1531	B1
Mill Creek Rd NE	DKbC	1670	E6
Milledge Av SE	ATLN	1891	A6
Milledge Pl NE	DKbC	1817	A3
Milledge St	EPNT	1975	E6
Milledge Gate Ct SE	CobC	1597	D7
Milledge Gate Dr SE	CobC	1597	D7
Milledge Gate Ter SE	CobC	1597	A6
Millen Dr SE	CobC	1738	A7
Millennium Wy NE	DKbC	1743	A5
Miller Av NE	ATLN	1891	E2
Miller Av SE	CobC	1666	C3
Miller Ct E	NRCS	1602	D4
Miller Ct NW	GwnC	1601	D4
Miller Ct W	NRCS	1602	D4
Miller Dr	CMBL	1671	D6
E Miller Dr SW	ATLN	1975	D4
N Miller Dr SW	ATLN	1975	D3
S Miller Dr SW	ATLN	1975	D4
	EPNT	1975	D4
W Miller Dr SW	ATLN	1975	D3
Miller Dr NE	CobC	1527	B3
Miller Ln SW	ATLN	1975	D3
Miller Rd	FulC	2146	B1
Miller Reed Av SE	ATLN	1976	C3
Millet Wy NW	GwnC	1601	E1
Millford Pl SW	ATLN	1974	A2
Mill Gate Ct	DKbC	1600	B3
Mill Gate Dr	DKbC	1600	A3
Mill Glen Ct	DKbC	1600	A2
Mill Glen Dr	DKbC	1600	A2
Millhouse Ln NW	GwnC	1533	D6
Milligan Ct	ClyC	2147	B5
Milligan Dr	DKbC	1819	B6
Milliken Ct	DKbC	2066	D1
Millinocket Rd NE	CobC	1528	B1
Mill Lake Wy	ClyC	2150	E7
Mill Pond Blvd NE	CobC	1596	E2
Mill Pond Ct NE	CobC	1596	D2
Mill Pond Ct SE	SMYR	1738	D3
Mill Pond Dr SE	SMYR	1738	D3
Mill Pond Rd SE	SMYR	1738	D3
Mill Race Ct	DKbC	1600	A3
Millridge Ln SE	CobC	1668	A1
Mill Ridge Tr NE	DKbC	1744	E4
Mill Ridge Wk NE	DKbC	1744	B4
Millrons Dr	ATLN	1976	A5
	EPNT	1976	A5
Mill Run Dr NE	CobC	1598	D1
Mill Run Trc NE	CobC	1598	D1
Mill Run Wy NE	CobC	1598	D1
Mills Bnd	DKbC	1979	A3
Mills Ln SE	CobC	1666	B4
Mills Pl SW	FulC	1887	C3
Mills St NW	ATLN	1890	D2
Mill Shire Ln	DKbC	1600	A2
Millside Ct SE	CobC	1739	A5
Millside Dr SE	CobC	1739	A5
Millside Trc SE	CobC	1739	A4
Millside Wk SE	CobC	1739	A5
Millstone Ct NW	GwnC	1533	D6
Mill Stone Dr NE	CobC	1596	B2
Mill Stream Ct	DKbC	1600	D6
Mill Trace Ct	DKbC	1600	A3
Mill Trace Dr	DKbC	1600	A2
Mill Vale Ct	DRVL	1672	C3
Mill Valley Rd SW	ATLN	1974	A3
Mill View Av	RSWL	1530	C3
Millview Dr NE	CobC	1596	B1
Millwood Ct	DKbC	1818	C2
Millwood Tr SE	SMYR	1739	A2
Millwood Wy	DKbC	1818	C1
Milmar Dr NW	ATLN	1740	E6
Milowyn Pl NE	DKbC	1743	B3
Milscott Dr	DKbC	1818	B5
Milstead Cir NE	CobC	1527	A4
Milstead Trc NE	CobC	1527	A4
Milton Av NW	ATLN	1814	B7
Milton Av SE	ATLN	1976	E1
Milton Pl SE	ATLN	1891	E6
Milton St	DKbC	1818	D5
Milton St SW	ATLN	1890	B4
Milton Ter SE	ATLN	1977	A1
Mimms Dr NW	GwnC	1673	B2
Mimosa Blvd	RSWL	1530	C2
Mimosa Cir SE	SMYR	1667	A7
Mimosa Dr	DCTR	1893	A3
	FTPK	2149	C2
Mimosa Dr SE	CobC	1667	A2
	MRTA	1595	C5
Mimosa Pl	DCTR	1893	A3
Mims St SW	ATLN	1889	D4
Mindy Dr	FulC	1887	B3
Mine Creek Ln NE	CobC	1528	D3
Minette Pl	DKbC	1819	D2
Minhinette Dr	RSWL	1530	C1
S Minister Dr NW	GwnC	1673	E6
Minnewil Ln NE	CobC	1596	B4
Minnow Rd	ClyC	2151	D5
Miriam Ct	DKbC	1979	D1
Miriam Ln	DKbC	1893	C7
	DKbC	1979	C1
Mirrabeau Ct NE	CobC	1527	A5
Miss Astor Pl NE	ATLN	1816	C3
Missbach Ct NE	CobC	1527	E4
Missendell Ln NW	GwnC	1533	D5
Missionary Ct	DCTR	1893	B2
Missionary Dr	DCTR	1893	B2
Mission Ridge Cir SE	CobC	1739	E1
Mission Ridge Ct SE	CobC	1739	E1
Mission Ridge Ln SE	CobC	1739	E1
Mission Ridge Rd SE	CobC	1739	E1
Missy Dr NE	CobC	1528	C2
Mistletoe Rd	DKbC	1818	C3
Mistral Wy	ClyC	2149	B3
Mistwater Trc	RSWL	1532	A3
Mistwater Close	RSWL	1531	C6
Misty Gln	DKbC	2064	E1
Misty Lk	DKbC	2064	E1
Misty Ln SE	CobC	1739	C7
Misty Wk NE	CobC	1597	B1
Misty Creek Dr	DKbC	1818	E3
Misty Forest Dr NE	CobC	1597	B1
Misty Forest Wy NE	CobC	1597	B1
Misty Harbour Tr	DKbC	1673	D6
Misty Hollow Dr NE	CobC	1597	B1
Misty Morning Ln	RSWL	1532	B7
Misty Oaks Dr	FulC	1531	B7
	FulC	1600	B1
Misty Ridge Mnr NW	FulC	1669	E5
Misty River Run	RSWL	1531	D6
Misty Valley Rd	DKbC	1893	E5
Mistyview Dr	ClyC	2151	C4
Misty Waters Dr	DKbC	1979	C2
Mitchell Ct NE	CobC	1528	B5
Mitchell Dr	DKbC	1893	C6
Mitchell Dr NE	MRTA	1526	C6
Mitchell Pl	DKbC	1893	C7
Mitchell Rd	ClyC	2065	C7
	ClyC	2151	B1
Mitchell Rd NE	CobC	1528	B4
Mitchell Rd NW	FulC	1669	D3
	NRCS	1602	E6
Mitchell Rd SE	SMYR	1813	B2
Mitchell St	FTPK	2063	C7
	FTPK	2149	C1
Mitchell St SW	ATLN	1890	C4
Mitchell Cove NE	DKbC	1742	E1
Mitchells Glenn Ct	ClyC	2065	C7
Mitchells Meadow Ln	ClyC	2065	C7
Mitchells Ridge Dr	ClyC	2065	C7
Mitchells Valley Ct	ClyC	2065	C7
Mitscher Blvd	CobC	1666	C3
Mitsey Pt	CobC	1597	A2
Mitsy Lake Ct NE	CobC	1597	B1
Mitsy Ridge Dr NE	CobC	1597	A2
Mize Rd	ClyC	2148	C6
Mizel Dr	DKbC	1817	B6
Mobile Av NE	ATLN	1815	E2
Mobile Av SW	ATLN	1976	C4
Mobile Ln SW	CobC	1595	A7
Mobile St NW	ATLN	1889	E3
Mobley Ct SE	ATLN	1977	A6
Mobley Dr SE	ATLN	1976	E6
Mockingbird Ln	DCTR	1817	D7
Mockingbird Ln NE	CobC	1597	A2
Mockingbird Ln SE	SMYR	1738	B4
Mockingbird Ln SW	ATLN	1888	C7
Mockwell Ct	DKbC	1600	A5
Moffat Ct	DKbC	1894	D6
Mohawk Dr NE	MRTA	1595	B2
Mohawk Pl SE	SMYR	1739	A2
Mohawk St NE	ATLN	1891	D4
Mohican Tr	DKbC	1894	D3
Mohon Cir SE	CobC	1666	B4
Mollie St SE	ATLN	1891	C5
Monaco Run SW	FulC	1973	A2
Monarch Ct	DKbC	2065	B2
Monarch Ct NE	CobC	1527	B7
Monarch Dr	DKbC	2065	B1
Monarch Dr NE	CobC	1527	C7
Moncrief Cir	DKbC	1744	D7
Monet Ct NW	ATLN	1815	A2
Monica Ct SW	ATLN	1888	D5
Monica Dr	ClyC	2150	D6
Monica Wy	ClyC	2150	D7
Monitor Ct	DKbC	1979	A4
Monmouth Dr	DKbC	1819	D4
Monroe Cir NE	ATLN	1816	B7
Monroe Dr NE	ATLN	1816	B7
	ATLN	1891	B1
Monroe Pl NE	ATLN	1816	B3
Monroe St	CGPK	2061	D3
Montague Av SW	FulC	1973	A3
Montague Rd NE	CobC	1528	D7
Montana Rd NW	ATLN	1741	B5
Montana Wy NE	CobC	1526	E1
Montcalm Dr SW	FulC	1973	A3
Montclair Cir SE	SMYR	1739	A1
Montclair Ct	DKbC	1601	C4
Montclair Ct SE	SMYR	1667	A7
	SMYR	1739	B1
Montclair Dr	FTPK	2063	D7
Montclair Dr NE	ATLN	1815	D4
Montclair Pl	HryC	2065	E7
Montcliff Ct	DKbC	1744	A7
Monte Carlo Dr NW	ATLN	1740	E1
Monteel Dr NW	ATLN	1813	D5
Montego Bay Dr	FulC	2059	C6
Monterey Ct	MRRW	2149	E5
Monterey Dr	DKbC	1893	C5
	MRRW	2149	E5
Monterey Dr NE	CobC	1596	D3
Monterey Dr NW	ATLN	1815	B3
Monterey Pkwy	FulC	1599	A3
Montevallo Cir	DKbC	1818	A2
Montevallo Dr NE	FulC	1670	A6
Montevista St SW	ATLN	1889	C6
Montezuma Cir	DKbC	2065	A4
Montford Dr	CMBL	1671	D4
	DKbC	1671	D4
Montgomery Cir NW	CobC	1526	A4
Montgomery St	DCTR	1892	E1
Montgomery St NE	ATLN	1891	E4
	MRTA	1595	B3
Montgomery St SE	ATLN	1891	E4
Montgomery Ferry Dr NE	ATLN	1816	A5
Monticello Coms NW	GwnC	1602	C3
Monticello Ct	FulC	1600	D2
Monticello Dr	FulC	1600	D1
Monticello Pl	DKbC	1893	C3
Monticello Wy	CGPK	2060	E5
Monticello Wy SE	CobC	1597	A7
Montilly Cir	FulC	2147	A4
Montilly Pl	FulC	2147	A4
Montre Sq NW	ATLN	1814	D7
Montreal Cir	DKbC	1744	E7
	DKbC	1818	E1
Montreal Ct	DKbC	1745	A7
Montreal Rd	CLKN	1819	B3
	DKbC	1744	E6
	DKbC	1818	E1
	DKbC	1819	A2
Montreal Sta	DKbC	1744	E7
Montreal Wy	DKbC	1819	A2
Montreal Creek Cir	CLKN	1819	A2
Montreal Creek Ct	CLKN	1819	B3
Montreal Industrial Wy	DKbC	1744	E6
Montreat Av SW	ATLN	1889	D7
Montreat Pl SW	ATLN	1889	D7
Montrose Av SW	ATLN	1975	B2
Montrose Ct SE	CobC	1812	C6
Montrose Dr	EPNT	1975	B7
Montrose Ln NW	FulC	1669	D3
Montvallo Ter SE	ATLN	1978	B1
Montview Dr NW	ATLN	1815	C2
Montwicke Chase NW	FulC	1669	C7
Monument Av SE	ATLN	1891	E5
Moody Dr SW	ATLN	1976	D4
Moon St	DKbC	1745	C5
Moon St NW	MRTA	1595	A4
Moonlight Ct	DKbC	1980	A6
Moonlight Tr	DKbC	1980	A7
Moonlight Forest Ct	DKbC	1980	A6

Atlanta Street Index

Street	City	Map #	Grid
Moonshadow Ct	RSWL	1530	B1
Moonstone Ct	DKbC	1744	B7
Moor Ct	ClyC	2151	C1
Moore Av	FTPK	2149	B2
Moore Av NE	MRTA	1595	C5
Moore Dr	CMBL	1671	E7
Moore Ln NW	NRCS	1602	E5
Moore Rd	DKbC	2064	C2
Moore St NW	ATLN	1814	A3
Moore St SE	ATLN	1891	A4
Mooregate Ct NE	CobC	1528	C6
Mooregate Dr NE	CobC	1528	C6
Mooregate Sq NW	ATLN	1741	B6
Moores Club Pl NE	ATLN	1742	C2
Moores Mill Rd NW	ATLN	1740	D7
	ATLN	1741	B6
	ATLN	1814	C1
Moorestown Cir	DKbC	1817	E3
Moran St NW	ATLN	1890	A1
Moran Wy NW	GwnC	1601	E3
Moray St SW	ATLN	1975	C2
Morehouse Dr NW	ATLN	1889	B3
Moreland Av	ClyC	2064	A4
	ClyC	2150	D2
	ClyC	2151	A5
	DKbC	2063	E1
	FTPK	2064	C6
	FTPK	2150	D2
Moreland Av SR-42	ClyC	2064	A4
	ClyC	2150	D2
	ClyC	2151	A5
	DKbC	2063	E1
	FTPK	2064	C6
	FTPK	2150	D2
Moreland Av US-23	ClyC	2064	A4
	ClyC	2150	D2
	ClyC	2151	A5
	DKbC	2063	E1
	FTPK	2064	C6
	FTPK	2150	D2
Moreland Av NE	ATLN	1891	D4
Moreland Av NE SR-42	ATLN	1891	D4
Moreland Av NE US-23	ATLN	1891	D4
Moreland Av SE	ATLN	1891	D7
	ATLN	1977	D6
	DKbC	1977	D6
	DKbC	2063	E1
Moreland Av SE SR-42	ATLN	1891	D7
	ATLN	1977	D6
	DKbC	1977	D6
	DKbC	2063	E1
Moreland Av SE US-23	ATLN	1891	D7
	ATLN	1977	D6
	DKbC	1977	D6
	DKbC	2063	E1
Moreland Dr SE	ATLN	1977	C3
Moreland Pl SE	ATLN	1891	D6
Moreland Wy	HPVL	2062	C1
Moreland Industrial Dr SE	ATLN	1977	D3
	DKbC	1977	D3
Morgan Pl SE	ATLN	1893	A5
	DKbC	1893	A5
Morgan Rd	DKbC	1745	D4
Morgan Rd NE	CobC	1526	E2
Morgan Rd NW	GwnC	1673	B1
Morgan St NE	ATLN	1891	B2
Morgan Chase Dr NE	CobC	1526	E2
Morgan Chase Ter NE	CobC	1526	E2
Morgan Falls Pl NE	FulC	1599	B3
Morgan Falls Rd	FulC	1599	A2
Morgan Farm Ct NE	FulC	1670	C6
Morgan Farm Dr NE	FulC	1670	C6
Morgan Lake Dr NE	CobC	1526	E3
Morgan Oak Cir NE	FulC	1670	C5
Morgan Place Ct NE	DKbC	1816	E1
Morgans Trc	HryC	2065	D5
Morganshire Pl	FulC	1601	B4
Morgans Landing Dr	FulC	1599	C2
Moriah Ln	FTPK	2149	B3
Morley Av SE	ATLN	1977	B1
Morning Tr	FulC	2145	D1
Morning Bird Ct	RSWL	1532	B6
Morning Creek Cir	FulC	2145	E4
Morning Creek Ct	FulC	2145	D3
Morning Creek Dr	FulC	2145	E3
E Morningside Dr NE	ATLN	1816	C5
N Morningside Dr NE	ATLN	1816	D6
Morningside Dr NE	MRTA	1595	C3
Morningside Pl NE	ATLN	1816	D3
Morningside Trc NE	MRTA	1527	A6
Morningside Village Ln	DKbC	1673	C6
Mornington Dr NW	ATLN	1741	B7
Morosgo Ct NE	ATLN	1816	C1
Morosgo Dr NE	ATLN	1816	B1
Morosgo Pl NE	ATLN	1816	B1
Morosgo Wy NE	ATLN	1816	B2
Morris Av	DKbC	1745	D5
	EPNT	2061	C1
Morris Cir SE	SMYR	1667	A7
Morris Ct NW	GwnC	1602	B2
Morris Rd	FulC	2147	A7
Morris St	ClyC	2062	D4
Morris St NE	FulC	1670	A6
Morris St NW	ATLN	1813	E7
Morris St SE	CobC	1666	D4
Morris St SW	ATLN	1890	C6
Morris Brown Av NW	ATLN	1889	B3
Morris Brown Dr SW	ATLN	1890	A4
Morris Landers Dr NE	DKbC	1743	D6
Morrow Rd	ClyC	2148	E5
	FTPK	2149	C5
	MRRW	2149	C5
Morrow Cove	ClyC	2149	C6
Mortimer Pl SE	ATLN	1891	D4
Mortimer St SE	ATLN	1891	D4
Mosley Rd	DKbC	2066	A3
Moss Dr	ClyC	2149	A5
Moss Ln SE	CobC	1667	E2
Moss Trc	ClyC	2151	D1
Moss Creek Dr NE	CobC	1528	B1
Moss Oak Dr	DRVL	1672	E3
Mosswood Ct SE	SMYR	1738	A4
Mosswood Ln SE	SMYR	1738	A4
Mossy Creek Dr SE	CobC	1596	C5
Mossyvale Wy NW	FulC	1598	C7
Moton Av SW	ATLN	1976	D1
Motors Industrial Wy	DRVL	1672	B4
Mountain Cir SE	CobC	1812	B4
Mountain Ct SE	CobC	1812	C4
Mountain Dr	DKbC	1893	E1
Mountain Dr SR-10	DKbC	1893	E1
Mountain Dr NE	ATLN	1742	B2
Mountain Rd SE	CobC	1812	B4
Mountain St SE	CobC	1740	A2
Mountain Tr SE	CobC	1812	B4
Mountain Trc NE	CobC	1529	B2
Mountain Wy NE	ATLN	1742	B2
Mountain Brook Ln NW	FulC	1669	B1
Mountain Brook Wy NW	FulC	1669	B1
Mountain Creek Cir NE	CobC	1529	B2
Mountain Creek Ct NE	CobC	1529	B2
Mountain Creek Dr NE	CobC	1529	A1
Mountain Creek Ln NE	CobC	1529	A2
Mountain Creek Rd NE	FulC	1670	A3
Mountain Creek Tr NW	FulC	1669	A1
Mountain Creek Trc NW	FulC	1669	A1
Mountain Laurel St NE	CobC	1529	C1
Mountain Oak Cove	DKbC	1819	D2
Mountain Top Dr NE	CobC	1596	A1
Mountain View Ct SW	CobC	1666	A6
Mountain View Dr NE	MRTA	1595	E2
Mountainview St	DCTR	1893	B1
Mountain View Wy	DKbC	2063	D4
Mt Airy Dr SW	ATLN	1889	A7
Mt Berry Ln NW	GwnC	1602	C2
Mt Bethel Dr NE	CobC	1597	D1
Mt Brian Rd NE	DKbC	1743	C7
Mountbury Ct	CLKN	1819	B4
Mountcreek Ct NW	GwnC	1602	A3
Mountcreek Pl NW	GwnC	1602	B3
Mt Everest Wy	FulC	1532	E5
Mt Gerizm Rd SE	CobC	1812	C5
Mt Gilead Pl SW	ATLN	1974	B5
Mt Gilead Rd SW	ATLN	1974	B4
Mt Mariah Rd NE	DKbC	1817	B1
Mt Mitchell Wy	FulC	1532	E4
Mt Olive Dr	DKbC	1818	C3
Mt Olive Rd	EPNT	2060	E2
Mt Paran Pkwy NW	ATLN	1741	A1
	FulC	1741	A1
Mt Paran Rd NE	FulC	1669	E5
Mt Paran Rd NW	ATLN	1669	D6
	ATLN	1740	D2
	FulC	1669	D6
	FulC	1741	A2
Mt Ranier Wy	FulC	1532	E5
Mt Repose Ln NW	GwnC	1533	A7
Mt Royal Dr NE	DKbC	1743	C7
Mt Rushmore Dr	FulC	1532	D5
Mt Shasta Ln	FulC	1532	D5
Mt Sinai Ct	DKbC	1745	C7
Mt Vernon Blvd	FulC	1599	D7
Mt Vernon Cir	DKbC	1673	C6
Mt Vernon Dr	DCTR	1818	A7
	EPNT	2060	D3
Mt Vernon Hwy	DKbC	1599	E6
Mt Vernon Hwy NE	DKbC	1599	D7
	FulC	1669	E1
Mt Vernon Hwy NW	FulC	1669	D2
Mt Vernon Pkwy NW	FulC	1669	B4
Mt Vernon Pl	DKbC	1600	D4
Mt Vernon Rd	DKbC	1599	E6
	DKbC	1600	A6
	FulC	1601	A3
Mt Vernon Wy	CGPK	2060	E5
	DKbC	1600	B5
Mt Vernon Forest Ct	DKbC	1600	B6
Mt Victoria Pl	FulC	1532	E4
Mt Washington Ln	FulC	1532	E4
Mt Whitney Pl	FulC	1532	E4
Mt Wilkinson Pkwy SE	CobC	1739	E1
	CobC	1740	A2
Mt Zion Blvd	ClyC	2150	E7
Mt Zion Rd SE	ATLN	2062	E1
Mt Zion Rd SW	ATLN	2062	C1
	HPVL	2062	C1
Moury Av SE	ATLN	1976	E3
Moury Av SW	ATLN	1976	D2
Mozart Ct	FulC	2147	A6
Mozart Dr	FulC	2147	B6
Mozelle Dr NE	CobC	1527	B4
Mozley Dr SE	CobC	1666	C4
Mozley Pl SW	ATLN	1889	D4
N Mt Dr	FulC	1532	E5
S Mt Dr	FulC	1532	E5
Muirfield Ct NE	CobC	1597	E2
Muirfield Dr NE	CobC	1597	E2
Muirfield Ln NE	CobC	1597	D2
Muirfield Rdg NE	CobC	1597	E2
Muirfield Tr NE	CobC	1597	E2
Muirfield Trc NE	CobC	1597	E2
Mulberry Ct	EPNT	1975	B5
	HryC	2152	D1
Mulberry Ct NE	CobC	1528	D7
	CobC	1598	A5
Mulberry Dr NE	CobC	1598	B4
Mulberry St	EPNT	1975	B5
Mulberry St NE	CobC	1526	C1
Mulberry Tr NE	CobC	1598	C4
Mulberry Creek Ct NE	CobC	1526	C2
Mulberry Creek Ln NE	CobC	1526	A2
Muncy Ct SE	SMYR	1667	B5
Mundy Dr	CMBL	1671	E6
Mural Cir	MRRW	2150	B6
Mural Dr	DKbC	1672	B7
	DKbC	1744	B1
	MRRW	2150	A6
Murdock Rd NE	CobC	1528	B7
Muriel Av NE	ATLN	1892	A2
Murphey St	DKbC	1818	D4
Murphy Av SW	ATLN	1890	B6
	ATLN	1975	E3
Murphy Cir SW	ATLN	1975	D3
Murphy Dr	MRRW	2150	A7
Murphy Candler Ct NE	DKbC	1671	B3
Murphy Mill Ct NE	CobC	1529	B5
Murray Dr	FTPK	2064	C7
Murray St SE	ATLN	1976	E3
Murray Hill Av NE	ATLN	1892	C3
Murray Lake Cir	ClyC	2063	D5
Murray Lake Ct	ClyC	2063	E6
Murren Dr SE	CobC	1739	C4
N Muscogee Av NW	ATLN	1815	D1
W Muscogee Av NW	ATLN	1815	D1
Muscogee Av NW	ATLN	1815	D1
Muscogee Wy NW	ATLN	1815	E1
Muse St SE	ATLN	1891	C6
Muse St SW	ATLN	1889	E6
Musket Entry	RSWL	1532	A4
Musket Ridge Rd NW	ATLN	1740	D2
Myers Av SE	CobC	1595	B7
	CobC	1666	B1
Myrtle Dr NE	MRTA	1526	C6
Myrtle Dr SW	ATLN	1975	B4
Myrtle Ln	CGPK	2061	D2
	DKbC	1817	E6
Myrtle St	CGPK	2061	D2
	HPVL	2062	B2
	RSWL	1530	D2
Myrtle St NE	ATLN	1816	A7
	ATLN	1891	A1
Myrtle Lee Ct	RVDL	2147	E7
Mystic Dr NE	ATLN	1741	E1
	FulC	1669	E7
	FulC	1741	E1
Mystic Pl NE	FulC	1669	E7
Calle Madrid	MRTA	1596	B7
N			
N N Av	FTPK	2149	E2
Nabell Av	EPNT	1975	D6
Nacoochee Dr NW	ATLN	1815	D2
Nacoochee Pl NW	ATLN	1815	D2
Nahunta Ct NW	GwnC	1602	B1
Nalley Cir	DKbC	1817	E1
Nalley Ct NE	CobC	1528	B4
Nancy Cir SE	SMYR	1739	C1
Nancy Dr SE	MRTA	1596	B5
Nancy Ln NE	DKbC	1744	A4
Nancy St NW	MRTA	1595	A3
Nancy Tr	RSWL	1530	B1
Nancy Creek Blf NW	ATLN	1740	C7
W Nancy Creek Ct NE	DKbC	1670	E4
E Nancy Creek Dr	DKbC	1671	C2
E Nancy Creek Dr NE	DKbC	1671	B3
W Nancy Creek Dr NE	DKbC	1670	E5
W Nancy Creek Pl NE	DKbC	1671	A4
Nancy Creek Rd NW	ATLN	1740	B6
Nancy Creek Rdg NW	ATLN	1740	D5
Nancy Creek Wy NE	DKbC	1671	C3
Nancy Hanks Dr NW	GwnC	1673	D2
Nancy Lee Wy	DKbC	1894	C3
Nandina Ln	DKbC	1600	A5
Nantahala Tr NE	CobC	1528	D7
Nantahalla Ct NE	DKbC	1817	B2
Nantucket Ct NE	CobC	1597	C1
Nantucket Dr NE	CobC	1597	C2
	DKbC	1744	A3
Nantucket Cove	DKbC	1894	E1
Napier Rd SE	CobC	1812	D2
Napier St SE	ATLN	1977	D2
Napoleon Dr SW	ATLN	1889	E5
Napoleon St	CGPK	2061	B2
Napoleon Stokes Cir	DKbC	1744	E7
Nappa Valley Ct SE	SMYR	1667	B7
Narmore Dr NE	ATLN	1742	D4
Narron Ct SW	ATLN	1974	A7
Narron Dr SW	ATLN	1974	A7
	ATLN	2060	A1
Narrow Av SE	ATLN	1891	B5
Nash Av SE	DKbC	1892	B7
Nash Dr SE	CobC	1812	A5
Nash Rd NW	ATLN	1813	C6
Nashua Ct NE	CobC	1528	B7
Nassau Ct NE	CobC	1598	A1
Nassau St	ClyC	2149	B6
Nassau St NW	ATLN	1890	D3
Nassau Wy NE	CobC	1597	E1
Natalie Ct	DKbC	2066	B3
Natalie Ln SE	SMYR	1666	B7
Natalie Tr	DKbC	2066	C2
Natalie Wy	DKbC	2066	B3
Natchez Tr	DKbC	2064	C3
Natchez Trc	FulC	1531	A6
Natham Dr SE	ATLN	1977	C6
Nathan Rd SW	ATLN	1888	B3
E National Cir NW	GwnC	1673	E5
S National Cir NW	GwnC	1673	E6
W National Cir NW	GwnC	1673	E5
National Dr	FulC	1887	D1
National Dr SW	FulC	1887	D1
National Data Plz NE	DKbC	1743	A6
Natoma Ct	FulC	1533	E4
Natoma Terr	FulC	1533	E3
Naturally Fresh Blvd	FulC	2145	E2
Nature Mill Ct	FulC	1533	B2
Nature Mill Rd	FulC	1533	C2
Nature Mill Wy	FulC	1533	C2
Nautica Wy	RSWL	1531	D5
Navaho Cir	FulC	2060	A7
Navaho Tr	MRRW	2149	D6
Navaho Tr SE	SMYR	1739	B2
Navajo Dr	MRRW	2149	D5
Navajo Pl NE	DKbC	1671	A3
Navajo Tr NE	DKbC	1671	A3
Navajo Tr SW	ATLN	1973	B6
Naval Forces Ct SE	CobC	1666	E1
Nawench Dr NW	ATLN	1741	A7
Naylor Ct NW	GwnC	1602	C1
Naylor Hall NE	CobC	1526	D2
Neal Av	ClyC	2150	C3
Neal Pl NW	ATLN	1890	A2
Neal St NW	ATLN	1890	A2
Nectarine Cir	DKbC	1979	E5
Needham Dr	DKbC	1818	E5
Needhams Ct	ClyC	2151	A3
Needle Dr	FTPK	2149	C5
Needle Rock Rdg NE	CobC	1596	B2
Neel Reid Dr	RSWL	1530	C3
Neely Av	EPNT	1975	B7
Neely Ct NW	GwnC	1602	A1
Neely Farm Dr NW	GwnC	1532	E7

INDEX 42

Neely Farm Dr NW — Atlanta Street Index — Norwich Ln

STREET	City	Map #	Grid
Neely Farm Dr NW	GwnC	1601	E1
Neely Meadows Ct NW	GwnC	1601	E1
Neely Meadows Dr NW	GwnC	1601	E2
Nekoma St NE	MRTA	1596	B4
Nekoma St NW	ATLN	1889	D2
Nelby Ct	DKbC	1894	E1
Nelby Dr	DKbC	1894	E1
Nell Ct NE	FulC	1670	B5
Nell Ln	ClyC	2150	D5
Nellie Brch SE	CobC	1812	A5
Nellie Ct SE	CobC	1812	A4
Nellie Trc SE	CobC	1812	A4
Nellie Brook Dr SE	CobC	1812	A5
Nellie Brook Dr SW	CobC	1812	A5
Nellwood Cir	EPNT	2060	E1
Nelms Av NE	ATLN	1892	A2
Nelms Ct	DKbC	1818	B2
Nelms Dr	DKbC	1818	B1
Nelms Dr SW	ATLN	1976	C5
Nelson Ln SE	SMYR	1666	E7
Nelson St SW	ATLN	1890	D4
Nelson Ferry Rd	DCTR	1892	D1
Neptune Pl	DKbC	1980	A3
Neptune Pl NW	ATLN	1813	A7
Nerine Cir	DKbC	1600	A6
Nesbit Al	NRCS	1602	D6
Nesbit Pl	FulC	1532	C5
	RSWL	1532	C5
Nesbit St NW	NRCS	1602	D6
Nesbit Tr	FulC	1532	B4
	RSWL	1532	B4
Nesbit Downs Ct	FulC	1601	C2
Nesbit Downs Dr	FulC	1601	C3
Nesbit Entry Dr	RSWL	1532	A4
Nesbit Ferry Ln	FulC	1601	C3
Nesbit Ferry Pl	FulC	1601	C3
Nesbit Ferry Rd	FulC	1532	C5
	FulC	1601	C2
	RSWL	1532	C5
Nesbit Lake Ct	FulC	1601	C3
Nesbit Lakes Dr	RSWL	1532	A3
Nesbit Ridge Ct	RSWL	1532	A4
Nesbit Ridge Dr	RSWL	1532	A4
Nesbitt Dr NE	DKbC	1743	B4
Nessa Ct SW	CobC	1738	A2
Nestle Creek Ct NE	CobC	1528	A6
Nestle Creek Dr NE	CobC	1528	A6
Nestor Ct	RSWL	1532	B7
Nettie Ct	DKbC	1893	C7
Nevels Rd	FulC	2146	E7
New St	DCTR	1893	B1
New St NE	ATLN	1892	A3
New St SE	CobC	1666	B2
New Bedford Ct NE	CobC	1598	D2
New Bedford Dr NE	CobC	1598	D2
New Bedford Ln NE	DKbC	1744	A2
New Bedford Pl NE	CobC	1598	D2
New Bedford Wy NE	DKbC	1744	A3
Newberry Ct	ClyC	2147	C6
Newberry Ct NE	CobC	1527	B6
Newberry Ln	ClyC	2147	C6
Newberry Tr	DKbC	1980	A4
Newberry Downs Ln	DKbC	1980	A4
Newbridge Trc NE	DKbC	1742	E1
New Britain Dr SW	FulC	1887	B7
	FulC	1973	A1
New Burks Rd	FTPK	2149	A1
Newcastle St SW	ATLN	1890	A4
New Cherry Ln	RSWL	1532	A2
Newcomb Rd	DKbC	2066	D2
Newell Dr NE	CobC	1529	B5
Newfield Wy	DKbC	1818	D6
Newgate Ct	FulC	1533	A4
Newgate Dr	DKbC	1894	C7
	DKbC	1980	D1
New Haven Cir NE	DKbC	1671	B4
New Haven Ct SE	SMYR	1739	B2
New Haven Dr NE	DKbC	1743	E3
New Heritage Dr	FulC	1532	E1
New Hope Rd SE	MRTA	1596	A7
New Hope Rd SW	FulC	1887	B7
	FulC	1973	B2
New Jersey Av NW	ATLN	1889	B2
New Kemp Rd NE	CobC	1526	E6
New London Trc NW	FulC	1669	C5
New Magnolia Ct	FulC	2146	B5
New Magnolia Pl	FulC	2146	B5
Newman Pl NW	ATLN	1814	C7
New Market Pkwy SE	MRTA	1667	B2
Newnan Av	EPNT	1975	D5
New Northside Dr NW	FulC	1668	E4
New Paces Ferry Rd SE	CobC	1740	A2
New Peachtree Rd	CMBL	1671	E6
	DKbC	1671	E6
	DKbC	1743	C1
	DRVL	1672	C4
Newport Pl NW	ATLN	1814	A1
Newport St	UNCT	2145	C6
Newport St NW	ATLN	1890	B3
New Snapfinger Woods Dr	DKbC	1980	E2
New South Dr NE	CobC	1526	D2
Newstead Trc NE	CobC	1528	C6
Newton Av SE	ATLN	1891	E6
Newton Dr NW	GwnC	1601	C4
Newton Dr SW	FulC	2059	A1
Newton Rd NE	CobC	1527	B4
New Town Cir SE	ATLN	1977	C3
New Trade Center Dr	ClyC	2062	B7
New Wellington Close NW	FulC	1669	C4
New York Av NE	ATLN	1892	B3
Neybrook Dr	MRTA	1596	A5
Nezhat Pl	FulC	1599	B1
Niagara Cir	FulC	1532	D6
Niblic Ct	FulC	1532	D6
Niblick Dr	FulC	1532	D6
Nicholas Ct NE	CobC	1527	D3
Nichols Dr	UNCT	2145	B5
Nichols Dr SE	CobC	1813	A4
Nichols Ln	DKbC	1893	C7
Nichols St SE	SMYR	1738	E1
Nicholson St	ATLN	1892	A7
Nickajack Rd SE	CobC	1738	B6
	SMYR	1738	B6
Nickajack Rd SW	CobC	1738	A6
Nickajack Park Rd SE	CobC	1813	A2
	SMYR	1813	A2
Nicolet Ct NE	CobC	1529	C3
Nielsen Ct	CLKN	1819	C3
	DKbC	1819	C3
Nielsen Dr	CLKN	1819	C3
	DKbC	1819	C3
Nifda Blvd SE	CobC	1740	A7
Nifda Dr SE	CobC	1740	A7
	CobC	1814	A1
Nile Dr	FulC	1532	C5
Niles Av NW	ATLN	1814	E7
Nimitz Dr SE	CobC	1666	C3
Ninas Trc SW	FulC	1973	C1
Nininger Wy SW	ATLN	1975	D3
Ninth Green Dr	RSWL	1532	A7
Niskey Dr SW	ATLN	1973	D3
Niskey Ovlk SW	ATLN	1973	C3
Niskey Cove Rd SW	ATLN	1973	D3
Niskey Lake Cir SW	FulC	1887	C7
	FulC	1973	C1
Niskey Lake Rd SW	ATLN	1973	C2
	FulC	1973	C1
Niskey Lake Tr SW	ATLN	1973	C2
Nivelle Dr	DKbC	1978	C1
NLVR SE	CGPK	2061	C6
	ClyC	2061	D7
	HPVL	2062	B4
Noahs Ln	ClyC	2065	A5
Noble Dr NE	ATLN	1816	E4
Noble Creek Dr NW	ATLN	1814	E2
	ATLN	1815	A2
Noble Forest Dr NW	GwnC	1602	A3
Nobleman Pt NW	GwnC	1533	E6
Noble Oak Dr NE	CobC	1598	C2
Noble Vines Dr	CLKN	1819	A3
Noel Dr NE	DKbC	1743	A4
Nogales Pl	ClyC	2151	B6
Nolan St SE	ATLN	1977	A2
Nonie Wy NE	CobC	1527	E7
Norbury Ct	CobC	1739	C4
Norbury Dr	CobC	1739	C4
Norbury Cove	CobC	1739	C5
Norcross St	RSWL	1530	D1
Norcross St SW	ATLN	1890	B5
N Norcross Tucker Rd NW	GwnC	1673	E2
	NRCS	1602	E7
S Norcross Tucker Rd NW	GwnC	1673	E6
Nordic Pl	ClyC	2150	C7
Nordic Trc NE	CobC	1529	C6
Norfleet Rd NW	ATLN	1815	B3
Norfolk St NW	ATLN	1890	A1
Norgate Ct	DKbC	1979	B4
Norgate Ln	DKbC	1979	B4
Norland Cir Ct	FulC	1533	B3
Norma Cir	DKbC	1979	A3
Normal St	DKbC	1893	A7
Norman Blvd	ClyC	2147	B2
Norman Cross	ClyC	2147	D4
Norman Ct	ClyC	2147	D4
Norman Dr	ClyC	2147	D3
Norman Rd	CLKN	1819	C3
	DKbC	1819	C3
Norman Berry Dr	EPNT	1975	D7
	EPNT	2061	E3
	HPVL	2061	E3
Normandy Cir NE	CobC	1528	B4
Normandy Ct NE	ATLN	1742	D7
	CobC	1528	B4
Normandy Dr NE	DKbC	1816	E6
Normandy Dr NW	ATLN	1741	C7
Norris Pl NW	ATLN	1889	D3
Norris St	DCTR	1818	A7
Norse Ct	DKbC	1819	D4
Norseman Cir NE	CobC	1529	C6
Norseman Dr SE	SMYR	1667	E6
North Av	DKbC	1818	D4
	FTPK	2149	B1
	HPVL	2062	C2
W North Av NW	ATLN	1889	E2
North Av NE	ATLN	1890	E1
	ATLN	1891	B2
North Av NE SR-8	ATLN	1890	E1
North Av NE US-29	ATLN	1890	E1
North Av NE US-78	ATLN	1890	E1
North Av NE US-278	ATLN	1890	E1
North Av NW	ATLN	1889	C2
	CobC	1595	A2
	MRTA	1595	A2
North Av NW SR-8	ATLN	1890	E1
North Av NW US-29	ATLN	1890	E1
North Av NW US-78	ATLN	1890	E1
North Av NW US-278	ATLN	1890	E1
North Av SE	CobC	1595	A7
	SMYR	1667	A7
North Ct	ClyC	2065	B6
North Dr	FulC	1530	E6
North Dr SW	FulC	1973	A4
North Pkwy	LKCY	2150	A4
North St	EPNT	2061	E1
North St NW	ATLN	1814	B6
Northaven Ln	DKbC	1673	A6
Northbelt Dr NW	NRCS	1673	D1
Northbelt Pkwy NW	NRCS	1673	D1
Northbrook Ct	DKbC	1673	B6
Northbrook Dr	DKbC	1673	B7
	DKbC	1745	B2
Northbrook Ln	DKbC	1600	D6
Northbrooke Cir	DKbC	1600	D7
Northchase Pkwy SE	MRTA	1667	D1
Northchester Ct	DKbC	1600	D4
Northcliff Trc	RSWL	1531	C6
Northcliffe Dr NW	ATLN	1815	A2
North Close SW	FulC	2059	B4
Northcrest Rd	DKbC	1673	A6
Northcrest Wy	DKbC	1672	E6
Northcut Ct	ClyC	2147	D3
Northcut Dr	ClyC	2147	D3
Northeast Expwy	ATLN	1815	E4
	DKbC	1672	C7
	DKbC	1673	A5
	DKbC	1742	E7
	FulC	1816	D1
Northeast Expwy I-85	ATLN	1815	E4
	DKbC	1672	C7
	DKbC	1742	E7
	DKbC	1816	D1
Northeast Expwy SR-403	ATLN	1815	E4
	DKbC	1672	C7
	DKbC	1742	E7
	DKbC	1816	D1
Northeast Expwy NE	ATLN	1816	C1
	DKbC	1743	D6
Northeast Expwy NE I-85	ATLN	1816	C1
Northeast Expwy NE SR-403	ATLN	1816	C1
Northeast Pkwy NW	GwnC	1672	D1
Northern Av	DCTR	1817	E7
	DKbC	1819	A7
	DKbC	1894	A1
Northern Av SE	ATLN	1891	C5
Northern Pl NW	GwnC	1601	D6
Northern St	ATLN	1892	D4
	DCTR	1892	D4
Northfield Blvd	FulC	2146	E2
Northfield Ct	ClyC	2150	D4
	FulC	2146	E2
Northfield Ct NE	CobC	1527	A5
Northfield Dr	ClyC	2150	D5
Northgate Dr NW	ATLN	1740	B3
Northgate Cove	ClyC	2065	C6
Northglenn Ct NE	FulC	1670	B4
Northgreen Dr NE	FulC	1599	C5
Northlake Ct NE	DKbC	1744	E4
Northlake Dr	DKbC	1673	B6
Northlake Pkwy	DKbC	1745	A5
Northlake Pkwy NE	DKbC	1744	E4
Northlake Tr	DKbC	1673	B6
Northlake Wy	DKbC	1673	B6
Northlake Center Dr	DKbC	1745	A5
Northlake Creek Ct	DKbC	1745	C3
Northlake Creek Dr	DKbC	1745	D3
Northlake Creek Cove	DKbC	1745	D3
Northlake Springs Ct	DKbC	1744	D7
Northland Ct NE	FulC	1670	C6
Northland Dr NE	FulC	1670	B5
Northland Ridge Ct NE	FulC	1670	C6
Northland Ridge Tr NE	FulC	1670	C6
Northmoor Ct NW	ATLN	1741	A7
Northpark Pl	FulC	1599	D7
Northplace Wy SE	CobC	1739	C2
Northridge Ct	ClyC	2065	B6
Northridge Dr	MRRW	2149	E6
	MRRW	2150	A7
Northridge Pkwy	FulC	1530	D7
Northridge Rd	FulC	1530	E7
Northridge Tr	ClyC	2065	B6
Northridge Wy	MRRW	2150	A7
Northridge Crossing Dr	FulC	1599	D1
Northrope Dr NE	ATLN	1816	C2
Northrup Dr	DKbC	1745	D3
Northside Cir NW	ATLN	1815	C5
Northside Dr	HPVL	2062	C2
Northside Dr NW	ATLN	1741	C7
	ATLN	1815	C1
	ATLN	1890	C2
	FulC	1668	E4
	FulC	1741	B1
Northside Dr NW SR-3	ATLN	1741	C7
	ATLN	1815	C1
	ATLN	1890	C2
Northside Dr NW SR-8	ATLN	1890	C1
Northside Dr NW SR-9	ATLN	1815	C7
	ATLN	1890	C2
Northside Dr NW US-19	ATLN	1815	C7
	ATLN	1890	C2
Northside Dr NW US-29	ATLN	1890	C4
Northside Dr NW US-41	ATLN	1741	C7
	ATLN	1815	C1
	ATLN	1890	C2
Northside Dr NW US-78	ATLN	1890	C1
Northside Dr NW US-278	ATLN	1890	C1
Northside Dr SW	ATLN	1890	C5
Northside Dr SW SR-3	ATLN	1890	C5
Northside Dr SW US-19	ATLN	1890	C5
Northside Dr SW US-29	ATLN	1890	C5
Northside Dr SW US-41	ATLN	1890	C5
Northside Pkwy NW	ATLN	1740	D3
	ATLN	1741	A6
	CobC	1740	B2
Northside Pkwy NW SR-3	ATLN	1740	D3
	ATLN	1741	A6
	CobC	1740	B2
Northside Pkwy NW US-41	ATLN	1740	D3
	ATLN	1741	A6
	CobC	1740	B2
Northside 75 NW	ATLN	1815	C4
Northside Chase NW	ATLN	1741	C1
Northspring Dr	ClyC	2150	E4
Northstrand Ct	DKbC	1980	D1
Northstrand Dr	DKbC	1980	C1
Northtowne Cove	HryC	2152	B2
Northview Av	DKbC	1893	B6
Northview Av NE	ATLN	1816	C5
Northview Dr	FTPK	2063	C7
Northview Pl SE	CobC	1739	A1
	SMYR	1739	A1
Northway Dr NE	FulC	1670	C6
E Northway Ln NE	FulC	1670	C6
W Northway Ln NE	FulC	1670	B6
Northwest Dr	CGPK	2061	A4
	MRTA	1667	B4
Northwest Dr NW	ATLN	1813	E6
Northwest Pkwy SE	CobC	1667	C2
	MRTA	1667	C2
Northwick Pass Wy	FulC	1533	A4
Northwind Dr	ClyC	2065	C6
Northwold Dr	FulC	1599	E1
	FulC	1600	A1
Northwood Av NE	ATLN	1815	E4
Northwood Dr NE	FulC	1669	E3
Northwoods Dr NE	CobC	1527	B2
Northwoods Pl	HPVL	2062	D3
Northyards Blvd NW	ATLN	1890	C2
Norton Cir SE	CobC	1666	A7
	CobC	1738	A1
Norton Ct SE	CobC	1738	A1
Norton Pl SE	CobC	1738	A4
Norwalk Rd	DKbC	1601	A7
Norway Ln	DKbC	1819	D3
Norwich Cir NE	ATLN	1742	D7
Norwich Ct	DKbC	1745	B4
Norwich Dr	DKbC	1745	B4
Norwich Ln	DKbC	1745	B4

INDEX 43

Norwich Wy

Olde DeKalb Wy

Atlanta Street Index

STREET	City	Map #	Grid
Norwich Wy	DKbC	1745	B4
Norwick Wy	FulC	1532	C4
Norwood Av NE	ATLN	1892	C4
Norwood Rd SE	ATLN	1977	C5
Nottaway Ct	DKbC	1673	B7
	DKbC	1745	B1
Nottingham Dr	AVES	1893	E2
	DKbC	1893	E2
Nottingham Ln NE	DKbC	1742	D5
Nottingham Wy NE	ATLN	1815	E4
Nottoway Tr NE	CobC	1527	A5
	MRTA	1526	E5
Notty Pine Tr NE	CobC	1528	A1
Nova N	DKbC	1980	D3
Nova S	DKbC	1980	D3
Nowlin Dr SE	CobC	1738	C4
	SMYR	1738	C4
Nunnally Pl	FulC	1531	B7
Nursery Rd SE	CobC	1666	B7
	CobC	1738	B1
	SMYR	1666	B7
	SMYR	1738	B1
Nuthatch Ct NE	CobC	1527	D6
Nutmeg Ct SE	CobC	1812	A4
O			
Oak Av	ClyC	2150	C4
	DKbC	1745	E3
Oak Cir	ClyC	2063	E6
	ClyC	2150	D1
	FTPK	2150	D1
W Oak Cir NE	MRTA	1526	E6
Oak Ct	ClyC	2150	D1
N Oak Ct	DKbC	1979	D7
Oak Dr	ClyC	2150	D1
	HPVL	2062	C2
W Oak Dr NE	MRTA	1526	D6
Oak Dr NE	CobC	1527	B1
Oak Dr SE	ATLN	2062	E2
	SMYR	1813	C1
Oak Dr SW	ATLN	2062	D2
Oak Gln NE	CobC	1598	C4
Oak Ln	ClyC	2063	E6
	DCTR	1893	B1
Oak Ln NE	CobC	1528	D4
	DKbC	1743	C7
Oak Lndg NW	FulC	1669	A4
W Oak Pkwy NE	CobC	1526	D6
	MRTA	1526	D6
Oak Pl	ClyC	2148	C2
Oak Rd NW	GwnC	1673	B1
Oak St	AVES	1893	C1
	ClyC	2150	A3
	EPNT	1975	C7
	FTPK	2149	B1
	HPVL	2062	B3
	LKCY	2150	A3
	RSWL	1530	C2
N Oak St	FTPK	2149	B1
Oak St NW	ATLN	1814	D5
Oak St SE	CobC	1666	B3
Oak St SW	ATLN	1889	E6
Oak Alley Ct	FulC	1532	E2
Oak Alley Wy	FulC	1532	E2
Oakawana Dr NE	DKbC	1743	E4
Oak Bluff Ct	FulC	1601	C2
Oak Bridge Tr	FulC	1532	E3
Oakbrook Ln	DKbC	1818	E3
Oakbrook Wy NE	DKbC	1742	E2
Oak Chase Ct NE	CobC	1527	A3
Oak Chase Dr NE	CobC	1529	C2
Oak Chase Dr NW	GwnC	1673	E6
Oak Chase Ln	RVDL	2148	A7
Oak Chase Pt NE	CobC	1529	D2
Oakcliff Ct NW	ATLN	1888	B3
Oakcliff Rd	DKbC	1672	D2
	DKbC	1673	A4
	DRVL	1672	E3
Oakcliff Rd NW	ATLN	1888	B3
Oakcliff Industrial Ct	DKbC	1673	A4
Oakcliff Industrial St	DKbC	1672	E5
W Oak Commons Ct NE	MRTA	1526	D7
W Oak Commons Ln NE	MRTA	1526	D7
Oak Creek Dr NE	CobC	1527	A1
Oak Creek Wy	HryC	2065	D5
Oakcrest Ct	DKbC	1745	D7
Oak Crest Ct NE	CobC	1527	B1
Oakcrest Dr	DKbC	1745	D7
Oakcrest Dr SW	ATLN	1974	B1
Oak Crest Tr NE	CobC	1527	B1
Oak Crossing Dr	DKbC	1818	B1
Oakdale Ct SE	SMYR	1813	B1
Oakdale Dr	FTPK	2149	B5
Oakdale Dr SE	SMYR	1738	D2
Oakdale Rd	HPVL	2062	B2
Oakdale Rd NE	ATLN	1817	A7
	ATLN	1891	E3
	ATLN	1892	A1
	DKbC	1817	A7
Oakdale Rd SE	CobC	1739	C6
	CobC	1812	E4
	CobC	1813	B2
	SMYR	1739	C7
	SMYR	1813	B2
Oakdale St NW	ATLN	1813	E3
Oakdale Vinings Cir SE	CobC	1739	B5
Oakdale Vinings Lndg SE	CobC	1739	B5
Oakengate Dr	DKbC	1819	D2
Oakfield Dr SE	DKbC	1891	E7
Oak Forest Cir NE	CobC	1528	E5
Oak Forest Ct NE	DKbC	1671	A2
Oak Forest Dr NE	CobC	1528	E6
	DKbC	1671	A3
Oak Forest Dr SE	CobC	1738	A2
	SMYR	1738	A2
Oak Forest Wy NE	DKbC	1671	A2
Oak Grove Av SE	ATLN	1891	E5
Oak Grove Dr	DKbC	1818	A2
Oak Grove Mdw	DKbC	1818	A1
Oak Grove Mnr NE	MRTA	1595	B3
Oak Grove Rd	DKbC	1744	A7
	DKbC	1818	A1
Oak Grove Rd NE	DKbC	1744	A6
Oak Grove Valley Rd NE	DKbC	1744	A6
Oakham Pl	AVES	1893	D1
Oak Harbor Ct NE	MRTA	1526	B6
Oak Harbor Tr NE	MRTA	1526	B5
Oakhill Av SW	ATLN	1890	B7
Oak Hill Cir	DKbC	1819	E6
Oak Hill Cir SE	CobC	1597	E6
Oak Hill Dr NE	CobC	1527	E2
Oakhill Pl	DKbC	1818	E2
Oakhurst Ct	ClyC	2150	C7
Oakhurst Dr	ClyC	2150	C7
	MRTA	1526	C6
Oakhurst Dr NE	MRTA	1526	C6
Oak Knoll Cir SE	ATLN	1977	A3
Oak Knoll Ct SE	SMYR	1738	A2
Oak Knoll Dr NE	CobC	1597	C4
Oak Knoll Ter SE	ATLN	1977	A3
Oakland Av SE	ATLN	1891	A5
Oakland Dr SE	CobC	1596	C7
Oakland Dr SW	ATLN	1889	E7
	ATLN	1975	E1
Oakland Ln SW	ATLN	1975	E2
Oakland St	DCTR	1817	D7
Oakland Ter	DKbC	1893	C7
Oakland Ter SW	ATLN	1975	E1
Oakland Trc NE	DKbC	1742	E1
Oakland Park Av SE	ATLN	1891	A5
Oak Laurel Ct	FulC	1533	D2
Oaklawn Av NE	DKbC	1743	A3
Oak Lea Ct NE	CobC	1529	A1
Oakleaf Ln	MRRW	2150	A7
Oakleaf Wy	MRRW	2150	A7
Oakleaf Cove	DKbC	1980	E7
Oakleigh Ct NE	DKbC	1744	A7
Oakleigh Dr	EPNT	1975	E6
Oakley Cir	UNCT	2145	C6
Oakley Ct	UNCT	2145	C6
Oakley Pl	UNCT	2145	C6
Oakley Rd	FulC	2145	C7
	UNCT	2145	C7
Oakley Trc SE	SMYR	1667	D6
Oakley Commons Blvd	UNCT	2145	C6
Oaklhill Dr	CGPK	2061	A5
Oak Mill Ct	ClyC	2150	E7
Oakmont Av	DRVL	1672	B5
Oakmont Cir SE	CobC	1597	E6
Oakmont Ct	DKbC	1819	D2
Oakmont Dr NW	ATLN	1889	C3
Oakmont Ln NW	GwnC	1673	D4
Oakmoor Pl NE	CobC	1527	B6
Oak Park Cir NE	DKbC	1817	A1
Oak Park Dr	ClyC	2148	B3
Oak Park Dr NE	DKbC	1816	E6
Oak Park Ln	DKbC	1893	E7
Oak Park Sq	FulC	2147	A4
Oak Park Ter	FulC	2147	A4
Oak Park Tr	DKbC	1818	B1
Oak Park Cove	DKbC	1818	C1
Oakpointe Pl	DKbC	1599	E3
Oak Quarters SE	SMYR	1739	C1
Oak Ridge Av	HPVL	2062	A4
Oakridge Av NE	ATLN	1893	A4
	DCTR	1893	A4
Oakridge Av SE	ATLN	1893	A4
Oakridge Cir	DKbC	1818	B1
Oakridge Ct	DKbC	1818	B1
	DKbC	1978	E2
Oak Ridge Ct NE	CobC	1596	B1
Oakridge Dr	HryC	2065	E7
	MRRW	2149	D6
Oak Ridge Dr SE	CobC	1666	B1
Oakridge Ln	EPNT	1974	D7
Oakridge Pl	DKbC	1818	B1
Oakrill Ct NE	CobC	1527	E4
Oakrill Pt NE	CobC	1527	D4
Oakrill Rd NE	CobC	1527	D4
Oakrill Wy NE	CobC	1527	D4
Oak Run St	EPNT	2060	B6
	FulC	2060	B6
Oaks Pkwy SE	CobC	1666	B7
	SMYR	1666	B7
Oak Shadow Ct NE	DKbC	1743	D3
Oak Shadow Dr NE	DKbC	1743	D3
Oak Shadow Ln NE	DKbC	1743	D3
Oakshire Ct	DKbC	1818	A1
Oakside Dr SW	ATLN	1888	A3
Oak Springs Ct NE	CobC	1527	A1
Oak Springs Dr NE	CobC	1526	E1
Oak Springs Trc NE	CobC	1526	E1
Oak Springs Wy NE	CobC	1526	E1
Oak Terrace Dr SE	DKbC	1978	D6
Oak Trail Ct	DKbC	1599	E6
	DKbC	1600	A6
Oak Trail Dr	DKbC	1599	E5
	DKbC	1600	A6
Oak Trail Dr NE	CobC	1596	B2
Oak Tree Ct	EPNT	2060	C5
Oak Tree Rd	DKbC	1818	C3
Oakvale Av	DKbC	1979	C7
Oakvale Hts	DKbC	1979	D7
Oakvale Pl	DKbC	1745	B3
Oakvale Rd	DKbC	1979	C7
	DKbC	2065	D1
Oakvale Cove	DKbC	1979	C7
Oakvale Falls Ct	DKbC	1979	C7
Oakvale Falls Dr	DKbC	1979	C7
Oak Valley Dr	RVDL	2148	C6
Oak Valley Rd	DKbC	1894	D7
Oak Valley Rd NE	ATLN	1742	C4
Oakview Cir	ClyC	2063	E6
Oakview Dr	ClyC	2063	E6
	FTPK	2063	E6
Oakview Dr SE	SMYR	1738	D2
Oakview Rd	ATLN	1892	D4
	DCTR	1892	D4
Oakview Rd NE	ATLN	1892	C4
	DCTR	1892	C4
Oakview Rd SE	ATLN	1892	C4
Oak Village Ct NE	CobC	1527	D3
Oak Village Dr NE	CobC	1527	D3
Oak Village Pl NE	CobC	1527	D3
Oakwood Ct NE	CobC	1527	A3
	CobC	1528	D4
Oakwood Dr	LKCY	2149	C4
	RSWL	1529	D2
Oakwood Mnr	DKbC	1894	B3
Oakwood Trc SE	SMYR	1739	B1
Oakwood Wy SE	SMYR	1739	B1
Oakwood Manor Ct	DKbC	1894	B3
Oakwood Manor Cove	DKbC	1894	B3
Oakwoods Ct	DKbC	1819	E2
Oakwood Village Ln	DKbC	1672	E7
Oana St SW	ATLN	1976	B4
Oberlin Ct	DKbC	1745	C6
Oberlin Wy NE	CobC	1529	B7
Oberon Ct SE	CobC	1739	C4
Oberon Dr SE	CobC	1739	C4
Oberon Wk SE	CobC	1739	C4
Ocala Av SW	ATLN	1889	D7
	ATLN	1975	D1
Ocasta Ct	DKbC	1894	C2
Occidental Ct	DKbC	2066	B1
Occidental Wy	DKbC	2066	B1
Ocean Valley Dr	FulC	2146	D5
Ocoee Ct NE	CobC	1597	D1
Oconee Pass NE	DKbC	1671	A3
O'Connor Wy SW	CobC	1738	A6
Octavia Cir NE	CobC	1597	A1
Octavia Ct NE	CobC	1527	E7
Octavia Ln NE	CobC	1596	D1
Octavia Pl	DKbC	1673	C7
	DKbC	1745	C1
Octavia St SE	ATLN	1977	D5
Odean Dr NE	CobC	1527	A4
Odins Wy NE	CobC	1529	C6
Ogden St SW	ATLN	1890	B4
Ogilvie Dr NE	ATLN	1816	D3
	DKbC	1816	D3
Oglesby Rd	FulC	2145	E4
Oglethorpe Av NE	DKbC	1742	E4
Oglethorpe Av SW	ATLN	1889	D6
Oglethorpe Cir NE	DKbC	1743	A3
Oglethorpe Dr NE	DKbC	1743	A1
O'Hara Dr	FTPK	2063	B5
O'Hara Pl SE	ATLN	1977	C6
O'Hara Rd	FTPK	2063	B5
O'Henry St SW	ATLN	1976	D1
Ohm Av	DKbC	1818	D7
OJ Hurd Ct	EPNT	2061	E1
Okawana Ct NE	CobC	1596	E3
Okawana Dr NE	CobC	1596	E3
Okemah Tr SE	CobC	1666	B5
Oland Cir NE	CobC	1526	D4
Old Alabama Pl	RSWL	1531	E2
Old Alabama Rd	FulC	1532	C2
	RSWL	1531	C3
Old Alabama Rd Connector	ALPT	1532	A2
	RSWL	1532	A2
Old Allgood Cir	DKbC	1819	E6
Old Anvil Block Rd	ClyC	2064	D7
Old Bee Tree Cir NE	MRTA	1595	E4
Old Bee Tree Dr NE	MRTA	1595	E4
Old Bells Ferry Rd NW	CobC	1526	A7
	MRTA	1526	A7
Old Bill Cook Rd	CGPK	2146	E2
	FulC	2146	E2
Old Bolton Rd NW	ATLN	1814	B7
Old Branch Ct	DKbC	1599	E6
Old Briarcliff Rd NE	DKbC	1817	A4
Old Briarcliff Wy NE	DKbC	1817	A4
Old Briarwood Rd NE	DKbC	1743	B6
Old Bridge Ln NW	GwnC	1601	E1
Old Brooke Ln	DKbC	1600	E4
Old Brooke Pt	DKbC	1601	A4
Old Burlington Cir	FulC	1533	C4
Old Burlington St	FulC	1533	C4
Old Cabin Ln SE	SMYR	1739	C1
Old Cabin Rd NW	FulC	1598	C7
Old Campus Ct NE	FulC	1599	A4
Old Campus Tr NE	FulC	1599	A3
Old Canton Ct NE	CobC	1597	A3
Old Canton Rd NE	CobC	1527	E5
Old Car Line Av	DKbC	1818	D6
Old Carriage Dr	FulC	2146	D5
Old Cascade Rd	FulC	1973	E2
Old Chamblee Tucker Rd	DKbC	1673	A7
Old Chartwell Cross	FulC	1532	C2
Old Chartwell Dr	FulC	1532	C3
Old Chattahoochee Av NW	ATLN	1814	E4
Old Chelsea Cir SE	CobC	1597	A6
Old Chestnut Wy NE	CobC	1528	C7
Old Clark Howell Hwy	ClyC	2148	C1
Old Clay St SE	MRTA	1595	B6
Old Coach Ct	DKbC	1894	E3
Old Coach Rd	DKbC	1894	E3
Old Cobblestone Dr	FulC	1600	D2
Old College Wy NE	CobC	1528	D7
	FulC	1599	B4
Old Colonial Ln	FulC	1532	E1
Old Colony Rd	EPNT	1974	E6
Old Concord Rd SE	CobC	1666	B4
	CobC	1738	B1
	SMYR	1666	B5
	SMYR	1738	B1
Old Conley Rd	ClyC	2063	D5
Old Conley Rd SE	ATLN	2063	C4
	ClyC	2063	C4
Old Constitution Rd SE	DKbC	1977	E6
Old Cooledge Rd	DKbC	1745	A6
Old Creek Rd NE	FulC	1742	B1
Old Creek Tr NW	FulC	1669	B2
Old Decatur Cir	DCTR	1818	A6
Old Decatur Rd NE	ATLN	1742	B6
Old Dixie Hwy	ClyC	2062	D6
	FTPK	2062	D6
	FTPK	2148	E1
Old Dixie Rd	ClyC	2062	E7
	ClyC	2149	A6
	FTPK	2062	E7
	FTPK	2148	E1
Old Dixie Rd SR-3	ClyC	2062	E7
	ClyC	2149	A6
	FTPK	2062	E7
	FTPK	2148	E1
Old Dixie Rd US-19	ClyC	2062	E7
	ClyC	2149	A6
	FTPK	2062	E7
	FTPK	2148	E1
Old Dixie Rd US-41	ClyC	2062	E7
	ClyC	2149	A6
	FTPK	2062	E7
	FTPK	2148	E1
Old Dixie Wy	ClyC	2149	A6
Old Dogwood Rd	RSWL	1531	B2
Old Dominion Dr	FulC	1600	D2
Old Dominion Rd	FulC	1600	E2
Old Dunn Ct	ClyC	2064	D7
Olde Clubs Dr	FulC	1532	D6
Olde DeKalb Wy	DKbC	1673	C7

Olde Lauren Ct Atlanta Street Index Paces Lake Ct SE

INDEX 47

Pine Bark Ln — Atlanta Street Index — Pontiac Cir

Atlanta Street Index

STREET / City / Map # / Grid

- Pine Bark Ln — DKbC 1599 E5
- Pinebark Wy — MRRW 2150 A7
- Pinebloom Dr — RSWL 1532 B2
- Pine Bluff Dr — DKbC 1818 B4
- Pine Branch Ct — DKbC 1979 A5
- Pine Branch Pt — DKbC 1599 E5
- Pine Branch Wy — DKbC 1979 A6
- Pine Branches Close — DKbC 1599 E5
- Pinebreeze Ct NE — MRTA 1526 E6
- Pinebreeze Dr NE — MRTA 1526 E6
- Pinebreeze Wy NE — MRTA 1526 E6
- Pine Brook Rd NE — FulC 1670 B3
- Pine Canyon Dr SW — ATLN 1974 C7
- Pinecliff Dr NE — DKbC 1744 D5
- Pine Cone Dr SW — ATLN 1974 B4
- Pine Cone Ln NE — DKbC 1743 B5
- Pine Cove SW — ATLN 1973 B7
- Pine Cove Ct — DKbC 1745 D3
- Pine Cove Dr — DKbC 1745 D3
- Pinecreek Rd — FTPK 2149 C5
- Pinecrest Av — DCTR 1818 A7
- Pinecrest Cir SE — SMYR 1667 A7; SMYR 1739 A1
- Pinecrest Dr — ClyC 2149 C6; ClyC 2150 B7; RVDL 2148 B7
- Pinecrest Dr NE — ATLN 1742 A2
- Pinecrest Cove — ClyC 2149 C6
- Pinedale Dr — ClyC 2063 D7; ClyC 2149 E1
- Pinedale Dr NW — ATLN 1889 C2
- Pinedale Dr SE — SMYR 1738 D2
- Pinedale Pl — DKbC 1893 E7
- Pine Forest Dr NE — DKbC 1817 D1
- Pine Forest Dr SE — ATLN 2063 D3
- Pine Forest Rd NE — FulC 1742 A1
- Pine Forest Wy SE — MRTA 1595 E5
- Pine Gate Dr — ClyC 2148 A3
- Pine Glen Cir — DKbC 1894 E5
- Pineglen Ct — ClyC 2147 E5
- Pineglen Dr — ClyC 2147 E5; ClyC 2149 C6
- Pine Glen Wy — ClyC 2147 D4
- Pineglen Cove — ClyC 2149 C6
- Pine Grove Av NE — DKbC 1742 E4
- Pine Grove Cir SE — DKbC 1978 D6
- Pine Grove Ct — ClyC 2150 E7
- Pine Grove Ct SE — CobC 1597 A7
- Pine Grove Dr NW — ATLN 1814 C2
- Pine Grove Rd — CobC 1529 D1; RSWL 1529 D1
- Pinegrove Rd — ClyC 2148 C6; RVDL 2148 C6
- Pine Grove Ter NE — DKbC 1743 A1
- Pine Haven Ln NE — FulC 1670 B7
- Pine Heights Dr NE — ATLN 1742 C7; ATLN 1816 C3
- Pinehill Dr — DKbC 1893 E4
- Pinehill Dr SE — SMYR 1666 C7
- Pinehill Pl NW — ATLN 1741 D3
- Pine Hill Rd — DKbC 1979 A5
- Pinehurst Cir SE — CobC 1598 A6; SMYR 1738 E2
- Pinehurst Ct — DKbC 1980 D6
- Pinehurst Dr — EPNT 1975 B5
- Pinehurst Dr SE — SMYR 1738 D1
- Pinehurst Dr SW — ATLN 1975 B2
- Pinehurst Ln NE — CobC 1597 B5
- Pinehurst Pl — DKbC 1980 D6
- Pinehurst St — DCTR 1818 B7; DKbC 1818 B7
- Pinehurst Ter SW — ATLN 1889 E7
- Pinehurst Cove — DKbC 1980 C6
- Pinehurst Valley Dr — DKbC 1980 C6
- Pine Island Ct — RSWL 1531 B4
- Pine Knoll Av SW — ATLN 1974 A5
- Pineknoll Ct — HryC 2152 E1
- Pine Lake Dr NW — FulC 1669 E6
- Pine Lake Pl — DKbC 1745 E3
- Pine Lake Rd — DKbC 1745 E3
- Pineland Av — DRVL 1672 B5
- Pineland Dr SE — CobC 1738 A2
- Pineland Rd NW — ATLN 1741 D3
- Pine Leaf Ct — FulC 1533 A1
- Pinella Dr SW — ATLN 1973 C7
- Pinellas Tr — DKbC 1817 E2
- Pine Manor Ct SE — DKbC 1978 C5
- Pine Meadow Dr NE — CobC 1527 A3
- Pine Meadow Ln NE — CobC 1527 A3
- Pine Meadow Rd NW — ATLN 1740 E5
- Pine Meadows Ct — DKbC 1745 C4; LKCY 2149 D4
- Pine Meadows Dr — LKCY 2149 D4
- Pine Meadows Ln — ATLN 1974 C5
- Pine Mill Ln NE — FulC 1598 E7
- Pine Mist Cir — FulC 1533 A1
- Pine Mountain Dr — FTPK 2149 C5
- Pine Mountain Dr NE — CobC 1527 A1
- Pine Needle Ct — EPNT 1974 D6
- Pine Needle Dr — EPNT 1974 D6
- Pine Oak Dr SW — ATLN 1889 B6
- Pine Orchard Dr — DKbC 1745 C3
- Pine Point Trc NE — CobC 1597 E3
- Pineridge Cir — DKbC 1671 E1
- Pineridge Dr — FTPK 2149 C4; LKCY 2149 C4
- Pine Ridge Dr NE — ATLN 1816 C4
- Pineridge Pl — FTPK 2149 B4
- Pine Ridge Rd NE — ATLN 1742 D5; DKbC 1742 D5
- Pine Ridge Tr SE — CobC 1596 D6
- Pine Shoals Ct — ClyC 2148 B4
- Pine Shoals Dr — ClyC 2148 A4
- Pineside Dr — FulC 2146 D5
- Pine Springs Ct — DKbC 1979 A6
- Pine Springs Ln SE — CobC 1596 E6
- Pine Springs Mnr — DKbC 1979 A6
- Pine Springs Tr SE — CobC 1596 E6
- Pinestream Dr NE — CobC 1596 E4
- Pinestream Rd NW — ATLN 1741 A5
- Pine Thicket Wy — RSWL 1530 A2
- Pinetree Cir — DKbC 1893 E1
- Pinetree Cir NE — DKbC 1817 C2
- Pinetree Dr — DCTR 1892 D1
- Pine Tree Dr NE — ATLN 1742 A7
- Pinetree Dr NE — CobC 1597 B4
- Pinetree Dr SE — CobC 1739 A2; SMYR 1739 A2
- Pinetree Ln — ClyC 2151 D5
- Pine Tree Rd NE — ATLN 1816 C1
- Pine Tree St — ClyC 2148 D2
- Pine Valley Cir — EPNT 2060 D1
- Pine Valley Dr — ClyC 2150 B7; FTPK 2063 C7
- Pine Valley Dr NE — MRTA 1595 E1
- Pine Valley Dr SE — CobC 1597 E7
- Pine Valley Ln — EPNT 2060 D1
- Pine Valley Rd — DKbC 1745 D5
- E Pine Valley Rd NW — ATLN 1741 D6
- W Pine Valley Rd NW — ATLN 1741 C6
- Pine Valley Rd NW — ATLN 1741 C6
- Pine Valley Rd SE — CobC 1597 E6
- N Pineview Ct — DKbC 1818 B6
- S Pineview Ct — DKbC 1818 A6
- Pineview Dr — DKbC 1818 A6; FTPK 2149 C2
- Pineview Dr SE — CobC 1739 C4; SMYR 1738 B3
- Pine View Ter — ClyC 2148 A6; RVDL 2147 E6
- Pineview Ter — HryC 2065 C5
- Pineview Ter SW — ATLN 1889 D7
- Pine Warbler Ct NE — CobC 1527 D6
- Pine Warbler Wy NE — CobC 1527 D6
- Pineway Dr NE — DKbC 1817 A2
- Pine Wood Ct NE — CobC 1598 C4
- Pinewood Dr — DKbC 1978 E1
- Pinewood Dr NE — CobC 1596 E5
- Pine Wood Close — RSWL 1532 A2
- Piney Ct SW — FulC 1973 A4
- Piney Wy SW — FulC 1973 A4
- Piney Point Ln SE — CobC 1739 E2
- Piney Ridge Wk — FulC 1532 D1
- Piney Wood Dr — EPNT 1974 D7
- Piney Wood Ln — EPNT 1974 D6
- Piney Wood Ter — EPNT 1974 D6
- Pinhurst Dr SE — CobC 1740 A1
- Pinkney Dr NE — CobC 1527 C4
- Pinnacle Ct — DKbC 1980 D5
- Pinnacle Pl NE — CobC 1596 B2
- Pin Oak Cir — DKbC 1672 E4; DRVL 1672 E4
- Pin Oak Tr — DKbC 1980 D6
- Pin Oak Wy — DRVL 1672 E4
- Pin Oaks Dr NW — GwnC 1673 D5
- Pintail Pt NE — CobC 1529 B6
- Pioneer Ct — DKbC 1744 A2
- S Pioneer Dr SE — SMYR 1813 B1
- Pioneer Tr NE — CobC 1596 C5
- Piper Cir SE — ATLN 1978 A1
- Piper Dr — DKbC 1818 D2
- Pirnmill Pl NE — CobC 1527 B1
- Pitch Lake Ln — RSWL 1532 B5
- Pitner Dr SE — CobC 1666 A3
- Pittman St NW — ATLN 1814 A4
- Pitts Rd — FulC 1599 D2
- Pixley Dr — ClyC 2147 E6; RVDL 2147 E6
- Plains Ct NE — CobC 1527 E1
- Plains Wy NE — CobC 1527 E1
- Plainview Dr NE — CobC 1526 D5
- Plainview St — DCTR 1817 E7
- Plainville Cir SW — ATLN 1887 E6
- Plainville Ct SW — ATLN 1887 E5
- Plainville Dr SW — ATLN 1887 E6
- Plainville Pl SW — ATLN 1887 E6
- Plainville Ter SW — ATLN 1887 E6
- Plainville Tr SW — ATLN 1887 D6
- Plainville Wy SW — ATLN 1887 E6
- Plant Dr NW — GwnC 1601 E3
- Plant Rd NW — ATLN 1814 B1
- Plant St — CGPK 2061 D1; EPNT 2061 D1
- Plantation Cir — CLKN 1819 A3
- Plantation Dr — CLKN 1819 A3; EPNT 1975 A5
- Plantation Dr NE — ATLN 1742 C7; CobC 1528 D1
- Plantation Ln — DKbC 1671 E4; RSWL 1529 E3
- Plantation Crossing Apartments — MRTA 1667 E2
- Plantation Hill Rd SE — CobC 1812 D6
- Plant Atkinson Rd SE — CobC 1739 D7
- Planters Ct — ClyC 2150 E7
- Planters Mill Ln NE — CobC 1596 D1
- Plasamour Dr NE — ATLN 1816 B3
- Plaster Av NE — ATLN 1815 E2
- Plaster Rd NE — DKbC 1743 E2; DKbC 1744 A3
- Plaster Bridge Rd NE — ATLN 1816 B3
- Plasters Av NE — ATLN 1816 A3
- Platina Park Ct — DKbC 2066 C1
- Play Ln NW — ATLN 1890 B3
- Plaza Av SW — ATLN 1889 E7
- Plaza Dr — ClyC 2148 C1
- Plaza Dr SE — CobC 1666 C7; SMYR 1666 C7
- Plaza Ln SW — ATLN 1975 B4
- Plaza Wy — CMBL 1671 E5
- Plaza Wy NW — CobC 1595 A2; MRTA 1595 A2
- Pleas Dr — DKbC 2066 A4
- Pleasant Av — RSWL 1530 C3
- Pleasant St NE — CobC 1527 A1
- Pleasant Tr — DKbC 1672 D4
- Pleasantbrook Village Ln — DKbC 1673 C5
- Pleasantdale Cross — DKbC 1673 B5
- Pleasantdale Pkwy — DKbC 1673 C6
- Pleasantdale Rd — DKbC 1673 B5
- Pleasant Forest Ct — DKbC 1980 E3
- Pleasant Forest Dr — DKbC 1980 E3
- Pleasant Hill Rd — ClyC 2147 A4; FulC 2146 E4
- E Pleasant Hill Rd — ClyC 2147 C4
- Pleasant Hill St — RSWL 1530 C2
- Pleasant Point Dr — DKbC 1980 E3
- Pleasant Ridge Dr — DKbC 1980 E4
- Pleasant Ridge Rd — DKbC 1980 E4
- Pleasant Shade Ct — DKbC 1673 C7
- Pleasant Shade Dr — DKbC 1673 C6
- Pleasant Valley Dr — ClyC 2150 B7; DKbC 1672 D4
- Pleasant View Cir NE — CobC 1528 B7
- Pleasantwood Dr — DKbC 1980 E3
- Plover Ct — DKbC 1979 D2
- Plum Ct — ClyC 2148 A3
- Plum St — RSWL 1530 C1
- Plum St NW — ATLN 1815 D7
- Pluma Dr SE — ATLN 1977 D5; DKbC 1977 D5
- Plumcrest Cir SE — SMYR 1738 B4
- Plumcrest Rd SE — SMYR 1738 C4
- Plymouth Av NW — ATLN 1814 D4
- Plymouth Ln NE — CobC 1527 C4
- Plymouth Rd NE — ATLN 1816 C5
- Plymouth Rd NW — ATLN 1814 D4
- Plymouth Colony Dr NE — DKbC 1744 A3
- Plymstock Ln NW — ATLN 1740 C6
- Plymwood Ct — RSWL 1532 A2
- Pocono Ct — DKbC 1894 C2
- Poinset Pl — DKbC 1818 C2
- Poinsetta Dr NE — CobC 1527 B5
- W Point Av — CGPK 2060 E7; CGPK 2146 E1
- W Point Cir NE — CobC 1529 D6
- E Point Dr NE — CobC 1529 E6
- N Point Dr — RSWL 1529 E3
- W Point Dr NE — CobC 1529 D6
- W Point Pl NE — CobC 1529 D6
- N Point Wy — RSWL 1529 E2
- Pointe Pkwy NW — GwnC 1602 C4
- Pointe Ter SE — CobC 1740 A2
- N Pointe Trc — RSWL 1532 A1
- Pointe Bleue Ct — DKbC 1980 C6
- Pointe Bleue Dr — DKbC 1980 C6
- Pointer Rdg NW — GwnC 1673 E7
- Pointe Ridge Dr NW — FulC 1598 C6
- Point Pleasant SE — SMYR 1739 B3
- Pointview Dr — EPNT 1975 C5
- Poland St NW — ATLN 1890 A2
- Polar Rock Av SW — ATLN 1976 D6
- Polar Rock Dr SW — ATLN 1976 D6
- Polar Rock Pl SW — ATLN 1976 D5
- Polar Rock Rd SW — ATLN 1976 D5
- Polar Rock Ter SW — ATLN 1976 D5
- Polk St NW — MRTA 1595 A4
- Pollard Blvd SW — ATLN 1890 E6
- Pollard Dr SW — ATLN 1975 B2
- Pollard St — EPNT 2061 B2
- Polo Dr NE — ATLN 1816 A5
- Polo Ln SE — CobC 1739 E5
- Polo Run Cir SE — CobC 1738 A2; SMYR 1738 A2
- Polytechnic Ln SE — MRTA 1595 E7
- Pomeroy St SW — MRTA 1595 A5
- Pommel Pl SE — CobC 1597 B6
- Pomona Cir SW — ATLN 1976 C6
- Pomona Wy — EPNT 2060 C3
- Pompey Dr SW — EPNT 2059 D3
- S Ponce Ct NE — ATLN 1892 A1
- S Ponce Ln NE — ATLN 1892 A1
- E Ponce de Leon Av — CLKN 1819 A4; DCTR 1892 E1; DKbC 1818 D6; DKbC 1893 A1
- N Ponce de Leon Av NE — DKbC 1892 B1
- S Ponce de Leon Av NE — ATLN 1891 D1; ATLN 1892 A1; DKbC 1892 A1
- W Ponce de Leon Av — DCTR 1892 D1; DKbC 1892 D1
- Ponce de Leon Av NE — ATLN 1890 E1; ATLN 1891 B1; ATLN 1892 B1; DKbC 1892 B1
- Ponce de Leon Av NE SR-8 — ATLN 1891 B1; ATLN 1892 B1; DKbC 1892 B1
- Ponce de Leon Av NE SR-410 — DKbC 1892 C2
- Ponce de Leon Av NE US-23 — ATLN 1891 B1; ATLN 1892 B1; DKbC 1892 B1
- Ponce de Leon Av NE US-29 — ATLN 1891 B1; ATLN 1892 B1; DKbC 1892 B1
- Ponce de Leon Av NE US-78 — ATLN 1891 B1; ATLN 1892 B1; DKbC 1892 B1
- Ponce de Leon Av NE US-278 — ATLN 1891 B1; ATLN 1892 B1; DKbC 1892 B1
- Ponce de Leon Av NW — ATLN 1890 E1
- Ponce de Leon Cir NW — GwnC 1673 B3
- Ponce de Leon Ct — DCTR 1893 A1
- Ponce de Leon Ct NE — ATLN 1891 B1
- Ponce de Leon Mnr NE — DKbC 1892 B1
- Ponce de Leon Pl — DCTR 1817 E7
- Ponce de Leon Pl NE — ATLN 1816 C7
- Ponce de Leon Ter NE — ATLN 1816 C7
- N Pond Cir — RSWL 1531 C3
- N Pond Ct — RSWL 1531 C3
- Pond Ln NE — CobC 1529 B3
- Pond St NW — ATLN 1890 B3
- N Pond Tr — RSWL 1531 D3
- N Pond Wy — RSWL 1531 C3
- Ponderosa Cir — DKbC 1744 C7
- Ponderosa Ct — FulC 2146 B6
- Ponderosa Pl — FTPK 2149 D5
- Ponderosa Park Dr — FTPK 2149 D5
- Ponders Wy — EPNT 1975 D5
- Pondside Ct NE — CobC 1527 D3
- Pondside Pl NE — CobC 1527 D3
- Pond View Ct NE — CobC 1528 C2
- Ponte Vedra Ct — DKbC 1979 E1
- Ponte Vedra Dr SE — CobC 1598 A6
- Pontiac Cir — DRVL 1672 B3

INDEX 48

Pontiac Pl SE — Atlanta Street Index — Rainier Falls Dr NE

STREET	City	Map #	Grid
Pontiac Pl SE	ATLN	1977	C2
Pool Rd	ATLN	1741	D1
Poole Cir	HryC	2065	E6
Poole Pl SW	ATLN	1890	B6
Poole Rd SW	ATLN	1975	A2
Pope Cir	DCTR	1817	D7
Pope St SW	ATLN	1976	E1
Poplar Cir	DCTR	1893	A2
Poplar Dr	CLKN	1819	B4
	GwnC	1672	E2
Poplar Ln	HryC	2152	E6
Poplar Pt SE	SMYR	1666	B7
Poplar St	ClyC	2150	C4
	DCTR	1893	B1
	DKbC	1672	C5
	DRVL	1672	C5
	EPNT	2062	A1
Poplar St NW	ATLN	1890	E3
	GwnC	1673	C1
Poplar St SE	CobC	1666	B3
Poplar Bluff Cir NW	GwnC	1602	A1
Poplar Bluff Ct NW	GwnC	1602	A1
Poplar Chase Ct	DKbC	2066	A2
Poplar Chase Ln	DKbC	2066	A2
Poplarcrest Cir SE	DKbC	1977	E1
Poplar Grove Dr NE	DKbC	1816	E5
Poplar Hollow Ct NE	CobC	1528	E1
Poplar Ln Wy	DKbC	1818	B6
Poplar Pointe Dr	ClyC	2147	C4
Poplar Shoals	DKbC	2066	A1
Poplar Shoals Ln	DKbC	2066	A2
Poplar Spring Ct NW	GwnC	1602	A1
Poplar Spring Dr NW	GwnC	1601	E1
Poplar Springs Dr NE	DKbC	1743	B4
Poplar Springs Rd	ClyC	2148	A6
Poppleford Ln	DKbC	1600	D4
Port Blvd S	FulC	2145	E3
N Port Cir	FulC	2145	E2
Portabello Ln NE	CobC	1598	D2
Portal Pl NW	GwnC	1533	C6
Port Antonio Ct	FulC	2059	C5
Port A Prince Ct	ClyC	2149	C7
Port A Prince Dr	ClyC	2149	B7
Port Chester Ct	DKbC	1980	E6
Port Chester Wy	DKbC	1980	D6
Port Cobb Dr SE	CobC	1814	A1
Porter Ct	DKbC	1894	B2
Porter Dr NW	ATLN	1889	C4
Porter Ln NE	CobC	1527	E5
Porter Pl	DKbC	1893	C7
Porter Pl NE	ATLN	1890	E2
Porter Rd	DKbC	1894	B2
Porter Glade Ct	DRVL	1672	B3
Portland Av SE	ATLN	1891	E6
Portland Ct NE	CobC	1528	D2
Port Patrick Ln SE	CobC	1738	A6
Port Royal Ln	DKbC	1979	A4
Portsmouth Ct	UNCT	2145	C7
Portsmouth Dr	UNCT	2145	B7
Post Rd	ClyC	2062	A5
Post Creek Ct NE	CobC	1527	D3
Postell St NW	ATLN	1890	C3
Post House Ct SE	CobC	1597	C6
Post Oak Ct NE	CobC	1527	D2
Post Oak Dr	DKbC	1819	C1
Post Oak Dr NE	CobC	1527	D3
Post Oak Tr NW	GwnC	1602	A5
Post Oak Tritt Rd NE	CobC	1527	D3
Post Springs Ct NE	CobC	1528	C3
Post Village Dr SE	SMYR	1667	B6
Post Woods Dr SE	CobC	1740	B1
Potomac Av NE	ATLN	1815	E1
Potomac Ct	EPNT	2060	D3
W Potomac Dr	EPNT	2060	D3
Potomac Rd	FulC	1599	E7
Potomac Ter	EPNT	2060	D3
Potter Av	AVES	1893	E1
Potter Ct	ClyC	2150	C4
Potters Wk NE	ATLN	1742	B2
Potts Cir	UNCT	2145	B7
Pounds Ln	DKbC	1819	C2
Powderdam Dr	RSWL	1532	C5
E Powderhorn Rd NE	FulC	1670	C7
W Powderhorn Rd NE	FulC	1670	B7
Powderhorn Rd NE	FulC	1670	C7
Powder Mill Pl SE	CobC	1597	B7
Powder Ridge Rd	RSWL	1532	A5
Powder Springs St SE	SMYR	1666	C6
Powder Springs St SW	MRTA	1595	A5
Powder Springs St SW SR-360	MRTA	1595	A7
Powell Ct SE	DKbC	1977	E1
Powell Ln	DKbC	1817	D6
Powell St SE	ATLN	1891	B5
Powell Cove	DCTR	1892	D1
Powell-Wright Rd NE	CobC	1526	D4
Power Dr	DKbC	1600	E7
Powerplant Dr NW	ATLN	1890	D1
S Powers Ct NW	FulC	1669	B5
Powers Pl NE	CobC	1598	B4
Powers Rd NE	CobC	1598	A4
Powers St	RVDL	2148	B7
Powers Chase Cir NW	FulC	1669	B5
Powers Cove NE	CobC	1598	B4
Powers Cove NW	FulC	1669	D6
Powers Ferry Ct SE	CobC	1596	D7
Powers Ferry Dr SE	CobC	1596	C7
	CobC	1667	D1
Powers Ferry Mnr SE	MRTA	1596	A5
Powers Ferry Pl SE	MRTA	1667	D1
N Powers Ferry Rd NW	FulC	1669	B5
Powers Ferry Rd NW	ATLN	1741	D2
	FulC	1668	D5
	FulC	1741	D2
Powers Ferry Rd SE	CobC	1596	C7
	CobC	1667	E1
	MRTA	1596	A5
	MRTA	1667	E1
Powers Ferry Trc SE	MRTA	1596	D7
Powers Ferry North SE	CobC	1596	C7
Powers Ford SE	CobC	1668	B1
Powers Lake Dr NW	FulC	1669	B4
Powers Overlook Ct NW	FulC	1669	A4
Powers Park Ct NE	CobC	1598	B4
Powers Park Wy NE	CobC	1598	B4
Powers Point Ct NW	FulC	1669	A4
Powers Ridge Ct NW	FulC	1669	A4
Powers Ridge Pl NW	FulC	1669	A4
Powhatan Rd	DKbC	1978	D7
S Prado NE	ATLN	1816	A6
Prado Ln	CobC	1526	A3
Prairie View Dr SW	ATLN	1889	A5
Prairie View Pl SW	ATLN	1889	A5
Pratt St	RSWL	1530	C2
Pratt St SE	ATLN	1891	A4
Preakness Ct NE	CobC	1597	B1
Preakness Dr	DKbC	1980	B4
	RSWL	1532	B4
Prentiss Dr	DKbC	2066	D2
Prentiss Pt SE	CobC	1597	D7
Prescott St NE	ATLN	1890	E2
Prescott Wk NE	ATLN	1892	A1
Presidential Dr	DKbC	1672	D7
Presidential Pkwy	DKbC	1672	D6
	DKbC	1744	D1
Presley Wy NE	ATLN	1892	C3
Pressley Dr	DKbC	1818	E6
Presswyck Ct NE	CobC	1529	A5
Prestige Sq	ClyC	2150	C6
Prestige Valley Ct	ClyC	2150	D5
Prestige Valley Dr NE	CobC	1527	B7
Prestige Valley Rd	ClyC	2150	D6
S Preston Ct	FulC	1532	E2
W Preston Ct	FulC	1532	E2
Preston Ct NE	DKbC	1670	E3
Preston Dr	DKbC	1979	B3
S Preston Tr	FulC	1532	E2
Preston Wy	DKbC	1979	B3
Preston Chase Apartments	MRTA	1667	B1
Preston Lake Dr NW	GwnC	1673	C4
Preston Oaks Dr	FulC	1532	E2
Preston Woods Tr	FulC	1599	D6
Prestwick Dr	DKbC	1745	B3
Prestwick Pl SE	SMYR	1739	B1
Prestwood Ct	DKbC	1600	E6
Pretty Branch Dr SE	CobC	1738	E2
Prettyview Ln SE	CobC	1738	B2
Price Ln NW	CobC	1526	A6
Prichard Wy NE	ATLN	1742	C4
Priestcliff Dr SE	SMYR	1667	A6
Primrose Ln NW	GwnC	1602	A2
Primrose Pl	DKbC	1894	A6
Primrose Pth NE	CobC	1598	D3
Primrose Hill Ct NW	GwnC	1601	E3
Prince Av NE	MRTA	1526	D7
Prince Pl NW	ATLN	1814	A5
Prince Rd SE	CobC	1739	A7
	SMYR	1739	A7
Prince Ter NE	MRTA	1526	D6
Prince Wy	DKbC	1819	B1
Prince Charles Pl	FulC	1532	C3
Prince George Dr	ClyC	2147	C6
Prince George St	EPNT	2060	C3
Prince Howard Dr NE	CobC	1528	A3
Prince Howard Ln NE	CobC	1528	A4
Prince Howard Tr NE	CobC	1528	A4
Prince Howard Wy NE	CobC	1528	A4
Princess Av SW	ATLN	1976	A1
Princess Cir NE	DKbC	1743	D7
	DKbC	1817	D1
Princess Ln NW	GwnC	1602	B3
Princess Ln SE	CobC	1596	D6
Princess Square Ct SE	CobC	1596	D6
Princess Tammy Cove	DKbC	1745	A3
Princeton Av	CGPK	2061	A4
	ClyC	2150	B6
Princeton Dr	CGPK	2061	B3
Princeton Ln NE	CobC	1527	E2
Princeton Pl SW	ATLN	1887	D3
Princeton Ter	DKbC	1980	E2
Princeton Trc NE	FulC	1599	B4
Princeton Wk NE	CobC	1597	E1
Princeton Wy NE	DKbC	1817	D6
	FulC	1599	A4
Princeton Corners Dr NE	CobC	1528	B7
Princeton Corners Ln NE	CobC	1597	B1
Princeton Lakes Dr NE	CobC	1529	A7
Princeton Mill Ct NE	CobC	1596	E3
Princeton Mill Run NE	CobC	1596	E2
Princeton West Tr NE	CobC	1528	C6
Prince Williheme Ter	EPNT	2060	C3
Priscilla Ct	ClyC	2150	E7
Priscilla Dr NE	CobC	1527	D2
Priscilla Wy	ClyC	2150	E7
Pristine Pl	RSWL	1601	C1
Pritchard Dr NE	CobC	1597	E2
Pritchard Wy NE	ATLN	1742	C5
Pro Dr NW	GwnC	1602	B1
Proctor Av	DKbC	1818	D6
Proctor St NW	ATLN	1890	A2
Professional Ct	RVDL	2148	C7
Professional Pl	ClyC	2148	D7
	RVDL	2148	D7
Promenade Dr SW	FulC	1973	A3
Promenade Wy SW	FulC	1973	A3
Promontory Cir NE	CobC	1596	B1
Promontory Ct	DKbC	1599	E7
Promontory Dr NE	CobC	1527	C7
Promontory Ln NE	CobC	1527	D7
Promontory Pth NE	CobC	1527	C7
Prospect Av SE	ATLN	1891	D7
Prospect Pl NE	ATLN	1891	B3
	FulC	1670	B3
Prospect St	RSWL	1530	D1
Providence Ln	DKbC	1745	D2
Providence Pl	DKbC	1817	D3
Providence Rd NE	CobC	1528	C7
Providence Church Rd	CobC	1528	D7
Providence Corners Dr NE	CobC	1528	D7
Pryor Cir SW	ATLN	1976	D4
Pryor Rd SW	ATLN	1890	D7
	ATLN	1976	D1
Pryor St SW	ATLN	1890	E4
Public Pl	FulC	1532	E3
Puckett St	FTPK	2063	B7
	FTPK	2149	B1
Pueblo Dr SW	ATLN	1973	B6
Pullen Ln	FulC	2059	C6
Pulliam St SW	ATLN	1890	D6
Pullman Ct	DKbC	1599	E7
Pumpco Ct	ClyC	2148	D3
Purple Heart Hwy	DKbC	1980	B2
Purple Heart Hwy I-20	DKbC	1980	B2
Purple Heart Hwy SR-402	DKbC	1980	B2
Putnam Cir NE	ATLN	1741	E3
Putnam Dr NW	ATLN	1741	E3
Putters Ct	FulC	1532	E6
Pylant St NE	ATLN	1816	B7
Pyrenees Ct	DKbC	1601	B7
Pyrite Cir SW	ATLN	1974	C7
	ATLN	2060	C1
Q			
N Q Av	FTPK	2149	E2
Quail Ct	DKbC	1980	A5
Quail Run	RSWL	1531	C4
Quailbrook Ct	DKbC	1745	E7
Quailridge Ct NE	CobC	1597	A4
Quail Ridge Wy NW	GwnC	1532	E7
	GwnC	1601	C2
Quaker St SW	ATLN	1976	B6
Qualmish Av	ATLN	1975	E3
Quarles Av SE	SMYR	1667	A7
	SMYR	1738	E1
Quarry Lake Ct NE	FulC	1669	E4
Quarter Horse Ct NE	CobC	1529	D3
Quarter Horse Dr NE	CobC	1529	C1
Quarter Horse Wy NE	CobC	1529	C1
Quebec Ct	DKbC	1819	A1
Queen St NW	ATLN	1814	C2
Queen St SW	ATLN	1890	A6
Queen Ann Ct	DKbC	1894	E1
Queen Anne Ct	FulC	1531	A4
Queen Anne Ct SE	CobC	1738	A6
Queen Anne Dr SE	CobC	1738	A5
Queen Anne Pl NW	ATLN	1814	A1
Queen Elizabeth St	EPNT	2060	C2
Queen Elizabeth Wy	ClyC	2149	C7
Queen Ester Ct	ClyC	2151	C3
Queen Mill Rd SE	CobC	1812	C5
Queens Ct	ClyC	2147	C6
Queens Ct NW	NRCS	1602	D5
Queens Wk NE	DKbC	1744	D4
Queens Wy	DKbC	1671	D2
Queensborough Dr	DKbC	1599	E3
Queensbury Ln NW	ATLN	1741	C7
Queensferry Dr SE	CobC	1812	B7
Queensferry Pl SE	CobC	1812	B7
Queensgate Ct SE	SMYR	1738	D4
Queensgate Dr SE	SMYR	1738	D4
Queens Meadow Dr SE	CobC	1812	C4
Queens River Dr SE	CobC	1812	D4
Queen Victoria Pl NE	ATLN	1741	B3
Querulous St	ClyC	2064	B6
Quiet Water Ln	FulC	1600	D1
Quillian Av	ATLN	1892	E6
	DKbC	1892	E6
Quincetree Ln	DKbC	1979	E5
Quincy Ln	DKbC	1979	B3
	RSWL	1532	B5
Quinto Dr SW	CobC	1666	A5
Quondam Cir NE	CobC	1529	C4
R			
N R St	FTPK	2149	E1
Rabun Dr SW	ATLN	1888	B6
Rabun Rd	ClyC	2150	D7
Raccoon Run NE	CobC	1597	D1
Rachael St SE	ATLN	1977	C5
Rachel Ct NE	CobC	1527	B3
Rachel Rdg NW	GwnC	1601	E1
Racine St SW	ATLN	1889	D4
Radar Cir NE	MRTA	1595	E5
Radar Dr	HPVL	2062	C3
Radar Rd NE	DKbC	1743	D5
Radcliffe Blvd	DKbC	1980	D7
	DKbC	2066	D2
Radcliffe Ct	DKbC	1980	D7
Radcliffe Dr NW	ATLN	1815	B2
Radford Cir SW	CobC	1738	A1
Radford Ct	ClyC	2147	B6
Radford Ct SW	CobC	1738	A1
Radford Dr	ClyC	2147	B5
Radium St NW	MRTA	1595	A3
Ragin River Ct	DKbC	2065	C1
Ragley Hall Rd NE	DKbC	1671	A6
Railroad Av	DKbC	1745	D4
Railroad Av SE	ATLN	1891	C6
Railroad St	ClyC	2151	B3
Rainbow Cir	DKbC	1979	D3
Rainbow Ct	DKbC	1980	C3
Rainbow Dr	DKbC	1979	D3
S Rainbow Dr	DKbC	1979	D3
Rainbow Pkwy	DKbC	1980	C3
Rainbow Wy	DKbC	1979	C3
Rainbow Creek Dr	DKbC	1980	C3
Rainbow Forest Cir	DKbC	1979	D3
Rainbow Forest Ct	DKbC	1980	B3
Rainbow Forest Dr	DKbC	1980	A3
Rainbow Ridge Rd	DKbC	1980	A3
Rainbow Ridge Wy	DKbC	1980	A3
Rainbow Row Ct	FulC	1532	D4
Rainbow Village Ln	NRCS	1602	D7
Raindrop Ct	DKbC	1980	C3
Raines Ct NE	CobC	1528	B4
Rainey Av	FulC	2062	A3
	HPVL	2062	A3
Rainforest Cir	DKbC	1978	E7
Rainforest Cir NW	GwnC	1602	A3
Rainier Falls Dr NE	DKbC	1817	B3

INDEX 51

Riverthur Pl NW — Atlanta Street Index — Roswell Farms Ln

STREET	City	Map #	Grid
Riverthur Pl NW	GwnC	1533	E7
Riverton Park Pl SE	SMYR	1812	C1
River Trace Dr	FulC	1530	E5
	FulC	1532	E3
Rivertrail Ct	FulC	1531	E7
River Tree Dr	DKbC	1979	B7
River Valley Dr SE	SMYR	1738	D4
River Valley Rd NW	FulC	1598	C7
	FulC	1669	C1
Riverview Bnd	DKbC	2066	A2
Riverview Dr NW	GwnC	1533	E5
Riverview Dr SE	CobC	1668	D1
Riverview Fy	DKbC	2066	A2
Riverview Rd NW	FulC	1668	D6
Riverview Rd SE	CobC	1813	C1
	SMYR	1813	B3
River View Tr	RSWL	1530	C4
Riverview Wy NW	GwnC	1533	E5
Riverview Approach	DKbC	2066	A2
Riverview Chase Blf	DKbC	2066	A2
Riverview Chase Dr	DKbC	2066	A2
Riverview Chase Wy	DKbC	2066	A2
Riverview Club Dr	DKbC	2066	A2
Riverview Industrial Dr SE	CobC	1813	B2
Riverview Industrial Wy SE	CobC	1813	C3
Riverview Spring Ct	DKbC	2066	A2
River Walk Ct	ClyC	2147	D2
River Walk Dr	ClyC	2147	D2
Riverwalk Dr	RSWL	1530	C4
River Walk Ln	ClyC	2147	D2
River Walk Pl	CGPK	2147	D2
	ClyC	2147	D2
River Walk Tr	ClyC	2147	D3
Riverwalk Cove	DKbC	2065	C1
Riverwood Cir	DKbC	1980	E1
Riverwood Ct	ClyC	2147	C4
Riverwood Ct NW	FulC	1669	D1
Riverwood Dr NW	FulC	1669	D2
Riverwood Ln	RSWL	1531	A1
Riverwood Pkwy SE	CobC	1668	B7
	CobC	1740	B1
Riverwood Pl NW	FulC	1669	A4
Riverwood Spr	DKbC	2065	A1
Riverwood Wy	DKbC	1980	E2
Riviera Ct	DKbC	1744	C6
Riviera Dr	ATLN	1974	C7
Riviera Rd	RSWL	1530	E4
Rivoli Cir NE	FulC	1670	C4
RN Martin St	EPNT	2061	D1
Roach St SW	ATLN	1890	B5
Roanoke Av NE	ATLN	1815	E2
Roanoke Dr NE	CobC	1526	D3
Roanoke Pl SE	CobC	1667	E3
Robbie Ln SW	CobC	1666	B6
Robert Dr SE	CobC	1667	B6
Robert Ln NE	CobC	1528	A7
Robert St NW	ATLN	1888	E1
Roberta Dr NW	ATLN	1741	A6
Roberta Dr SW	CobC	1666	A3
Robert Nash Ct	DKbC	1745	C4
Roberts Dr	DKbC	1600	A3
	FulC	1530	E5
Roberts Dr SE	ATLN	1977	B1
	CobC	1812	E3
Roberts Rd SE	CobC	1667	B2
Roberts Tr NW	CobC	1526	A3
Roberts Wy NE	DKbC	1671	B6
Roberts Landing Cove	FulC	1530	E5
Robertson Rd	ClyC	2063	E7
Roberts Park Rd	DKbC	1600	A4
Robeson Ct NE	MRTA	1595	B4
Robin Ln	FTPK	2063	C7
	FulC	2059	B6
	HryC	2152	E5
Robin Ln NE	ATLN	1816	D4
Robin Ln SE	CobC	1596	D6
	SMYR	1666	D5
Robin Rd	DKbC	1893	D4
Robin Rd SE	CobC	1598	B5
Robin St	DCTR	1892	E1
Robindale Ct	DKbC	1980	B5
Robindale Rd	DKbC	1980	B5
Robinhill Ct	DKbC	1745	B6
Robinhill Dr	DKbC	1745	B6
Robinhood Dr	ClyC	2150	D5
Robin Hood Pl NE	CobC	1596	D2
Robin Hood Rd NE	ATLN	1815	E5
Robin Point Dr	DKbC	1980	A7
Robins Landing Wy	DKbC	1893	C6
Robinson Av	DKbC	1818	D6
Robinson Av SE	ATLN	1891	B7
Robinson Dr SW	FulC	1887	B3
Robinson Rd NE	CobC	1596	D2
Robinson Farms Ct NE	CobC	1597	B3
Robinson Farms Dr NE	CobC	1597	B2
Robinson Farms Trc NE	CobC	1597	C3
Robinson Farms Wy NE	CobC	1597	B2
Robinson Oaks Wy NE	CobC	1528	B3
Robinson Walk Ct NE	CobC	1597	C1
Robinson Walk Dr NE	CobC	1597	C1
Robinwood Ln	RSWL	1529	E2
Robinwood Pl	DKbC	1980	E5
Robinwood Rd	DKbC	1818	D2
Robinwood Tr	DKbC	1980	D5
Rob Roy Ln	ClyC	2064	A6
Robson Pl NE	ATLN	1892	C4
Robyn Wy NE	CobC	1528	E3
Rochelle Ct	DKbC	1671	B1
Rochelle Dr	DKbC	1671	B1
Rochelle Dr SW	ATLN	1889	E7
Rochelle Wy	ClyC	2147	A2
Rock St NE	MRTA	1595	C5
Rock St NW	ATLN	1890	B3
Rockaway Ct	DKbC	1745	A1
Rockaway Rd	DKbC	1673	A7
	DKbC	1745	A1
Rock Bridge Ct NE	CobC	1526	B2
Rockbridge Rd	DKbC	1818	D7
Rock Bridge Rd NE	CobC	1526	B2
Rockbridge Tr	DKbC	1819	C6
Rockbridge Heights Dr	DKbC	1819	D6
Rock Cliff Dr SW	CobC	1738	A3
Rockcliff Pl SE	DKbC	1978	B3
Rockcliff Rd SE	DKbC	1978	C3
Rock Creek Ln	RSWL	1530	E1
Rockcrest Ct	DKbC	2065	A2
Rockcrest Ct NE	CobC	1596	A1
Rockcrest Dr NE	CobC	1527	A7
Rockcrest Tr	DKbC	2065	A2
Rockcrest Wy NE	CobC	1596	A2
Rock Cut Pl	ClyC	2064	B6
Rock Cut Rd	ClyC	2063	D6
	FTPK	2063	D6
Rockdale Dr	DKbC	1978	D3
Rockdale St NW	ATLN	1814	D6
Rockey Valley Dr	DKbC	2064	E2
Rockford Ct	ClyC	2147	C6
Rockfort Ct	FulC	2146	A7
Rockfort Dr	FulC	2146	A7
Rockgarden Ct	DKbC	2065	A2
Rockglen Ct NW	GwnC	1673	D6
Rockhaven Cir	DKbC	1892	E7
Rockhaven Cir NE	ATLN	1742	D5
Rockhaven Dr	DKbC	1892	E7
Rock Hill Dr	ClyC	2148	B4
Rock Hill Rd	FulC	2146	C1
Rock Hollow Ct	DKbC	2065	A1
Rock Hollow Dr	DKbC	2065	A1
Rocking Ter	ClyC	2064	B6
Rocking Wy	DKbC	2064	E2
Rocking Chair Ln	DKbC	1819	E3
Rockingham Dr NW	ATLN	1741	B7
Rockingham St	FulC	1533	A4
Rockingham Wy NE	CobC	1598	A1
Rockingwood Dr	ClyC	2148	B4
Rockingwood Ln	ClyC	2148	B4
Rockingwood Trc	ClyC	2148	A4
Rock Island Ln	HryC	2152	A1
Rockland Ct NE	CobC	1528	E5
Rockland Dr SE	ATLN	1892	B7
	DKbC	1892	B7
Rocklane Ct	DKbC	2064	E1
Rocklane Dr	ClyC	2064	B6
Rockledge Rd NE	ATLN	1816	B3
Rockmart Dr NW	ATLN	1889	E4
Rockmart Dr SW	ATLN	1889	E4
Rockmill Dr	DKbC	2065	E3
Rockmill Cove	DKbC	2066	A3
Rockmont Dr NE	ATLN	1816	B4
Rockmont Ln NE	CobC	1526	C1
Rockmoor Tr NE	CobC	1526	B1
Rocknoll Ct	DKbC	2065	A2
Rocknoll Dr	DKbC	2065	A2
Rockport Pl SW	ATLN	1888	A3
Rock Quarry Rd	FulC	2146	B3
Rockridge Pl NE	ATLN	1816	B4
Rock Ridge Rd NE	CobC	1527	E5
Rockridge Tr	CobC	1668	B5
Rock Shoals Ct	ClyC	2148	B4
Rock Shoals Wy	ClyC	2148	A4
Rock Springs Cir NE	DKbC	1816	E5
E Rock Springs Ct NE	DKbC	1816	E6
Rock Springs Pl NE	DKbC	1816	E6
E Rock Springs Rd NE	ATLN	1816	D5
	DKbC	1816	D5
N Rock Springs Rd NE	ATLN	1816	B4
Rock Springs Rd NE	ATLN	1816	A4
Rocksprings St	ClyC	2063	D6
	FTPK	2063	D6
E Rock Springs Ter NE	DKbC	1816	E5
Rockwell St SW	ATLN	1890	C7
Rockwood Av NW	ATLN	1888	E1
Rockwood Ct NE	CobC	1597	D4
Rockwood Dr SE	CobC	1596	C6
Rockwood Rd	EPNT	1974	D7
	EPNT	2060	D1
Rocky Creek Dr	RSWL	1530	D1
Rocky Creek Rd	FulC	2059	A2
Rockyford Rd NE	ATLN	1892	C3
Rockyford Rd SE	ATLN	1892	C4
Rocky Springs Ct NE	CobC	1528	C3
Rocky Springs Dr NE	CobC	1528	C3
Rocky Valley Ct	DKbC	2065	A2
Rod Ct	FulC	1532	C3
Rod Rd	FulC	1532	C3
Rodeo Ct SE	DKbC	1978	D4
Rodney Dr SW	ATLN	1888	E7
Rogeretta Dr NE	DKbC	1817	B3
Rogers Av SW	ATLN	1889	B6
Rogers St	CLKN	1819	B4
	DKbC	1819	A4
Rogers St NE	ATLN	1892	B4
	MRTA	1595	C5
Rogers St SE	ATLN	1892	B4
Rokefield Wy NW	GwnC	1533	C5
Rolland St NE	CobC	1528	D4
Rolling Pl	DKbC	2064	E1
Rolling Brook Tr	EPNT	2060	E1
Rolling Green Rdg SW	ATLN	1974	A3
Rolling Hill Rd SW	ATLN	1973	C6
Rolling House Ln NE	CobC	1529	D5
Rolling Meadows Dr	ClyC	2151	C1
Rolling Rock Ct	DKbC	2065	A1
Rolling Rock Dr	DKbC	2064	E1
Rolling Rock Rd SE	CobC	1598	A6
Rollingview Dr	DKbC	1894	B7
	DKbC	1980	B1
Rolling View Dr SE	SMYR	1667	D6
Rollingwood Ct SE	DKbC	1978	C5
Rollingwood Dr SE	DKbC	1978	C5
Rollingwood Ln SE	DKbC	1978	C4
Rollins Wy NE	DKbC	1817	B5
Romain Wy	EPNT	1974	E5
Roman Ct	DKbC	1745	C6
Romans Dr NE	CobC	1527	B6
Rome Dr NW	ATLN	1889	D3
Romelie Dr	DKbC	1673	C7
Ronald Rd	DKbC	1745	B7
Rondak Cir SE	SMYR	1739	B2
Rondo Rd SE	ATLN	2062	E4
Rondon Ct SE	DKbC	1978	C4
Ronnie Dr	ClyC	2151	A5
Ronnie Dr NE	CobC	1527	E7
Roosevelt Cir NE	MRTA	1595	B4
Roosevelt Dr SE	ATLN	2063	C3
Roosevelt Hwy	CGPK	2060	E7
	CGPK	2146	B1
	FulC	2145	B4
	FulC	2146	B1
	UNCT	2145	B4
Roosevelt Hwy SR-14	CGPK	2060	E7
	CGPK	2146	B1
	FulC	2145	B4
	FulC	2146	B1
	UNCT	2145	B4
Roosevelt Hwy SR-139	CGPK	2061	A6
Roosevelt Hwy US-29	CGPK	2060	E7
	CGPK	2146	B1
	FulC	2145	B4
	FulC	2146	B1
	UNCT	2145	B4
Roosevelt St	CGPK	2061	A3
Root St NE	MRTA	1595	A4
Rosaire Pl NW	ATLN	1814	E2
Rosalia St SE	ATLN	1891	B6
Rosalind Dr NE	DKbC	1743	C7
Rosalyn Dr NE	MRTA	1595	E2
Rosalyn Ln SE	SMYR	1666	C6
Rosalyn St NW	ATLN	1815	C7
Rose Cir	DKbC	1893	A5
Rose Cir SW	ATLN	1890	A7
Rose Ct NE	ATLN	1741	E2
Rose Ct SE	SMYR	1666	B7
Rose Dr SE	MRTA	1595	D6
Rose Ln SE	MRTA	1595	D6
Rose Rdg	DKbC	1672	E6
Rose Ter	HPVL	2062	B2
Rose Arbor	DKbC	1673	A6
Rose Arbor Ct	DKbC	1673	A6
Rosebriar Dr NE	MRTA	1527	A5
Rosebrook Cross SE	CobC	1739	E6
Rosebrook Ct	DKbC	1818	D3
Rosebrook Ct SE	CobC	1739	E7
Rosebrook Dr	DKbC	1818	D3
Rosebrook Pl SE	CobC	1739	E7
Roseclair Dr SE	ATLN	1892	E4
Rosecliff Dr NE	DKbC	1743	D7
Rosecommon Dr NW	GwnC	1601	C2
Rosecrest Pl NE	DKbC	1743	D4
Rosedale Av SE	ATLN	1891	B7
Rosedale Dr	ClyC	2150	D6
Rosedale Dr NE	ATLN	1816	D7
	CobC	1526	D3
Rosedale Dr SE	SMYR	1738	C3
Rosedale Rd NE	ATLN	1816	D7
	DKbC	1816	D7
Rosedown Wy	FulC	1532	E1
Rose Gate Dr NE	ATLN	1741	E2
Roselawn Ln SE	CobC	1667	B3
Rose Ln St NW	CobC	1595	A2
	MRTA	1595	A2
Rosemary Av SW	ATLN	1889	C7
Rosemary Dr NW	ATLN	1813	E3
Rose Mill Wy SE	SMYR	1739	A1
Rosemont Dr	ATLN	1892	E6
	DKbC	1892	E6
Rosemont Pl NE	DKbC	1817	C3
Rosemoore Wk NE	CobC	1527	C2
Rosemoore Wy NE	CobC	1527	C2
Rose Moss Ct SE	SMYR	1738	A4
Rose Petal Ln	FulC	1532	E2
Roses of Picardy	ClyC	2147	B2
Rosette Lndg NE	CobC	1597	A1
Rosette Wy NE	CobC	1597	A1
Rosewell Oaks Pkwy NE	CobC	1529	C2
Rosewood Cir SE	MRTA	1596	A5
Rosewood Dr NE	ATLN	1816	D6
Rosewood Grv	DKbC	1980	E7
Rosewood Rd	DKbC	1893	D7
	DKbC	1979	D1
Rosewood Creek Dr NE	MRTA	1527	A5
Rosewood Plantation Rd NE	ATLN	1741	B3
	ATLN	1742	A4
Rosie Ln SE	CobC	1812	E3
Ross Av	CGPK	2061	A3
Ross Dr	CGPK	2060	E2
	EPNT	2060	E2
Ross Rd NE	CobC	1527	A5
	MRTA	1527	A5
Ross Rd NW	GwnC	1673	A3
Ross St SW	ATLN	1976	C4
Rossburn Ct	DKbC	2065	D1
Rosser St SW	ATLN	1890	A5
Roswell Ct NE	ATLN	1742	A5
Roswell Rd	FulC	1530	D6
	FulC	1599	D2
	RSWL	1530	D6
Roswell Rd SR-9	FulC	1530	D6
	FulC	1599	D1
	RSWL	1530	D6
Roswell Rd NE	ATLN	1741	E5
	ATLN	1742	A2
	CobC	1528	E7
	FulC	1599	A6
	FulC	1670	A2
	FulC	1742	A2
	MRTA	1596	A4
Roswell Rd NE SR-9	ATLN	1741	E5
	ATLN	1742	A2
	FulC	1599	A6
	FulC	1670	A2
	FulC	1742	A2
Roswell Rd NE SR-120	CobC	1528	E7
	MRTA	1596	A4
Roswell Rd NE US-19	ATLN	1741	E5
	ATLN	1742	A2
	FulC	1670	A3
	FulC	1742	A2
Roswell Rd SE	MRTA	1595	E5
Roswell Rd SE SR-120	MRTA	1595	E5
Roswell St NE	MRTA	1595	B5
Roswell St NE SR-120	MRTA	1595	B5
Roswell St SE	CobC	1667	A6
	MRTA	1595	C5
	SMYR	1666	E7
Roswell St SE SR-120	MRTA	1595	C5
Roswell St SW	ATLN	1973	E5
Roswell Farms Cir	RSWL	1530	B2
Roswell Farms Ct	RSWL	1530	B2
Roswell Farms Dr	RSWL	1530	B2
Roswell Farms Ln	RSWL	1530	B2

INDEX 53

Sanford Rd — Shannon Ridge Ct

Atlanta Street Index

STREET	City	Map #	Grid
Sanford Rd	DKbC	1817	E5
Sanford Rd SE	SMYR	1666	D7
Sanfords Wk NW	GwnC	1673	E7
San Gabriel Av	DKbC	1893	D5
Sanibel Ln SE	CobC	1666	A7
Sanibel Wy SE	CobC	1666	A6
San Jose Dr	DKbC	1893	D6
San Juan Dr	DKbC	1893	D5
San Juan St	ClyC	2149	B6
Sanlee Ln	DKbC	1601	C5
San Marco Dr	DKbC	2064	E1
San Marino Ct	FulC	2146	C7
San Remo Ct	FulC	2146	C6
Sans Souci Ct	DKbC	1819	C3
Sans Souci Wy	DKbC	1819	C3
Santa Barbara Dr	ClyC	2149	A6
	DKbC	1893	C5
Santa Barbara Dr NW	ATLN	1888	E2
Santa Cruz Dr	DKbC	1893	D6
Santa Fe Pkwy	FulC	1599	B3
Santa Fe Sta	DKbC	1599	E6
Santa Fe Tr	DKbC	1672	C6
	HryC	2152	A1
Santa Fe Tr SW	ATLN	1973	B6
Santa Leta Dr	DKbC	1978	E7
	DKbC	2064	E1
Santa Lucia Ter NW	ATLN	1888	E2
Santa Monica Dr	DKbC	1893	C5
Santa Monica Dr NW	ATLN	1888	E2
Santa Rosa Dr SW	ATLN	1973	B6
Santeelah Tr	DKbC	1894	C2
Sapelo Tr NW	GwnC	1533	C7
Sapphire Cir	ClyC	2150	C3
Sapphire Ct	ClyC	2150	C3
	DKbC	2066	C1
Sapphire Dr NE	CobC	1598	D1
Sapphire Lp	ClyC	2150	C3
Sapphire St	FulC	2146	D7
Sara Dr NE	CobC	1527	E4
Sarah St NW	ATLN	1889	B1
Sarah Frances Cir NE	CobC	1526	D4
Sarah M Harden Dr SW	ATLN	1975	D2
Sarahs Ln	DKbC	1745	B7
Saratoga Ct NE	CobC	1528	B7
Saratoga Dr	DKbC	1979	E1
	RSWL	1532	B5
Saratoga Pl NE	ATLN	1816	D1
Saratoga Rd	RSWL	1530	D1
Sardis Wy NE	ATLN	1742	A6
Saren Ct	DKbC	1745	B5
Sargent Av SE	ATLN	1978	A1
	DKbC	1978	A1
Sargent Dr SE	ATLN	1977	A6
Sargent Pl SE	ATLN	1977	A6
Sargent St	FTPK	2149	C2
Sarnia Ln SW	ATLN	1887	E3
Sarr Pkwy	DKbC	1745	E7
Sasanqua Ct	DKbC	1745	E6
Sassafras Ln	RSWL	1532	A5
Sassafras Rd	RSWL	1532	A6
Satellite Blvd	DKbC	1978	E7
	DKbC	2064	E1
Satellite Ter	DKbC	1978	E7
Satellite Wy	DKbC	1978	E7
Satinwood Dr	RSWL	1532	B7
	RSWL	1601	B1
N Satinwood Pl	RSWL	1532	A2
S Satinwood Pl	RSWL	1532	A2
Satisfaction Wy	DKbC	1818	B4
Saturn Ct NW	GwnC	1602	E3
Saturn Dr	DKbC	1818	B4
Saturn Dr NW	ATLN	1888	A1
Saul Dr	HryC	2065	D6
Saunders St NE	ATLN	1892	B4
Sautee Tr	DKbC	2064	C2
Savannah Ct SE	CobC	1739	A4
Savannah Sq E	DKbC	1673	B7
Savannah Sq W	DKbC	1673	B7
Savannah St SE	ATLN	1891	B4
Savannah Estates Dr	FulC	1601	B3
Savey Dr	ClyC	2150	B5
	MRRW	2150	B5
W Savey Dr	MRRW	2150	A5
Savoy Dr	DKbC	1671	D2
Sawmill Ter NE	CobC	1528	C1
Sawtell Av SE	ATLN	1977	A3
Sawtell Av SE SR-54 CONN	ATLN	1977	A3
Sawtooth Cir	FulC	1532	C6
Sawyer Rd NE	MRTA	1526	C7
Saxon Pl NE	DKbC	1742	E7
Saxon Wy NE	CobC	1528	C7
Saxon Valley Cir NE	DKbC	1742	E7
Saxony Gln NE	CobC	1527	E1
Saxony Ln	FulC	1533	A1
Saxony Sq	DKbC	1819	E2
Saybrook Ct NE	CobC	1596	C3
Saybrook Dr NE	DKbC	1671	A7
Sayers St SW	ATLN	1975	E3
Scarborough Ct	HryC	2066	E6
Scarborough Ct SE	CobC	1597	B5
Scarborough Rd	DKbC	2066	D7
	FulC	2059	B7
	FulC	2145	A1
	HryC	2152	E1
Scarborough Wy	FulC	1532	E2
Scarlet Oak Ct	DRVL	1672	E3
Scarlet Oak Dr	DRVL	1672	E3
Scarlet O'Hara Dr	DKbC	2066	C5
Scarsdale Dr	ClyC	2148	D6
Scenic Dr	EPNT	2060	D3
Scenic Ter	EPNT	2060	D3
Scenic View Ct SE	CobC	1740	A2
Scenic View Dr SE	CobC	1740	A2
Schoel Dr	DKbC	1818	A4
Schoen St SE	ATLN	1977	A4
School Dr	DRVL	1672	B4
	FTPK	2149	B3
School Dr SE	ATLN	2063	A1
School Ln	LKCY	2149	C3
School Pl SW	ATLN	1889	D4
School St	CMBL	1671	D5
Schooner Cir NW	FulC	1598	D6
Schuyler Av SE	ATLN	1977	B1
Scientific Dr NW	GwnC	1602	D3
Sciple Ter NW	ATLN	1890	B3
Scofield Pl	DKbC	1894	D1
Scofield Rd	CGPK	2147	A2
	FulC	2147	A2
Scotland Pl NW	ATLN	1814	D1
Scotney Glen Cir	FulC	1532	C2
Scott Blvd	DCTR	1817	D7
	DKbC	1817	D7
	FTPK	2063	A7
Scott Blvd SR-8	DCTR	1817	D7
	DKbC	1817	D7
Scott Blvd SR-410	DCTR	1817	D7
	DKbC	1817	D7
Scott Blvd US-23	DCTR	1817	D7
	DKbC	1892	D1
Scott Blvd US-29	DCTR	1817	D7
	DKbC	1817	D7
Scott Blvd US-78	DCTR	1817	D7
	DKbC	1817	D7
Scott Cir	DKbC	1817	E4
	EPNT	2060	B6
Scott Cir SE	MRTA	1596	B5
Scott Coms	DKbC	1818	A6
Scott Cross	RSWL	1531	E3
Scott Ct SE	SMYR	1667	B7
Scott Dr	ClyC	2063	D5
Scott Dr SE	MRTA	1596	B5
Scott Ln	HryC	2152	C1
Scott Rd	FTPK	2063	B5
	RSWL	1531	E4
	RSWL	1532	B4
Scott Rd NE	CobC	1526	C1
Scott St NW	ATLN	1889	E3
	ATLN	1890	E2
Scott St SW	ATLN	1888	B4
	ATLN	1976	C4
Scottdale Rd	DKbC	1818	C5
Scottie Ln SW	CobC	1666	A7
Scottish Mill Run NE	CobC	1596	E3
Scottish Mill Wy NE	CobC	1596	E2
Scottridge Dr NW	ATLN	1889	A3
Scotts Pkwy NE	CobC	1527	D5
Scott Valley Rd NW	FulC	1598	D7
Scotty Cir	DKbC	1978	E1
Scout St	HPVL	2062	C3
Screven St NE	ATLN	1891	D4
Scribner Ct NE	CobC	1529	B5
Scruggs Ct NE	ATLN	1892	A4
Scufflegrit Rd NE	CobC	1527	A7
	MRTA	1527	A7
Scyler Pl	DKbC	1673	D7
Scyler Wy	DKbC	1673	E7
Seabass Rd	DKbC	2065	C1
Seaboard Av NE	ATLN	1891	D3
Seaboard Av NW	ATLN	1815	A3
Seaboard Pl NW	ATLN	1815	A3
Seaboard Industrial Blvd NW	ATLN	1814	E3
Seaborn Pl	ClyC	2147	D2
Seaborn Rd NW	ATLN	1888	D1
Sea Holly Cir	RSWL	1531	D3
Seal Pl NE	ATLN	1816	B7
Seaman Cir	DKbC	1671	D3
Seaman Wy	DKbC	1671	E3
Seamarsh Ct NW	FulC	1598	C7
Sean Wy NE	CobC	1527	A2
Seasons Pkwy NW	GwnC	1673	C4
Seaton Dr	DKbC	1600	E4
Seaton Wy	DKbC	1600	E4
Seatton Ct NE	CobC	1527	D2
Seavey Dr	DKbC	1893	C7
	DKbC	1979	C1
Seay Av SE	CobC	1666	A3
Sebring Ct	DKbC	1980	E5
Sebring Wk	DKbC	1980	E5
Secluded Pines Dr NE	CobC	1598	C2
Secretariat Ct	DKbC	1980	C4
Sedalia Ct SE	CobC	1596	C5
Sedberry Hill Ct SE	CobC	1739	E5
Sedgefield Rd NE	MRTA	1595	D1
Sedgewick Pl NE	CobC	1529	A2
Seine Ct	FulC	1532	C5
Selig Dr SW	FulC	1887	B4
Selkirk Dr NE	FulC	1599	A4
Sells Av SW	ATLN	1889	D5
	ATLN	1890	A5
Selman St SE	ATLN	1891	C4
Selwin Av SW	ATLN	1975	E1
Selwyn Dr	DKbC	1894	D7
Seminole Av NE	ATLN	1891	D2
Seminole Dr NE	MRTA	1595	B3
Seminole Pl NE	MRTA	1595	C3
Seminole Rd	DKbC	2065	C3
Semmes St	EPNT	1975	C5
	EPNT	2061	C1
Semra St SW	FulC	1887	A6
Seneca Ct SE	SMYR	1739	B2
Seneca St	DCTR	1817	E7
Seneca Wy	DKbC	1894	D3
Sentinae Chase Dr	RSWL	1531	D6
Sentinae Close	FulC	1601	A2
Sentinel Pl NE	CobC	1597	D5
Sentinel Vw NW	ATLN	1740	D1
Sentinel Post Rd NW	ATLN	1740	D1
Sentry Cross NE	CobC	1597	D2
Sentry Dr	DKbC	1745	E7
Sentry Wk NE	CobC	1597	D2
Sentry Hill Tr NE	FulC	1599	B7
September Chase	DKbC	1817	E1
September Eve NW	GwnC	1601	D6
September Morn NW	GwnC	1601	E5
Sequoia Dr	FTPK	2149	C4
Sequoia Dr NE	MRTA	1595	B2
Sequoyah Dr NW	ATLN	1740	D7
Serendipity Wy	FulC	1530	E5
Serpentine Dr NE	DKbC	1744	D5
Serramonte Dr NE	CobC	1598	C3
Service Rd	ClyC	2062	D5
S Service Rd	CobC	1887	A1
N Sessions St NW	MRTA	1595	A3
Sessions St NE	MRTA	1595	A3
Sessions St NW	MRTA	1595	A3
Seton Hall Dr	DKbC	2066	B1
Seton Hall Wy	DKbC	2066	B1
Settendown Tr SE	CobC	1738	A6
Settle Cir SE	DKbC	1892	B7
Settlement Ln	DKbC	1819	C4
Settlement Rd	DKbC	1819	A1
Settlement Rd SE	CobC	1739	E6
Settlers Ct SE	CobC	1597	D5
Seven Hills Ct	DKbC	1894	D1
Seven Hills Tr	DKbC	1894	C1
Seven Oaks Cir	DKbC	2064	E2
Seven Oaks Ct	DKbC	2064	E2
Seven Oaks Dr NW	GwnC	1673	D5
Seven Oaks Ln	EPNT	2060	C5
Seven Pines Ct SE	CobC	1739	E2
Seven Pines Ln SE	CobC	1739	E2
Seven Springs Cir NE	CobC	1528	D6
Seventeenth Fairway	RSWL	1532	B7
Seville Dr	DKbC	1818	E3
Seville Wy	EPNT	2060	B6
Seville Chase NW	FulC	1598	E5
Sewage Plant Service Rd	DKbC	2066	D2
Sewanee Av NW	ATLN	1889	A4
Sewell Ln NE	CobC	1596	C5
Sewell Mill Rd NE	CobC	1527	D7
Sewell Park Dr NE	CobC	1596	C5
Sexton Woods Dr	CMBL	1671	D5
	DKbC	1671	D5
Shabromat Wy	DKbC	1745	A1
Shade Dr	ClyC	2150	E5
Shadecrest Dr NE	DKbC	1743	C1
Shaded Oaks Ln SE	MRTA	1596	B5
Shadow Bnd	DKbC	1600	B7
Shadow Ct	DKbC	1600	C7
Shadow Ln NE	DKbC	1671	B5
Shadow Bluff Ct N	CobC	1527	E5
Shadow Bluff Ct S	CobC	1527	E5
Shadow Bluff Dr NE	CobC	1527	D5
Shadowbrook Ct	RSWL	1530	E2
Shadowbrook Dr	DKbC	1980	D3
	RSWL	1530	E2
Shadowbrook Dr NE	MRTA	1596	A3
Shadowbrook Pl	DKbC	1980	C3
Shadow Creek Chase	RSWL	1532	A4
Shadow Glen Ct	DKbC	1600	D5
Shadowlake Ct SE	CobC	1597	C6
Shadowlake Ln SE	CobC	1597	C5
E Shadowlawn Av NE	ATLN	1742	A6
W Shadowlawn Av NE	ATLN	1742	A5
Shadowlawn Rd SE	CobC	1597	C6
Shadow Ledge Ln	RSWL	1532	B7
Shadowmoor Dr	DCTR	1893	A2
Shadowood Ct	RSWL	1530	E1
Shadowood Dr NE	CobC	1527	C1
Shadowood Ln NE	CobC	1527	A1
Shadowood Pkwy SE	CobC	1668	B5
Shadow Park Dr NW	GwnC	1673	C1
Shadow Pine Dr	RSWL	1532	B2
Shadowridge Dr SE	ATLN	1891	E7
	DKbC	1891	E7
	DKbC	1977	E1
Shadowrock Ct NE	CobC	1596	A1
Shadowrock Dr NE	CobC	1596	A1
Shadowrock Hts NE	CobC	1596	A1
Shadow Walk Ln	DKbC	1673	D7
Shadow Woods Cir NE	CobC	1527	E5
Shadow Woods Pl NE	CobC	1527	E5
Shady Ln	ClyC	2149	A5
	DKbC	1745	C5
Shadybrook Dr NE	CobC	1526	D5
Shadybrook Ln SW	FulC	1887	B6
Shady Creek Ln NE	CobC	1528	C2
Shadydale Av SE	ATLN	1976	E4
Shadydale Ln	DKbC	1818	A4
Shady Hill Rd NE	CobC	1529	B6
Shady Ln Cir	ClyC	2149	A5
Shady Ln Dr SE	CobC	1739	D4
Shady Ln Wy	FTPK	2063	D6
Shady Oak Ct	DRVL	1672	E3
Shady Oak Dr	DRVL	1672	E3
Shady Pine Ter	HryC	2065	B5
Shady River Trc	RSWL	1531	D6
Shady Shoals Ct	DKbC	1979	A3
Shady Valley Dr NE	ATLN	1742	D7
	ATLN	1816	D1
	DKbC	1742	D7
Shady Valley Pl NE	DKbC	1742	D7
Shagbark Ct SE	CobC	1596	E7
Shaker Hllw	FulC	1532	C6
Shalimar Dr NE	DKbC	1743	D4
Shallowford Pl	CMBL	1744	A1
	DKbC	1744	A1
Shallowford Rd	RSWL	1529	D1
N Shallowford Rd	DKbC	1671	E2
	DKbC	1672	A3
Shallowford Rd NE	CMBL	1672	B7
	CMBL	1744	A3
	CobC	1528	D1
	CobC	1529	A1
	DKbC	1672	B7
	DKbC	1744	A3
	DRVL	1672	B7
	RSWL	1529	A1
Shallowford Ter	CMBL	1744	A1
	DKbC	1744	A1
Shamrock Cir SW	ATLN	1888	C6
Shamrock Ct	DKbC	1893	E7
	DKbC	1979	E1
Shamrock Dr	DKbC	1893	E7
	DKbC	1979	E1
Shamrock Tr SE	CobC	1739	A4
	SMYR	1739	A4
Shamrock Cove	ClyC	2150	D6
Shancey Ln	FulC	2147	A3
Shandra Wy	FulC	2145	D6
Shane Ct	DKbC	2066	C2
Shane Tr	DKbC	2066	C2
Shannon Blvd	UNCT	2145	C7
Shannon Ct	UNCT	2145	B6
Shannon Dr NE	CobC	1526	C1
Shannon Dr SW	ATLN	1976	C2
Shannon Pkwy	UNCT	2145	B7
Shannon Ridge Ct	DKbC	1893	D7

INDEX 54

Shanter Tr SW — Soaring Tr NE

Atlanta Street Index

STREET	City	Map #	Grid
Shanter Tr SW	FulC	1974	B1
Shared Dr NE	FulC	1670	B7
	FulC	1742	C1
Shareese Ct SE	CobC	1597	C5
Sharon Cir SE	SMYR	1738	D2
Sharon St	FTPK	2149	B3
Sharon St NW	ATLN	1889	D4
Sharon Wy	DKbC	1979	C1
Sharondale Cir NE	ATLN	1816	B1
Sharondale Ct NE	ATLN	1816	A1
Sharondale Dr NE	ATLN	1816	A1
Sharonton Dr	DKbC	1894	E3
Sharonton Wy	DKbC	1894	E3
Sharon Valley Ct	DKbC	1601	A7
Sharp Mountain Cr SE	CobC	1597	C7
	CobC	1668	C1
Sharpsburg Ct	DKbC	1979	A4
Shasta Wy NE	CobC	1529	D4
	DKbC	1744	C4
E Shaw Ct NE	CobC	1527	A3
W Shaw Ct NE	CobC	1527	A2
Shaw Dr NE	CobC	1527	A3
Shaw Rd NE	CobC	1527	A2
Shaw St SW	ATLN	1976	D3
Shawn Ct NW	GwnC	1533	B7
Shawn Ter NW	GwnC	1533	B6
Shawnee Ln NE	DKbC	1671	A3
Shawnee Pl SE	SMYR	1739	B1
Shawnee Tr SE	CobC	1596	C5
	SMYR	1739	A2
Shawn Wayne Ct SE	DKbC	1978	D1
Shaw Park Rd NE	CobC	1526	D1
Sheba Dr	ClyC	2151	C3
Sheepberry Ct	DKbC	1980	D7
	DKbC	2066	E1
Sheffield Dr NE	DKbC	1817	A2
Sheffield Dr SW	ATLN	1888	D4
Sheffield Pkwy NE	CobC	1527	B7
Sheffield Pl	DKbC	1745	B7
Sheffield Rd NW	NRCS	1673	E1
Sheffield Glen Wy NE	DKbC	1817	A2
Sheila Ln NE	CobC	1596	E1
Shelborne Dr	DKbC	1672	B1
Shelburn Dr	ClyC	2148	D6
Shelburne Rdg NE	CobC	1529	C5
Shelburne Cove NE	CobC	1529	C6
Shelby Ln NE	CobC	1528	C2
Shelby Pl SE	ATLN	1977	D1
Sheldon Ct	ClyC	2147	B4
Sheldon Dr NE	ATLN	1742	A3
Shelia Robin Tr NE	CobC	1527	B1
Shell Rd SE	ATLN	1976	E5
Shelley Ct NE	CobC	1527	E6
Shelley Ln	ClyC	2150	E6
Shellnut Dr	FTPK	2149	B4
Shelly Dr SW	ATLN	1888	D5
Shelton Av SW	ATLN	1890	B7
Shelton St SE	ATLN	1891	B4
Shenandoah Av NE	ATLN	1816	A2
Shenandoah Valley Dr NE	DKbC	1744	D3
Shenandoah Valley Ln SE	SMYR	1667	B7
Shenfield Dr	FulC	2145	E6
	UNCT	2145	E6
Shenfield Ln	FulC	2145	E6
Shepherd Cir SW	ATLN	1975	C4
	EPNT	1975	C4
Shepherds Ln NE	DKbC	1816	E3
Shepherds Pth	DKbC	1980	B7
Sheppard Dr	ClyC	2064	A6
Sheppard Pl NE	ATLN	1892	A3
Sheppard Crook	DKbC	1819	E7
Sheppard Crossing Ct	DKbC	1819	E7
Sheppard Crossing Wy	DKbC	1819	E7
Sheraton Wy SE	CobC	1812	A4
Sheraton Wy SW	CobC	1812	A3
Sherborne Chase NE	CobC	1528	B6
Sherbrooke Ct NE	DKbC	1744	B4
Sherbrooke Dr NE	DKbC	1744	A3
Sherbrooke Wy SW	ATLN	2060	A1
Sheridan Dr NE	ATLN	1741	E7
Sheridan Ln	DKbC	1600	E5
Sheridan Pk NE	DKbC	1816	E1
Sheridan Rd NE	ATLN	1816	D2
	DKbC	1816	D2
Sheridan Wk NE	DKbC	1816	E2
Sheridan Chase SE	CobC	1597	C5
Sheridan Point Ln NE	FulC	1670	B4
Sheriff Rd	FulC	2147	A5
Sherifield Dr NE	CobC	1598	C2
Sheringham Ct	RSWL	1532	A1
Sheringham Dr	RSWL	1532	A2
Sherington Pl	FulC	1601	A1
Sherlock Dr	DKbC	1978	E3
Sherlock Dr NE	CobC	1526	E1
Sherman Rd	HPVL	2062	C3
Sherman Wy	DKbC	1817	E6
Sherrell Dr NE	FulC	1670	B4
Sherrie Ln SW	ATLN	1973	C4
Sherrydale Ln	DKbC	1894	A5
Sherwood Av	DKbC	1894	D7
Sherwood Cir	FTPK	2149	C4
Sherwood Dr SE	CobC	1596	C6
Sherwood Ln SE	CobC	1598	B5
Sherwood Pl	ClyC	2150	D5
S Sherwood Rd SE	SMYR	1738	C2
Sherwood Rd NE	ATLN	1816	B5
Sherwood Rd SE	SMYR	1666	C7
Sherwood St SE	ATLN	1891	D5
Sherwood Oaks Ct	DKbC	1980	D5
Sherwood Oaks Dr	DKbC	1980	D6
Sherwood Oaks Ln	DKbC	1980	D5
Sherwood Oaks Wy	DKbC	1980	E5
Sheryl Dr	DKbC	1979	B1
Shetland Dr	DKbC	1818	B2
Shieldcrest Wy	ClyC	2063	C4
Shillingford Ct SE	CobC	1597	A7
Shiloh Dr	DKbC	1979	A4
Shining Armor Dr	ClyC	2064	A5
Shirley Ct	FTPK	2149	D5
Shirley Dr	MRRW	2149	E6
Shirley Dr SW	FulC	1887	D2
Shirley Pl NW	ATLN	1889	B4
Shirley St SE	SMYR	1738	D2
Shirley St SW	ATLN	1889	B7
Shirley Wy SW	FulC	1887	E3
Shiver Smt NE	FulC	1670	C4
Shoal Creek Rd	DKbC	1979	E4
Shoals Ct	ClyC	2148	A4
	DKbC	1979	B3
Shoals Ter	DKbC	1979	A3
Shoals Wy	DKbC	1978	E3
Shoals Creek Dr	FulC	2146	D6
Shoemaker Ct	HryC	2152	D1
N Shore Ct	RSWL	1530	E3
S Shore Ct	RSWL	1531	B5
N Shore Dr	RSWL	1531	B4
N Shore Dr SW	ATLN	1888	D7
	ATLN	1974	D1
Shore Dr SE	MRTA	1595	D5
Shore Dr SW	ATLN	1974	D1
S Shore Pl	RSWL	1531	C5
Shoreham Dr	ClyC	2147	E3
Shorelake Dr	DKbC	1673	D6
Shoreland Dr SW	ATLN	1973	C7
	CobC	1973	C7
Shoreline Wk	FulC	1532	E2
Short Av	EPNT	1975	C7
Short St	CobC	1595	B7
Short St SE	ATLN	1891	C4
	DKbC	1892	A7
Shorter Ter NW	ATLN	1888	C1
Shorter Wy	DKbC	2066	D1
Shortleaf Dr	FTPK	2149	D6
Shoshonee Tr	FulC	2060	B7
Shoshone Valley Rd NE	CobC	1597	E1
Shoup Ct	DKbC	1817	D5
Showcase Wy NE	CobC	1529	A2
Shurburne Dr	RSWL	1532	C5
Sibley St NE	MRTA	1595	D4
Sibley Forest Dr SE	CobC	1597	C7
Sibley Mill Ct SE	CobC	1668	B1
E Side Dr	DKbC	1980	E3
W Side Dr	RSWL	1530	B4
W Side Pl	DKbC	1978	B6
	DKbC	2064	C1
Sidestreet	DKbC	1671	C4
Sidestreet Cir	DKbC	1671	C4
Sidestreet Ct	DKbC	1671	C4
Sidis Ct	DKbC	1673	C7
Sidney Marcus Blvd	ATLN	1816	D1
Sidney Marcus Blvd NE	ATLN	1816	B1
Sienna Ct NW	GwnC	1601	E5
Sierra Dr	FTPK	2063	B6
Sierra Dr NE	CobC	1527	B5
Siesta Ct NE	CobC	1527	D7
Siesta Ln NE	CobC	1527	D7
Siloam Av SE	ATLN	1891	D6
Silva Ct	DKbC	2064	E3
Silva Dr	DKbC	2064	E3
Silva Wy	DKbC	2064	D3
Silvapine Tr NE	DKbC	1744	D5
Silvastone Dr	DKbC	1744	C6
Silvastone Dr NE	DKbC	1744	D6
Silver Ln NE	FulC	1670	B3
Silverdale Rd	FulC	2060	C7
	FulC	2146	C1
Silver Lace Ct NE	DKbC	1744	B3
Silver Lake Dr NE	DKbC	1671	A7
Silver Mine Cross SE	CobC	1812	A7
Silver Mine Ct	CobC	1812	A7
Silver Mine Tr SE	CobC	1812	A7
Silver Mine Pass	CobC	1812	A7
Silver Mist Cir	FulC	1533	B1
Silver Petal Wy	ClyC	2147	D5
Silver Pine Tr	RSWL	1531	E4
Silver Queen Rd	ClyC	2150	E5
Silversmith Ct NE	CobC	1529	A3
Silver Springs Cir SW	ATLN	1889	A5
Silver Springs Ct	DKbC	2066	C1
Silverstone Ct NE	CobC	1529	A1
Silverwood Dr	ClyC	2148	A4
Silverwood Rd NE	FulC	1669	E5
Simca St SE	ATLN	2063	A2
Simcoe Cir NE	CobC	1529	C4
Simmons Cir	GwnC	1672	E2
Simmons Dr	CGPK	2061	B3
Simmons St NW	ATLN	1890	A1
Simmons Wy	HryC	2066	A6
Simms Dr NE	MRTA	1526	D7
Simon St SE	ATLN	2063	A3
E Simon Ter NW	ATLN	1888	E3
W Simon Ter NW	ATLN	1888	E3
Simon Ter NW	ATLN	1888	E3
Simpson Dr	DKbC	1744	E7
Simpson Rd	ClyC	2063	D7
	FTPK	2063	D7
Simpson Rd NW	ATLN	1889	D2
Simpson Rd SE	CobC	1739	C3
Simpson St	ATLN	1890	C2
Simpson St NW	ATLN	1890	D3
Simpson Ter NW	ATLN	1889	C2
Simpson Farm Dr SE	CobC	1739	D3
Simpson Farm Wy SE	CobC	1739	D2
Sims Av NW	ATLN	1814	B7
Sims Cir NE	ATLN	1742	A6
Sims Ct	CGPK	2061	A4
Sims Rd	DKbC	2066	A4
Sims St	HPVL	2062	B2
Sims St SW	ATLN	1890	C7
	ATLN	1976	C1
Simsbury Ln	DKbC	1671	D1
Sinclair Av NE	ATLN	1891	D2
Sinclair Pl	ClyC	2150	D7
Sioux Pth SE	SMYR	1739	B2
Sioux Wy	DKbC	1894	D3
Sir Henry St	EPNT	2060	C2
Sirocco Ct	ClyC	2149	B3
Sirron Ct	DKbC	1600	B7
Sir Walter Ct SE	CobC	1738	B6
Sisk St NW	ATLN	1814	A7
Sisson Av NE	ATLN	1892	C3
Sister Ln	ClyC	2147	B5
Six Branches Ct	RSWL	1531	D3
Six Branches Dr	RSWL	1531	D4
Six Branches Ln	RSWL	1531	E4
Six Flags Dr SW	CobC	1887	A1
Six Flags Pkwy SE	CobC	1812	B7
Six Flags Pkwy SW	CobC	1812	A7
Six Flags Wy SW	CobC	1887	A2
Six Oaks Ct	DKbC	1979	D7
Sizemore Av NW	ATLN	1814	A6
Skidmore Ct	DKbC	2066	C2
Skidmore Dr	DKbC	2066	C2
Skin Alley St NW	NRCS	1602	B7
Skipper Dr NW	ATLN	1813	C7
Skipper Pl NW	ATLN	1813	C7
Sky Haven Rd SE	ATLN	1977	D1
	DKbC	1977	D1
Skyland Ct NW	GwnC	1673	C3
Skyland Dr	FTPK	2149	C4
	RSWL	1530	B4
Skyland Dr NE	ATLN	1742	B1
	CMBL	1743	C1
	DKbC	1743	C3
Skyland Rd NE	DKbC	1743	C3
Skyland Ter NE	DKbC	1743	C3
Skyland Tr NE	DKbC	1743	C3
Skyland Trc	RSWL	1530	B3
Skyland Wy NE	DKbC	1743	C3
Skylane Dr NE	CobC	1527	E7
Skylark Dr	DKbC	1818	D2
	MRRW	2149	D6
Skyline Dr	CGPK	2060	E5
	ClyC	2151	D7
Skyline Pl	ClyC	2151	D7
Skyline Tr	CobC	1739	D3
Skyridge Ct NE	CobC	1528	D2
Skyridge Dr	FulC	1600	C1
Skyridge Tr	FulC	1600	D1
Sky View Dr NE	MRTA	1595	C4
Skyview Ln NE	CobC	1526	E1
Slane Trc	RSWL	1531	D6
Slash Pine Rd	FTPK	2149	C5
Slate Rd	ClyC	2064	B7
Slater Mill Ct NE	CobC	1596	E3
Slaton Dr NW	ATLN	1741	E6
Slaton St	FTPK	2063	C7
Sleeping Fawn Knl	DKbC	1979	E7
Sleepy Hllw	ClyC	2150	D7
Sleepy Ln SE	SMYR	1739	C1
Sloan Cir SE	ATLN	1977	C2
Sloan Pl NE	DKbC	1817	A3
Sloan Rd NE	CobC	1526	C4
Sloan Sq NE	DKbC	1817	A3
Sloan St	RSWL	1530	C3
Sloans Wy NE	CobC	1527	D2
Sloop Wy	FulC	2060	A5
Slopewood Bnd NE	CobC	1527	C6
Slumber Tr	DKbC	1980	C4
N Smead Ct	RSWL	1531	E6
S Smead Ct	RSWL	1531	D6
Smith Rd	FulC	2146	B4
Smith St	CLKN	1819	A4
W Smith St	CLKN	1819	B3
Smith St NW	ATLN	1813	E3
Smith St SE	ATLN	1978	A1
	DKbC	1978	A1
Smith St SW	ATLN	1890	C6
	ATLN	1976	C1
Smithdun Ln	FulC	1599	E1
Smithfield Ct SE	SMYR	1738	E3
Smithfield Dr	DKbC	1745	D6
Smithpointe Dr NW	GwnC	1602	D4
Smithson Creek Dr	DKbC	2066	E3
Smithsonia Ct	DKbC	1745	E2
Smithsonia Dr	DKbC	1745	E2
Smithsonia Wy	DKbC	1745	E2
Smithstone Ct SE	CobC	1596	E7
Smithstone Rd SE	CobC	1596	E7
Smithstone Trc SE	CobC	1596	E7
Smithstone Wy SE	CobC	1596	E6
Smithwood Dr NE	CobC	1527	C7
Smokecreek Ct NE	DKbC	1744	D2
Smokeridge Ct NE	CobC	1528	D1
Smokerise Cir SE	CobC	1668	A2
Smoke Rise Ct NE	CobC	1529	B4
Smoke Rise Ln NE	CobC	1529	A4
Smoke Stone Cir NE	CobC	1529	A4
Smoke Stone Ct NE	CobC	1529	A5
Smokestone Ct NE	DKbC	1744	D2
Smoketree Ct NE	DKbC	1744	E3
Smoketree Rd NE	DKbC	1744	D3
Smoketree Wy NE	DKbC	1744	E3
Smyrna Hill Dr SE	SMYR	1738	C2
Smyrna Powder Springs Rd SE	CobC	1666	A6
	SMYR	1666	A6
Smyrna Powder Springs Rd SW	CobC	1666	A7
Snake Ct	ClyC	2150	D4
Snapfinger Cir	DKbC	1980	C2
Snapfinger Pkwy	DKbC	1980	C2
Snapfinger Rd	DKbC	1894	A7
	DKbC	1980	D3
Snapfinger Wy	DKbC	1980	C2
Snapfinger Woods Dr	DKbC	1980	E3
Snow Rd SW	ATLN	1889	B7
Snowmass Tr NE	CobC	1529	A2
Snug Hbr NE	CobC	1526	E5
	MRTA	1526	E5
Snug Harbor Ct NE	CobC	1526	E5
Snyder St NW	ATLN	1815	C7
Soapstone Ct	DKbC	2065	C1
Soapstone Rd	DKbC	2065	C1
Soaring Cir NE	MRTA	1596	A2
Soaring Dr NE	CobC	1596	A2
	MRTA	1596	A2
Soaring Rdg NE	MRTA	1596	A1
Soaring Tr NE	CobC	1596	A1
	MRTA	1596	A1

Atlanta Street Index

INDEX 56

SR-3 Cobb Pkwy NW — Atlanta Street Index — Stanford Wy

Atlanta Street Index

STREET	City	Map #	Grid
SR-3 Cobb Pkwy NW	CobC	1595	A1
SR-3 Cobb Pkwy SE	CobC	1667	A1
	CobC	1668	B7
	CobC	1740	B1
	MRTA	1595	E5
	MRTA	1667	A1
	SMYR	1667	D5
SR-3 Crown Rd SE	ATLN	2062	D4
SR-3 Dogwood Dr	HPVL	2062	B1
SR-3 Metropolitan Pkwy SW	ATLN	1890	C7
	ATLN	1976	C2
	ATLN	2062	B2
SR-3 Northside Dr NW	ATLN	1741	C7
	ATLN	1815	C2
	ATLN	1890	C1
SR-3 Northside Dr SW	ATLN	1890	C6
SR-3 Northside Pkwy NW	ATLN	1740	E5
	ATLN	1741	B6
	CobC	1740	B2
SR-3 Old Dixie Rd	ClyC	2062	E7
	ClyC	2149	A5
	FTPK	2062	E7
	FTPK	2148	E1
SR-3 Ralph D Abernathy Frwy	ATLN	1890	C6
SR-3 Tara Blvd	ClyC	2149	B7
SR-5	CobC	1526	A6
	CobC	1595	B6
	MRTA	1526	A6
SR-5 Atlanta St SE	CobC	1595	B6
	MRTA	1595	B6
SR-5 Austell Rd SE	CobC	1666	A2
SR-5 Austell Rd SW	CobC	1666	A3
SR-5 SPUR Canton Rd NE	CobC	1526	C6
SR-5 Canton Road Connector NE	CobC	1595	A1
	MRTA	1526	B7
SR-5 SPUR Canton Road Conn NE	CobC	1526	D5
	MRTA	1526	D5
SR-5 Cherokee St NE	MRTA	1595	B3
SR-5 Church St NE	MRTA	1595	A3
SR-5 S Cobb Dr SE	CobC	1595	B7
	CobC	1666	A2
SR-5 W Dixie Av SE	MRTA	1595	B6
SR-5 Larry McDonald Mem Hwy	CobC	1526	A6
	MRTA	1526	A6
SR-5 N Marietta Pkwy NE	MRTA	1595	A4
SR-5 N Marietta Pkwy NW	MRTA	1595	A5
SR-5 S Marietta Pkwy SE	MRTA	1595	A5
SR-5 S Marietta Pkwy SW	MRTA	1595	A5
SR-5 Pearl St SE	CobC	1595	B7
SR-8 Bankhead Hwy SE	CobC	1812	E4
SR-8 Bankhead Hwy SW	CobC	1812	A3
SR-8 D L Hollowell Pkwy NW	ATLN	1813	D7
SR-8 Juniper St NE	ATLN	1890	E1
SR-8 Lawrenceville Hwy	DKbC	1745	E4
	DKbC	1818	B5
	DKbC	1819	A1
SR-8 North Av NE	ATLN	1890	E1
SR-8 North Av NW	ATLN	1890	C2
SR-8 Northside Dr NW	ATLN	1890	D1
SR-8 Piedmont Av NE	ATLN	1891	A1
SR-8 Ponce de Leon Av NE	ATLN	1891	D1
	ATLN	1892	B1
	DKbC	1892	C1
SR-8 Scott Blvd	DCTR	1817	D7
	DKbC	1817	D7
SR-9 14th St NW	ATLN	1815	E6
SR-9 Alpharetta St	RSWL	1530	D1
SR-9 Atlanta St	RSWL	1530	C2
SR-9 S Atlanta St	RSWL	1530	D6
SR-9 Northside Dr NW	ATLN	1815	C7
SR-9 Peachtree Rd NE	ATLN	1742	A6
SR-9 Peachtree Rd NW	ATLN	1741	E7
	ATLN	1815	E1
SR-9 W Peachtree St NW	ATLN	1815	D6
SR-9 Peachtree St NW	ATLN	1815	E5
SR-9 Roswell Rd	FulC	1530	D7
	FulC	1599	B4
	RSWL	1530	D4
SR-9 Roswell Rd NE	ATLN	1741	E4
	ATLN	1742	A1
	FulC	1599	A7
	FulC	1670	A4
	FulC	1742	A1
SR-9 Spring St NW	ATLN	1815	E6
SR-10 N Avondale Plz	AVES	1893	D1
SR-10 N Avondale Rd	AVES	1893	E1
SR-10 E College Av	AVES	1893	A1
	DCTR	1892	E2
	DKbC	1893	A1
SR-10 W College Av	DCTR	1892	E2
SR-10 College Av NE	ATLN	1892	C2
SR-10 Covington Rd	AVES	1893	D1
	DKbC	1893	D1
SR-10 Freedom Pkwy NE	ATLN	1891	B3
SR-10 E Lake Dr	DCTR	1892	D2
	DKbC	1892	D2
SR-10 E Lake Rd NE	DKbC	1892	D2
SR-10 Memorial Dr	DKbC	1819	B7
	DKbC	1894	A1
SR-10 Mountain Dr	DKbC	1893	E1
SR-10 Park Pl	DCTR	1892	D2
SR-10 Park Pl NE	ATLN	1892	C2
	DCTR	1892	D2
SR-12 Covington Hwy	AVES	1893	E1
	DKbC	1893	E1
SR-12 Covington Rd	AVES	1893	E1
	DKbC	1893	E1
SR-13	ATLN	1815	E4
SR-13 Buford Hwy NE	ATLN	1816	D1
	CMBL	1672	A7
	CMBL	1744	A1
	DKbC	1672	B5
	DKbC	1742	E7
	DKbC	1744	A1
	DKbC	1816	D1
	DRVL	1672	B5
SR-13 Buford Hwy NW	DRVL	1672	E2
	GwnC	1602	C7
	GwnC	1672	E2
	NRCS	1602	C7
SR-13 Buford Hwy Connector NE	ATLN	1816	D1
SR-14 SPUR	CGPK	2146	B2
	FulC	2146	B2
SR-14 Roosevelt Hwy	CGPK	2060	E7
	CGPK	2146	D1
	FulC	2145	A6
	FulC	2146	D1
	UNCT	2145	A6
SR-42	ClyC	2151	A5
SR-42 CONN	ATLN	1891	D2
SR-42 Briarcliff Rd NE	ATLN	1816	E7
	DKbC	1816	E7
SR-42 N Druid Hills Rd NE	DKbC	1742	E7
	DKbC	1817	A1
SR-42 CONN E Freedom Pkwy NE	ATLN	1891	C2
SR-42 Macon Hwy	ClyC	2151	A7
SR-42 SPUR McDonough Blvd SE	ATLN	1976	E2
SR-42 Moreland Av	ClyC	2064	C6
	ClyC	2150	D1
	ClyC	2151	A6
	DKbC	2063	E1
	FTPK	2064	C6
	FTPK	2150	D1
SR-42 Moreland Av NE	ATLN	1891	D7
SR-42 Moreland Av SE	ATLN	1891	D4
	ATLN	1977	E7
	DKbC	1977	E7
	DKbC	2063	E1
SR-54 CONN	FTPK	2063	C7
SR-54 Jonesboro Rd	FTPK	2063	B4
	FTPK	2149	D1
	LKCY	2149	D1
	MRRW	2149	E6
SR-54 Jonesboro Rd SE	ATLN	1976	E2
	ATLN	2063	B1
SR-54 McDonough Blvd SE	ATLN	1976	E1
SR-54 CONN Sawtell Av SE	ATLN	1977	A3
SR-54 CONN Thurmond Rd	ClyC	2063	E5
	DKbC	2064	A3
	FTPK	2063	E5
SR-54 University Av SW	ATLN	1976	D1
SR-70 Fulton Ind Blvd NW	ATLN	1813	A6
	FulC	1813	A6
SR-70 Fulton Ind Blvd SW	ATLN	1887	C3
	FulC	1887	C3
SR-85	ClyC	2148	B5
	RVDL	2148	B5
SR-120 Alpharetta St	RSWL	1530	D1
SR-120 Atlanta St	RSWL	1530	C2
SR-120 S Atlanta St	RSWL	1530	C3
SR-120 Marietta Hwy	RSWL	1529	B6
SR-120 N Marietta Pkwy NE	CobC	1595	E3
	MRTA	1595	E3
SR-120 N Marietta Pkwy NW	MRTA	1595	A5
SR-120 S Marietta Pkwy NE	CobC	1596	B4
	MRTA	1596	B3
SR-120 S Marietta Pkwy SE	CobC	1596	B5
	MRTA	1595	C6
SR-120 S Marietta Pkwy SW	MRTA	1595	A5
SR-120 S Park Sq SE	MRTA	1595	A4
SR-120 Roswell Rd NE	CobC	1528	E7
	MRTA	1596	B4
SR-120 Roswell Rd SE	MRTA	1595	E5
SR-120 Roswell St NE	MRTA	1595	A4
SR-120 Roswell St SE	MRTA	1595	D5
SR-120 Whitlock Av NW	MRTA	1595	A4
SR-139 Best Rd	CGPK	2061	B7
SR-139 Church St	EPNT	1975	D7
SR-139 East Point St	EPNT	1975	D7
	EPNT	2061	D1
SR-139 Lee St SW	ATLN	1890	B7
	ATLN	1975	E4
SR-139 Legion Wy	EPNT	2061	D1
SR-139 Lesley Dr	CGPK	2061	A7
SR-139 Mableton Pkwy SE	CobC	1812	A6
SR-139 Mableton Pkwy SW	CobC	1812	A6
SR-139 Main St	ATLN	1975	E5
	CGPK	2061	A6
	EPNT	1975	E4
	EPNT	2061	A6
SR-139 Martin L King Jr Dr SW	ATLN	1887	E2
	ATLN	1889	D5
	FulC	1812	C7
SR-139 R D Abernathy Blvd SW	ATLN	1889	E6
SR-139 Riverdale Rd	CGPK	2061	C7
	CGPK	2147	C1
	ClyC	2147	C1
	ClyC	2148	A6
	RVDL	2148	A6
SR-139 Roosevelt Hwy	CGPK	2061	C2
SR-139 Tom Murphy Frwy SW	ATLN	1888	A2
SR-139 T Owen Smith Blvd	CGPK	2061	B7
SR-139 W Whitehall St SW	ATLN	1890	B7
SR-140 Holcomb Bridge Rd	FulC	1532	B5
	FulC	1601	D1
	RSWL	1530	E1
	RSWL	1532	B5
	RSWL	1601	D1
SR-140 Holcomb Bridge Rd NW	FulC	1601	E3
	GwnC	1602	B6
SR-140 Jimmy Carter Blvd NW	GwnC	1602	D7
	NRCS	1602	D7
SR-141 CONN Lenox Rd NE	ATLN	1742	B4
SR-141 Medlock Bridge Rd NW	GwnC	1533	E7
SR-141 Paul Duke Pkwy NW	GwnC	1601	E7
SR-141 Peachtree Pkwy NW	GwnC	1533	E7
	GwnC	1602	D2
SR-141 Peachtree Rd	CMBL	1671	C7
SR-141 Peachtree Rd NE	ATLN	1742	E4
	CMBL	1671	C7
	DKbC	1671	C7
	DKbC	1742	E4
SR-141 Peachtree Rd NW	ATLN	1742	A6
SR-141 Peachtree Ind Blvd	CMBL	1671	C7
	DKbC	1601	D7
	DKbC	1671	E4
	DRVL	1672	A3
SR-141 Peachtree Ind Blvd NW	DKbC	1601	E7
	GwnC	1602	B6
SR-154 Campbellton Rd SW	ATLN	1973	E5
	FulC	1973	A4
SR-154 Knotts Av	EPNT	1975	E5
SR-154 Langford Memorial Hwy	ATLN	1974	C5
	EPNT	1974	E5
SR-154 Lee St SW	ATLN	1890	B7
	ATLN	1975	E4
SR-154 Main St	ATLN	1975	E4
	EPNT	1975	E4
SR-154 Memorial Dr	AVES	1893	D3
	AVES	1894	A1
	DKbC	1893	D3
SR-154 Memorial Dr SE	ATLN	1890	E5
	ATLN	1891	E5
	ATLN	1893	A5
	DKbC	1892	B5
	DKbC	1893	B5
SR-154 Memorial Dr SW	ATLN	1890	E5
SR-154 Peters St SW	ATLN	1890	D4
SR-154 Trinity Av SW	ATLN	1890	C5
SR-154 W Whitehall St SW	ATLN	1890	B7
SR-154 Womack Av	EPNT	1975	E4
SR-155 Candler Rd	DKbC	1893	A6
	DKbC	1979	C1
SR-155 Candler Rd NE	ATLN	1893	A4
	DCTR	1893	A4
SR-155 Candler Rd SE	ATLN	1893	A4
	DKbC	1893	A5
SR-155 S Candler St	DCTR	1893	A4
SR-155 Clairemont Av	DCTR	1817	E7
	DKbC	1817	D6
SR-155 Clairmont Rd	DKbC	1817	D6
SR-155 Clairmont Rd NE	DKbC	1743	C5
	DKbC	1817	D1
SR-155 E College Av	DCTR	1893	A1
SR-155 Commerce Dr	DCTR	1893	A1
SR-155 Flat Shoals Pkwy	DKbC	1979	E6
SR-155 Flat Shoals Rd	DKbC	1979	C4
SR-160 Jonesboro Rd	FTPK	2149	D1
SR-166 Campbellton Rd SW	ATLN	1973	E5
	FulC	1973	A4
SR-166 Langford Memorial Hwy	ATLN	1974	C5
	EPNT	1974	E5
SR-236 Hugh Howell Rd	DKbC	1745	E4
SR-236 Lavista Rd	DKbC	1744	C7
	DKbC	1745	B5
	DKbC	1817	E1
SR-236 Lavista Rd NE	ATLN	1816	D2
	DKbC	1816	D2
	DKbC	1817	C2
SR-236 Lawrenceville Hwy	DKbC	1745	E4
SR-236 Lindbergh Dr NE	ATLN	1815	E1
SR-236 Lindbergh Wy NE	ATLN	1816	B2
SR-237 Piedmont Rd NE	ATLN	1742	B6
	ATLN	1816	B1
SR-260 Glenwood Av SE	ATLN	1891	E6
	ATLN	1892	E6
	DKbC	1892	E6
SR-260 Glenwood Rd	DKbC	1893	A6
SR-260 Ralph D Abernathy Frwy	ATLN	1892	B6
	DKbC	1892	B6
SR-279 Old National Hwy	CGPK	2060	E7
	CGPK	2146	E4
	FulC	2146	E7
	FulC	2147	A5
SR-280 S Cobb Dr SE	ATLN	1813	D2
	CobC	1595	B7
	CobC	1666	A2
	CobC	1667	A2
	CobC	1739	A5
	CobC	1813	C1
	MRTA	1667	A2
	SMYR	1666	B4
	SMYR	1738	C1
	SMYR	1813	C1
SR-280 Delk Rd SE	CobC	1667	C2
	MRTA	1667	C2
SR-280 Hightower Rd NW	ATLN	1888	E2
	ATLN	1889	A4
SR-280 James Jackson Pkwy NW	ATLN	1813	E7
SR-314 W Fayetteville Rd	CGPK	2147	C5
	ClyC	2147	C5
SR-331 Forest Pkwy	ClyC	2148	E1
	FTPK	2148	E1
	LKCY	2149	D2
SR-360 Powder Springs St SW	MRTA	1595	A6
SR-400 T Harvey Mathis Pkwy	ATLN	1742	C6
	ATLN	1816	C1
	FulC	1670	C3
SR-400 Turner McDonald Pkwy	FulC	1530	E7
	FulC	1670	C5
	RSWL	1531	C1
SR-401	ATLN	1815	E7
	ClyC	2149	B6
	CobC	1740	C1
	MRRW	2149	B6
SR-401 Horace E Tate Frwy	ATLN	1740	E6
	ATLN	1815	A3
	FulC	1740	D2
SR-401 James W George Pkwy	ATLN	1815	D7
SR-401 Larry McDonald Mem Hwy	CobC	1526	A6
	CobC	1667	D3
	CobC	1740	C1
	MRTA	1526	B7
	MRTA	1667	C1
SR-402 Purple Heart Hwy	DKbC	1980	D3
SR-402 Ralph D Abernathy Frwy	ATLN	1888	D3
	ATLN	1978	B1
	DKbC	1892	A5
	DKbC	1978	B1
SR-402 Southeast Expwy	DKbC	1980	A2
SR-402 Tom Murphy Frwy	ATLN	1887	E2
	CobC	1887	E2
SR-403	ATLN	1815	E4
	CGPK	2061	D3
	CGPK	2146	D1
	FulC	2145	D7
	UNCT	2145	D7
SR-403 James W George Pkwy	ATLN	1815	D7
SR-403 Northeast Expwy	ATLN	1815	E4
	DKbC	1672	D7
	DKbC	1742	E7
	DKbC	1816	A4
SR-403 Northeast Expwy NE	ATLN	1816	D1
SR-403 Veterans Pkwy	GwnC	1673	B4
SR-407	ATLN	1813	C2
	ATLN	1974	B2
	ATLN	2060	B2
	CGPK	2146	D1
	ClyC	2062	D7
	ClyC	2147	E1
	CobC	1667	E7
	CobC	1739	D3
	CobC	1813	C2
	DKbC	1670	E3
	DKbC	1744	E7
	DKbC	1818	E1
	DKbC	1978	E6
	DKbC	2064	A2
	DRVL	1672	A2
	EPNT	2060	B2
	FTPK	2063	B5
	FulC	1669	A3
	FulC	1888	B6
	FulC	1974	B2
	FulC	2060	C7
	FulC	2146	D1
	SMYR	1667	E7
	SMYR	1813	C2
SR-410 Lawrenceville Hwy	DKbC	1818	A5
SR-410 Ponce de Leon Av NE	DKbC	1892	C1
SR-410 Scott Blvd	DCTR	1817	D7
	DKbC	1817	D7
SR-410 William Evans Hwy	DKbC	1745	D7
	DKbC	1818	E3
Staci Ln	EPNT	2060	B6
Stacks Rd	FulC	2145	D3
Stacy Ct NE	CobC	1528	A3
Stacy Ln	ClyC	2065	B5
Stadium Ct NW	GwnC	1602	A3
Stadium Dr	CMBL	1671	D5
Staff Row SW	ATLN	1975	E2
Stafford Pl	DRVL	1672	B6
Stafford Pl NE	CobC	1528	E5
Stafford St NW	ATLN	1889	E4
Stafford St SW	ATLN	1889	E4
Stagecoach Rd	ClyC	2065	B7
	ClyC	2151	D4
	HryC	2152	A7
Stagecoach Rdg	HryC	2152	A7
Stagecoach Tr	HryC	2152	A7
Stagecoach Pass	ClyC	2151	C3
Staghorn Ct NE	CobC	1528	B1
Stalcup Dr SW	CobC	1666	A6
Stallings Av SE	ATLN	1892	A7
Stamford Rd SW	ATLN	1888	A4
Stancil Rd NE	CobC	1526	C4
Standard Dr NE	DKbC	1742	E4
Standing Rock Dr SW	FulC	1973	A4
Standish Av NW	ATLN	1815	D4
Stanford Cir	DKbC	2066	D1
Stanford Dr	ClyC	2150	D5
Stanford Dr NE	CobC	1528	E4
Stanford Wy	DKbC	1893	C5

Atlanta Street Index

STREET	City	Map #	Grid
Stanhope Cir NE	CobC	1528	D3
Stanhope Cir NW	ATLN	1889	E3
Stanley Wy SE	DKbC	1978	D4
Stanrich Ct NE	CobC	1528	A5
Stansbury Dr NE	CobC	1526	D2
Stansell Rd	FulC	2146	C1
Stanton Cir	EPNT	1975	C5
Stanton Ct	EPNT	1975	C5
Stanton Rd	EPNT	1975	C4
Stanton Rd SW	ATLN	1975	C3
Stanton St	DKbC	1893	A7
Stanton Tr NE	CobC	1528	D7
Stantondale Dr	DKbC	1672	D7
	DKbC	1744	D1
Stanwood Av SE	ATLN	1892	A4
Stanwyck Ter	DKbC	1745	C7
Stapleton Ct	DKbC	1600	D3
Stapleton Dr	DKbC	1600	D3
Stapp Dr	DKbC	1819	A1
Star Dr NE	DKbC	1742	D3
Star Ln	DKbC	1980	C3
N Star Tr SW	FulC	1973	B7
Starboard Pt	RSWL	1531	C4
Starcross Ct	DKbC	1600	E5
Stardust Cir	DKbC	1979	E3
Stardust Ct	DKbC	1980	A4
Stardust Tr	DKbC	1980	A3
Starfire Dr NE	DKbC	1744	B6
Stark Ln	DKbC	1671	D4
Starlight Cir NE	FulC	1670	C7
Starlight Ct NE	FulC	1670	C7
Starlight Dr NE	ATLN	1742	C1
	CobC	1527	C6
	FulC	1670	C7
	FulC	1742	C1
Starlight Ln NE	FulC	1670	C7
	FulC	1742	C1
Starline Dr	DKbC	1979	A1
Starline Dr SE	SMYR	1738	D2
Star Mist Dr SW	ATLN	1974	C4
E Starmount Wy	DKbC	1892	E7
W Starmount Wy	DKbC	1892	E7
Starvine Wy	DKbC	1817	D5
State St	ClyC	2150	A5
	MRRW	2150	A5
State St NW	ATLN	1815	D7
	ATLN	1890	D1
State Bridge Rd	FulC	1533	E1
Statewood Rd NE	ATLN	1742	B2
Station Mill Ct NW	GwnC	1601	E2
Station Mill Dr NW	GwnC	1601	E2
Staunton Dr SE	CobC	1596	E7
Staverly Ln NW	GwnC	1533	D5
Steel Dr	DKbC	1745	B5
Steele Av SW	ATLN	1976	D7
Steele Dr NW	ATLN	1815	C5
Steele Rd	ClyC	2151	D1
Steeplechase Dr	RSWL	1532	A6
Steeplechase Ln	RSWL	1531	E7
	RVDL	2148	A7
Steeple Gate Ln	RSWL	1532	A6
Steeple Point Dr	RSWL	1532	A7
Steepleridge Ct	RVDL	2148	A6
Stella Dr NW	ATLN	1741	D1
	FulC	1669	D7
	FulC	1741	D1
Stella Burns Dr	DKbC	1745	E3
Stephanie Dr SW	ATLN	2059	D1
Stephen Long Dr NE	ATLN	1816	A2
Stephens Ct	DKbC	1745	C5
Stephens Dr NE	DKbC	1817	A3
Stephens St	DKbC	1745	C4
Stephens St NW	ATLN	1814	A4
Stephens St SE	SMYR	1666	D7
Stephens St SW	ATLN	1890	C6
Stephens Wk	DKbC	1600	E5
Stephens Lake Rd	FTPK	2150	B1
Stephens Mill Run NE	ATLN	1742	A3
Stepney Ct SE	CobC	1596	D7
Sterling Rd NE	CobC	1526	D5
Sterling St	DCTR	1892	E3
Sterling St NE	ATLN	1891	E2
Sterling St SE	ATLN	1977	A4
Sterling Forest Dr	DKbC	1980	E4
Sterling Ridge Ct	DKbC	1980	B1
Sterling Ridge Rd	DKbC	1980	B1
Sterling Ridge Wy	DKbC	1980	B1
Sterling Ridge Chase NE	CobC	1596	E1
Sterwart Pl	ATLN	1976	C7
Stethem Fy	FulC	1533	D4
Stetson Pl NW	ATLN	1888	C1
Stevann Dr NE	CobC	1527	D6
Steve Dr NW	GwnC	1672	E2
Steve Dr SW	ATLN	2062	B1
Stevens Rd NW	NRCS	1602	D7
Stevens St SE	SMYR	1666	D7
Stevens Wy NE	DKbC	1817	A3
Stewart Av NW	MRTA	1595	A3
Stewart Ct	DRVL	1672	C5
Stewart Dr NE	FulC	1669	E4
Stewart Rd	DRVL	1672	C4
Stiff St NW	ATLN	1889	E1
Stillbrook Wy NE	CobC	1528	B1
Stillbrook Pass NE	CobC	1528	B1
Stillhouse Rd SE	CobC	1740	A1
Stillman St SE	ATLN	1977	A4
Stillwater Ct NE	CobC	1529	A4
Stillwater Dr	RVDL	2148	B6
Stillwater Cove NE	CobC	1527	B2
Stillwater Lake Ct NE	CobC	1527	B3
Stillwater Lake Ln NE	CobC	1527	B3
Stillwater Park Ct NE	CobC	1527	B2
Stillwater Park Dr NE	CobC	1527	B2
Stillwood Dr	HPVL	2062	B2
Stillwood Dr NE	ATLN	1816	D7
	DKbC	1816	D7
Stillwood Chase Dr NE	DKbC	1816	E7
Stillwood Cove	FTPK	2063	A7
	FTPK	2149	A1
Stilson Cir NW	GwnC	1533	C6
Stimson Ln	ClyC	2147	D6
Stimson Wy	ClyC	2147	D6
Stirling Ct NE	CobC	1529	B6
Stirrup Ln SE	DKbC	1978	D5
Stockbridge Dr SE	DKbC	1892	A7
	DKbC	1978	A1
Stockbridge Rd NE	CobC	1529	A3
Stockton St	DKbC	1893	B6
Stokes Av SE	MRTA	1595	B6
Stokes Av SW	ATLN	1889	C6
Stokes Dr	HryC	2152	B5
Stokes Crossing Ct	HryC	2152	B4
Stokeswood Av SE	ATLN	1891	E7
	DKbC	1891	E7
	DKbC	1977	E1
Stoland Dr NE	DKbC	1743	D3
Stone Rd	CGPK	2061	A2
	EPNT	2060	D2
Stone Rd SW	ATLN	1973	E6
	ATLN	2060	A1
Stone Ter	MRRW	2149	E7
Stone Wy	MRRW	2149	D7
Stonebridge Dr	RSWL	1530	D1
Stonebridge Tr	RSWL	1530	D2
Stonebrook Ct NE	CobC	1529	B3
Stone Brook Pk NE	DKbC	1742	E1
Stonebrook Pl NE	CobC	1529	B3
Stone Brook Prk NE	DKbC	1742	E1
Stonecliff Ct	DKbC	1744	B7
Stonecliff Dr	DKbC	1744	B7
Stone Creek Dr	ClyC	2150	E6
Stone Creek Ln	ClyC	2151	A6
Stonecreek Rd SE	SMYR	1666	C6
Stone Creek Wy	ClyC	2151	A6
Stonecrest Ct	DKbC	1672	E6
Stone Edge Ct NE	CobC	1597	D2
Stonefield Ct	ClyC	2151	C5
Stonegate Dr	DKbC	1745	C1
Stonegate Tr	DKbC	1745	C1
Stonegate Wy NW	ATLN	1740	E2
Stone Gate Wy SE	CobC	1738	B7
	CobC	1812	B1
Stoneglen Close	RSWL	1531	C6
Stoneham Ct	ClyC	2147	E2
Stoneham Ter NE	CobC	1597	E2
Stoneheath Mw NE	CobC	1529	D6
Stonehenge Ct	DKbC	1601	B7
Stonehenge Dr	DKbC	1601	B7
Stonehenge Pl	DKbC	1601	B7
Stonehenge Wy	DKbC	1601	B7
Stone Hogan Rd Connector SW	ATLN	1974	B7
	ATLN	2060	B1
Stone Hollow Ct NE	CobC	1529	B4
Stone Hollow Wy NE	CobC	1529	B5
Stonehouse Ct	DKbC	1600	D4
Stonehurst Pl	ATLN	1888	E4
Stonelake Ct	RSWL	1532	A5
Stonemeade Ct SW	FulC	2059	B5
Stone Mill Tr NE	FulC	1598	E6
Stonemill of E Cobb Apartments	CobC	1667	D1
Stonemill of E Cobb Apartments	MRTA	1667	D1
Stonemist Ct	RSWL	1531	C6
Stonemist Trc	RSWL	1531	C6
Stone Pond Ln	FulC	1533	D3
Stoneridge Ct	ClyC	2148	D7
Stonesmith Ct	DKbC	1745	E2
Stoneview Cir	DKbC	1819	C4
Stoneview Ct NE	CobC	1597	E2
Stoneview Ter	EPNT	2060	E2
Stonewall Cir SE	CobC	1740	A1
Stonewall Ct SE	CobC	1740	A1
Stonewall Dr SE	ATLN	1977	C6
	CobC	1739	E1
Stonewall Pl SE	CobC	1740	B1
Stonewall St SW	ATLN	1890	C4
Stonewall Ter SE	CobC	1740	A1
Stonewall Tell Rd	FulC	2145	A3
	UNCT	2145	A3
Stoneybrook Ct SE	CobC	1812	E2
Stoneybrook Dr NE	MRTA	1596	A4
Stoneybrook Dr NW	GwnC	1673	D6
Stoneybrook Dr SE	ATLN	1891	D7
	DKbC	1891	D7
Stoney Brook Ln NE	CobC	1527	E4
Stoneybrook Rd	FTPK	2063	D6
Stoneybrook Wy	CobC	1812	B1
Stoney Creek Ct SE	CobC	1597	D6
Stoney Creek Rd SE	MRTA	1596	B7
Stoney Creek Wy	RSWL	1529	D2
Stoneyfork Ct SE	CobC	1812	A1
Stoneykirk Close	FulC	1601	A3
E Stoneykirk Close	FulC	1601	A3
Stoney Ridge Ct	FulC	1532	E3
Stoney Ridge Dr	FulC	1532	D4
Stoneyridge Dr NE	CobC	1526	E2
Stoney Ridge Ln	FulC	1532	D4
Stoneywood Cir SE	CobC	1812	B1
Stoneywood Trc SE	CobC	1812	B1
Stonington Cir	DKbC	1672	A1
Stonington Dr NE	FulC	1599	A5
Stonington Pl NE	CobC	1597	A5
Stonington Rd	DKbC	1672	A1
	DRVL	1672	A1
Stonington Trc	DKbC	2066	A3
Stovall Blvd NE	ATLN	1742	C3
Stovall Ln SW	ATLN	1975	D3
Stovall Pl NE	ATLN	1742	C3
Stovall St SE	ATLN	1891	D5
Stovall Ter NE	ATLN	1742	C3
Stovehill Ct SE	CobC	1597	B7
Strait St	DRVL	1672	B6
Strasburg Ct	DKbC	1600	E6
Stratfield Cir NE	DKbC	1671	B6
Stratfield Dr NE	DKbC	1671	B6
Stratford Cir	ClyC	2150	D7
Stratford Ct	FulC	1599	E2
Stratford Dr NW	ATLN	1888	C3
Stratford Grn	DKbC	1893	E1
Stratford Ln	ClyC	2150	D7
Stratford Ln	FulC	1599	E2
Stratford Pl NE	ATLN	1742	C2
Stratford Pl SE	MRTA	1596	D7
Stratford Rd	AVES	1893	D2
N Stratford Rd NE	ATLN	1742	B3
Stratford Rd NE	ATLN	1742	B4
Stratford Arms Cir	MRRW	2150	B6
Stratford Arms Ct	MRRW	2150	A6
Stratford Arms Dr	DKbC	1672	B7
	DKbC	1744	B1
	MRRW	2150	A6
Stratford Chase SE	SMYR	1738	C4
Stratford Green Ct	DKbC	1893	E1
Stratford Green Ln	DKbC	1893	E1
Stratford Green Pl	DKbC	1893	D1
Stratford Green Wy	DKbC	1893	E1
Stratford Hall Pl NE	ATLN	1741	B3
Stratham Dr	DKbC	1600	C5
Strathmoor Rd SE	SMYR	1667	B7
Strathmoor Wy	ClyC	2149	B7
Strathmore Dr NE	ATLN	1816	C2
Stratmore Pl	HryC	2152	E2
Straton Trc SW	FulC	1887	C7
Straton Chase SE	CobC	1597	B7
Stratton Ln	DKbC	1818	E5
Stratton Place Wy	FulC	1973	B3
Strauss Ln	FulC	1601	C1
Strawberry Ct	HryC	2152	C1
Strawberry Dr	HryC	2066	C7
Strawberry Ln	DKbC	1979	E5
	HryC	2066	D7
	HryC	2152	C1
Strawberry Tr	HryC	2066	C7
Streamside Ct	DKbC	1980	C3
Streamside Dr SE	CobC	1597	D6
Stream View Wy NE	CobC	1596	A1
Street Deville NE	DKbC	1743	E5
Strickland Dr SW	CobC	1812	B2
Strickland Rd	RSWL	1530	D1
Strong St NW	ATLN	1890	C2
Stroud Ct SW	CobC	1812	A5
Stroud Dr SE	CobC	1812	A5
Stroud Dr SW	CobC	1812	A5
Stuart Rdg	FulC	1533	A4
Sturbridge Cres NE	CobC	1529	C2
Sturbridge Ct	DKbC	1745	B5
Sturbridge Wy	FulC	2146	D3
Sturges Wy	FulC	1533	C4
Stutz Ct	DKbC	1745	D7
Substation Dr NW	ATLN	1890	B1
E Sudbury Ct	DKbC	1672	C1
W Sudbury Ct	DKbC	1672	C1
Sudbury Ct NE	CobC	1528	C2
Sudbury Rd	DKbC	1601	C7
Sudbury Rd NE	FulC	1599	C4
Sudbury Trc NE	CobC	1528	C3
Sue Ln	DKbC	1894	C3
Sue Ln Ct	DKbC	1894	D3
Suffex Green Ln SE	CobC	1739	D4
Suffolk Ct NE	CobC	1528	C2
Suffolk Dr	UNCT	2145	C6
Suffolk Sq	UNCT	2145	B6
Sugar Creek Ln SE	DKbC	1978	B4
Sugar Creek Pl SE	DKbC	1978	B2
Sugar Creek Trc SE	DKbC	1978	E6
Sugar Creek Close SE	DKbC	1978	D6
Sugar Creek Falls Av SE	DKbC	1978	E6
Sugar Creek Falls Ct SE	DKbC	1978	E6
Sugar Creek Falls Dr SE	DKbC	1978	D6
Sugar Creek Golf Dr SE	DKbC	1978	D7
Sugar Downs Ct SE	DKbC	1978	B4
Sugar Hill Dr NW	MRTA	1595	A3
Sugar Maple Ct	ClyC	2147	D5
Sugar Mill Rd	FulC	1530	D7
Sugarplum Ct NE	DKbC	1744	E3
Sugarplum Rd NE	DKbC	1744	E3
Suholdon Cir NE	CobC	1526	C1
Suholdon Dr NE	CobC	1526	C1
Sulene Dr	FulC	2145	E1
Sulky Cir SE	CobC	1597	B6
Sullivan Rd	CGPK	2061	C7
	CGPK	2146	D1
	CGPK	2147	E2
	ClyC	2061	C7
	ClyC	2147	E2
	ClyC	2148	A1
	FulC	2146	D1
Sullivan Hill Rd	FulC	1599	C1
Sumac Cir SE	CobC	1738	E5
Sumac Dr	DKbC	1601	D5
Sumac Dr NW	GwnC	1601	D5
Sumlin St NW	ATLN	1814	B7
Summer Cross	FulC	1531	A5
Summer Dr NE	FulC	1670	D1
Summer Ln	ClyC	2148	A3
Summer Wy	FulC	1531	A6
Summerbrook Dr	FulC	1531	A6
Summer Brook Rd	ClyC	2147	E3
Summer Chase Ct	DKbC	1980	D4
Summerford Ct	DKbC	1600	B6
Summerford Dr	DKbC	1600	B6
Summer Glen Dr	UNCT	2145	C7
Summerglen Ln	ClyC	2147	B4
Summerhouse Ln	FulC	1601	C3
Summer Lake Dr	FulC	1531	A6
Summerland Dr	DKbC	1979	A2
Summerlin Ct SE	CobC	1738	E5
Summer Mist Ct	HryC	2152	C4
Summeroak Dr	DKbC	1745	D3
Summer Oaks Ct NE	CobC	1528	E7
Summer Oaks Dr	RSWL	1532	B3
Summer Oaks Close	RSWL	1532	B2
Summer Rose Ct	DKbC	1671	E2
Summer Rose Dr	DKbC	1671	E2
Summerset Dr	DKbC	1600	B3
Summerset Ln	DKbC	1600	D6
Summerset Ln NE	FulC	1599	C5
Summer Terrace Ln NE	FulC	1670	A6
Summertree Ct SE	SMYR	1738	C6

INDEX 60
Trailing Ivy Ct NE
US-19 Roswell Rd NE

Atlanta Street Index

STREET	City	Map #	Grid
Trailing Ivy Ct NE	CobC	1528	E6
Trailmark Dr	DKbC	1817	E2
Trailmore Ct	RSWL	1531	B3
Trailmore Dr	RSWL	1531	B3
Trailmore Pl	RSWL	1531	C3
Trailridge Ct	DKbC	1599	E5
Trailridge Dr	DKbC	1599	E6
Trailridge Ln	DKbC	1599	E6
Trailridge Pl	DKbC	1599	E6
Trailridge Wy	DKbC	1599	E5
	DKbC	1600	A5
Trailridge Pass	DKbC	1599	E6
Trails Wy NE	CobC	1527	B1
Trails End Ct NE	CobC	1529	C1
Trails End Rd NE	CobC	1529	C1
Trailwood Dr SE	SMYR	1666	C5
Trailwood Rd	DKbC	1978	D1
Tralyn Ct	DKbC	1979	E4
Trammell Rd	ClyC	2150	C5
	LKCY	2150	C5
Trammell St SW	MRTA	1595	A5
Transit Cir	FulC	2146	A5
Transport City Ct	DKbC	2063	E3
Transport City Dr	DKbC	2063	E3
Trapnell Ct	DKbC	1600	C4
Trapnell Dr	DKbC	1600	C4
Traver Dr	ClyC	2150	E5
Traverse Ct	FulC	2146	A4
Travertine Tr	FulC	1533	C4
Travis St NW	ATLN	1890	B2
Travis Trc	DKbC	1894	B2
Traymore Trc SE	SMYR	1738	C3
Traywick Dr NE	CobC	1529	B6
Treaddur Bay Ln NW	GwnC	1533	D7
Treadway Dr	DKbC	1980	E4
Treadwell Cir SW	ATLN	1888	B4
Treadwick Dr	FulC	1601	A3
Treasure Ct	DKbC	1980	C3
Treasure Cove	DKbC	1894	E5
Tree Bark Tr	DKbC	1980	B4
Tree Corners Pkwy NW	GwnC	1602	A4
Tree Creek Ct	DKbC	1819	C2
Tree Creek Ln	DKbC	1819	B2
Tree Fern Ct SE	CobC	1812	D3
Tree Fern Wy SE	CobC	1812	D3
Tree Haven Dr NE	ATLN	1742	B1
Treehouse Pkwy NW	GwnC	1673	E5
Tree Lodge Pkwy	FulC	1599	C3
Treeridge Ct	FulC	1531	D7
	FulC	1600	D1
Treeridge Pkwy	RSWL	1532	B6
Tree Top Bnd NE	CobC	1527	C5
Tree Top Ct NE	CobC	1527	C6
Tree Top Wy NE	CobC	1527	C6
Treewood Tr NE	MRTA	1526	E6
Tregoney Dr	DKbC	1979	A3
Trellis Ln SE	CobC	1596	D7
Trellis Pl	FulC	1601	B3
Tremont Dr NW	ATLN	1889	C3
Trenholm St SW	ATLN	1890	C5
Trent Ct	DKbC	1818	E1
Trent Dr NE	CobC	1527	B3
Trentham Ct	DKbC	1600	D4
Trentham Dr	DKbC	1600	D4
Trenton Ct	ClyC	2147	B6
Trenton St SE	ATLN	1891	E5
Trentwood Pl NE	DKbC	1743	B3
Tresillian Ct	FulC	1533	B1
Tressy Ct	ClyC	2064	A5
Trevelyan Wy	RSWL	1532	B1
Trevington Ct	FulC	1532	C2
Trevor Ct NE	CobC	1598	B1
Trexler Dr NE	FulC	1670	C4
Triad Ct NE	MRTA	1526	E7
Triangle Dr NW	GwnC	1602	D2
Triangle Pkwy NW	GwnC	1602	D1
Tribble Dr NW	ATLN	1813	D3
Tribble Ln NW	ATLN	1888	D3
Tribble St	CLKN	1819	B3
Tributary Wy	DKbC	1980	A5
Trickum Rd NE	CobC	1527	D1
Trilby St SE	ATLN	1891	D5
S Trimble Rd NE	FulC	1670	C5
Trimble Rd NE	FulC	1670	C4
Trimble Chase Ct NE	FulC	1670	C5
Trimble Crest Dr	FulC	1670	C6
Trimble Lake Ct NE	FulC	1670	D6
Trimble Walk Ln	FulC	1670	D6
Trinity Av SW	ATLN	1890	D4
Trinity Av SW SR-154	ATLN	1890	D4
Trinity Ct NE	CobC	1529	B7
E Trinity Pl	DCTR	1892	E1
W Trinity Pl	DCTR	1892	E1
Trinity Tr	HryC	2065	D6
Trion Cove NW	GwnC	1602	C1
Triple Crown Ln	HryC	2152	A2
Tripple Creek Ct NE	DKbC	1671	C2
Tristan Cir NE	DKbC	1744	B5
Tristan Dr SE	CobC	1739	B5
Tristan Wy NE	DKbC	1744	C5
Tritt Ln NE	CobC	1528	A3
Tritt Rd	FulC	2145	D2
Tritt Homestead Dr NE	CobC	1528	D3
Tritt Springs Cir NE	CobC	1528	C3
Tritt Springs Ct NE	CobC	1528	C3
Tritt Springs Dr NE	CobC	1528	C3
Tritt Springs Trc NE	CobC	1528	C4
Tritt Springs Wy NE	CobC	1528	C3
Triumph Cir SE	ATLN	2063	A3
Triumph Dr NW	ATLN	1815	A2
Trolley Ct SE	CobC	1739	E6
Trolley Square Cross NE	ATLN	1816	B7
Troop Row SW	ATLN	1975	E3
Trophy Dr NE	CobC	1527	B5
Trotters Ct SE	CobC	1597	C6
Trotters Cove	DKbC	1600	B4
Trotti St NE	ATLN	1892	B4
Troup St SW	ATLN	1976	D3
Trout St NE	MRTA	1595	D4
Troutdale Ct	DKbC	1980	A1
Troutdale Dr	DKbC	1894	A7
	DKbC	1980	A1
Trowbridge Ct	DKbC	1600	C4
Trowbridge Dr	DKbC	1600	C4
Trowbridge Lk NE	FulC	1599	C3
Trowbridge Pl	DKbC	1600	C4
Trowbridge Rd	FulC	1599	B3
Trowbridge Rd NE	FulC	1599	C4
Trowbridge Wk	FulC	1599	B3
Trowbridge Wy	DKbC	1600	D3
Trowbridge Cove	DKbC	1600	C3
Trowgate Ct	FulC	1599	B3
Trowgate Ln	FulC	1599	B3
Troy St NW	ATLN	1889	E3
Troy St SE	ATLN	1977	A4
Troy Cove Rd	DKbC	1980	B2
Truck Rd	HPVL	2062	A4
Truckers Blvd SE	CobC	1667	C2
Truehedge Trc	RSWL	1531	C3
Trumbull Ct	DKbC	1600	D5
Trumbull Dr	DKbC	1600	C5
Trumpet Vine Ct SE	CobC	1812	D2
Trumpet Vine Tr SE	CobC	1812	D2
Tryon Pl NE	DKbC	1743	C2
Tryon Rd NE	DKbC	1743	B1
Tsali Tr	LKCY	2149	D3
Tubeway Dr	ClyC	2148	D2
Tuckawanna Dr SW	ATLN	1888	D7
	ATLN	1974	D1
Tucker Av SW	ATLN	1976	A1
Tucker Pl SW	ATLN	1976	A1
Tucker St SW	ATLN	1976	C6
Tuckerbrook Ln	FulC	1532	D4
Tucker Norcross Rd	DKbC	1673	D7
Tucker North Ct	DKbC	1745	E2
Tucker North Dr	DKbC	1745	E3
Tucker Pointe Dr	DKbC	1673	D7
Tuckers Farm SE	CobC	1668	C1
Tuckersham Ct	DKbC	1673	E7
Tuckersham Ln	DKbC	1673	D7
Tucker Woods Ct NW	GwnC	1673	E6
Tucker Woods Dr NW	GwnC	1673	E5
Tucson Tr SW	ATLN	1973	B6
Tudor St SW	ATLN	1890	D7
Tufts Ct	DKbC	1980	E7
	DKbC	2066	D1
Tufts Run	DKbC	2066	E1
Tugaloo Blf	HryC	2152	B6
Tugaloo Dr NE	DKbC	1743	A4
Tula St NW	ATLN	1815	D3
Tulane Ct	ClyC	2147	B6
Tulip Dr	DKbC	1894	A5
Tulip Pl	DKbC	1894	B5
Tullamore Pl	FulC	1533	A3
Tullie Cir NE	DKbC	1743	A7
Tullie Rd NE	DKbC	1743	A7
Tullmore Dr	RSWL	1530	A4
Tumlin Dr SE	CobC	1666	B1
Tumlin St NW	ATLN	1815	C7
E Tupelo St SE	DKbC	1893	A5
Tupelo St SE	ATLN	1892	E5
Turbridge Ct	FulC	1533	B1
Turman Av SE	ATLN	1976	E3
Turnberry Ct	CobC	1667	E3
Turnberry Ln SE	CobC	1667	E3
Turnbury Oaks Dr NW	GwnC	1533	E7
	GwnC	1602	E1
Turner Dr SE	SMYR	1666	D5
Turner Ln NE	DKbC	1817	B4
Turner Pl NW	ATLN	1815	C7
Turner Rd	UNCT	2145	A6
Turner Rd NW	CobC	1526	A6
	MRTA	1526	A6
Turner Rd SE	ATLN	1977	D4
	CobC	1813	A4
Turner St	ClyC	2148	B1
	DRVL	1672	B3
Turner Tr	RSWL	1532	A1
Turner Heights Dr	DKbC	1894	B4
Turner McDonald Pkwy	FulC	1530	E7
	FulC	1670	C2
	RSWL	1531	A3
Turner McDonald Pkwy SR-400	FulC	1530	E7
	FulC	1670	C2
	RSWL	1531	A3
Turner McDonald Pkwy US-19	FulC	1530	E7
	FulC	1670	C2
	RSWL	1531	A3
Turners Mill Rd SE	CobC	1812	D6
Turpin Av SE	ATLN	1977	C1
Turpin Rd SE	SMYR	1667	B7
Turquoise Tr	FulC	2146	E7
Turtle Bend Ln	FulC	2146	D7
Turtle Cove Ct SE	CobC	1597	B5
Turtle Lake Ct SE	CobC	1597	B6
Turtle Lake Dr SE	CobC	1597	A6
Turtle Lake Club Dr SE	CobC	1597	B6
Tuscany Park Dr NE	CobC	1597	A2
Tuskegee St SE	ATLN	1890	E7
Tuxedo Av NE	ATLN	1892	B2
Tuxedo Ct	RSWL	1530	E1
Tuxedo Ct NW	ATLN	1741	C4
Tuxedo Dr	RSWL	1530	E1
Tuxedo Dr SE	CobC	1596	D7
	CobC	1667	D1
Tuxedo Pk NW	ATLN	1741	C4
Tuxedo Pl NW	ATLN	1741	B2
Tuxedo Rd NW	ATLN	1741	D3
Tuxedo Ter NW	ATLN	1741	D3
Tuxedo Tr	ClyC	2148	D7
Tuxworth Cir	DKbC	1818	A5
Twain Dr	ClyC	2150	D4
Tweed Pl	DKbC	1819	B1
Twelve Oaks Cir NW	ATLN	1740	E7
Twelvestone Dr	RSWL	1532	A5
Twiggs Cir SE	CobC	1667	E2
Twiggs St SW	ATLN	1976	D2
Twilight Tr	ClyC	2150	A5
	MRRW	2150	A5
Twilley Rd NW	ATLN	1889	B2
Twin Ct	DKbC	1978	D3
Twin Branch Ct NE	FulC	1599	D5
Twin Branch Dr NE	CobC	1527	B5
Twin Branch Ln NE	FulC	1599	D4
Twin Branch Rd NE	FulC	1599	D4
Twin Branches Cir SE	CobC	1667	E2
Twin Branches Wy	DKbC	1599	E6
Twin Brooks Ct SE	MRTA	1596	B7
Twin Brooks Dr SE	MRTA	1596	B7
Twin Brooks Rd NE	DKbC	1743	A2
Twin Brooks Wy SE	MRTA	1596	A7
Twin Creek Ct NE	CobC	1528	B3
Twin Creek Trc NE	CobC	1528	C3
Twin Creeks Ct	ClyC	2147	C5
Twin Dills SW	ATLN	1887	D4
Twin Falls Ct	DKbC	1894	A7
Twin Falls Rd	DKbC	1894	A7
	DKbC	1980	A1
Twingate Dr	FulC	1533	E3
Twin Lakes Ct NE	CobC	1528	B3
Twin Lakes Dr	FulC	2146	D4
Twin Lakes Dr NE	CobC	1528	B4
Twin Lakes Dr SE	CobC	1739	E3
Twin Lakes Tr	DKbC	1601	C6
Twin Lakes Trc NE	CobC	1528	B3
Twin Lakes Wy NE	CobC	1528	B3
Twin Leaf Ct NE	CobC	1528	D2
Twin Leaf Pl NE	CobC	1528	D3
Twin Leaf Tr NE	CobC	1528	D2
Twin Oaks Cir SE	CobC	1738	E2
Twin Oaks Dr	DKbC	1893	C1
E Twin Oaks Dr SE	SMYR	1739	A3
Twin Oaks Dr SE	CobC	1739	A3
	SMYR	1739	A3
Twin Springs Rd NW	ATLN	1669	C7
Twinspur Ct	RSWL	1531	D3
Twinspur Close	RSWL	1531	D3
Twin Tendrils SW	FulC	1887	C7
Tye St SE	ATLN	1891	C5
Tyewood Ln	EPNT	1974	D7
Tyler Ct	ClyC	2065	A5
Tyler Rdg SE	SMYR	1739	B3
Tyler St NW	ATLN	1890	C3
Tyler Wy	DKbC	1979	A1
Tyler Green Tr SE	SMYR	1739	A3
Tyndall Ct	DKbC	1600	C6
Tyne Ter SE	CobC	1739	C3
Tynebrae Ct	RSWL	1529	C1
Tynebrae Pl	RSWL	1529	D1
Tynecastle Dr	FulC	1600	A1
Tynecastle Wy	FulC	1531	B7
	FulC	1600	A1
Tynemoore Ct SE	CobC	1739	C4
Tynemoore Tr SE	CobC	1739	C4
Tynemoore Wk SE	CobC	1739	C4
Tynewick Dr NE	CobC	1529	C2
Tynewick Trc NE	CobC	1529	C2
Tynewick Wk NE	CobC	1529	C2
Tyson Cir	RSWL	1531	D1
Tyson Ct	RSWL	1531	D1
Tyson Knls	RSWL	1531	D1
Tyson Ln	RSWL	1531	D1
Tyson's Cor NE	MRTA	1527	B7
U			
S U Av	FTPK	2149	E2
Umberland Dr	DKbC	1745	C2
Umland Rd NE	CobC	1526	D2
Underwood Av SE	ATLN	1891	C7
	ATLN	1977	C1
Underwood Dr NW	FulC	1669	D1
Underwood St	DCTR	1892	E3
Union Av	HPVL	2062	B4
Union St	UNCT	2145	A7
Union Walk Cir SE	SMYR	1738	A4
United Dr SE	SMYR	1738	D6
University Av SW	ATLN	1976	C1
University Av SW SR-54	ATLN	1976	D1
University Dr NE	ATLN	1816	D6
	CobC	1598	A1
	DKbC	1816	D6
University Pl NW	ATLN	1890	C4
Upland Rd	DCTR	1892	D2
	DKbC	1892	D2
Upper Alabama St SW	ATLN	1890	E4
Upper Branden Pl NE	CobC	1598	B1
Uppergate Dr NE	DKbC	1817	C5
Upper Riverdale Rd	ClyC	2148	E7
SW Upper Riverdale Rd	ClyC	2148	E7
Upper Riverdale Rd SE	ClyC	2148	E7
Upper Riverdale Rd SW	ClyC	2148	D7
Upshaw St SW	ATLN	1976	D3
Upton Ct	ClyC	2065	D7
Upton Rd NW	ATLN	1815	B4
Urquart Ct NE	CobC	1529	B6
US-19	ClyC	2149	A7
	FulC	1670	B3
US-19 14th St NW	ATLN	1815	E6
US-19 N Central Av	ATLN	2062	D4
	HPVL	2062	D4
US-19 Crown Rd SE	ATLN	2062	D4
US-19 Dogwood Dr	HPVL	2062	B1
US-19 Metropolitan Pkwy SW	ATLN	1890	C7
	ATLN	1976	C1
	ATLN	2062	B2
US-19 Northside Dr NW	ATLN	1815	C6
US-19 Northside Dr SW	ATLN	1890	C6
US-19 Old Dixie Rd	ClyC	2062	E7
	ClyC	2149	A4
	FTPK	2062	E7
	FTPK	2148	E1
US-19 Peachtree Rd NE	ATLN	1742	A6
US-19 Peachtree Rd NW	ATLN	1741	E7
	ATLN	1815	E1
US-19 W Peachtree St NW	ATLN	1815	C6
US-19 Peachtree St NW	ATLN	1815	E5
US-19 Ralph D Abernathy Frwy	ATLN	1890	C6
US-19 Roswell Rd NE	ATLN	1741	E4
	ATLN	1742	A1
	FulC	1670	A4

INDEX 61

US-19 Roswell Rd NE — Atlanta Street Index — Vickery Ln

STREET	City	Map #	Grid
US-19 Roswell Rd NE	FulC	1742	A1
US-19 Spring St NW	ATLN	1815	E6
US-19 Tara Blvd	ClyC	2149	A7
US-19 Turner McDonald Pkwy	FulC	1530	E7
	FulC	1670	C1
	RSWL	1531	C1
US-23	ClyC	2151	A5
US-23 Buford Hwy NE	CMBL	1672	A7
	CMBL	1744	A1
	DKbC	1672	B5
	DKbC	1743	C5
	DKbC	1744	A1
	DRVL	1672	B5
US-23 Buford Hwy NW	DRVL	1672	D3
	GwnC	1602	E7
	GwnC	1672	D3
	NRCS	1602	E7
US-23 Clairemont Av	DCTR	1817	D6
	DKbC	1817	D6
US-23 Clairmont Rd	DKbC	1817	D6
US-23 Clairmont Rd NE	DKbC	1743	C5
	DKbC	1817	D1
US-23 Macon Hwy	ClyC	2151	A7
US-23 Moreland Av	ClyC	2064	A3
	ClyC	2150	D1
	ClyC	2151	A6
	DKbC	2063	E1
	FTPK	2064	C6
	FTPK	2150	D1
US-23 Moreland Av NE	ATLN	1891	D1
US-23 Moreland Av SE	ATLN	1891	D4
	ATLN	1977	E7
	DKbC	1977	E7
	DKbC	2063	E1
US-23 Ponce de Leon Av NE	ATLN	1891	E1
	ATLN	1892	B1
	DKbC	1892	D1
US-23 Scott Blvd	DCTR	1817	D7
	DKbC	1892	D1
US-29 Chapel St SW	ATLN	1890	B5
US-29 Church St	EPNT	1975	D7
US-29 East Point St	EPNT	1975	D7
	EPNT	2061	D1
US-29 Juniper St NE	ATLN	1890	E1
US-29 Lawrenceville Hwy	DKbC	1745	B7
	DKbC	1818	B5
	DKbC	1819	A1
US-29 Lee St SW	ATLN	1890	B7
	ATLN	1975	D5
US-29 Legion Wy	EPNT	2061	D1
US-29 Main St	ATLN	1975	E5
	CGPK	2061	A6
	EPNT	1975	E4
	EPNT	2061	A6
US-29 North Av NE	ATLN	1890	E1
US-29 North Av NW	ATLN	1890	D1
US-29 Northside Dr NW	ATLN	1890	C4
US-29 Northside Dr SW	ATLN	1890	C5
US-29 Peters St SW	ATLN	1890	B5
US-29 Piedmont Av NE	ATLN	1891	A1
US-29 Ponce de Leon Av NE	ATLN	1891	E1
	ATLN	1892	B1
	DKbC	1892	D1
US-29 Roosevelt Hwy	CGPK	2060	E7
	CGPK	2146	E1
	FulC	2145	A6
	FulC	2146	E1
	UNCT	2145	A6
US-29 Scott Blvd	DCTR	1817	D7
	DKbC	1817	E6
	DKbC	1818	A5
	DKbC	1892	D1
US-29 W Whitehall St SW	ATLN	1890	B7
US-41	ClyC	2149	A7
US-41 N Central Av	ATLN	2062	D4
	HPVL	2062	D4
US-41 Cobb Pkwy NE	CobC	1595	B1
	MRTA	1595	B1
US-41 Cobb Pkwy NW	CobC	1595	A1
US-41 Cobb Pkwy SE	CobC	1667	A1
	CobC	1668	A7
	CobC	1740	B1
	MRTA	1595	E5
	MRTA	1667	A1
	SMYR	1667	E7
US-41 Crown Rd SE	ATLN	2062	D4
US-41 Dogwood Dr	HPVL	2062	B1
US-41 Metropolitan Pkwy SW	ATLN	1890	C7
	ATLN	1976	C1
	ATLN	2062	B2
US-41 Northside Dr NW	ATLN	1741	C7
	ATLN	1815	C2
	ATLN	1890	C1
US-41 Northside Dr SW	ATLN	1890	C7
US-41 Northside Pkwy NW	ATLN	1740	E5
	ATLN	1741	B6
	CobC	1740	B2
US-41 Old Dixie Rd	ClyC	2062	E7
	ClyC	2149	A4
	FTPK	2062	E7
	FTPK	2148	E1
US-41 Ralph D Abernathy Frwy	ATLN	1890	C6
US-41 Tara Blvd	ClyC	2149	A7
US-78 Bankhead Hwy SE	CobC	1812	C3
US-78 Bankhead Hwy SW	CobC	1812	A3
US-78 D L Hollowell Pkwy NW	ATLN	1813	D7
US-78 Juniper St NE	ATLN	1890	E1
US-78 Lawrenceville Hwy	DKbC	1818	B5
US-78 North Av NE	ATLN	1890	E1
US-78 North Av NW	ATLN	1890	C2
US-78 Northside Dr NW	ATLN	1890	D1
US-78 Piedmont Av NE	ATLN	1891	A1
US-78 Ponce de Leon Av NE	ATLN	1891	E1
	ATLN	1892	A1
	DKbC	1892	D1
US-78 Scott Blvd	DCTR	1817	D7
	DKbC	1817	E6
US-78 William Evans Hwy	DKbC	1745	D7
	DKbC	1818	E3
US-278 N Avondale Plz	AVES	1893	D1
US-278 N Avondale Rd	AVES	1893	B1
US-278 Bankhead Hwy SE	CobC	1812	C3
US-278 Bankhead Hwy SW	CobC	1812	A3
US-278 E College Av	AVES	1893	C1
	DCTR	1892	E2
	DKbC	1893	C1
US-278 W College Av	DCTR	1892	E2
US-278 College Av NE	ATLN	1892	C2
US-278 Covington Hwy	AVES	1893	E1
	DKbC	1893	E1
US-278 Covington Rd	AVES	1893	E1
	DKbC	1893	E1
US-278 D L Hollowell Pkwy NW	ATLN	1813	D7
US-278 Juniper St NE	ATLN	1890	E1
US-278 E Lake Dr	DCTR	1892	D2
	DKbC	1892	D2
US-278 E Lake Rd NE	DKbC	1892	C2
US-278 North Av NE	ATLN	1890	E1
US-278 North Av NW	ATLN	1890	C2
US-278 Northside Dr NW	ATLN	1890	D1
US-278 Park Pl	DCTR	1892	D2
US-278 Park Pl NE	ATLN	1892	C2
	DCTR	1892	D2
US-278 Piedmont Av NE	ATLN	1891	A1
US-278 Ponce de Leon Av NE	ATLN	1891	E1
	ATLN	1892	A1
	DKbC	1892	A1
Utica Dr SE	CobC	1596	C5
Utoy Cir SW	ATLN	1887	D5
Utoy Ct SW	ATLN	1887	D5
Utoy Pl	FulC	1973	D1
Utoy Springs Rd SW	FulC	1974	A1
V			
S V Av	FTPK	2150	A2
Vada Dr NE	CobC	1596	E4
Vail Al	ClyC	2147	D4
Valaire Dr	DKbC	1818	E2
Valante Ter	EPNT	2060	D2
Valcouri Sq NW	ATLN	1741	E6
Valdez Dr	ClyC	2151	A6
Vale Ct	DKbC	1894	D7
Vale Close NE	ATLN	1742	D7
Valeland Av SW	ATLN	1974	A6
Valemont Dr	FulC	1530	C6
Valencia Dr NE	CobC	1527	E5
Valencia Rd	DKbC	1978	C1
Valentine Ct	RVDL	2147	E6
Valerie Woods Dr	DKbC	1894	E3
Valhalla Dr NE	DKbC	1744	A5
Valiant Dr NE	DKbC	1743	E5
Valiant Ln	RVDL	2148	C7
Vallejo Ct	FulC	2145	D5
Valley Cir	DKbC	1818	D4
Valley Cir NW	ATLN	1741	E5
Valley Ct	RVDL	2148	C6
Valley Dr	CobC	1596	D6
	EPNT	1975	C4
E Valley Dr NE	CobC	1596	E5
N Valley Dr	DKbC	1818	B3
Valley Dr SE	SMYR	1738	D1
Valley Ln NE	FulC	1670	B2
Valley Ovlk NE	ATLN	1816	D1
Valley Pkwy SE	SMYR	1739	B6
Valley Pl	DKbC	1818	C4
Valley Rd NW	ATLN	1741	C4
	NRCS	1602	D5
Valley Rd SE	SMYR	1667	A6
Valley Bend Ln	FulC	2146	C7
Valley Bend Rd	FulC	2146	C7
Valley Bluff Dr	DKbC	1673	C6
Valley Bluff Wy	DKbC	1673	C6
Valleybrook Cross	DKbC	1818	D4
Valley Brook Dr	FulC	2059	D7
	RVDL	2148	C6
Valley Brook Dr NE	ATLN	1742	A1
	FulC	1742	A1
Valley Brook Ln	FulC	2059	D6
Valley Brook Pl	DKbC	1818	D3
Valley Brook Rd	DKbC	1818	D4
N Valley Brook Rd	DKbC	1818	D2
Valleybrook Rd SE	CobC	1812	E2
Valley Brook Ter	FulC	2059	D6
Valley Brook Wy NE	DKbC	1742	E4
Valley Cove	FulC	1530	C6
Valley Creek Dr SE	CobC	1739	E4
Valleycrest Ct NW	GwnC	1533	C6
Valley Dale Dr	RVDL	2148	C6
Valleydale Dr SW	ATLN	1974	C1
Valley Field Ct NE	CobC	1528	C4
Valley Forest Ln SE	CobC	1738	A1
Valley Forge Pl NW	ATLN	1814	D1
Valley Glen Wy	DKbC	1600	A7
Valley Green Ct	ClyC	2063	E6
Valley Green Dr NE	ATLN	1742	B1
	CobC	1597	D3
Valley Green Trc NE	CobC	1597	D3
Valley Hall Dr	FulC	1600	E1
Valley Heart Dr NW	ATLN	1888	D3
Valley Lake Dr	ClyC	2147	D5
Valley Lake Ter	FulC	2059	C6
Valley Lakes Rd	FulC	2145	A4
Valleymeade Dr SE	CobC	1596	E7
	CobC	1667	C2
Valley Mist Ct NW	GwnC	1533	C6
Valley Mist Trc NW	GwnC	1533	C6
Valley Oaks Dr SE	SMYR	1666	C5
Valley Ridge Ct SE	CobC	1668	A1
Valley Ridge Dr	DKbC	1979	C1
	RSWL	1530	B4
Valley Ridge Dr SW	ATLN	1974	B3
Valley Ridge Ter SW	ATLN	1974	B4
Valleyside Dr	DKbC	1980	A2
Valley Stream Dr	DRVL	1672	B2
Valley Stream Dr NE	CobC	1596	A1
Valley Tarn	FulC	1531	A7
Valley Trail Dr SE	CobC	1739	D5
Valley View Ct	DKbC	1600	A6
Valley View Dr	EPNT	2060	D1
	FTPK	2149	B4
Valley View Dr NE	CobC	1597	B4
Valley View Dr SE	CobC	1739	D4
Valley View Rd	DKbC	1600	A7
Valley View Rd SE	ATLN	1977	D6
Valley Vista Rd SE	CobC	1739	C2
Vallo Vista Ct NE	FulC	1670	B6
Valmar Dr	DRVL	1672	B6
Valmont Ct NE	CobC	1526	E5
Valmont Trc NE	CobC	1526	E5
	MRTA	1526	E5
Valpariso Cir	DKbC	2066	D1
Valvedere Dr NE	DKbC	1743	B2
Van Buren St SW	ATLN	1975	E2
Vance Av NE	ATLN	1816	D7
Vance Cir NE	MRTA	1595	B4
Vance Dr	EPNT	1974	E7
Vance Dr NE	DKbC	1743	D5
Vancouver Dr	DKbC	1819	A1
Vancroft Ct	DKbC	1600	C4
Vanderbilt Ct NW	ATLN	1888	C1
Vanderbilt Ln NW	ATLN	1888	C1
Vanderbilt Wy NE	CobC	1529	C7
Vanderlyn Dr	DKbC	1600	C5
Vandiver Dr NE	CobC	1527	D1
Van Epps Av SE	ATLN	1891	E6
Vanessa Dr SE	CobC	1738	A3
Vanet Rd	CMBL	1671	D5
Van Eyck Wy	DKbC	1599	D3
Van Eyck Wy NW	GwnC	1673	E5
Van Fleet Cir	DKbC	1672	B2
	DRVL	1672	B2
Vanguard Cir SW	CobC	1666	A6
Van Heusen Blvd NW	ATLN	1814	E4
Van Horn Rd SW	ATLN	1975	D4
Vanira Av SE	ATLN	1890	E7
Vanity Joys Ln	ClyC	2151	C3
Vann St NE	MRTA	1595	A2
Vanneman Ct SE	CobC	1740	A2
Vannoy St SE	ATLN	1891	E5
Van Vleck Av SE	ATLN	1891	E6
Vanya Ln SE	CobC	1738	A2
Variations Dr NE	DKbC	1743	D4
Varner Dr NE	DKbC	1744	D3
Varner Rd NE	MRTA	1595	E4
Vassar St SW	CGPK	2061	D2
Vaughan St	CLKN	1819	B3
Vaughn Ct SW	ATLN	1890	C7
Vaughn St SE	ATLN	1891	E5
Vedado Wy NE	ATLN	1816	B7
Vel Ct SE	CobC	1812	D3
Velma Ct	DKbC	2066	A4
Velma Dr NE	CobC	1526	D3
Velma St SE	ATLN	1977	D4
Velma Burns Ct	DKbC	1745	E3
Veltre Cir SW	ATLN	1888	E7
	ATLN	1974	D1
Veltre Pl SW	ATLN	1974	D1
Venable St NW	ATLN	1890	D3
Veneta Wy SE	CobC	1739	A2
Venetian Dr SW	ATLN	1975	C2
Venetian Wy SW	CobC	1812	A4
Venetta Pl NW	ATLN	1813	C7
Venice Dr SE	ATLN	1893	B5
Ventana Cross NE	CobC	1527	B4
Ventana Pth NE	CobC	1527	B4
Ventana Rdg NE	CobC	1527	B4
Ventura Dr	ClyC	2149	B7
Ventura Pl SE	SMYR	1666	C5
Ventura Rd SE	SMYR	1666	C5
Venus Pl NW	ATLN	1888	A1
Venus Wy	DKbC	1980	A3
Ven Villa Rd NE	CobC	1596	C1
Vera Cir	DKbC	1745	D5
Vera St SE	ATLN	1891	C6
Veracruse Ct	ClyC	2150	D7
Veracruse Dr	ClyC	2150	D7
Veracruz Ct	DKbC	1980	D6
Veracruz Dr	DKbC	1980	C6
Veracruz Wy	DKbC	1980	D6
Verbena St NW	ATLN	1889	A4
Verde Dr	ClyC	2148	A6
Verdi Ln	FulC	1601	C1
Verdi Wy	DKbC	1818	E4
Verdon Ct	DKbC	1600	A4
Verdon Dr	DKbC	1599	E3
	DKbC	1600	A4
Verdun Dr NW	ATLN	1741	C6
Verlaine Pl NW	ATLN	1815	C2
Vermack Ct	DKbC	1600	C7
Vermack Pl	DKbC	1600	C7
Vermack Rd	DKbC	1600	C7
Vermack Rdg	DKbC	1600	C7
Vermont Rd NE	ATLN	1742	D3
Verna Ct	DKbC	1979	A4
Verna Dr	DKbC	1978	E4
Vernadean Dr SE	CobC	1740	A2
Verner St NW	ATLN	1815	B5
Verney Dr NE	CobC	1526	C1
Vernier Dr	FulC	2146	A5
Vernon Av SE	ATLN	1891	C6
Vernon Rd NW	ATLN	1741	E7
Vernon Wk NW	FulC	1669	A4
Vernon Glen Ct	FulC	1599	D6
Vernon Lake Dr	DKbC	1600	C4
Vernon North Dr	DKbC	1600	B5
Vernon Oaks Dr	DKbC	1600	C5
Vernon Oaks Wy	DKbC	1600	D4
Vernon Ridge Ct	DKbC	1600	B5
Vernon Ridge Dr	DKbC	1600	B5
Vernon Ridge Close	DKbC	1600	A5
Vernon Springs Ct NW	FulC	1669	A5
Vernon Springs Dr	DKbC	1600	B5
Vernon Springs Tr NW	FulC	1669	A5
Vernon Village Ct	DKbC	1600	A5
Vernon Woods Dr NE	FulC	1599	A7
	FulC	1670	A1
Vernon Wy Ct	DKbC	1600	B5
Verona Dr	DKbC	1818	E4
Versailles Ct NE	CobC	1527	A5
Versailles Dr SW	FulC	1973	A1
Vesta Av	CGPK	2061	C2
	EPNT	2061	C2
Vesta Av NW	ATLN	1889	B4
Vesta Ter	CGPK	2061	D2
	EPNT	2061	D2
Vester Dr NE	CobC	1597	A1
Veterans Pkwy	GwnC	1673	C4
Veterans Pkwy I-85	GwnC	1673	C4
Veterans Pkwy SR-403	GwnC	1673	C4
Veterans St	EPNT	1975	E7
	EPNT	2061	E1
VFW Wy	EPNT	1975	D7
Vic-AR Ct NW	GwnC	1601	D4
Vic-AR Rd NW	DKbC	1601	D4
Vickers Cir	DKbC	1817	C7
Vickers Dr	DKbC	1817	C7
Vickers Dr NE	DKbC	1817	C7
Vickers St SE	ATLN	1977	D1
Vickery Cir	RSWL	1531	A3
Vickery Dr NE	CobC	1526	C1
Vickery Ln	RSWL	1531	A3

Atlanta Street Index

STREET	City	Map #	Grid
Vickery St	RSWL	1530	C3
Vickery Wy	RSWL	1531	A3
Vickery Wy NE	CobC	1526	C1
Vickery Pass NE	CobC	1526	C1
Vicki Ln SE	DKbC	1978	C3
Vicksburg Ct	DKbC	1979	B4
Vicksburg Pl	FulC	1531	A6
Vickwood Ct NE	CobC	1597	B5
Victor Cir NW	ATLN	1889	D3
Victor Rd NE	ATLN	1742	D7
	DKbC	1742	D7
Victoria Ct	HryC	2152	C1
N Victoria Ct	HryC	2066	C7
Victoria Dr	DKbC	1819	A6
	EPNT	2060	C3
	HryC	2066	C7
	HryC	2152	C1
Victoria Dr NE	CobC	1597	A4
Victoria Ln	HPVL	2062	C3
Victoria Pl SW	ATLN	1890	B7
Victoria St	CGPK	2061	B2
Victoria St NE	DKbC	1670	E7
Victoria Falls Ct SW	ATLN	1974	C2
Victoria Falls Dr NE	DKbC	1817	B3
Victory Blvd	ClyC	2150	B4
Victory Cir	GwnC	1672	E2
Victory Dr SE	MRTA	1595	C5
Victory Dr SW	ATLN	1975	E3
Victory Ridge Ln	RSWL	1531	A1
Vidal Blvd	DCTR	1817	D7
Vidaulan Ct	FulC	1532	B3
Vienna Wy NE	CobC	1528	E3
View Hill Ct	FulC	1530	D7
Viewpoint Ln	DKbC	2066	A4
Viewpoint Tr	DKbC	2066	A4
Views Trc NW	GwnC	1602	A4
Vijay Dr	CMBL	1671	C7
Viking Ct	DKbC	1819	D4
Viking Ct NW	GwnC	1601	D4
Viking Dr	DKbC	1819	D3
Viking Dr SE	SMYR	1667	E6
Viking Wk NE	CobC	1529	C6
Vilenah Ln NE	DKbC	1817	A6
Villa Av SE	CobC	1812	B3
Villa Cir	DKbC	1893	C1
Villa Cir SE	ATLN	2063	A3
Villa Ct SE	ATLN	1977	C1
	SMYR	1739	B2
Villa Dr NE	DKbC	1816	E6
Villa Chase Ct NE	CobC	1529	A7
Villa Chase Dr NE	CobC	1529	A7
Villa Esta Dr	CMBL	1744	A1
	DKbC	1744	A1
Village Ct	DCTR	1893	B2
	DKbC	1600	D7
Village Ct SE	CobC	1812	E4
Village Dr	DKbC	1600	D7
Village Dr NE	CobC	1528	A4
Village Dr NW	GwnC	1673	E4
Village Dr SW	FulC	1973	E2
Village Ln	CobC	1598	B5
Village Pkwy NE	ATLN	1891	C2
	CobC	1598	B5
Village Pkwy SE	SMYR	1667	B7
Village Pl NE	CobC	1598	B5
Village Pt NE	DKbC	1742	E5
Village Run NE	DKbC	1742	E5
Village St NW	ATLN	1815	C6
Village Trc NE	CobC	1598	B5
Village at E Cobb Apartments	CobC	1596	B2
	MRTA	1596	C3
Village Cove NE	DKbC	1742	D6
Village Creek Ct	DKbC	1600	D6
Village Creek Dr	DKbC	1600	D6
Village Creek Trc NE	FulC	1599	D4
Village Green Cir SE	SMYR	1666	E7
Village Mill Dr	DKbC	1600	C7
Village Mill Rd	DKbC	1600	D7
Village North Ct	DKbC	1600	D7
Village North Rd	DKbC	1600	D7
Village Oaks Cir	DKbC	1671	C1
Village Oaks Ct	DKbC	1600	D7
Village Oaks Dr	DKbC	1600	C7
Village Oaks Ln	DKbC	1671	D1
Village Oaks Rdg	DKbC	1671	C1
Village Oaks Tr	DKbC	1671	D1
Village Oaks Wy	DKbC	1671	D1
Village On The Green Grn	RSWL	1601	A1
Village Park Dr NE	DKbC	1743	B3
Villager Wy	ClyC	2151	E4
Village Springs Pl	DKbC	1671	B1
Village Springs Run	DKbC	1671	B1
Village Square Ct	DKbC	1819	E4
Village Square Dr	DKbC	1819	E5
Village Square Ln	DKbC	1819	E6
Village Terrace Ct	DKbC	1600	A6
Village Terrace Dr	DKbC	1600	A6
Village Walk Dr	DCTR	1893	A1
Village Walk Dr NW	GwnC	1602	B2
Villa Ridge Rd NE	CobC	1529	B7
Ville St SE	ATLN	1977	C5
Vincent Dr	ClyC	2063	D5
Vine Cir	DKbC	1818	D4
Vine St NW	ATLN	1890	C3
Vine St SW	ATLN	1890	C4
Vinewood Pt NE	CobC	1597	B3
Vineyard Ct SE	SMYR	1666	A7
Vineyard Wy SE	CobC	1666	B7
	SMYR	1666	B7
Vinings Pkwy SE	CobC	1739	C2
	SMYR	1739	C2
Vinings Tr SE	CobC	1739	C2
Vinings Wk SE	CobC	1739	C2
Vinings Wy SE	CobC	1739	E6
Vinings Approach SE	SMYR	1738	C6
Vinings Central Dr SE	CobC	1739	D6
Vinings Central Run SE	CobC	1739	C7
Vinings Central Trc SE	CobC	1739	C7
Vinings Cove SE	CobC	1739	C2
Vinings Crest SE	CobC	1739	C3
Vinings Estates Ct SE	SMYR	1738	C7
Vinings Estates Dr SE	SMYR	1738	D7
Vinings Estates Pl SE	SMYR	1738	D7
Vinings Estates Run SE	SMYR	1738	C7
Vinings Estates Trc SE	SMYR	1738	D7
Vinings Estates Wy SE	SMYR	1738	C7
	SMYR	1812	C1
Vinings Falls Dr SE	SMYR	1739	A3
Vinings Ferry Dr SE	CobC	1740	A3
Vinings Forest Cir SE	SMYR	1739	A1
Vinings Forest Wy SE	CobC	1740	A3
Vinings Grove Wy SE	CobC	1738	D5
Vinings Lake Ct SW	CobC	1812	A2
Vinings Lake Dr SW	CobC	1812	A2
Vinings Lake Ln SW	CobC	1812	A2
Vinings Lake Vw SW	CobC	1812	A2
Vinings Lake Wy SW	CobC	1812	A2
Vinings Mill Ct SE	CobC	1739	B4
Vinings Mill Tr SE	CobC	1739	B4
	SMYR	1739	B4
Vinings Mill Wk SE	SMYR	1739	B4
Vinings North Ct SE	SMYR	1739	A3
Vinings North Ln SE	CobC	1739	C4
Vinings North Tr SE	SMYR	1739	A2
Vinings North Trc SE	SMYR	1739	A3
Vinings North Wy SE	SMYR	1739	A2
Vinings Oak Dr SE	CobC	1739	E6
Vinings Oaks Ct SE	CobC	1738	C5
Vinings Place Cir SE	CobC	1812	E3
Vinings Place Ct SE	CobC	1812	D3
Vinings Place Dr SE	CobC	1812	E3
Vinings Place Pt SE	CobC	1812	E2
Vinings Place Tr SE	CobC	1812	E2
Vinings Place Wy SE	CobC	1812	D3
Vinings Place Cove SE	CobC	1812	E2
Vinings Retreat Wy SW	CobC	1812	A2
Vinings Retreat Pass SW	CobC	1812	A2
Vinings Ridge Ct SE	CobC	1740	B2
Vinings Ridge Dr SE	CobC	1740	A2
Vinings Ridge Tr SE	SMYR	1738	C7
Vinings Slope SE	CobC	1739	E3
Vinings Springs Dr SE	CobC	1812	B1
Vinings Springs Tr SE	CobC	1812	C1
Vinings Springs Pointe SE	CobC	1812	C1
Vinington Ct	FulC	1601	B3
Vinson Dr SE	ATLN	1891	E4
Vinson Pl SW	ATLN	1976	B6
Vintage Ct	MRTA	1667	B5
Vintage Ln	DKbC	1672	A2
Vinton Woods Dr	ClyC	2149	C6
Vinyard Ct NE	CobC	1528	D4
Vinyard Trc NE	CobC	1528	D4
Vinyard Wy NE	CobC	1528	D4
Viola Ln	HryC	2152	D7
Violet Av NW	ATLN	1814	A6
Violet Ln	ClyC	2150	D6
Violet St SE	ATLN	1890	E7
	ATLN	1976	E1
Violet St SW	ATLN	1889	E7
	ATLN	1975	E1
Virgil St NE	ATLN	1891	C3
Virginia Av	CGPK	2061	D3
	EPNT	2061	D3
	FulC	2061	D3
	FulC	2062	A3
	HPVL	2061	D3
	UNCT	2145	A5
N Virginia Av NE	ATLN	1816	D7
Virginia Av NE	ATLN	1816	B7
Virginia Av NW	GwnC	1673	A1
Virginia Cir	FTPK	2149	B3
Virginia Cir NE	ATLN	1816	C7
Virginia Pl	HPVL	2062	B3
Virginia Pl NE	ATLN	1815	E2
Virginia Pl SE	CobC	1596	B6
Virginia Rd	DKbC	1599	D7
Virginia St	ATLN	1889	B1
Virginia Pine Ln	FulC	1532	D1
Viscount Ct	AVES	1893	E2
Vista Cir SE	MRTA	1595	C5
Vista Ct	RVDL	2147	E6
Vista Sq NW	ATLN	1815	C2
Vista Tr NE	DKbC	1816	E3
Vista Trc	DKbC	1744	C7
Vista Wy	DKbC	1818	D4
Vista Wy SE	CobC	1739	D2
Vista Brook Dr	DKbC	1818	D4
Vistadale Ct	DKbC	1745	B5
Vista Leaf Dr	DKbC	1818	A2
Vistamont Dr	DKbC	1817	E4
Vista Valley Dr NE	DKbC	1817	A2
Vistavia Cir	CobC	1817	C4
Vista View St NE	MRTA	1595	D1
Vistawood Ct	DKbC	1979	E6
Vistawood Dr NE	CobC	1526	B1
Vistawood Ln NE	CobC	1526	B2
Vivian Cir	DKbC	1818	A6
Vivian Ct	MRRW	2149	E7
Vivian Ln NE	ATLN	1741	D5
Volberg St NW	ATLN	1815	A4
Volley Ln NW	GwnC	1602	A1
Voltaire Ct SW	FulC	1973	A1
Voyles Dr	RVDL	2148	C7
W			
S W Av	FTPK	2150	A2
Wabash Av NE	ATLN	1891	B2
Wabash Ct	DKbC	2066	A2
Wabash Dr	HryC	2152	B1
Wabash Ln	DKbC	2066	A2
Waddell Rd	DKbC	2065	B2
Waddell St NE	ATLN	1891	C3
	MRTA	1595	B4
Waddell St SE	MRTA	1595	B5
Waddeston Wy NE	DKbC	1671	A6
Waddington Ct	FulC	1600	C1
Wade Av NE	ATLN	1892	A4
Wade St NE	ATLN	1891	D4
Wadley Av	EPNT	1975	D6
Wadley St NW	ATLN	1889	B3
Wadsworth Dr NW	ATLN	1815	A3
Wadsworth Mill Pl	DKbC	1893	D7
Waggoner Ct	ClyC	2151	B5
Waggoner Ln	ClyC	2151	B5
Waggoner Pl	ClyC	2151	B5
Waggoner Run	ClyC	2151	B5
Waggoner Tr	ClyC	2151	B5
Waggoner Wk	ClyC	2151	B5
Waggoner Wy	ClyC	2151	B5
Waggoner Cove	ClyC	2151	B5
Wagoner St	CLKN	1819	B4
Wagon Wheel Ct SE	CobC	1597	C5
Wagon Wheel Dr	HryC	2152	A4
Wahsega Wy	LKCY	2149	D3
Waikiki Wy	ClyC	2149	A7
Wainwright Dr SE	ATLN	1978	A1
	DKbC	1978	A1
Waits Av SW	ATLN	1973	D5
Waits Dr SE	CobC	1812	A1
Waits Dr SW	ATLN	1887	D4
	CobC	1812	A1
Wakefield Ct NW	GwnC	1673	E5
Wakefield Ct SE	SMYR	1738	C4
Wakefield Dr	DKbC	1980	C5
Wakefield Dr NE	ATLN	1815	E4
Wakefield Pl NE	CobC	1528	C6
Wakefield Cove	ClyC	2150	D6
Wake Forest Rd	DKbC	2066	C1
Wakehurst Pl	DKbC	1894	D2
Wake Robin Tr	DKbC	1744	E3
Wakita Ct SE	CobC	1666	B5
Wakita Dr SE	CobC	1666	A5
Walden Ct NW	GwnC	1533	B7
Walden Ln NE	CobC	1529	B3
Walden St NW	ATLN	1813	D7
Walden Trc NW	GwnC	1533	B7
Walden Wk NE	ATLN	1741	B3
Walden Wy	HryC	2152	D5
Walden Mill Dr NW	GwnC	1533	D6
Waldo St SE	ATLN	1891	B6
Waldorfs Ct	DKbC	1817	D3
Waldrep Cir SE	CobC	1666	A4
Waldrop Cir	DKbC	1979	E6
Waldrop Dr	FTPK	2063	B7
	FTPK	2149	B1
Waldrop Ln	DKbC	1979	E6
Waldrop Rd	DKbC	1979	E7
	DKbC	2065	E1
Waldrop Rd NE	CobC	1527	A2
Waldrop Tr	DKbC	1979	E7
Waldrop Cliff Cir	DKbC	2066	A1
Waldrop Cliff Ln	DKbC	1980	A7
Waldrop Creek Ct	DKbC	1980	A7
Waldrop Creek Tr	DKbC	1980	A7
Waldrop Farms Dr	DKbC	1979	D7
	DKbC	2065	D1
Waldrop Farms Wy	DKbC	1979	D7
Waldrop Hills Ct	DKbC	1980	A7
Waldrop Hills Dr	DKbC	1980	A7
Waldrop Hills Ter	DKbC	1980	A7
	DKbC	2066	A1
Waldrop Ridge Ct	DKbC	2066	A1
Waldrop Ridge Ln	DKbC	1980	A7
Waldwick Wy SE	CobC	1597	B7
Wales Av NW	ATLN	1813	D3
Wales Dr	FulC	1533	A1
Waleska Wy	EPNT	1974	D7
Walhalla Ct	FulC	1601	B4
Walker Av	CGPK	2061	D2
	EPNT	2061	E2
Walker Av SE	ATLN	1891	C7
	ATLN	1977	C1
Walker Av SW	ATLN	1975	E3
Walker Ct NE	CobC	1597	B1
Walker Ct SE	SMYR	1667	A7
Walker Dr	DKbC	1893	C3
Walker Dr NE	CobC	1527	E2
Walker Rd	ClyC	2147	E5
	DKbC	1893	B7
	RVDL	2147	E5
Walker St	UNCT	2145	B7
Walker St SE	CobC	1595	C7
	SMYR	1667	A7
Walker St SW	ATLN	1890	C4
Walker Ter NE	ATLN	1816	A6
Walker Wy SE	DKbC	1978	B3
Walker Creek Rd	CGPK	2147	C2
Walker Estates Dr	RVDL	2147	E7
Walker View Ct SE	DKbC	1978	B4
Wall St NE	CobC	1597	A3
Wall St SE	ATLN	1890	E4
Wall St SW	ATLN	1890	D4
Wallace Av SW	ATLN	1973	C5
Wallace Cir SE	CobC	1740	A3
Wallace Dr	DKbC	1671	E3
Wallace Rd NE	CobC	1595	E3
	MRTA	1595	E4
Wallace Rd SE	CobC	1812	A3
Wallace St NW	ATLN	1890	C1
Wallingford Dr	DKbC	1978	E2
Walnut Grv	FulC	1533	E4
Walnut St	DKbC	1818	D7
	HPVL	2062	C2
	RSWL	1530	C3
Walnut St NW	ATLN	1890	C2
Walnut St SW	ATLN	1890	C4
Walnut Hill Pl NW	ATLN	1814	A2
Walter Rd NE	CobC	1526	D6
Walter I Aaron Cir NW	ATLN	1813	E4
Walthal Rd SE	CobC	1666	A2
Walthall Ct NW	ATLN	1815	C4
Walthall Dr NW	ATLN	1815	C4
Walthall St NE	ATLN	1891	D4
Walthall St SE	ATLN	1891	D4
Waltham Cir NE	CobC	1529	A6
Waltham Pl SE	DKbC	1892	B6
Walton St NW	ATLN	1890	E4
Walton Wy SE	SMYR	1738	D3
Walton Wy SW	CobC	1666	B6
Walton Woods Cir	DKbC	1745	C6
Walton Woods Ct	DKbC	1745	C6

Willeo Creek Pt NE — Atlanta Street Index — **Wm Holmes Borders Sr Dr**

Woburn Ct

Atlanta Street Index

Wyngate Dr NW

Atlanta Points of Interest Index

INDEX 69

Entertainment & Sports

Atlanta Points of Interest Index

Libraries

FEATURE NAME CITY	MAP#	GRID
Georgia State University Sports-Arena, ATLN	1890	E4
Georgia World Congress Center, ATLN	1890	C3
Hermance Stadium, DKbC	1743	A1
Herndon Stadium, ATLN	1890	B3
Horizon Theatre, ATLN	1891	D3
Inforum, ATLN	1890	D3
John H Lewis Complex, ATLN	1890	C4
Jomandi Productions Tri-Cities-Auditorium, EPNT	1975	D6
Just Us Theater Company, ATLN	1889	C7
Lakewood Exhibition Center, ATLN	1976	E4
Little General Playhouse, CobC	1596	C5
MASK Center Studio Theatre, ATLN	1891	D3
Munroe Theater-Dobbs University-Center, DKbC	1817	B5
Neighborhood Playhouse, DCTR	1892	E1
Not Merely Players, ATLN	1891	D2
Off Off Peachtree Theatre, DKbC	1743	D3
Onstage Atlanta, DKbC	1818	A6
Peachtree Playhouse, ATLN	1815	E7
Philips Arena, ATLN	1890	D3
Polk Street Players, MRTA	1595	A4
Push Push Theater, DKbC	1816	E4
Rialto Theatre, ATLN	1890	E3
Robert Ferst Center for the Arts, - ATLN	1890	C1
Roswell Cultural Arts Center, RSWL	1530	D2
Roswell Mill Performing Arts-Center, RSWL	1530	C3
Russ Chandler Stadium, ATLN	1890	D1
Schwartz Center for the Performing-Arts, DKbC	1817	B6
Seven Stages Performing Arts-Centre, ATLN	1891	D2
Six Flags-Georgia, CobC	1887	A2
Six Flags Whitewater Park, MRTA	1595	E4
Spivey Hall-Clayton State College, - MRRW	2150	A5
Stage Door Players, DKbC	1600	A5
Storey Theatres, ATLN	1816	B1
Theatre Gael, ATLN	1891	C1
Theatrical Outfit, ATLN	1815	E7
The New American Shakespeare-Tavern, ATLN	1890	E2
The Square Globe Theatre, MRTA	1595	A4
The Tabernacle, ATLN	1890	D3
Tri-Cities Community Theatre, EPNT	1975	D7
Turner Field, ATLN	1890	E6
Variety Playhouse, ATLN	1891	D3
VisionQuest Theater, ATLN	1815	E7
Whet Acts, ATLN	1891	A1
Whole World Theatre, ATLN	1815	E6
Zoo Atlanta, ATLN	1891	A7

Golf Courses

FEATURE NAME CITY	MAP#	GRID
Alfred "Tup" Holmes GC, ATLN	1975	A2
Ansley GC, ATLN	1816	A4
Atlanta CC, CobC	1598	A6
Atlanta International Golf & CC, - DKbC	1980	E3
Bobby Jones GC, ATLN	1815	C2
Browns Mill GC, ATLN	1977	A6
Candler Park GC, ATLN	1892	A2
Capital City CC, DKbC	1742	D2
Cherokee Town & CC, ATLN	1741	E5
Cherokee Town & CC, FulC	1530	C6
City Club of Marietta GC, MRTA	1595	A6
College Park Municipal GC, CGPK	2061	A3
Country Club of Roswell, RSWL	1532	B2
Country Club of the South, FulC	1533	A4
Cross Creek GC, ATLN	1814	E1
Druid Hills GC, DKbC	1817	B7
Dunwoody CC, FulC	1600	D3
East Lake CC, DKbC	1892	E5
Fort McPherson GC, ATLN	1975	D2
Fox Creek GC, CobC	1667	A5
Heritage GC, DKbC	1745	E1
Horseshoe Bend CC, FulC	1531	E7
Indian Hills CC, CobC	1597	D3
John A White Park & GC, ATLN	1975	B1
Lakeside CC, EPNT	2059	C3
Legacy GC, CobC	1667	B5
North Fulton GC, ATLN	1741	D1
Peachtree GC, DKbC	1671	B7
Rivermont Golf & CC, FulC	1532	D5
Riverpines GC, FulC	1533	D3
Sugar Creek GC, DKbC	1978	E6

Historic Sites

FEATURE NAME CITY	MAP#	GRID
Agnes Lee Chapter House of the UDC,- DCTR	1893	A2
Albert E Thornton House, ATLN	1741	E6
American Heritage Gallery, DKbC	1671	A1
Ansley Park Historical District, - ATLN	1816	A5
Arnoldus Brumby House, MRTA	1595	A6
Atkins Park District, ATLN	1891	D1
Atlanta Stockade, ATLN	1891	C5
Atlanta University Historical-District, ATLN	1890	C5
Atlanta Waterworks Hemphill Avenue-Station, ATLN	1815	B6
Atlanta Womens Club, ATLN	1815	E6
Barrington Hall, RSWL	1530	B3
Bass Furniture Building, ATLN	1890	D4
Braves Monument Grove, ATLN	1890	E6
Briarcliff, DKbC	1816	E6
Brookhaven Historic District, ATLN	1742	C4
Brookwood Hills Historic District, - ATLN	1815	D5
Bulloch Hall, RSWL	1530	B3
Burns Cottage, ATLN	1891	D7
Cabbagetown District, ATLN	1891	C5
Candler Park Historical District, - ATLN	1891	D2
Canton Apartments, ATLN	1741	E7
Capital City Club, ATLN	1890	E3
Castleberry Hill Historic District,- ATLN	1890	C5
Church Street Historical District, - MRTA	1595	A3
DeKalb Avenue-Clifton Road Arch-Site, ATLN	1892	A2
Druid Hills Parks & Pkwys Historic-District, ATLN	1892	A1
East Point Industrial District, EPNT	1975	D7
Edward C Peters House, ATLN	1891	A1
E Van Winkle Gin & Machine Works, - ATLN	1815	B6
Faces of War Memorial, RSWL	1530	C2
Farlinger Building, ATLN	1890	E3
Ford Motor Company Assembly Plant, - ATLN	1891	C1
Garden Hills Historic District, ATLN	1816	A1
Garrison Apartments, ATLN	1815	E6
Glenridge Hall, FulC	1599	B7
Glover McLeod Garrison House, MRTA	1595	A6
Grant Park Historic District, ATLN	1891	A5
Habersham Memorial Hall, ATLN	1816	A6
Henry B Tompkins House, ATLN	1815	D1
Henry W Grady Monument, ATLN	1890	D4
Herndon Home, ATLN	1890	C4
Historic Scottish Rite Hospital-Site, DCTR	1892	E3
Hotel Row Historic District, ATLN	1815	C7
Hurt Building, ATLN	1890	E4
Inman Park, ATLN	1891	C3
Inman Park-Moreland Historic-District, ATLN	1891	D2
Jeremiah S Gilbert House, ATLN	1976	B5
Joel Chandler Harris House, ATLN	1890	A6
Johnston's Line-Historic Site, CobC	1813	A5
Judge William Wilson House, ATLN	1888	A6
Lost Mill Workers Monument, RSWL	1530	C3
Martin Luther King Jr Historic-District, ATLN	1891	B4
Martin Luther King Jr National-Historic Site, ATLN	1891	A3
Mary Gay House, DCTR	1892	E1
Mechanicsville Schoolhouse, GwnC	1673	A1
Mrs George A Howell Jr House, ATLN	1741	D5
Norcross Historic District, NRCS	1602	E6
North Grant Park Historic District,- ATLN	1891	A5
Northwest Marietta Historic-District, MRTA	1595	A3
Oakland Cemetery, ATLN	1891	A5
Old DeKalb County Courthouse, DCTR	1892	E1
Old Post Office & Courthouse, ATLN	1890	D4
Peachtree Heights Park, ATLN	1815	E1
Peachtree Highlands Historic-District, ATLN	1742	B5
Rex Mill, ClyC	2151	D4
Roswell Historic District, RSWL	1530	C3
Rufus M Rose House, ATLN	1890	E2
St. Mark United Methodist Church, - ATLN	1890	E1
Smith-Benning House, ATLN	1891	E2
Southern Bell Telephone Building, - ATLN	1742	A3
Southern Belting Company Building, - ATLN	1890	D5
Steele-Cobb House, DKbC	1818	B4
Stuart Witham House, ATLN	1741	D7
Swan House, ATLN	1741	D6
Techwood Homes Historic District, - ATLN	1890	D1
The Flair, ATLN	1890	C3
The Texas-Cyclorama Building, ATLN	1891	B6
Thomas H Pitts House & Dairy, ATLN	1974	C1
Thomas Talbot Monument, ATLN	1891	B6
Trygveson House, ATLN	1741	A5
Tullie Smith House, ATLN	1741	E6
Tyree Building, ATLN	1891	A1
Victor H Kriegshaber House, ATLN	1891	D3
Villa Lamar, ATLN	1741	B5
Washington Avenue Historic-District, MRTA	1595	B4
Whitlock Avenue Historic District, - MRTA	1595	A4
William G Raoul House, ATLN	1890	E1
William P Nicolson House, ATLN	1891	A1
Williams-Payne House, FulC	1669	E2
William T Genry House, ATLN	1892	E5
Wrens Nest, ATLN	1890	A6
Yonge Street School, ATLN	1891	A4

Hospitals

FEATURE NAME CITY	MAP#	GRID
Anchor Hosp, CGPK	2147	B3
Atlanta Med Ctr, ATLN	1891	A3
Atlanta Veterans Affairs Med Ctr, - DKbC	1817	C4
Childrens Healthcare of Atl at-Scottish Rite, FulC	1670	D4
Crawford Long Hosp-Emory-University, ATLN	1890	E2
Decatur Hosp, DCTR	1893	A1
DeKalb Med Ctr, DKbC	1818	B6
Egleston Childrens Hosp, DKbC	1817	C5
Emory-Adventist Hosp at Smyrna, SMYR	1738	E4
Emory Dunwoody Med Ctr, DKbC	1671	D1
Emory Northlake Regional Med Ctr, - DKbC	1819	A1
Emory University Hosp, DKbC	1817	B6
Georgia Regional Hosp-Atlanta, DKbC	1979	C5
Grady Memorial Hosp, ATLN	1891	A4
HCA West Paces Ferry Hosp, ATLN	1740	E6
Hillside Hosp, ATLN	1816	B6
Hughes-Spalding Childrens Hosp, ATLN	1891	A4
Kindred Hosp-Atlanta, ATLN	1890	E1
Marietta Health Center, MRTA	1666	A3
Metropolitan Hosp, ATLN	1740	E6
Northlake Regional Med Ctr, DKbC	1818	E1
Northside Hosp, FulC	1670	D3
Piedmont Hosp, ATLN	1815	D3
Ridgeview Institute, SMYR	1739	A4
St. Josephs Hosp of Atlanta, DKbC	1670	D4
St. Josephs Hosp of Atlanta, FulC	1670	D4
Shepherd Center, ATLN	1815	D3
Southern Regional Med Ctr, ClyC	2148	D7
South Fulton Med Ctr, EPNT	1975	E7
Southwest Hosp & Med Ctr, ATLN	1888	A5
Wellstar Kennestone Hosp, MRTA	1595	A2
Wellstar Windy Hill Hosp, MRTA	1667	D4

Law Enforcement

FEATURE NAME CITY	MAP#	GRID
Atlanta Police Dept, ATLN	1890	E3
Atlanta Police Dept, ATLN	1891	B1
Atlanta Police Dept Academy, ATLN	2062	E4
Atlanta Police Dept-Airport-Precinct, CGPK	2061	D6
Atlanta Police Dept-Auburn Avenue-Precinct, ATLN	1891	A4
Atlanta Police Dept-City Precinct, - ATLN	1890	E4
Atlanta Police Dept-Fair Street-Precinct, ATLN	1890	B5
Atlanta Police Dept Headquarters, - ATLN	1890	E4
Atlanta Police Dept Helicopter-Unit, FulC	2061	E3
Atlanta Police Dept-Homicide Unit, - ATLN	1891	C2
Atlanta Police Dept-Midtown-Precinct, ATLN	1815	E7
Atlanta Police Dept-Mounted Patrol,- ATLN	1977	A1
Atlanta Police Dept-School-Division, ATLN	1890	D5
Atl Police Dept-Stewart & Lakewood-Precinct, ATLN	1976	B5
Atlanta Police Dept-Zone 1, ATLN	1889	A1
Atlanta Police Dept-Zone 2, ATLN	1816	B1
Atlanta Police Dept-Zone 3, ATLN	1891	B7
Atlanta Police Dept-Zone 4, ATLN	1975	C1
Atlanta Police Dept-Zone 5, ATLN	1890	D2
Atlanta Police Dept-Zone 6, ATLN	1892	A5
Avondale Estates Police Dept, AVES	1893	D1
Chamblee Police Station, CMBL	1671	E5
Clarkston Police Station, CLKN	1819	B3
Cobb County Police Dept, MRTA	1595	A4
Cobb County Sheriffs Dept, MRTA	1595	B4
College Park Police Dept, CGPK	2061	C4
Decatur Police Station, DCTR	1892	E1
DeKalb County Police Dept-Center-Precinct, DKbC	1894	A1
DeKalb County Police Dept-North-Precinct, DKbC	1671	A2
DeKalb County Police Dept-South-Precinct, DKbC	1979	C3
DeKalb County Sheriff, DKbC	1894	A1
DeKalb County Sheriffs Headquarters-& Jail, DKbC	1894	A1
Dept of Public Safety-Agnes Scott-College, DCTR	1893	A2
Doraville Police Station, DRVL	1672	B5
East Point Police Dept, EPNT	1975	D7
Emory University Police Dept, DKbC	1817	C6
Forest Park Police Station, FTPK	2149	A3
Fulton County Police Dept, ATLN	1890	D4
Fulton County Police Dept-Northside-Precinct, FulC	1599	C3
Fulton County Public Safety-Training Center, FulC	2060	B7
Fulton County Sheriffs Dept, ATLN	1890	E4
Georgia State Patrol Post #48, FulC	1887	D1
Hapeville Police Station, HPVL	2062	C3
Lake City Police Dept, LKCY	2150	A3
Marietta Police Dept, MRTA	1595	B4
Mercer University Police Dept, DKbC	1744	D1
Morrow Police Station, MRRW	2150	A7
Norcross Police Station, NRCS	1602	E6
Roswell Police Station, RSWL	1530	C2
Smyrna Police Station, SMYR	1666	E7
Union City Police Dept, UNCT	2145	A7

Libraries

FEATURE NAME CITY	MAP#	GRID
Atlanta-Fulton-Adams Park, ATLN	1975	A2
Atlanta-Fulton-Bankhead Courts, ATLN	1813	B5
Atlanta-Fulton-Bowen Homes, ATLN	1813	D7
Atlanta-Fulton-Buckhead, ATLN	1742	A6
Atlanta-Fulton-Carver Homes, ATLN	1976	D3
Atlanta-Fulton-Cleveland Avenue, - ATLN	1976	E7

Atlanta Points of Interest Index

Libraries   **Parks & Recreation**

Atlanta Points of Interest Index

Parks & Recreation | **Schools**

Atlanta Points of Interest Index

✦ RAND M℃NALLY

Thank you for purchasing this Rand McNally Street Atlas!
We value your comments and suggestions.

Please help us serve you better by completing this postage-paid reply card.
This information is for internal use ONLY and will not be distributed or sold to any external third party.

Street Atlas Title: **Get Around™ Atlanta**　　ISBN# **0-528-85842-4**　　**1st Edition**　　**MKT: ATL**

Date: _____　Gender ☐M ☐F　　Age Group ☐18-24 ☐25-31 ☐32-40 ☐41-50 ☐51-64 ☐65+

1. Where did you purchase this Street Atlas? (store name & city) _____

2. Why did you purchase this Street Atlas? _____

   Please explain: _____

3. Does this Street Atlas meet your expectations? ☐Yes ☐No

4. Do you primarily use this Street Atlas for the ☐City Maps ☐Regional Maps

5. Where do you use it? ☐Primarily in the car ☐Primarily in the office ☐Primarily at home ☐Other: _____

6. How do you use it? ☐Primarily for business ☐Both work and personal evenly ☐Primarily for personal use

7. What do you use the Street Atlas for? (mark all that apply)
   ☐Finding addresses ☐In route navigation ☐Planning routes ☐Other (please specify) _____

   ☐Finding points of interest (please specify)_____

8. Do you own a car? ☐Yes ☐No

9. How often do you use your car? ☐Daily ☐Weekly ☐Monthly ☐Other: _____

10. How often do you use public transportation? ☐Daily ☐Occasionally ☐Never

11. Do you use any of the following mapping products in addition to your Street Atlas?

    ☐Folded paper maps ☐Folded laminated maps ☐Wall maps ☐Other street atlases ☐Internet maps ☐Phone maps

12. What features or information do you find most useful in your Rand McNally Street Atlas? (please specify)

    _____

    _____

13. Please provide any additional comments or suggestions you have: _____

    _____

We strive to provide you with the most current updated information available. If you know of a map correction, please notify us here.

Where is the correction?　Map Page #: _____　　Grid #: _____　　Index Page #: _____

Nature of the correction:　☐Street name missing ☐Street name misspelled ☐Street information incorrect
　　　　　　☐Incorrect location for point of interest ☐Index error ☐Other: _____

Detail: _____

Yes, I would like to receive information about updated editions and special offers from Rand McNally.

☐via e-mail　E-mail address: _____

☐via postal mail

Your name: _____　　Company (if used for work): _____

Address: _____　　City/State/ZIP: _____

Thank you for your time and help. We are working to serve you better.
This information is for internal use ONLY and will not be distributed or sold to any external third party.

get directions at
randmcnally.com

RAND McNALLY
The most trusted name on the map.

You'll never need to ask for directions again with these Rand McNally products!

- EasyFinder® Laminated Maps
- Folded Maps
- Street Guides
- Wall Maps

- CustomView Wall Maps
- Road Atlases
- Motor Carriers' Road Atlases
- Rand McNally Traffic

SA06